FALKLANDS WAR AIRCRAFT

Books LLC®, Reference Series, Memphis, USA, 2011. ISBN: 9781155351131. www.booksllc.net.
Copyright: http://creativecommons.org/licenses/by-sa/3.0/deed.en

Table of Contents

Aermacchi MB-339 1	British Aerospace Sea Harrier............ 66	Hawker Siddeley Nimrod................. 127
AgustaWestland AW109 3	Dassault-Breguet Super Étendard 71	IAI Nesher 131
Avro Vulcan.. 6	Dassault Mirage 5 73	Learjet 35 132
Aérospatiale Alouette III.................... 15	Dassault Mirage III 76	Lockheed C-130 Hercules 134
Aérospatiale Gazelle 21	Douglas A-4 Skyhawk 84	Lockheed L-188 Electra.................... 143
Aérospatiale SA 330 Puma 25	Embraer EMB 110 Bandeirante........ 92	Lockheed P-2 Neptune 146
Beechcraft T-34 Mentor..................... 28	English Electric Canberra 95	Short SC.7 Skyvan 153
Bell UH-1N Twin Huey..................... 31	FMA IA 58 Pucará 103	Sikorsky SH-3 Sea King 154
Bell UH-1 Iroquois 36	Fokker F27 Friendship.................... 105	Westland Lynx 158
Boeing 707 44	Fokker F28 Fellowship 107	Westland Scout 164
Boeing CH-47 Chinook 53	Grumman S-2 Tracker 109	Westland Sea King........................... 171
Boeing Chinook (UK variants)......... 60	Handley Page Victor 114	Westland Wasp................................. 175
British Aerospace 125....................... 64	Hawker Siddeley Harrier 119	Westland Wessex 178

Introduction

Purchase of this book entitles you to a free trial membership in the publisher's book club at www.booksllc.net. (Time limited offer.) Simply enter the barcode number from the back cover onto the membership form. The book club entitles you to select from hundreds of thousands of books at no additional charge. You can also download a digital copy of this and related books to read on the go. Simply enter the title or subject onto the search form to find them.

Each chapter in this book ends with a URL to a hyperlinked online version. Type the URL exactly as it appears. If you change the URL's capitalization it won't work. Use the online version to access related pages, websites, footnotes, tables, color photos, updates. Click the version history tab to see the chapter's contributors. Click the edit link to suggest changes.

A large and diverse editor base collaboratively wrote the book, not a single author. After a long process of discussion and debate, the chapters gradually took on a neutral point of view reached through consensus. Additional editors expanded and contributed to chapters striving to achieve balance and comprehensive coverage. This reduced the regional or cultural bias found in many other books and provided access and breadth on subject matter otherwise little documented.

Aermacchi MB-339

The **Aermacchi MB-339** is an Italian military trainer and light attack aircraft. It was developed as a replacement for the earlier MB-326.

Design and development

The MB-339 is of conventional configuration, and shares much of the 326's airframe. It has a low, un-swept wing with tip tanks and jet intakes in the roots, tricycle undercarriage, and accommodation for the student and instructor in tandem. The most significant revision was a redesign of the forward fuselage to raise the instructor's seat to allow visibility over and past the student pilot's head.

The first flight took place on 12 August 1976 and deliveries to the Italian Air Force commenced in 1979. Still in production in 2004 in an enhanced version with a much-modernised cockpit. Over 200 MB-339s have been built, with roughly half of them going to the Italian Air Force.

The Lockheed-Aermacchi MB-339 T-Bird II was a losing contender in the USA's Joint Primary Aircraft Training System (JPATS) aircraft selection. Among the seven to enter, the Raytheon/Pilatus entry won, which became the T-6 Texan II.

According to an article posted on the Italian website 'Il Porto Franci', called 'Armi e finanziamenti nel corno d'Africa', Eritrea paid about $US 50 million for six MB-339 CEs in 1997. This is the original MB-339 with more advanced avionics for the ground attack role, RWR, uprated Viper 680-43 engine, and larger wingtip tanks. It is capable of carrying Sidewinder AAMs, AGM-65 Maverick AGMs, and laser-guided bombs. Unit price of the MB-339C would have to be somewhere around $US 8.3 million in 1997 dollars.

Variants

Italian Air Force Boeing 707 refuelling MB-339s

A MB-339PAN

MB-339X
Two prototypes
MB-339A
Original production variant for Italy
MB-339PAN
Variant for Frecce Tricolori aerobatic team
MB-339RM
Radio and radar calibration variant
MB-339AM
MB-339A version built for Malaysia.
MB-339AN
MB-339A version built for Nigeria.
MB-339AP
MB-339A version built for Peru.
MB-339K *Veltro II*
Single-seat dedicated attack version, first flew 30 May 1980.
MB-339B
Trainer with enhanced attack capabilities

MB-339C
More powerful engine
MB-339CB
New Zealand version (weapons training with laser designation, radar detection, AIM-9L and AGM-65 Maverick capability - 17 survivors - in storage at RNZAF Base Ohakea, New Zealand)
MB-339CE
MB-339C version built for Eritrea.
MB-339CM
MB-339C version being built for Malaysia.
MB-339CD
Modernised flight controls and instrumentation.
MB-339FD ("Full Digital")
Export version of the MB-339CD
MB-339 T-Bird II (Lockheed T-Bird II)
Version for U.S. JPATS competition.

Operational history

Argentina

Argentine Naval Aviation MB-339

The Argentine Naval Aviation (*Comando de Aviación Naval*) was the first foreign user of the forerunner MB-326GB, buying eight in 1969.

In 1980, *Comando de la Aviación Naval Argentina* (CANA), or Argentine naval air command, ordered ten MB-339As, advanced trainer and light attack aircraft. The MB339 were delivered in 1981 and were operated by the *III Escuadra Naval* 's 1 *Escuadrilla de Ataque*. During the Falklands War, late in April 1982, six of them were located at Port Stanley Airport, renamed *Base Aérea Militar* (BAM) Malvinas. They were the only attack jets to operate from the Falklands, along with four Beech T-34 Mentors armament trainer and light attack aircraft, and 24 turboprops FMA IA 58 Pucará light attack aircraft of *Grupo 3 de Ataque*. Other Airmacchis operated from three mainland bases, at Almirante Zar, Bahia Blanca and Río Grande, Tierra del Fuego naval air station. On 21 May during a routine reconnaissance flight and flown by Lieutenant Owen Crippa, a MB-339A was the first one to attack the Royal Navy amphibious force. The Aermacchi hit the frigate HMS *Argonaut*, causing light damage. On 27 May, a MB-339A (4-A-114) was shot down by a Blowpipe missile during the Battle for Goose Green, while attempting to attack British ships and landed troops. The Pilot, *Teniente* (Lt) Miguel, was killed. Three MB-339 airframes were captured by the British.

Eritrea

During tensions between Eritrea and Ethiopia in the late 1990's, Eritrea started to rebuild its air force. In 1995-1996, the Eritreans ordered six Aermacchi MB.339FD strike fighters, with which the first combat unit of the ERAF was founded in 1997. They have proved their worth as training aircraft and even during the early fighting in 1998.

Their initial deployment started on 5 June 1998 (the same day in which the ETAF also started its operations). During the same afternoon, the Ethiopians reported two attacks of Eritrean MB.339FDs on the city of Mekelle, the capital of Ethiopian province Tigray. Reportedly, as many as 44 civilians were killed and 135 injured as cluster bombs were used.

However, on 6 June one of the Macchis was shot down north of Mekelle. The pilot ejected and was rescued by a Mi-8 of the ERAF. The Eritrean Macchis were deployed again on the next day during the fighting around Erde Mattios.

On the morning of 12 June 1998, two Eritrean Mi-8 appeared in low level over Addis Pharmaceutical works, in Adigrat, attempting to bomb it. Their weapons, however, fell a few yards from the plant and caused only minor damage. Only a couple of hours later, four MB.339s rocketed and cluster-bombed against several targets in the city as well. According to Ethiopian sources four people died and 30 other were injured during those attacks.

On 5 February 1999 the Ethiopian government claimed that two Eritrean MB.339FDs attacked a fuel depot in Adigrat, some 48 kilometres inside the Ethiopian border, important for the supply of the Ethiopian army with fuel.

Operators

Frecce Tricolori at RIAT 2005 in their anniversary year

Dubai
- Dubai Air Wing operates 7 MB-339A.

Eritrea
- Eritrean Air Force operates 5 MB-339CE.

Ghana
- Ghana Air Force operates 4 MB-339A

Italy
- Italian Air Force operates 72 MB-339A and 30 MB-339CD.

Malaysia
- Royal Malaysian Air Force operated 13 MB-339AM - 8 survivors. An order for 8 MB-339CM replacements was placed in 2006.

Nigeria
- Nigerian Air Force operates 12 MB-339AN.

Peru
- Peruvian Air Force operates 14 MB-339AP.

Former operators

Argentina
- Argentine Naval Aviation 10 originally delivered, widthdraw 1990s

New Zealand
- Royal New Zealand Air Force received 18 MB-339CB used by No. 14 Squadron RNZAF between 1991 and 2002. 17 aircraft are now stored

Specifications (MB-339A)

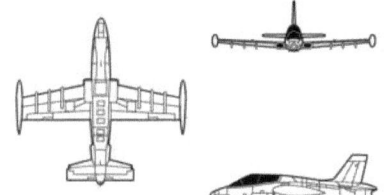

Data from Jane's All The World's Aircraft 1980-81

General characteristics
- **Crew:** two, student and instructor
- **Length:** 10.97 m (36 ft 0 in)
- **Wingspan:** 10.86 m (35 ft 7½ in)
- **Height:** 3.60 m (11 ft 9¾ in)
- **Wing area:** 19.3 m² (208 ft²)
- **Airfoil:** NACA 64A-114 (mod) at centreline, NACA 64A-212 (mod) at tip
- **Empty weight:** 3,075 kg (6,780 lb)
- **Loaded weight:** 4,400 kg (9,700 lb)
- **Max takeoff weight:** 5,897 kg (13,000 lb)
- **Powerplant:** 1 × Rolls-Royce Viper Mk. 632 turbojet, 4,000 lb (17.8 kN)

Performance
- **Never exceed speed:** Mach 0.82 (926 km/h, 500 knots, 575 mph)
- **Maximum speed:** 898 km/h (485 knots, 558 mph) at sea level
- **Stall speed:** 148.5 km/h (80 knots, 92.5 mph)
- **Range:** 1,760 km (950 NMI, 1,093 mi)
- **Service ceiling:** 14,630 m (48,000 ft)
- **Rate of climb:** 33.5 m/s (6,595 ft/min)
- **Wing loading:** 228 kg/m² (46.6 lb/ft)

Armament

Source (edited): "http://en.wikipedia.org/wiki/Aermacchi_MB-339"

AgustaWestland AW109

An Helisureste Agusta AW109S Grand

Agusta A109 K2 of the Rega over Mount Pilatus

The **AgustaWestland AW109** is a light-weight, twin-engine, eight-seat multi-purpose helicopter manufactured AgustaWestland of Italy. First flown as the Agusta A109 in 1971, the craft has proven itself in light transport, medivac, search-and-rescue, and military roles.

The AgustaWestland AW119 Koala is a more economical single-engine variant.

Design and development

In the late 1960s Agusta designed the **A109** as a single-engined commercial helicopter. It was soon realised that a twin-engined design was needed and it was re-designed in 1969 with two Allison 250-C14 turboshaft engines. A projected military version (the **A109B**) was not developed and the company concentrated on the eight-seat version the **A109C**. The first of three prototypes made its maiden flight on 4 August 1971. A protracted development then followed and the first production aircraft was not completed until April 1975. Delivery of production machines started in early 1976. The aircraft soon became a success and was soon used for roles other than as a light transport including as an air ambulance and search-and-rescue. In 1975 Agusta returned again to the possibility of a military version and trials were carried out between 1976 and 1977 with five A109As fitted with Hughes Aircraft TOW missiles. Two military versions were then developed, one for light attack or close support and another for naval operations.

Fuselages of A109 are made by PZL-Świdnik. In June 2006 the 500th fuselage was delivered by this manufacturer, marking 10 years of co-operation between the two companies.

The sale of the Agusta A109 to the Belgian armed forces in 1988 gave rise to a bribery scandal when it was alleged the company had given the Belgian Socialists over 50 million Belgian francs to get the sale. This scandal led to the resignation and conviction of NATO Secretary General Willy Claes.

The Agusta A109 became renamed the AW109 following the July 2000 merger of Finmeccanica S.p.A. and GKN plc's respective helicopter subsidiaries Agusta and Westland Helicopters to form AgustaWestland.

In August 2008, Scott Kasprowicz and Steve Sheik broke the round-the-world speed record using a factory-standard AgustaWestland Grand, with a time of 11 days, 7 hours and 2 minutes. The A109S Grand is also the fastest helicopter from New York to Los Angeles.

Variants

A U.S. Coast Guard MH-68A Stingray

Dyfed-Powys Police Air Support Unit Helicopter (X-Ray 99) Demonstration at Dyfed-Powys Police HQ Open Day 2008

- **A109A**: The first production model, powered by two Allison Model 250-C20 turboshaft engines. It made its first flight on 4 August 1971. Initially, the A109 was marketed under the name of "Hirundo" (Latin for the swallow), but this was dropped within a few years.
  - **A109A EOA**: Military version for the Italian Army.
  - **A109A Mk II**: Upgraded civilian version of the A109A.
  - **A109A Mk.II MAX**: Aeromedical evacuation version based on A109A Mk.II with extra wide cabin and access doors hinged top and bottom, rather than to one side
- **A109B**: Unbuilt military version.
- **A109C**: Eight-seat civil version, powered by two Allison Model 250-C20R-1 turboshaft engines.
  - **A109C MAX**: Aeromedical evacuation version based on A109C with extra-wide cabin and access doors hinged top and bottom, rather than to one side
- **A109D**: One prototype only
- **A109E Power**: Upgraded civilian version, initially powered by two Turbomeca Arrius 2K1 engines. Later the manufacturer introduced an option for two Pratt & Whitney PW206C engines to be used - both versions remain known as the A109E Power
  - **A109E Power Elite**: stretched cabin version of A109E Power. This variant, which is operated by the RAF, has a glass cockpit with two complete sets of pilot instruments and navigation systems, including a three-axis autopilot, an auto-coupled Instrument Landing System and a satellite-based Global Positioning System. There is also a Moving Map Display, weather radar and a Traffic Alerting System.
  - **A109LUH**: Military LUH "Light Utility Helicopter" variant based on the A109E Power. Operators include South African Air Force as well as Sweden and Malaysia
  - **MH-68A Stingray**: Eight A109E Powers were used by the United States Coast Guard Helicopter Interdiction Tactical Squadron Jacksonville (HITRON Jacksonville) as short range armed interdiction helicopters from 2000 until 2008 when they were replaced with MH-65C Dolphins.
- **A109K**: Military version.
- **A109K2**: High-altitude and high-temperature operations with fixed wheels rather than the retractable wheels of most A109 variants. Typically used by police, search and rescue, and air ambulance operators
- **A109M**: Military version.
  - **A109KM**: Military version for high altitude and high temperature operations.
  - **A109KN**: Naval version.
  - **A109CM**: Standard military version.
  - **A109GdiF**: Version for Guardia di Finanza, the Italian Finance Guard

- **A109BA**: Version created for the Belgian Army.
- **AW109S Grand**: Lengthened cabin-upgraded civilian version with two Pratt & Whitney Canada PW207 engines and lengthened main rotor blades with different tip design to the Power version.
- **CA109**: Chinese version of A109, manufactured by Changhe Aircraft Industries Corporation under license.
- **AW109 Grand New** (or AW109 SP) : single IFR, TAWS and EVS, especially for EMS

Operators

Military operators

Belgian Air Component A109BA anti-tank variant

South African Air Force AW109LUH

Helinet Agusta A-109 over Los Angeles, California.

A109E of the Empire Test Pilots' School

Albania
- Albanian Air Force - Used for VIP transport.

Argentina
- Argentine Army

Australia
- Royal Australian Navy
  - 723 Squadron RAN

Bangladesh
- Bangladesh Navy

Belgium
- Belgian Air Component
- Belgian Army - Former operator.

Benin

People's Republic of China
- CA109 Variant

Chile
- Carabineros de Chile

Ghana

Greece
- Hellenic Air Force

Honduras

Italy

New Zealand
- Royal New Zealand Air Force Five aircraft will be delivered from October 2010 to replace Bell 47 Sioux. In 2010 the NZ government signaled the future purchase of three additional aircraft, which would bring the total to eight.

Dominican Republic
- Dominican Fire and Rescue Department

Latvia

Malaysia
- Malaysian Army
- Malaysian Maritime Enforcement Agency
- Malaysian Fire and Rescue Department

Mexico

Nigeria
- Nigerian Navy Three originally bought; one lost in 2007; two more commissioned in 2009.

Paraguay
- Paraguayan Air Force
  - Grupo Aéreo de Helicópteros/ GAH - 1 A.109 for Presidential transport (1993–1998)

Peru

South Africa

Sweden

United Kingdom
- Army Air Corps - out of service 2007
- Empire Test Pilots' School
- Royal Air Force
  - No. 32 Squadron RAF

Venezuela

United States
- United States Coast Guard (Replaced by the MH-65C)

Former Military operators

Slovenia
- Slovenian Air Force

Civilian and government operators

The Agusta A109E Power operated by CareFlight International Air Ambulance

Australia
- CareFlight International Air Ambulance

Bulgaria
- Bulgarian Border Police

Poland
- Polish Air Emergency

Slovenia
- Slovenian Police

Japan
- Police services

Portugal
- Emergency medical services in Portugal

Iran
- TARA Airlines

Malaysia
- Sabah Air operate one A109S Grand

Mexico
- FlyMex

Saudi Arabia
- Saudi Aramco - 7 used for offshore and medical use.

Montenegro
- Vektra Aviation operates one A109

Slovakia
- Slovak HEMS - ATE

United Kingdom
- Warwickshire and Northamptonshire Air Ambulance
- Derbyshire, Leicestershire & Rutland Air Ambulance
- Dyfed-Powys Police Air Support Unit

United States
- Summit Air Ambulance operates a two patient A109 Power out of Elko, Nevada serving all of northern Nevada.
- AirMed Georgia operates an A109 Power for their primary aircraft for medical evacuation
- North Memorial Medical Center (Minneapolis/St. Paul, MN) has a fleet of A109s
- Shands at The University Of Florida's Medevac Helicopter is an Augusta A109
- Careflite operates four A109s in the Dallas/Fort Worth Metroplex.
- Intermountain Life Flight operates Two A109 K2's including Mountain Hoist Rescue Operations in Utah, Idaho, Wyoming.
- Lifeflight of Maine operates two A109Es, one out of Central Maine Medical Center in Lewiston (able to handle two patients), one out of Eastern Maine Medical Center in Bangor (one patient, extended fuel tanks).
- Arctic Air Service Inc. operates an A109E, out of Astoria, Oregon performing offshore marine pilot transfers for the Columbia River Bar Pilots.

Specifications

Agusta A109 Power

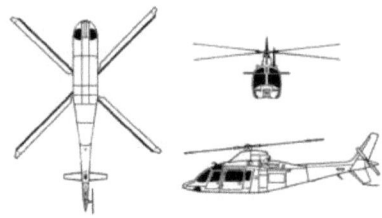

Data from www.agustawestland.com

General characteristics
- **Crew:** 1 or 2 pilots
- **Capacity:** 7/6 passengers
- **Length:** 42 ft 9 in (13.04 m)
- **Rotor diameter:** 36 ft 2 in (11.00 m)
- **Height:** 11 ft 6 in (3.50 m)
- **Empty weight:** 3,461 lb (2,000kg)
- **Max takeoff weight:** 6,283 lb (2,850 kg–3,000 kg (depending on version))
- **Powerplant:** 2× Pratt & Whitney Canada 206C **or** Turbomeca Arrius 2K1 turboshafts, 567 hp or 571 hp (423 kW or 426 kW) each

Performance
- **Maximum speed:** 177 mph (154 knots, 285 km/h)
- **Ferry range:** 599 mi (521 NM, 964 km)
- **Service ceiling:** 19,600 ft (6,000 m)
- **Rate of climb:** 1,930 ft/min (9.8 m/s)

Armament
(Agusta A109 LUH only)
- **Guns:** possibilities include 12.7 mm machine gun (250 rounds) in pod, pintle mounted 7.62 mm machine gun, door gunner post 12.7 mm machine gun
- **Missiles:** possibilities include 2 × TOW missile launchers (2 or 4 missiles each), unguided rockets in pods (2.75 in or 81 mm rockets with 7 or 12 tubes per pod), rocket/machine gun pod (70 mm × 3 rockets and 12.7 mm machine gun (200 rounds))

Source (edited): "http://en.wikipedia.org/wiki/AgustaWestland_AW109"

Avro Vulcan

The **Avro Vulcan**, sometimes referred to as the **Hawker Siddeley Vulcan**, is a delta wing subsonic jet strategic bomber that was operated by the Royal Air Force (RAF) from 1953 until 1984. It was developed by Avro in response to a specification released by the Air Ministry. At the time, both jet engines and delta wings were considered cutting-edge and relatively unexplored; thus, the small-scale Avro 707 was produced to test the principles of the design. In flight, the Vulcan was an agile aircraft for its size.

The Vulcan **B.1** was first delivered to the RAF in 1956. In service, the Vulcan was armed with nuclear weapons and was a part of the RAF's V bomber force, the United Kingdom's airborne deterrent against aggression from other powers such as the Soviet Union during the Cold War. In addition to an extensive electronic countermeasures suite, the Vulcan had a small radar cross-section, aiding its deterrent role by evading detection and therefore increasing the likelihood of penetrating Soviet airspace and deploying its weapons load successfully. A second batch of aircraft, the **B.2**, was produced with new features, including a larger wing and greater fuel capacity, along with more advanced electronics and radar systems.

The B.2s were adapted into several other variants, the **B.2A** carrying the Blue Steel missile, the **B.2 (MRR)** for Marine Radar Reconnaissance use, and the **K.2** tanker for aerial refuelling. The Vulcan was also used in the secondary role of conventional bombing near the end of its service life in the 1982 Falklands War against Argentina during Operation Black Buck. One example, XH558, was recently restored for use in display flights and commemoration of the employment of the aircraft in the Falklands conflict.

Development

Design work began at A. V. Roe in 1947 under Roy Chadwick, however, the delta wing design built upon the wartime work of Professor Alexander Lippisch, and the first design studies featured a radical tailless delta wing design. The Air Ministry specification B. 35/46 required a bomber with a top speed of 575 mph (925 km/h), an operating ceiling of 50,000 ft (15,000 m), a range of 3,452 miles (5,556 km) and a bomb load of 10,000 lb (4,500 kg); intended to carry out delivery of Britain's nuclear-armed gravity bombs to strategic targets within Soviet territory. Design work also began at Vickers and Handley Page. All three designs were approved – aircraft that would become the Valiant, the Victor, and the Avro Vulcan.

The Type 698 as first envisaged by Chadwick, and upon his death in the crash of the Avro Tudor 2 prototype on 23 August 1947, later refined by his successor, Stuart Davies in March 1949, was a more conventional delta wing design initially with tail surfaces at the ends of the wing and finally with a "full" tail unit. Avro felt this would be able to give the required combination of large wing area and sweepback to offset the transonic effects and a thick wing root to embed the engines. The thick wing gave considerable space for the engines and made allowances for future larger models to be installed. Wingtip rudders provided the control instead of the traditional rear fuselage and tail, which were unnecessary on this design. This design was reworked multiple times to reduce weight, a restriction which was later loosened, and became more conventional, adopting a centre fuselage with four paired engines and a tail.

The prototype Vulcans (VX777 front, VX770 rear) with four Avro 707s at Farnborough in September 1953

As the delta wing was an unknown quantity, Avro began scale prototype testing in 1948 with a series of single-seater Avro 707 "proof-of-concept" aircraft. Despite the crash of the first 707 prototype on 30 September 1949, work continued and eventually four additional 707s were built to test low-speed as well as high-speed characteristics of the delta wing design.

The first full-scale prototype Type 698 made its maiden flight piloted by Avro Chief Test Pilot retired Wing Commander Roly Falk on 30 August 1952. The Vulcan name was not chosen until 1952, after the Valiant had already been named. The 698's fourth flight was its appearance at the 1952 Farnborough airshow when Roly Falk demonstrated an "almost vertical bank". Falk made another public demonstration of the Vulcan's high performance and agility at the 1955 Farnborough Airshow; while flying the second production Vulcan, *XA890*, he performed an upward barrel roll shortly following takeoff. After the second occasion he rolled it at the show, the SBAC requested he stop as it was "inappropriate".

Two prototypes were built and subsequently modified for development purposes. Both flew with a straight leading edge, which was then modified to have a kink further out towards the wingtip; this was to remove the occurrence of high frequency buffeting during flight. The production Vulcan bomber in service was fitted with a delta wing, but these were not pure delta wings for reason of better flying characteristics, and successive variants saw the wing altered and expanded again.

Design

Overview

Vulcan B.1 XA890 in early silver scheme landing at Farnborough in September 1955 after Roly Falk's "aerobatic" display

The Vulcan normally operated with a crew of five: two pilots, two navigators and an Air Electronics Operator (AEO), with the AEO responsible for all electrical equipment in a role similar to that of flight engineer on earlier propeller aircraft. Only the pilot and co-pilot were provided with ejection seats; the fact that the rear crew were not provided ejection seats led to considerable criticism. There were several instances of the pilot and co-pilot ejecting in an emergency and the rear crew being killed because there was not enough time for them to bail out.

Despite its large size, it had a relatively small radar cross-section (RCS) as it had a fortuitously stealthy shape apart from the tail fin; at certain angles, it would vanish from the radar altogether. The Vulcan used entirely powered control surfaces; this allowed a joystick to be used instead of a larger yoke. This system provided a synthetic controls "feel"; flying conditions were fed back to pilot flying as a proportional resistance to his control inputs based upon the aircraft's dynamic flight configuration.

Engine

The Rolls-Royce Olympus, originally known as the *Bristol Olympus* prior to Bristol Siddeley merging with Rolls-Royce, is the axial-flow turbojet engine that powered the Vulcan. As the Vulcan was ready prior to the engine completing development, the aircraft was first launched with the Rolls-Royce Avon, which were quickly replaced in turn by Armstrong Siddeley Sapphires. Each Vulcan had four engines buried in the wings, positioned in pairs close to the center of the fusalage. Developed specifically for the Vulcan to operate at sub-sonic speeds, it would later be redeveloped into a supersonic powerplant for the cancelled BAC TSR-2 strike bomber and the supersonic passenger transport Concorde.

Avionics and power systems

The main navigation and bombing aid on the Vulcan was the Navigation and Bombing System, (NBS) the main element being a H2S radar with a nose-mounted scanner. In order to assist in low level flying, which became a common bomber tactic as Soviet SAM capabilities and numbers grew in the late 1950s, the Vulcans were outfitted with Terrain Following Radar (TFR) in 1966. The TFR used was created for the American General Dynamics F-111

Aardvark. The Red Steer tail-warning radar was also amongst the tools available to the AEO, increasing the likelihood of spotting an enemy fighter and effectively using chaff and flares to negate missile attacks. The extensive electronic countermeasures (ECM) suite installed on the Vulcans kept them a viable option, capable of successfully penetrating Soviet air defenses if need be, throughout the 1960s.

Electrical power was DC supplied from generators on each engine. Backup power was available from batteries if the generators failed; however, these had little capacity in event of power loss. The power systems were revised for the B.2, switching from DC to AC, the inclusion of a Ram Air Turbine (RAT) that would operate at higher altitude, and an Airborne Auxiliary Power Unit (AAPU) which could be started once the aircraft had reached a lower altitude of 30,000 ft (9,100 m) or less.

Aerial view of a Vulcan B.2 in late RAF markings on static display at RAF Mildenhall

Colour schemes

Early Vulcans left the factory in an overall silver finish, with a black fibreglass radome for the H2S Mk 9 Navigation and Bombing System (NBS) under the nose. This was later changed to an overall finish of anti-flash white with the radome remaining black. With the transfer to low-level operations, Vulcans were re-painted in a two-tone grey/green disruptive pattern camouflage on the upper surfaces with grey undersides. This was later changed to initially, a "wraparound" version with the camouflage continuing under the leading and trailing edges of the wings, before being changed to a full continuation of the

disruptive pattern on the entire undersurfaces. This was because in low-level flight in the US during "Red Flag" combined exercises, defending US SAM forces had stated that the grey-painted undersides of the Vulcan became much more visible against the ground at high angles of bank.

Operational history

Introduction

In September 1956, the RAF received its first Vulcan B.1, *XA897*, which immediately went on a round-the-world tour; this was done due to a great emphasis placed upon the provision of goodwill visits and tours abroad during the early years of Vulcan operation, as they were seen as highly effective propaganda; many Vulcans were utilised in this role. Misfortune struck on 1 October 1956, however; while landing at London Heathrow Airport at the completion of the world tour, *XA897* was destroyed in a fatal accident.

The first two aircraft were delivered to 230 OCU in January 1957 and the training of crews started on 21 February 1957, in the following months more aircraft were delivered to the OCU. The first OCU course to qualify was No. 1 Course, on the 21 May 1957, and they went on to form the first flight of No. 83 Squadron. No. 83 Squadron was the first operational squadron to use the bomber, at first using borrowed Vulcans from the OCU and on 11 July 1956 it received the first aircraft of its own. By September 1957, several Vulcans had been handed over to No.83 Squadron The second OCU course also formed a Flight of 83 Squadron, but subsequent trained crews were also used to form the second bomber squadron, 101 Squadron. The last aircraft from the first batch of 25 aircraft had been delivered by the end of 1957 to 101 Squadron.

In order to increase the mission range and flight time for Vulcan operations, in-flight refuelling capabilities were added in 1959 onwards; several Valiant bombers were refurbished as tankers to refuel the Vulcans. Continuous airborne patrols proved untenable, however, and the refuelling mechanisms across the

Vulcan fleet fell into disuse in the 1960s.

XH558 taking off; 2008 Farnborough Airshow

Vulcans frequently visited the United States during the 1960s and 1970s to participate in air shows and static displays, as well as to participate in the Strategic Air Command's Annual Bombing and Navigation Competition at such locations as Barksdale AFB, Louisiana and the former McCoy AFB, Florida, with the RAF crews representing Bomber Command and later Strike Command. Vulcans also took part in the 1960, 1961, and 1962 Operation Skyshield exercises, in which NORAD defences were tested against possible Soviet air attack, the Vulcans simulating Soviet fighter/bomber attacks against New York, Chicago and Washington. The results of the tests were classified until 1997.

Nuclear deterrent

As part of Britain's independent nuclear deterrent, the Vulcan initially carried Britain's first nuclear weapon, the *Blue Danube* gravity bomb. Blue Danube was a low-kiloton yield fission bomb designed before the United States detonated the first hydrogen bomb. The British then embarked on their own hydrogen bomb programme, and to bridge the gap until these were ready the V-bombers were equipped with an Interim Megaton Weapon based on the Blue Danube casing and Green Grass, a large pure-fission warhead of 400 kt (1.7 PJ) yield. This bomb was known as *Violet Club*. Only five were deployed before a better weapon was introduced as *Yellow Sun Mk.1*.

A later model, *Yellow Sun Mk 2*, was fitted with *Red Snow*, a British-built variant of the U.S. Mk-28 warhead. *Yellow Sun Mk 2* was the first British thermonuclear weapon to be deployed, and was carried on both the Vulcan and Handley Page Victor. Only the Valiant carried U.S. thermonuclear bombs assigned to NATO under the dual-key arrangements. *Red Beard* (a smaller, lighter low-kiloton yield) bomb was pre-positioned in Cyprus and Singapore for use by Vulcan and Victor bombers, and from 1962, 26 Vulcan B.2As and the Victor bombers were armed with the Blue Steel missile, a rocket-powered stand-off bomb, which was also armed with the 1.1 Mt (4.6 PJ) yield *Red Snow* warhead.

Operationally, RAF Bomber Command and the US Strategic Air Command cooperated together in the *Single Integrated Operational Plan* (SIOP) to ensure coverage of all major Soviet targets from 1958, 108 aircraft of the RAF's V-Bombers were assigned targets under SIOP by the end of 1959. From 1962 onwards, two jets in every major RAF base were armed with nuclear weapons and on standby permanently under the principle of Quick Reaction Alert (QRA). Vulcans on QRA standby were to be airborne within four minutes of receiving an alert, as this was identified as the amount of time between warning of a USSR nuclear strike being launched and it arriving in Britain. The closest the Vulcan came to take part in potential nuclear conflict was during the Cuban missile crisis in October 1962, where Bomber Command was moved to Alert Condition 3, an increased state of preparedness from normal operations, however stood down in early November.

Royal Air Force Avro Vulcan B.2

The Vulcans were intended to be equipped with the American Skybolt Air Launched Ballistic Missile to replace the Blue Steel, with Vulcan B.2s carrying two Skybolts under the wings; the last 28 B.2s were modified on the production line to fit pylons to carry the Skybolt. Also proposed was a stretched version of the Vulcan, with increased wingspan to carry up to six Skybolts. When the Skybolt missile system was cancelled by U.S. President John F. Kennedy on the recommendation of his Secretary of Defense, Robert McNamara in 1962, Blue Steel was retained. To supplement it until the Royal Navy took on the deterrent role with Polaris submarines, the Vulcan bombers adopted a high-low-high mission profile using a rapidly introduced parachute-retarded "laydown" bomb, *WE.177B*. After the British Polaris submarines became operational and Blue Steel was taken out of service in 1970, WE.177B continued in use on the Vulcan in a low-level tactical strike role in support of European NATO ground forces. It outlived the Vulcan bombers, being used also on Buccaneer, Panavia Tornado, and Jaguar until retirement in 1998. While not a like-for-like replacement, the multirole Tornado is the successor for the positions filled by the Vulcan following its retirement.

Conventional role

Vulcan over Ascension Island on 18 May 1982

Although the primary weapon for the aircraft was nuclear, Vulcans could carry up to 21 1,000 lb (454 kg) bombs in a secondary role, and squadrons had been conducting training for conventional bombing and strike roles since the

1960s.

The only combat missions involving the Vulcan took place in 1982 during the Falklands War with Argentina. This was also the only time V-bombers took part in conventional warfare. The Vulcans flew missions knows as the *Black Buck* raids, 3,889 mi (6,259 km) from Ascension Island to Stanley on the Falklands. The first raid struck on 1 May when a lone Vulcan bomber flew over Port Stanley and dropped bombs across the main airfield. This was quickly followed up by strikes against anti-air installations made by carrier-based British Aerospace Sea Harriers.

In total, there were three missions to bomb the airfield at Stanley and two to attack Argentine radar installations with missiles, while two missions were cancelled. Victor aircraft were used for air-to-air refuelling in a complex scheme, and approximately 1.1 million gal (5 million L) of jet fuel were used in each mission. The Vulcan's ECM system was effective at jamming Argentine radars, greatly reducing the likelihood of British airborne elements coming under effective fire.

Five Vulcans were selected for the operation; their bomb bays were modified, the flight refuelling system that had long been out of use was reinstated, the electronics updated, and new wing pylons fitted to carry an ECM pod and Shrike anti-radar missiles at wing hardpoint locations originally installed for carrying Skybolt missiles. The engineering work began on 9 April 1982 with the first mission on 30 April–1 May. At the time, these missions held the record for the world's longest-distance raids; reaching the islands required extensive in-flight refuelling operations.

Avro Vulcan from Operation Black Buck at the National Museum of Flight, showing mission markings

Maritime radar reconnaissance

On 1 November 1973, the first of nine B.2 (MRR) aircraft was delivered to No. 27 Squadron at RAF Scampton, reformed for its main role of maritime radar reconnaissance. The main external visual difference was the presence of a gloss paint finish, with a light grey undersurface, which was made due to the secondary role of air sampling. Only five of the B.2 (MRR)s were capable of air sampling, and these aircraft were distinguished by the additional hardpoints outside the Skybolt points.

Aerial refuelling role

After the end of the Falklands War in 1982, the Vulcan was due to be withdrawn from RAF service that year. However, the Falklands campaign had consumed much of the airframe fatigue life of the RAF's Victor Tankers. While Vickers VC10 and Lockheed TriStar tankers would be ordered as a result of lessons learned from the conflict, six Vulcan B.2s were converted to a tanker configuration as a stopgap measure. The Vulcan Tanker conversion was accomplished by removing the jammers from the ECM bay in the tail of the aircraft, and replacing them with a single Hose Drum Unit (HDU).

The go-ahead for converting the six aircraft was given on 4 May 1982. Just fifty days after being ordered, the first Vulcan Tanker, *XH561*, was delivered to RAF Waddington. The additional fuel load in the Vulcan K.2 Air Tanker was carried in three large tanks fitted in the bomb bay, giving a total fuel capacity of 100,000 lb (45,000 kg). The Vulcan K.2s were operated by No.50 Squadron, along with three Vulcan B-2s, in support of UK air defense activities.

Engine test beds

The first Vulcan prototype, *VX770*, was also the first Vulcan to serve as an engine test bed. Initially refitted with Armstrong Siddeley Sapphires, four 15,000 lbf (67 kN) Rolls-Royce Conway R.Co.7 were later installed. It flew with the Conways, the first turbofans in the world, from 1957–8 until its fatal crash. Its place was taken by Vulcan B.1 *XA902*, which was powered by the R.Co.11 variant. In 1961 the two inner Conways were replaced with Rolls-Royce Speys, flying for the first time on 12 October 1961.

XA894 flew with five Olympus engines, the standard four plus an underbelly supersonic Olympus 320 fed from a bifurcated intake starting just aft of the wing leading edge and inboard of the main intakes, in a mock-up of the BAC TSR-2 installation. This aircraft was destroyed on a fire on the ground on 3 December 1962. Another Vulcan, B.1 *XA903*, was converted to a similar layout. The Olympus test engine mounted was a 35,080 lbf (156.0 kN) Olympus 593, the type later used on the Concorde, mounted underbelly in a mockup of a single Concorde nacelle. The first flight was on 1 October 1966 and testing continued through to June 1971.

In April 1973, *XA903* flew with an underbelly Rolls-Royce RB.199 turbofan destined for the Panavia Tornado. The RB.199 engine included both the reheat and thrust reverser functions.

Variants

B.1
The initial production aircraft, with the straight wing leading edge, with wide undercarriage track and four overwing airbrakes. Early examples finished in silver, later changed to "anti-flash" white. Unlike the B.2 production batch, the B.1s did not undergo extensive wing strengthening for low-level flying.

B.1A
The B.1 with an Electronic Countermeasures (ECM) system in a new larger tail cone.

B.2
Developed version of the B.1. Larger, thinner wing than the B.1 and fitted with Olympus 201 engines of 17,000 lbf (76 kN) each, or Olympus 301 engines of 20,000 lbf (89 kN) each. Terrain-following radar in nosecone and passive radar warning in tail fin giving it a

square top from mid-1970s. Uprated electrics with Airborne Auxiliary Power Unit and emergency Ram Turbine generator.

B.2A
Also known as B.2BS. B.2 with Olympus 301 engines to carry Blue Steel in recessed bomb doors.

B.2 (MRR)
Nine B.2 converted to Maritime Radar Reconnaissance. Five aircraft further modified for Air Sampling Role. Distinctive gloss finish with light grey underside.

K.2
Six B.2 converted for air-to-air refuelling with Mark 17 hose drum mounted semi-recessed in tail cone. It was fitted with three bomb-bay drum tanks, and was the only mark of Vulcan that could jettison fuel in an emergency.

'Avro Atlantic'
A civilian variant of the Vulcan, to be known as the Avro Atlantic, was proposed and discussions were held with BOAC and Armstrong-Siddeley in the early 1950s about payload requirements.

Production
A total of 134 production Vulcans were manufactured at Woodford Aerodrome, 45 to the B.1 design and 89 were B.2 models, the last being delivered to the RAF in January 1965.

Operators

The Vulcan to the Sky Trust's Avro Vulcan XH558

- United Kingdom
  - Aeroplane and Armament Experimental Establishment aircraft used for trials and evaluation
  - Royal Air Force
    - No. 9 Squadron RAF (Operated the B.2 from 1962 to 1982)
    - No. 12 Squadron RAF (Operated the B.2 from 1962 to 1967)
    - No. 27 Squadron RAF (Operated the B.2 from 1961 to 1972 and the B.2 (MRR) from 1973 to 1982)
    - No. 35 Squadron RAF (Operated the B.2 from 1962 to 1982)
    - No. 44 Squadron RAF (Operated the B.1 from 1960 to 1967 and the B.2 from 1966 to 1982)
    - No. 50 Squadron RAF (Operated the B.1 from 1961 to 1966, the B.2 from 1966 to 1984 and the B.2 (K) from 1982 to 1984)
    - No. 83 Squadron RAF (the first Vulcan squadron operated the B.1 from 1957 to 1960 and the B.2 from 1960 to 1969)
    - No. 101 Squadron RAF (Operated the B.1 from 1957 to 1967 and the B.2 from 1967 to 1982)
    - No. 617 Squadron RAF (Operated the B.1 from 1958 to 1961 and the B.2 from 1961 to 1981)
    - No. 230 Operational Conversion Unit RAF
    - Bomber Command Development Unit
  - Vulcan To The Sky Trust (flying XH558)
  - Aircraft were also operated at various times under the direction of the Ministry of Aviation for trials and evaluation by Avro, Bristol Siddeley Engines and Rolls-Royce.

Bases
- RAF Akrotiri in Cyprus was the base for two operational B.2 squadrons from 1969 to 1975
  - 9 Squadron 1969-1975, moved from Cottesmore in 1969 it returned to the UK in 1975 to Waddington.
  - 35 Squadron 1969-1975, moved from Cottesmore in 1969 it returned to the UK in 1975 to Scampton.
- RAF Coningsby was the base for three operational squadrons from 1962 to 1964
  - 9 Squadron 1962-1964, formed in 1962 to operate the B.2 it moved to Cottesmore in 1964.
  - 12 Squadron 1962-1964, formed in 1962 to operate the B.2 it moved to Cottesmore in 1964.
  - 35 Squadron 1962-1964, formed in 1962 to operate the B.2 it moved to Cottesmore in 1964.
- RAF Cottesmore was the base for three operational squadrons from 1964 to 1969.
  - 9 Squadron 1964-1969, moved in from Coningsby in 1964, it moved to Akrotiri in 1969.
  - 12 Squadron 1964-1967, moved in from Coningsby in 1964 until it disbanded in 1967.
  - 35 Squadron 1964-1969, moved in from Coninsgby in 1964, it moved to Akrotiri 1969.
- RAF Finningley
  - 101 Squadron 1957-1961, formed in 1957 to be the second operational B.1 squadron, moved to Waddington in 1961.
  - 230 OCU 1961-1969, moved from Waddington in 1961, moved to Scampton in 1969.
- RAF Scampton was the base for three operational squadrons at different times between 1961 and 1981
  - 27 Squadron 1961-1972, formed in 1961 to operate the B.2 until it disbanded in 1972.
  - 83 Squadron 1960-1969, a former B.1 squadron formed in 1960 to operate the B.2 until disbanded in 1969.
  - 617 Squadron 1958-1981, formed in 1958 to operate the B.1, converted to the B.2 in 1961 until disbanded in 1981.
  - 230 OCU 1969-1981, moved from Finningley in 1969 until disbanded in 1981.
- RAF Waddington was the base for a number of operational squadrons at different times between 1957 and

1984, it was the first and last operational Vulcan base.
- 9 Squadron 1975-1982, moved in from Akrotiri in 1975 until it was disbanded 1982.
- 27 Squadron 1973-1982, formed in 1973 to operate the B.2 (MRR) variant until 1982.
- 44 Squadron 1960-1982, formed in 1960 to operate the B.1, it converted to the B.2 in 1966 until disbandd in 1982.
- 50 Squadron 1961-1984, formed in 1961 to operate the B.1, it converted to the B.2 in 1966, from 1982 it also flew the tanker version until disbanding in 1984.
- 83 Squadron 1957-1960, formed in 1957 to be the first operational squadron to operate the B.1 until 1960, it reformed at Scampton later in the year as a B.2 unit.
- 101 Squadron 1961-1982, moved from Finningley in 1961 with the B.1, converted to B.2 in 1967 until disbanding in 1982.
- 230 OCU 1956-1961, formed in 1956 to train Vulcan crews it moved to Finningley in 1961.

V-Bomber dispersal airfields

In the event of transition to war the Vulcan squadrons were to deploy four aircraft at short-notice to each of a 26 pre-prepared dispersal airfields around the United Kingdom. In the early 1960s the RAF ordered 20 Beagle Basset communication aircraft to move the Vulcan crews to dispersal airfields; the importance of these aircraft was only brief, diminishing when the primary nuclear deterrent switched to the Royal Navy's Polaris submarines.

- On 1 October 1956, Vulcan B.1 *XA897* crashed at London Heathrow Airport after an approach in bad weather, striking the ground 700 yd (640 m) short of the runway just as engine power was applied. The impact probably broke the drag links on the main undercarriage, allowing the undercarriage to be forced backwards and damage the trailing edge of the wing. After the initial impact, the aircraft rose back in the air. The pilot, Squadron Leader D. R. Howard, and co-pilot Air Marshal Sir Harry Broadhurst both ejected. The aircraft then hit the ground and broke up. Howard and Broadhurst survived but the other four occupants, including Howard's usual co-pilot, were killed. *XA897* was the first Vulcan to be delivered to the RAF. AOC-in-C Bomber Command, Air Marshal Broadhurst, had taken the aircraft with a full Vulcan crew of four and an Avro technician on a round-the-world tour. At the conclusion of the tour, Broadhurst was to land at Heathrow Airport in front of the assembled aviation media. RAF aircraft were not equipped to use the Instrument Landing System installed at Heathrow and other civil airports so a Ground-controlled approach was carried out.
- In 1957, a Vulcan B.1 *XA892* attached to the Aeroplane and Armament Experimental Establishment (A&AEE) at Boscombe Down for acceptance testing was unintentionally flown to an Indicated Mach Number (IMN) above 1.04, alarming the crew that it had reached supersonic speed. The aircraft commander, Flt Lt Milt Cottee (RAAF) and co-pilot Flt Lt Ray Bray (RAF) were tasked to fly at 478 mph (769 km/h) and 0.98 IMN, to take the aircraft to a load factor of 3 g. The Vulcan was climbed to 35,000 ft (11,000 m) and then dived with the intention of reaching the target speed at 27,000 ft (8,200 m). Approaching the target altitude, the crew closed the throttles and were applying full up-elevator, the aircraft continued to pitch nose-down. Flt Lt Cottee contemplated pushing forward to go inverted and then rolling upright; instead, he opened the speed brakes even though the airspeed was above their maximum operating speed. The speed brakes were not damaged and succeeded in reducing the Mach number. The aircraft came back past the vertical at about 18,000 ft (5,500 m) and regained level flight at 8,000 ft (2,400 m). There was no report of a sonic boom in the vicinity; as such, it is unlikely a true Mach Number of 1.0 was reached. (At Mach 1.0, the Vulcan had position error of about 0.07.) After the flight a rear bulkhead was found to be deformed.

The prototype Vulcan *VX770* in 1954 when powered by Sapphires but retaining the original "pure delta" wing shape

- On 20 September 1958, a Rolls-Royce test pilot was authorised to fly *VX770* on an engine performance sortie with a fly past at RAF Syerston Battle of Britain "At Home" display. The Vulcan flew along the main runway then started a roll to starboard and climbed slightly. During this roll the starboard wing disintegrated, resulting in a collapse of the main spar and wing structure. The Vulcan went into a dive with the starboard wing on fire and struck the ground. Three occupants of a controllers' caravan were killed by debris, all four of the Vulcan crew were also killed. The cause may have been pilot error; analysis of amateur cine film suggested the aircraft had flown over the airfield at 472–483 miles per hour (760–777 km/h) instead of the briefed 288–345 miles per hour (463–555 km/h); it had also descended to a height of 65–70 ft (20–21 m) instead of 200–300 ft (61–91 m). Rolling the Vulcan to starboard while flying at this speed imposed a load or stress of 2–3 g; it should have remained below 1.25 g. The *VX770* was a prototype with construction and materials not to production standard, which was the primary reason for imposing low flight performance

- limits.
- On 24 October 1958, Vulcan B.1 *XA908* of No. 83 Squadron crashed into the residential neighborhood of Grosse Pointe Park on the East side of Detroit, Michigan, USA after a complete electrical systems failure. The failure occurred at around 30,000 ft (9,100 m) and the backup system should have provided 20 minutes of emergency power to allow the aircraft to divert to Kellogg Airfield, at Battle Creek, Michigan. Due to a short circuit in the service busbar, backup power only lasted three minutes before expiring and locking the aircraft controls. *XA908* then went into a dive of between 60–70° before it crashed, leaving a 40-ft (13 m) crater in the ground, which was later excavated to 70 ft (21 m) deep in an unsuccessful attempt to find the cockpit of the aircraft. All six crew members were killed, including the co-pilot, who had ejected. The co-pilot's ejector seat was found in Lake St Clair, but his body was not recovered until the following spring. There were no ground fatalities, and only one person on the ground required hospitalization, though property damage was extensive.
- On 24 July 1959, Vulcan B.1 *XA891* crashed due to an electrical failure during an engine test. The aircraft commander was Avro Chief Test Pilot Jimmy Harrison. Shortly after take-off the crew observed generator warning lights and loss of busbar voltage. The aircraft commander climbed *XA891* to 14,000 ft (4,300 m) and steered a course away from the airfield and populated areas while the AEO attempted to solve the problem. When it became clear that control of the aircraft would not be regained the aircraft commander instructed the crew in the rear compartment to exit the aircraft, and the co-pilot to eject. The aircraft commander then also ejected. All the crew survived, making them the first complete crew to escape successfully from a Vulcan. The aircraft crashed near Kingston upon Hull.
- On 12 December 1963, Vulcan B.1A *XH477* of No. 50 Squadron crashed in Scotland during an exercise at low level (not less than 1,000 ft (300 m) above ground.) *XH477* had struck the ground while climbing slightly, and it was assumed it crashed due to poor visibility.
- On 11 May 1964, Vulcan B.2 *XH535* crashed during a low speed demonstration. The test pilot was demonstrating a very low speed and high rate of descent when the aircraft began to spin. The landing parachute was deployed and the spin stopped briefly, but the aircraft then began to spin again. At around 2,500 ft (760 m) the aircraft commander instructed the crew to abandon the aircraft. The aircraft commander and co-pilot ejected successfully but none of the crew in the rear compartment did so, presumably due to the g forces in the spin.
- On 16 July 1964, Vulcan B.1A *XA909* crashed in Anglesey after a midair explosion, causing both No. 3 and No. 4 engines to be shut down. The explosion was caused by failure of a bearing in No. 4 engine. The starboard wing was extensively damaged, the pilot had insufficient aileron power, and both airspeed indications were highly inaccurate. The whole crew successfully abandoned *XA909* and were found within a few minutes and rescued.
- On 7 October 1964, Vulcan B.2 *XM601* crashed during overshoot from an asymmetric power practice approach at Coningsby. The copilot had executed the asymmetric power approach with two engines producing thrust and two at idle. He was being checked by the Squadron Commander, who was unfamiliar with the aircraft. When he commenced the overshoot the copilot moved all the throttles to full power. The engines that had been producing power reached full power more quickly than the engines at idle and the resultant asymmetric thrust exceeded the available rudder authority, causing the aircraft to spin and crash. All the crew perished. Sqn Ldr Ron Dick, later Air Cdre, said it had happened to him once where the horizon passed rapidly across his field of view; the only recovery was to retard all 4 engines to idle and then increase them together.
- On 25 May 1965, Vulcan B.2 *XM576* crash-landed at Scampton, causing it be written off within a year of delivery.
- On 11 February 1966, Vulcan B.2 *XH536* of the Cottesmore Wing crashed in the Brecon Beacons during a low level exercise. The aircraft struck the ground at 1,910 ft (580 m) near the summit of Fan Bwlch Chwyth 1,978 ft (603 m), 20 mi (32 km) northeast of Swansea. All crew members died. Hilltops at the time were snow-covered and cloud extended down to 1,400 ft (430 m).
- On 6 April 1967, Vulcan B.2 *XL385* burnt out on the runway at RAF Scampton during its takeoff run. It was enroute for Goose Bay. All crew survived. The accident was caused by failure of a compressor blade on the inner port engine. The aircraft was carrying a dummy Blue Steel missile, and fire was a difficult one for the fire crews to deal with as it involved a running fuel fire and high cross winds. Subsequently, the aircraft was completely engulfed in flames and totally destroyed; only the nose of the aircraft survived.
- On 7 January 1971, Vulcan B.2 *XM610* of No.44 Squadron crashed after fatigue failure of a blade in the No. 1 engine that damaged the fuel system and led to an engine fire. The crew abandoned the aircraft safely, and the aircraft crashed harmlessly in Wingate.
- On 14 October 1975, Vulcan B.2 *XM645* of No.9 Squadron lost its left undercarriage and damaged the airframe when it undershot the runway at Luqa airport in Malta. After a runway had been covered

with fire prevention foam, the aircraft was turning inbound for a landing when it broke up over the village of Zabbar. The pilot and co-pilot escaped, using their ejection seats, but the other five crew members were killed. Large pieces of the aircraft fell on the village. One woman, was hit by an electric cable and killed. Some 20 others were injured.
- On 17 January 1977, Vulcan B2 XM600 of 101 Squadron at RAF Waddington crashed near the town of Spilsby in Lincolnshire. The Vulcan was returning to Waddington after an exercise over the North Sea when fire broke out in one of the engines. Fire extinquishers in the engine bays failed to douse the fire. The captain stayed with the aircraft until the last seconds and was credited with saving Spilsby. After the fire started, the three rear crew members baled out through the hatch and the co-pilot ejected. The Vulcan crashed into a field at 3.45pm - only half a mile from the town where it was market day. Lincolnshire police said it was a miracle that no-one on the ground was hurt. Wreckage was scattered over 20 acres. Thick fog enveloped the scene shortly after the crash, hampering early investigations. By coincidence, the captain knew the first person he met after parachuting down. He was walking along a lane when he met a former Vulcan AEO who had retired to the area four years earlier. He took the Vulcan captain to his home where he telephoned Waddington to tell them what had happened. Details from report in Lincolnshire Standard newspaper by reporter Mike Curtis. Verified by MC March 2011.
- On 12 August 1978, Vulcan B.2 XL390 of No. 617 Squadron crashed during an air display at Naval Air Station Glenview, Illinois in the United States. The accident sequence began at about 400 ft (120 m) after a possible stall during a wing-over. The Vulcan crashed into a landfill just north of the base and all crew members aboard perished.

Aircraft on display

Avro Vulcan *XL361* on display at CFB Goose Bay in 1988

Avro Vulcan *XL319* on display at North East Aircraft Museum

- *XJ823* Vulcan B.2A – Solway Aviation Museum, Carlisle, Cumbria, England.
- *XJ824* Vulcan B.2A – Imperial War Museum, Duxford Aerodrome, England.
- *XL318* Vulcan B.2 – Royal Air Force Museum London, Hendon, England.
- *XL319* Vulcan B.2 – North East Aircraft Museum, Sunderland, England.
- *XL360* Vulcan B.2 – Midland Air Museum, Coventry, England.
- *XL361* Vulcan B.2 – CFB Goose Bay (Happy Valley), Labrador, Canada
- *XL426* Vulcan B.2 (G-VJET) preserved in taxiable condition at Southend Airport, England.
- *XM573* Vulcan B.2 – Strategic Air and Space Museum – relocated from Offutt AFB to a site near Ashland, Nebraska, United States.
- *XM575* Vulcan B.2A – East Midlands Airport Aeropark, England.
- *XM594* Vulcan B.2 – Newark Air Museum, Newark-on-Trent, England.
- *XM597* Vulcan B.2 – National Museum of Flight, East Fortune, Scotland.
- *XM598* Vulcan B.2 – Royal Air Force Museum Cosford, Cosford, England.
- *XM603* Vulcan B.2 – Woodford Aerodrome, some parts removed for support of *XH558*, *XM655* and *XL426*.
- *XM605* Vulcan B.2 – Castle Air Museum (former Castle AFB), Atwater, California, United States.
- *XM606* Vulcan B.2 – Barksdale AFB, United States.
- *XM607* Vulcan B.2 – RAF Waddington, England.
- *XM612* Vulcan B.2 – City of Norwich Aviation Museum, Norwich, England.
- *XM655* Vulcan B.2 (G-VULC) preserved in taxiable condition at Wellesbourne Mountford Airfield, England.

XH558

XH558 performs its first post-restoration public display on 5 July 2008

The last airworthy Vulcan (XH558) has been restored to flying condition by the "Vulcan to the Sky Trust" after years of effort and fundraising. The first post-restoration flight, which lasted 34 minutes, took place on 18 October 2007.

Being the sole airworthy Vulcan, the aircraft's airworthiness status was in peril as maintenance funding was in need before the end of February, 2010. At the last moment an anonymous benefactor presented £458,000 to the foundation, ensuring its airworthiness for both its 50th birthday and the prospect of a flight performance for the 2012 Summer Olympic Games opening ceremony in London.

Specifications

Specifications (Vulcan B.1)

Data from Polmar, Laming

General characteristics
- **Crew:** 5 (pilot, co-pilot, AEO, Navigator Radar, Navigator Plotter)
- **Length:** 97 ft 1 in (29.59 m)
- **Wingspan:** 99 ft 5 in (30.3 m)
- **Height:** 26 ft 6 in (8.0 m)
- **Wing area:** 3554 ft² (330.2 m²)
- **Empty weight:** 83,573 lb (including crew) (37,144 kg)
- **Max takeoff weight:** 170,000 lb (77,111 kg)
- **Powerplant:** 4 × Bristol Olympus 101, or 102 or 104 turbojet, 11,000 lbf (49 kN) each

Performance
- **Maximum speed:** Mach 0.96 (607 mph (1,040 km/h)) at altitude
- **Cruise speed:** Mach 0.86 (567 miles per hour (912 km/h)) at 45,000 ft
- **Range:** 2,607 mi (4,171 km)
- **Service ceiling:** 55,000 ft (17,000 m)
- **Thrust/weight:** 0.31

Armament
- 21 x 1,000 pounds (454 kg) of conventional bombs
- 1 x Blue Danube nuclear gravity bomb
- 1 x Violet Club 400-kiloton nuclear gravity bomb
- 1 x Yellow Sun Mk.1 400-kiloton nuclear gravity bomb
- 1 x Yellow Sun Mk 2 400-kiloton nuclear gravity bomb
- 1 x Red Beard nuclear gravity bomb
- 1 x Blue Steel rocket-propelled 1.1 megaton nuclear stand-off missile

Notes
Source (edited): "http://en.wikipedia.org/wiki/Avro_Vulcan"

Aérospatiale Alouette III

The **Aérospatiale Alouette III** (French pronunciation: [alwɛt], *Lark*) is a single-engine, light utility helicopter developed by Sud Aviation. It was manufactured by Aérospatiale of France, and under license by Hindustan Aeronautics Limited in India as Hal Chetak and Industria Aeronautică Română in Romania.

The Alouette III is the successor to the Alouette II, being larger and having more seating. Originally powered by a Turbomeca Artouste IIIB turboshaft engine, the Alouette III is recognised for its mountain rescue capabilities and adaptability.

Development

The first version of the Alouette III, the SE 3160 prototype, first flew on 28 February 1959. Production of the SA 316A (SE 3160) began in 1961 and remained in production until 1968, when it was replaced by the SA 316B. The last and 1437th Alouette III left the Marignane assembly lines in 1979, when the main production line in France was closed down. The last Alouette III from Aérospatiale was delivered in 1985.

Over 500 units were manufactured under license in Romania, India and Switzerland. Hindustan Aeronautics Limited (HAL) obtained a licence to build Alouette IIIs as the **HAL Chetak** in India. Over 300 units were produced by HAL as it continued to independently update and indigenize the helicopter over the years, and a variant is still in production though in diminishing volumes. Versions of the Alouette III were also either licence-built or assembled by IAR in Romania (as the IAR 316), F+W Emmen in Switzerland, and by Fokker and Lichtwerk in the Netherlands.

Production numbers are as follows:
- France: 1453
- India: 300+ (Still in production)
- Romania: 230
- Switzerland: 60

Operational history

French Navy *Alouette III* on the frigate *La Motte-Picquet*

The Alouette III entered in service with the French Armed forces in 1960. From April 1964-1967, three machines were delivered from France for local assembly in Australia, and were used by Royal Australian Air Force (RAAF) at the Woomera Rocket Range for light passenger transport and recovery of missile parts after test launches at the Range.

2 Alouette III of the Pakistan Air Force (PAF) were shot down in Indo-Pakistani War of 1971.

The helicopter saw service in the Portuguese Colonial War, during 60's and 70's with large utilization in Angola, Mozambique and Guinea, where it proved its qualities.

In June 2004, the Alouette III was retired from the French Air Force after 32 years of successful service being replaced by the Eurocopter EC 355 Ecureuil 2. In the same year, the Swiss Armed Forces announced the retirement of the Alouette III, from the front line by 2006, and entirely by 2010. Venezuelan Air forces retired their Alouette IIIs in the late 90s.

At Baldonnel 21 September 2007 the Alouette III was retired from the Irish Air Corps. During 44 years of successful service, the fleet amassed over 77,000 flying hours. As well as routine military missions, the aircraft undertook some 1,717 Search and Rescue Missions, saving 542 lives and flew a further 2,882 Air Ambulance flights. The oldest of the Alouettes, 195, is currently being kept in 'rotors running' condition for the Air Corps Museum.

Combat History

Argentina

The Argentine Naval Aviation purchased 14 helicopters. One SA316B was on board the *ARA General Belgrano* when she was sunk by the *HMS Conqueror's* torpedoes during the Falklands (Islas Malvinas) War with Great Britain in 1982 and a second one played an important role during the Invasion of South Georgia. On 2 December 2010, the last example was retired at a ceremony held at BAN Comandante Espora, Bahía Blanca.

France

The French Army needed a fast, well-armed machine for the war in Algeria. So during this war ALAT (Aviation Légère de l'Armée de Terre) used Alouette IIIs armed with Nord AS.10 and AS.11 wire-guided antitank missiles. The missiles were first used against guerillas who had holed up in heavily fortified mountain caves. Alouette IIIs could carry four missiles each, often operating in mixed formations with gun-armed Alouette IIIs.

India

Hindustan Aeronautics Limited built over 300 units of the helicopter under licence as the **HAL Chetak**. They were primarily in service with the Indian Armed Forces in training, transport, CASEVAC (Casualty Evacuation), communications and liaison roles. The Chetak is being replaced by HAL Dhruv in the armed forces. An option to re-engine the HAL Chetak with the Turbomeca TM 333-2B engine for high-altitude operations in the Himalayas was considered, but not pursued.

In 1986 the Government constituted the Army's Aviation Corps and most Chetak operating in AOP Squadrons were transferred from the Air Force on 1 November 1986. The Air Force continues to fly armed Chetaks in the antitank role as well as for CASEVAC and general duties.

HAL also exported Chetak helicopters to Namibia and Suriname. India has also donated used Chetak helicopters to other countries such as Bangladesh and Nepal.

Namibia

In 2009, India sold two of their Chetak and one Cheetah helicopters to Namibia, for a total price of $10 million.

Pakistan

Simultaneously with acquisition of Mirage IIIs Pakistan purchased 35 Alouette III helicopters and used them in the Indo-Pakistani War of 1971, mainly for liaison and VIP-transport.

Portugal

Portuguese Air Force's helicopter operating in African theatre during the war.

The war in Guinea Bissau began in earnest in August 1961. From 1967 the situation changed considerably, when the Organisation of African Unity (OAU), officially provided its full support to the PAIGC, de-facto recognising this organisation as an official representation of Guinea Bissau. The Portuguese reaction to these developments was an intensive campaign of building schools, hospitals, housing, and roads, in an effort to improve the living conditions of the local population. Until then, communications were almost non-existent in Guinea. To improve the means of communication, 12 SA.316B Alouette III helicopters were permanently deployed, in order to support the civilians. Several of these helicopters were equipped with 20mm cannons, carried in the rear cabin and fired over the side. Portugal used their Alouettes against guerrillas in Africa. During the 60's and 70's Portugal used large numbers of helicopters in Angola, Mozambique and Guinea, where Alouettes proved its qualities for use in dusty and hot flying conditions. The versatile Alouette III bore the brunt of COIN operations in Africa: Wherever the troops were sent, the helicopters led or transported them, flew reconnaissance and liaison, CASEVAC/MEDEVAC and other missions. The Portuguese Air Force would be the first to use them with French 20mm cannons.

The Portuguese needed some time until they learned how to make best use of their Alouettes. They started regularly sitting five of six armed troops aboard, in addition to the crew of two, despite the fact that the Alouette III was built to carry only four passengers. This placed especially the gearbox of the helicopters under strain, causing quite some maintenance problems in return.

After some time the French technicians assigned to FAP instructed the Portuguese to be more careful, and the practice was changed so the number of troops usually transported was reduced. This was causing some problems especially if there were casualties to recover, but there was no way around. The lack of facilities for evacuation of casualties (CASEVAC), however, was one of the main reasons for the low morale among the Portuguese soldiers. The FAP personnel was also highly praised and most of the successes during the war in Angola were achieved either by elite units or the air force. However, the Portuguese pilots had no means to communicate with ground troops: even the most elementary equipment – like smoke-grenades for marking targets, and mirrors – was not available, and the troops were not trained to communicate with pilots.

Rhodesia and South Africa, both of which were concerned about their own future in the case of the Portuguese defeat gave military support. They initially limited their participation on shipments of arms and supplies. However, by 1968 South Africa begun providing SA.316B Alouette III helicopters with crews to the FAP, and finally several companies of South African Defence Forces (SADF) infantry were deployed in southern central Angola. There were reports that a some Rhodesian pilots were recruited to fly FAP helicopters, however Rhodesian pilots were considered too valuable by the RRAF/RhAF to be deployed in support of the Portuguese, while the SADF had pilots and helicopters operating out of "Centro Conjunto de Apoio Aéreo" (CCAA – Joint Air Support Centre), set up in Cuito Cuanavale, in 1968.

FAP deployed a large number of SA.316B Alouette IIIs in Angola, and used them for all possible purposes. All the helicopters of this type were operated by Esquadra 94 and were camouflaged in overall green colour. This camouflage would soon be quite worn out to different shades of olive green due to the sun, sand and rain. In some operations a piece of tarpauline with a large number 1, 2, 3, or 4 was applied on the lower window of the cockpit doors. Several Rhodesian and South African "advisers" supported the Portuguese COIN operations, but these never succeeded in goading the Portuguese into employing some effective Rhodesian combat tactics.

The Alouette III was originally purchased by the Rhodesians pre UDI. Later a large number of Alouette IIIs were covertly obtained from various sources to increase the capability of No. 7 Squadron and also to replenish the squadron for various losses suffered both by accidents and while on combat missions.

In the 1970s South African Air Force (SAAF) Alouette III helicopters were attached to No. 7 Squadron, Rhodesian Air Force. The Alouette III was also the choice of the South African Air Force which meant that training facilities and expertise could be shared. The Portuguese Air Force had also purchased Alouette IIIs.

For Fireforce missions a gunship version of the Alouette III was fitted with a Matra MG 151/20 20 mm cannon. The 'K-Car', as it was known, was operated usually with a crew of three, (pilot, gunner and fireforce commander). The 'K-Car' was used as a mobile command post to allow the army commander of the heli-borne troops to direct their operations from the air above them.

Ammunition for the 20mm Cannon was carried in a special bin in the left hand baggage compartment and fed to the cannon via a feed tray through the rear bulkhead. The spent brass was collected in a compartment below the cabin floor. The ammunition bin was supposed to be able to carry 440 rounds of 20mm ammuninition, but typically, only 400-410 rounds were loaded. The gunner in the 'K-Car' was also a technician and therefore he was not only the gunner, but also responsible for all the maintenance of his aircraft.

A Rhodesian Alouette III, 'K-Car' had the distinction of shooting down a Botswana Defence Force Islander on 9 August 1979 with its 20mm cannon.

The standard troop carrying/utility version of the Alouette III in the Rhodesian Air Froce were called 'G-Cars'. They were used by No. 7 Squadron for the troop transport, light air/ground fire support, SAR, casualty evacuation (CASEVAC) and a variety of other roles.

Rhodesian practice was to operate the 'G-Car' with a gunner/technician and to mount twin Mk 2 .303 Brownings machine guns, with about 400 rounds per gun. As with the 'K-Car', not only did the technician fly in combat and operate the aircraft's weapons, he was also responsible for all the maintenance of the helicopter too.

In the troop carrying role, a "Stick" of four soldiers was the standard load for the RhAF Alouette III. The seating configuration was two in the rear of the cabin, beside the gunner/technician and behind the pilot, with the "Stick commander" in the centre and his MAG gunner beside him. The other two riflemen were in the front on the rear-facing bench seat. Experience in combat led the Rhodesians to remove all but the pilot's door on the 'G-Car' and to reverse the front passengers to widen the available floorspace and gain flexibility. With the doors removed, it was easier for the soldiers to leave the helicopter quickly. Reversing the front seats opened up floor area and therefore more space for internal cargo was available.

The standard Sud Aviation front seats in the 'G-Car' were replaced in the Rhodesian Air Force by a "home made" rear-facing bench seat. While carrying troops, casualties on a stretcher could be carried laterally across the rear of the cabin, one on the floor and another stretcher on a rack above it.

In September 1974 Rhodesian Air Force Alouette IIIs were fitted with anti-STRELA shrouds on the engines, the tail pipe was turned up to deflect the hot exhaust gasses into the rotor downwash and they were given matt paint finishes. This was done to reduce the Infra Red signature of the helicopter and proved to be highly successful for the type.

Several Alouettes were brought down by fire from the ground, but considering the intensity of operations, losses were surprisingly low. This was probably due to the highly skilled pilots' tactics of using ultra low level flying and terrain to keep out of the line of enemy fire.

At one stage, 27 SAAF helicopters were deployed in Rhodesia. Within No. 7 Squadron, the SAAF Alouettes were designated as belonging to Alpha Flight.

South Africa
The Alouette III helicopter served for 44 years and flew more than 346.000 hours in the South African Air Force (SAAF).

SAAF received its first examples in 1962, delivered to the SAAF's 17 Squadron. In all, 118 were delivered between 1962 and the late 1970s. The last eight were received from Rhodesia, possibly as replacements for SAAF helicopters lost during operations in that country. Used in the SAAF in many roles, the Alouette III primary role was qualifying helicopter pilots and flight engineers for the SAAF, its secondary roles of SAR and supporting internal security in South Africa. The Alouette saw service with almost all SAAF helicopter units at one time or another. It was also used extensively throughout the Bush War in Namibia, Angola and Rhodesia. In these countries was used mainly in search-and-rescue, reconnaissance roles, providing top-cover for the Pumas during troop deployments and extractions and close air-support with Koevoet and army units. The Aloutte proved its durability in the demanding African environment.

by 1968 SAAF began providing Alouette III helicopters with crews to the FAP. SAAF was also deeply involved in Rhodesia from 1975 to 1980, at least 20 to 30 Alouette III helicopters were based in Rhodesia at any one time, initially under the South African Police name.

The Alouette III configurations used operationally by the SAAF during the Bush War were:
- The K-car Gunship: armed with a Ga1, MG151 or Mk V Hispano 20mm cannon with AP and HE rounds. The most prominent feature of the K-car was the specially developed Heat shield around the turbine which vented the exhaust gasses up towards the rotors. This minimised the heat signature of the helicopter making it difficult for the Russian SAMs to lock onto target.
- The G-car: Transport version, armed with 7.62mm FN MAG for Fireforce type and COIN operations.

An Alouette III powerplant and dynamics system were used as the basis for an engineering and development capability demonstrator as a precursor to the Rooivalk programme. It was designated the Alpha XH-1, and it first flew in 1984 and is preserved at the SAAF Museum. this Missile Gunship was armed with two AS12 Missiles and laser designator.

The official withdrawal of Alouette III in SAAF took place on 30 June 2006 at Swartkop in Pretoria.

Variants

- **SA 316A**: the first production version. Original designation **SE 3160**.
- **SA 316B**: powered by a 425 kW (570 shp) Turboméca Artouste IIIB turboshaft engine, with strengthened main and tail rotor for greater performance. The SA 316B was built under licence in India as the HAL Chetak, and again under licence in Romania as the IAR 316.
- **HAL Chetak**: Indian production version of the SA 316B.
- **IAR 316**: Romanian production version of the SA 316B.
- The **SA 319B** was a direct development of the SA 316B, it was powered with a 649 kW (870 shp) Turboméca Astazou XIV turboshaft engine, but it was derated to 447 kW (660 hp).
- The **SA 316C** was powered by a Turbomeca Artouste IIID turboshaft engine. The SA 316C was only built in small numbers.
- **G-Car** and **K-Car**: Helicopter gunship versions for the Rhodesian Air Force. The G-Car was armed with two side-mounted Browning .303 or a single 7.62mm MAG machine guns. The K-Car was armed with a 20 mm MG 151 cannon, fitted inside the cabin, firing from the port side of the helicopter.
- **SA.3164 Alouette-Canon**: Modified in 1964 as a gunship version armed with a 20mm gun in the nose and external hardpoints for missiles mounted on each side of the fuselage. Only one prototype was built.
- **IAR 317 Airfox**: A Romanian helicopter gunship project based on the IAR 316. Only three prototypes were ever built.
- **Atlas XH-1 Alpha**: A Two-seat attack helicopter project. It was used in the development of the Denel AH-2 Rooivalk.

When used as an aerial ambulance, the Alouette III can accommodate a pilot, two medical attendants and two stretcher patients.

Operators

Current military operators

Albania
- Albanian Air Force - (SA 319)

Angola
- People's Air and Air Defence Force of Angola 20× SA316Bs

Austrian *Alouette III* over the Alps

Austria
- Austrian Air Force Twenty-six (12× SE3160, 14× SA316B).

Bangladesh
- Bangladesh Air Force Four former Indian Air Force *HAL Chetak*

Belgium
- Belgian Navy 3× SA316B

Bolivia

Burkina Faso

Burma
- Burma Air Force Fourteen (13× SE3160 and 1× SE316B)

Burundi
- Four (1× SE3160 and 3× SA316Bs)

Cameroon
- Cameroon Air Force 2× SA319

Chad
- Chad Air Force Ten former French SE3160s

Republic of the Congo
- Congolese Air Force 4× SA316B

Côte d'Ivoire
- Côte d'Ivoire Air Force Four (3× SE3160, 1× SA316B)

Dominican Republic
- Dominican Air Force 1× SE3160

Ecuador
- Ecuadorian Air Force (SA 316)
- Ecuadorian Army

El Salvador
- Air Force of El Salvador 1× SA316B

Equatorial Guinea
- Military of Equatorial Guinea

Ethiopia
- Ethiopian Air Force Eleven (5× SE3160 & 6× Romanian-built SA316B).

France
- French Navy 23 in active service
- Sécurité Civile Six (SA316)

Gabon
- Gabonese Air Force Five (1× SE3160, 1× SA316B, 3× SA319B)

Ghana
- Ghana Air Force 4× SA316B

Greece
- Hellenic Naval Aviation Two SA319B for rotary flying training

Guinea
- Guinean Air Force 1× SA316B

Guinea-Bissau
- Military of Guinea-Bissau (SA 316)

HAL Chetak from Indian Navy's INS *Rana*.

India
- Indian Air Force 87+ (55× French-built SE3160 and SA316B, 32+ Indian-built SA319B Chetak)
- Indian Navy 18+ (7× French-built SE3160, 7× French-built SA316B plus Indian built Chetaks)
- Indian Army over 120 in active service.

Indonesia
- Indonesian Army 7× SE3160

Iran
Laos
Libya
- Libyan Arab Jamahiriyah Army Aviation 13× SA316B, three later to Malta

Madagascar
- Malagasy Air Force Two (SE3160, one former French Army)

Malawi
- Malawi Army Air Wing One SA316

Malaysia
- Royal Malaysian Air Force 26× SA316B and 10× SA319B (not including 7× SA316B transferred from Republic of Singapore Air Force in 1978/9), 20× SA316Bs were later transferred to the Malaysian Army's Air Wing

Malta
- Armed Forces of Malta 3× SA316B (all former Libyan Air Force).

Mexico
- Mexican Air Force 3× SE3160
- Mexican Naval Aviation Five (SA319B)

Morocco
- Royal Moroccan Gendarmie Air Squadron 2× SA316B.

Mozambique
- Mozambique Air Force 4× SA316B (former Portugal Air Force).

Namibia
- Namibian Air Force

Nepal
- Nepal Royal Flight 1× SE3160
- Air Battalion, 11th Brigade Nepal Army At least 4 HAL Cheetak.

Netherlands
- Royal Netherlands Air Force 4 in active service for VIP transport

Nicaragua
- Nicaraguan National Guard Two

Pakistan Naval Air Arm Alouette III on board PNS Tippu Sultan at Portsmouth in 2005

Pakistan
- Pakistan Air Force Thirteen (7× SE3160, 4× SA316B, 2 x SA319B plus local production)
- Pakistan Army Twelve (11× SE3160, 1× SA316B)
- Pakistan Navy
- Pakistan Naval Air Arm (SA316, SA319)

People's Republic of China
- People's Liberation Army Ground Force

Peru
- Peruvian Air Force Twelve (4× SE3160, 8× SA316C)
- Peruvian Naval Aviation 6× SA316B

Portuguese *Alouette III* in Africa during a MEDEVAC

Portugal
- Portuguese Air Force 12× SA316B

Romania
- Romanian Air Force (IAR 316) 8× IAR316B in service for rotary flying training

Rwanda
- Rwanda Air Force 2× SE3160

Saudi Arabia
- Royal Saudi Air Force Five (4× SE3160, 1× SA316B)

Seychelles
South Korea
- Republic of Korea Navy (SA319B) One Alouette III on display at the War Memorial of Korea, Seoul, Republic of Korea

South Vietnam
- Vietnam Air Force (SA319)

Sri Lanka (SA316)
Suriname
- Military of Suriname (SA316)

Swaziland
- Umbutfo Swaziland Defence Force 3 ex SAAF

20 - Aérospatiale Alouette III

Tunisia
- Tunisian Air Force Eight (4× SE3160, 4× SA316B)

Venezuela
- Venezuelan Air Force 20× c
  - Special Helicopter Squad of 1st Corps of AF and AD used two SA 316 helicopters.

Zaire
- Zaire Air Force Ten (SE3160 and SA316B)

Zambia
- Zambian Air Force

Zimbabwe
- Air Force of Zimbabwe - (SA 316)

Former military operators

Argentine Navy Alouette III aboard USS *Bunker Hill*

Argentina
- Argentine Naval Aviation Fourteen (3× SE3160, 7× SA316B and 4× SA319B). Last surviving aircraft retired on 2 December 2010.

Australia
- Royal Australian Air Force - Three Alouette IIIs (RAAF serials *A3-165 to 167*) were in service from 1964 to 1967. The helicopters were used for general transport and support duties at the Woomeria Rocket Range in South Australia.

United Arab Emirates (Abu Dhabi)

Upper Volta

Bophuthatswana
- Bophuthatswana Air Force
- Upper Volta Air Force Two SA316B

Biafra
- Biafran Air Force operated few helicopters.

Chile
- Chilean Navy 10× SA319Bs, retired in 1991

Denmark
- Danish Navy 8× SE3160

France
- French Air Force Entire fleet retired
- French Army Light Aviation Entire fleet retired

Hong Kong
- Royal Hong Kong Auxiliary Air Force Three (2× SE3160, 1× 316B)

Iraq
- Iraq Air Force 44× SA316C

Irish Air Corps SA-316B Alouette III, 212 from 3 Operations Wing at RNAS Yeovilton in July 2006

Ireland
- Irish Air Corps Eight (3× SE3160 and 5× SA316B) in service between 1963 and 2007.

Jordan
- Jordanian Air Force 16× SA316B

Lebanon
- Lebanese Air Force Eighteen (11× SE3160, 7× SA316B) retired from military service; currently being used for crop spraying

Rhodesia
- Rhodesian Air Force

Retired *Alouette III* (SA316B) of the Republic of Singapore Air Force on static display at RSAF Museum.

Singapore
- Republic of Singapore Air Force (8× SA316B delivered in 1968/9, one preserved at RSAF Museum while remaining 7 were retired and transferred to Royal Malaysian Air Force in 1978/9)

South Africa (SA 316)
- South African Air Force 120 (58× SE3160, 40× SA316B plus others)

Spain
- Spanish Air Force 5× SA319B
- Spanish Army 3× SA319B

Aérospatiale SA 316 *Alouette III* of the Swiss Air Force

Switzerland
- Swiss Air Force Total of 84: 24× SE3160 first delivered in 1964 (minus 6 accident write-offs) plus 60× SA316B first delivered in 1972 (minus 13 accident write offs). In late August 2010, 10 airframes were donated to Pakistan's National Disaster Management Authority (NDMA) for search and rescue (SAR) work. On 10 December 2010, all the remaining 55 airframes (of which 20 were still airworthy) were retired at Alpnache Aerodome, replaced by 20× Eurocopter EC635

P2+

Civilian operators

SA316B-1 used by Nagoya Fire Department, Kagamihara Aviation Museum.

Chile
- ALFA Helicópteros

Italy
- Air Walser srl
- GIANA Helicopter - RTI

Japan
- Tokyo Fire Department
- Some Local firefighting service

Pakistan
- Askari Aviation

United States
- Flight for Life

Specifications (SA 316B)

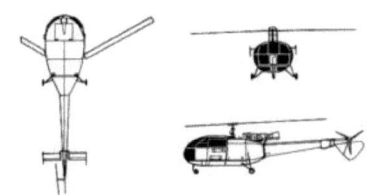

Close-up of the turbine of an *Alouette III*

Data from Jane's All The World's Aircraft 1976-77

General characteristics
- **Crew:** 2
- **Capacity:** 5 passengers
- **Length:** 10.03 m (32 ft 10¾ in)
- **Main rotor diameter:** 11.02 m (36 ft 1¾ in)
- **Height:** 3.00 m (9 ft 10 in)
- **Main rotor area:** 95.38 m² (1026 ft²)
- **Empty weight:** 1,143 kg (2,520 lb)
- **Gross weight:** 2,200 kg (4,850 lb)
- **Powerplant:** 1 × Turbomeca Artouste IIIB turboshaft, 649 kW (870 shp) derated to 425 kW (570 hp)

Performance
- **Maximum speed:** 210 km/h (130 mph)
- **Cruising speed:** 185 km/h (115 mph)
- **Range:** 540 km (335 miles)
- **Service ceiling:** 3,200 m (10,500 ft)
- **Rate of climb:** 4.3 m/s (850 ft/min)

Source (edited): "http://en.wikipedia.org/wiki/A%C3%A9rospatiale_Alouette_III"

Aérospatiale Gazelle

The **Aérospatiale Gazelle** is a French-designed five-seat light helicopter, powered by a single turbine engine, manufactured by Sud Aviation (later Aérospatiale), and its licensees (Westland Aircraft and SOKO).

Design and development

The Aérospatiale Gazelle originated in a French Army requirement for a lightweight utility helicopter. The design quickly attracted British interest, leading to a development and production share out agreement with British company Westland Helicopters. The deal, signed in February 1967, allowed the production in Britain of 292 Gazelles and 48 Aérospatiale Pumas ordered by the British armed forces; in return Aérospatiale was given a work share in the manufacturing programme for the 40 Westland Lynx naval helicopters for the French Navy.

Though the general layout resembles that of the Alouette series, the Gazelle featured several important innovations. This was the first helicopter to carry a Fenestron or fantail, which allows considerable noise reduction. Also, the rotor blades were made of composite materials, a feature now widely used in modern helicopters.

In service with the French Army Light Aviation (ALAT), the Gazelle is used primarily as an anti-tank gunship (**SA 342M**) armed with Euromissile HOT missiles. A light support version (**SA 341F**) equipped with a 20 mm cannon is used as well as anti-air variants carrying the Mistral air-to-air missile (**Gazelle Celtic** based on the **SA 341F**, **Gazelle Mistral** based on the **SA 342M**). The latest anti-tank and reconnaissance versions carry the Viviane thermal imagery system and so are called **Gazelle Viviane**. The Gazelle is being replaced in frontline duties by the Eurocopter Tiger, but will continue to be used for light transport and liaison roles.

It also served with all branches of the British armed forces—the Royal Air Force, Royal Navy (including Royal Marines) and the British Army in a variety of roles. Four versions of the Gazelle were used by the British forces. The **SA.341D** became the **Gazelle HT.3** in RAF service, equipped as a helicopter pilot trainer (hence HT). The **SA 341E** was used by the RAF for communications duties and VIP transport as the **Gazelle HCC.4**. The **SA 341C** was purchased as the **Gazelle HT.2** pilot trainer for the Royal Navy. The training variants have now been replaced by the Squirrel HT1. The **SA 341B** was equipped to a specification for the Army Air Corps as the **Gazelle AH.1** (from Army Helicopter Mark 1). It was used as an Air Observation Post (AOP) for directing artillery fire, Airborne Forward Air Controller (ABFAC) directing ground-attack aircraft, casualty evacuation, liaison, and command and control, and communications relay.

The Gazelle flown by the British Army Air Corps has recently been enhanced with a Direct Voice Input (DVI) system developed by QinetiQ. It allows for voice control of avionics equipment using standard aircrew helmet microphones and intercom. Being speaker independent, the system does not need to be trained to recognize a specific user. This means high command recognition rates may be achieved whether or not the user has operated the system before. It gives aircrew the ability to control aircraft systems using voice commands and access information without removing their hands from the flight controls or their eyes from the outside world.

Gazelles were also manufactured in Egypt by ABHCO and in Yugoslavia by SOKO.

Operational history
France
The French army deployed the Gazelle on many occasions, especially during interventions in Africa and peacekeeping operations. This includes Chad (1980s), the former Yugoslavia (1990s), Djibouti (1991-1992), Somalia (1993) and Cote d'Ivoire (2002-Present). During Operation Desert Storm, HOT-carrying Gazelles were used against Iraqi armour.
Iraq
Iraq received a number of Gazelles and HOT missiles in the 1970s and 1980s. They were used intensively in the Iran–Iraq War. During the Gulf War they saw little use, because of Allied air supremacy.
Syria
Syrian Gazelles were used during 1982 Lebanon War. Syrian Army claimed they had large success against Israeli armour (30 kills), while suffering medium losses. One was captured by Israeli forces, tested and now is displayed in IAF museum.
Kuwait
Kuwait said its Gazelles were used during the Iraqi invasion, destroying some Iraqi trucks or APCs. Several were captured and used by Iraqi Army.
United Kingdom
The Gazelle was used in combat in the Falkland Islands, Kuwait, Iraq and Kosovo, and with 8 Flight Army Air Corps in support of 22 Special Air Service Regiment. It was also used for air patrols in Northern Ireland. British Gazelles were only armed when used in the Falklands, where they were fitted with machine guns and rocket pods, but these were not used. Three Gazelles were lost in action in 1982, two due to ground fire, and one shot down by a Sea Dart surface to air missile fired by HMS Cardiff. British Gazelles performed as scouts for other attack platforms in 1991 Gulf War.

Yugoslav Air Force Soko Gazelle

Ex-Yugoslavia
SA 341/342 Gazelle GAMA (Yugoslav version) was used by Republika Srpska Air Force and Republika Srpska Krajna Militia Air Force during the Yugoslav civil wars (1991-1995), and by the Yugoslav air force during the Kosovo war.
Lebanon
Gazelles armed with machine guns, were used by the Lebanese Air Force against the Al Qaeda-inspired militants of Fatah al-Islam during the battle of Nahr el-Bared.
Morocco
24 SA342L Gazelle helicopters were bought, half of them armed with HOT missiles and the other half with 20mm guns. Some were used in Western Sahara to fight Polisario columns.
Ireland
The Irish Air Corps formerly operated two Gazelle helicopters as pilot training aircraft.

Variants
SA 340
First prototype, first flown on 7 April 1967 with a conventional Alouette type tail rotor.
SA 341
Four pre-production machines. First flown on 2 August 1968. The third was equipped to British Army requirements and assembled in France as the prototype Gazelle AH.1. This was first flown on 28 April 1970.
SA 341.1001
First French production machine. Initial test flight 6 August 1971. Featured a longer cabin, an enlarged tail unit and an uprated Turbomeca Astazou IIIA engine.
SA 341B (*Westland Gazelle AH.1*)

A Westland Gazelle AH.1 of the British Army in 1983.

Version built for the British Army; Featured the Astazou IIIN engine, a nightsun searchlight and Decca Doppler 80 Radar. First Westland-assembled version flown on 31 January 1972, this variant entered service on 6 July 1974. A total of 158 were produced.
SA 341C (*Westland Gazelle HT.2*)
Training helicopter version built for British Fleet Air Arm; Features included the Astazou IIIN engine, a stability augmentation system and a hoist. First flown on 6 July 1972, this variant entered operational service on 10 December 1974. A total of 30 were produced.
SA 341D (*Westland Gazelle HT.3*)
Training helicopter version built for British Royal Air Force; Featuring the same engine and stability system as the 341C, this version was first delivered on 16 July 1973. A total of 14 were produced.

SA 341E (*Westland Gazelle HCC.4*)
Communications helicopter version built for British Royal Air Force; Only one example of this variant was produced.

SA 341F
Version built for the French Army; Featuring the Astazou IIIC engine, 166 of these were produced. Some of these were fitted with an M621 20-mm cannon.

Aerospatiale SA 341G Gazelle

SA 341G
Civil variant, powered by an Astazou IIIA engine. Officially certificated on 7 June 1972; subsequently became first helicopter to obtain single-pilot IFR Cat 1 approval in the US. Also developed into "Stretched Gazelle" with the cabin modified to allow an additional 8 inches (20cm) legroom for the rear passengers.

SA 341H
Military export variant, powered by an Astazou IIIB engine. Built under licence agreement signed on 1 October 1971 by SOKO in Yugoslavia.

SOKO HO-42
Yugoslav-built version of SA 341H.

SOKO HI-42 Hera
Yugoslav-built scout version of SA 341H.

Control panel of a Gazelle SA 342M of the French Army's Light Aviation (ALAT)

SOKO HN-42M Gama
Yugoslav-built attack version of SA 341H.

SOKO HN-45M Gama 2
Yugoslav-built attack version of SA 342L.

SOKO HS-42
Yugoslav-built medic version of SA 341H.

SA 342J
Civil version of SA 342L. This was fitted with the more powerful 649kW (870shp) Astazou XIV engine and an improved Fenestron tail rotor. With an increased take-off weight, this variant was approved on 24 April 1976, and entered service in 1977.

SA 342K
Military export version for "hot and dry areas". Fitted with the more powerful 649-kW (870-shp) Astazou XIV engine and shrouds over the air intakes. First flown on 11 May 1973; initially sold to Kuwait.

SA 342L
Military companion of the SA 342J. fitted with the Astazou XIV engine. Adaptable for many armaments and equipment, including six Euromissile HOT anti-tank missiles.

SA 342M
French Army anti-tank version fitted with the Astazou XIV engine. Armed with four Euromissile HOT missiles and a SFIM APX M397 stabilised sight.

SA 342M1
Standard SA 342M retrofitted with three Ecureuil main blades to improve performance.

Operators

Cypriot National Guard Aérospatiale Gazelle armed with HOT missiles.

Bosnian Soko Gazelle

French Army Gazelle SA 342L1 at RIAT 2010

24 - Aérospatiale Gazelle

Serbian Soko Gazelle

Military operators

Angola
- People's Air and Air Defence Force of Angola operates about 7 aircraft.

Bosnia and Herzegovina
- Air Force and Anti-Aircraft Defense operates 4 aircraft

Burundi
- Burundi Army Aviation operates 2 aircraft.

Cameroon
- Cameroon Air Force operates 3 aircraft. 4 were ordered but 1 crashed

People's Republic of China

Cyprus
- Cypriot National Guard's Air Component operates 4 aircraft.

Ecuador
- Ecuadorian Army operates about 20 aircraft.

Egypt
- Egyptian Air Force operates about 84 aircraft.

France
- French Army

Gabon
- Gabon Air Force operates 5 aircraft.

Guinea
- Guinea Air Force operates 1 aircraft.

Iraq
- Iraqi Air Force operates 6 aircraft.

Jordan

Kenya
- Kenya Air Force, 1 in service in 2009

Kuwait
- Kuwait Air Force operates 13 aircraft.

Lebanon
- Lebanese Air Force operates 8 helicopters equipped with HOT missiles, 68 mm rocket pods, and heavy machine guns. Lebanon signed a contract with Eurotech in January 2010 to revamp and upgrade 13 Gazelles of the original and ex-UAE deliveries.

Montenegro
- Air Defense operates 11 aircraft

Morocco
- Royal Moroccan Air Force operates 24 aircraft.

Qatar
- Qatar Emiri Air Force

Rwanda

Senegal

Serbia
- Serbian Air Force operates 61 aircraft
  - 252. Mixed-Aviation Squadron
  - 138. Mixed-Transport-Aviation Squadron
  - 714. Anti-Armour Helicopter Squadron
  - 119. Combined-Arms Helicopter Squadron

Syria
- Syrian Air Force operates 38 aircraft.

Trinidad and Tobago
- Trinidad and Tobago Defence Force

Tunisia
- Tunisian Air Force

United Arab Emirates
- United Arab Emirates Air Force operates 1 aircraft.

United Kingdom
- Army Air Corps - Current Units;
  - 2 Regiment AAC (Trg), *671 Sqn*
  - 5 Regiment AAC (NI), *665 Sqn*
  - Canada, *29 (BATUS) Flight*
  - Germany, *12 Flight*

Law Enforcement operators

Bosnia and Herzegovina
- **Republika Srpska**
- Republika Srpska Police operates 4 aircraft

Montenegro
- Montenegro Police operates 3 aircraft

Serbia
- Serbian Police Helicopter unit operates 13 aircraft

Former military operators

Ireland
- Irish Air Corps - Two aircraft operated between 1979–2005

Republika Srpska
- Republika Srpska Air Force operated 20 aircraft

United Kingdom
- Royal Air Force - 32
- Royal Marines
- Royal Navy - Fleet Air Arm

Yugoslavia
- FR Yugoslav Air Force
  - 890. Mixed-Helicopter Squadron *Pegazi*
  - 897. Mixed-Helicopter Squadron *Stršljeni*
  - 712. Anti-Armour Helicopter Squadron *Škorpioni*
  - 714. Anti-Armour Helicopter Squadron *Senke*

Yugoslavia
- SFR Yugoslav Air Force operated about 207 helicopters, passed to successor states
  - 890. Transport Helicopter Squadron
  - 782. Helicopter Squadron
  - 782. Helicopter Squadron
  - 783. Helicopter Squadron
  - 712. Anti-Armour Helicopter Squadron
  - 714. Anti-Armour Helicopter Squadron
  - 333. Aviation Squadron
  - 711. Anti-Armour Helicopter Squadron
  - 713. Anti-Armour Helicopter Squadron
  - EIV of 1st Army region
  - EIV of 2nd Army region
  - EIV of 3rd Army region
  - EIV of Navy region

Slovenia
- Slovenian Air Force and Air Defence operated 1 aircraft from 1991 to 1996

Specifications (SA 341)

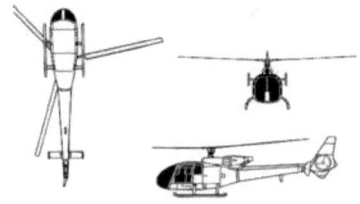

Data from Airplane Magazine Vol 1 Issue 6

General characteristics
- **Crew:** 2
- **Capacity:** 3 Passengers
- **Length:** 11.97 m (39 ft 0 in)
- **Main rotor diameter:** 10.5 m (34 ft 6 in)
- **Height:** 3.15 m (10 ft 3 in)
- **Main rotor area:** 86.5 m² (931 ft²)
- **Empty weight:** 908 kg (2,002 lb)
- **Gross weight:** 1,800 kg (3,970 lb)
- **Powerplant:** 1 × Turbomeca Astazou IIIA turboshaft, 440 kW (590 hp)

Performance
- **Maximum speed:** 310 km/h (193 mph)
- **Cruising speed:** 264 km/h (164 mph)
- **Range:** 670 km (416 miles)
- **Service ceiling:** 5,000 m (16,405 ft)
- **Rate of climb:** 9 m/s (1,770 ft/min)

Popular culture
Two Gazelles were modified to star as a high-tech attack/surveillance helicopter in the 1983 action-thriller film *Blue Thunder*, and in its short-lived television series spinoff. A Gazelle was used as part of the futuristic semi-truck in the television series *The Highwayman*.
Source (edited): "http://en.wikipedia.org/wiki/A%C3%A9rospatiale_Gazelle"

Aérospatiale SA 330 Puma

The **Aérospatiale SA 330 Puma** is a four-bladed, twin-engined medium transport/utility helicopter. The Puma was originally manufactured by Sud Aviation of France.

Development

The SA 330 Puma was originally developed by Sud Aviation to meet a requirement of the French Army for a medium-sized all-weather helicopter. The helicopter also had to be capable of operating by day and night as well as in a wide variety of climates.

In 1967, the Puma was also selected by the Royal Air Force (RAF) and given the designation **Puma HC Mk 1**. As a result of this decision, the SA 330 was included in a joint production agreement between Aerospatiale and Westland Helicopters of the UK, which also resulted in the purchase of Aérospatiale Gazelle by the United Kingdom and the Westland Lynx by France. This resulted in Westland building components for the Puma, and assembling the RAF's Pumas.

The first of two Puma prototypes flew on 15 April 1965. Six pre-production models were also built, the last of which flew on 30 July 1968. The first production SA 330 Puma flew in September 1968, with deliveries to the French Army starting in early 1969.

Production of the SA 330 Puma by Aérospatiale ceased in 1987, by which time a total of 697 had been sold. The Puma was then replaced by an upgraded and improved version, the Eurocopter AS332 Super Puma.

Variants

Portuguese Air Force Puma in support of a Space Shuttle Recovery Exercise at Lajes Field, Azores

Aerospatiale SA 330B Puma of the French Army at RIAT 2010

Aérospatiale versions

SA 330A
Prototypes, originally called "Alouette IV".

SA 330B
Initial production version for the French Army Aviation. Powered by 884 kW (1,185 hp) Turbomeca Turmo IIIC4 engines. 132 purchased by France.

SA 330 *Orchidée*
SA 330 modified to carry an *Orchidée* battlefiled surveillance radar system with a rotating underfuselage antenna, for the French Army. One demonstrator was built, flying in 1986. The *Orchidée* programme was cancelled in 1990, but the prototype rushed back into service in 1991 to serve in the Gulf War, leading to production of a similar system based on the Eurocopter Cougar.

SA 330C
Initial export production version. Powered by 1,044 kW (1,400 hp) Turmo

IVB engines.
SA 330E
Version produced by Westland Helicopters for the RAF under the designation Puma HC Mk. 1.
SA 330F
Initial civilian export production version with Turbomeca Turmo IIIC4 turboshaft engines.
SA 330G
Upgraded civilian version with 1175 kW (1,575 hp) Turbomeca Turmo IVC engines.
SA 330H
Upgraded French Army and export version with Turbomeca IVC engines and composite main rotor blades. Designated SA 330Ba by the French Air Force. All surviving French Army SA 330Bs converted to this standard.
SA 330J
Upgraded civil transport version with composite rotor blades and with higher maximum takeoff weight.
SA 330L
Upgraded version for so-called "hot and high" conditions. Military equivalent to civil SA 330J.
SA 330S
Upgraded SA 330L (themselves converted from SA 330C) version for the Portuguese Air Force. Powered by Turbomeca Makila engines.
SA 330Z
Prototype with "fenestron" tail rotor.

Versions by other manufacturers
Atlas Aircraft Corporation Oryx
This is a remanufactured and upgraded SA 330 Puma built for the South African Air Force.
IPTN NAS 330J
This is a version that was assembled by IPTN of Indonesia under the local designation NAS 330J and the Aerospatiale designation of SA 330J. Eleven units were produced.
IAR 330
This is a licence-built version of the SA 330 Puma manufactured by Industria Aeronautică Română of Romania. Designated as the SA 330L by Aerospatiale.
IAR-330 Puma SOCAT
24 modified for antitank warfare.
IAR-330 Puma Naval
3 modified for the Romanian Navy, using the SOCAT avionics.
Westland Puma HC Mk 1
This is the SA 330E version assembled by Westland Helicopters for the RAF and first flown on 25 November 1970. This is basically similar to the SA 330B used by France. The RAF placed an initial order for 40 Pumas in 1967, with a further eight attrition replacement aircraft in 1979. 30 of these are planned to be upgraded to **Puma HC Mk 2** standard, with new Turbomeca Makila engines, revised cockpit displays and new communications, navigation and defensive systems.

Operators
Military operators

The SA 330J Puma.

Aérospatiale Puma of the 801 Squadron of Spanish Air Force.

RAF Westland SA-330E Puma HC1 at RIAT 2009

Philippine Air Force Puma greeted by US and Philippine Marines at Subic Bay

 Albania
- Albanian Police

Argentina
- Argentine Army - Former operator.
- Argentine Coast Guard

 **Belgium**
- Federal Police (Belgium)
- Gendarmerie (Belgium) - Former operator

Brazil
- Brazilian Air Force - Former operator.

Cambodia

Cameroon
- Cameroon Air Force operates 3.

 **Chad**
- Chad Air Force - Former operator.

Chile
- Chilean Army
- Chilean Air Force - Former operator.

Côte d'Ivoire
- Cote d'Ivoire Air Force

Democratic Republic of the Congo
- Air Force of the Democratic Repub-

lic of the Congo

Ecuador
- Ecuadorian Army

Ethiopia
- Ethiopian Air Force - Former opeator

France
- French Air Force
- French Army

Gabon
- Military of Gabon

Gambia

Germany
- Federal Police (Germany)

Greece
- Hellenic Air Force
- Hellenic Coast Guard
- Hellenic Fire Service

Guinea
- Military of Guinea (1 helicopter)

Indonesia
- Indonesian Air Force

Ireland
- Irish Air Corps - Former operator.

Iran

Iraq
- Iraqi Air Force - Former opeator.

Kenya
- Kenya Air Force, 9 in service in 2009

Kuwait
- Kuwait Air Force 62nd Sqd

Lebanon
Lebanese Air Force - 7 active, 3 ex-UAE TBD. Additionally 7 SA330L are currently in storage.

Malawi
- Military of Malawi

Mexico
- Mexican Air Force - Former operator.

Morocco
- Royal Moroccan Air Force
- Royal Moroccan Gendarmerie

Nepal
- Nepalese Army Air Service

Nigeria
- Nigerian Air Force

Oman
- Royal Air Force of Oman

Pakistan
- Pakistan Army

Philippines
- Philippine Air Force - Former operator.

Portugal
- Portuguese Air Force

Romania
- Romanian Air Force
- Romanian Navy

Senegal
- Senegalese Air Force - Former operator.

Slovenia

South Africa
- South African Air Force:
  - On the 31 January 1972 the SAAF Puma became involved with operations in Namibia and Angola, remaining involved until 1988. This first deployment to the Eastern Caprivi led to the first member of the SAAF to be awarded the Honoris Crux, one of several to be awarded to Puma crews. The Puma was to be involved in normal trooping, rapid deployment during "follow up" operations, radio relay, evacuation of casualties, rescuing downed aircrew, insertion of Special Forces (Ops Backlash and Kodak etc.) and large scale cross border operations such as Savannah, Uric, Protea, Super, Moduler etc. The Puma also saw action in Rhodesia, Zambia, Botswana and Mozambique.
  - 13 Pumas were deployed and played a critical roles in the rescue efforts during the sinking of the MTS Oceanos

Spain
- Spanish Air Force

Sudan
- Sudan Air Force

Switzerland
- Swiss Air Force

Togo
- Military of Togo - Former operator.

United Arab Emirates
- United Arab Emirates Air Force

United Kingdom
- Royal Air Force - The RAF ordered 48 Puma HC Mk 1 and in addition received a single ex-Argentine SA 330J Used by Prefectura Naval Argentina captured in the Falklands War, and six ex-South African SA 330L purchased in 2002.
  - No. 33 Squadron RAF
  - No. 230 Squadron RAF
  - No. 1563 Flight RAF

Venezuela

Zaire
- Zairian Air Force - Former operator.

Civil operators

Germany
Helog KG - SA 330J

South Africa
Starlite Aviation - SA 330J

United States
Presidential Airways - SA 330J
Evergreen Aviation - SA 330J

Specifications (SA 330H Puma)

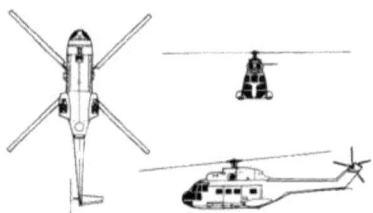

Data from Jane's All The World's Aircraft 1976-77

General characteristics
- **Crew:** 3
- **Capacity:** 16 passengers
- **Length:** 18.15 m (59 ft 6½ in)
- **Rotor diameter:** 15.00 m (49 ft 2½ in)
- **Height:** 5.14 m (16 ft 10½ in)
- **Disc area:** 177.0 m² (1,905 ft²)
- **Empty weight:** 3,536 kg (7,795 lb)
- **Max takeoff weight:** 7,000 kg (15,430 lb)
- **Powerplant:** 2× Turboméca Turmo IVC turboshafts, 1,175 kW (1,575 hp) each

Performance
- **Never exceed speed:** 273 km/h (147

knots, 169 mph)
- **Maximum speed:** 257 km/h (138 knots, 159 mph)
- **Cruise speed:** 248 km/h (134 knots, 154 mph) econ cruise
- **Range:** 580 km (313 nm, 360 mi)
- **Service ceiling:** 4,800 m (15,750 ft)
- **Rate of climb:** 7.1 m/s (1,400 ft/min)

Armament

- **Guns:**
  - Coaxial 7.62 mm (0.30 in) machine guns
  - Side-firing 20 mm (0.787 in) cannon
  - Various others

Popular culture

In Red Dawn (1984) and most notably Rambo: First Blood Part II (1985) and Rambo III (1988), an SA 330 Puma was equipped with stub wings and a gun turret to mimic a Soviet Mil Mi-24 Hind. Source (edited): "http://en.wikipedia.org/wiki/A%C3%A9rospatiale_SA_330_Puma"

Beechcraft T-34 Mentor

The **Beechcraft T-34 Mentor** is a propeller-driven, single-engined, military trainer aircraft derived from the Beechcraft Model 35 Bonanza. The earlier versions of the T-34, dating from around the late 1940s to the 1950s, were piston-engined. These were eventually succeeded by the upgraded **T-34C Turbo-Mentor**, powered by a turboprop engine. The T-34 remains in service almost six decades after it was first designed.

Design and development

The T-34 was the brainchild of Walter Beech, who developed it as the **Beechcraft Model 45** private venture at a time when there was no defense budget for a new trainer model. Beech hoped to sell it as an economical alternative to the North American T-6/NJ Texan, then in use by all services of the U.S. military.

A YT-34 on display at the Castle Air Museum in Atwater, California

Piston-engined T-34s of the March Field Aero Club at the March Air Reserve Base (ARB) in California in 2004

Three initial design concepts were developed for the Model 45, including one with the Bonanza's signature V-tail, but the final design that emerged in 1948 incorporated conventional tail control surfaces for the benefit of the more conservative military (featuring a relatively large unswept vertical fin that would find its way onto the Travel Air twin-engine civil aircraft almost ten years later). The Bonanza's fuselage with four-passenger cabin was replaced with a narrower fuselage incorporating a two-seater tandem cockpit and bubble canopy, which provided greater visibility for the trainee pilot and flight instructor. Structurally, the Model 45 was much stronger than the Bonanza, being designed for +10g and -4.5g, while the Continental E-185 engine of 185 horsepower (hp) at takeoff (less than a third of the power of the T-6's engine) was the same as that fitted to contemporary Bonanzas.

Following the prototype were three **Model A45T** aircraft, the first two with the same engine as the prototype and the third with a Continental E-225, which would prove to be close to the production version. Production did not begin until 1953, when Beechcraft began delivering **T-34As** to the United States Air Force (USAF) and similar **Model B45** aircraft for export. Production of the **T-34B** for the United States Navy (USN) began in 1955, this version featuring a number of changes reflecting the different requirements of the two services. The T-34B had only differential braking for steering control on the ground instead of nosewheel steering, additional wing dihedral and, to cater for the different heights of pilots, adjustable rudder pedals instead of the moveable seats of the T-34A. T-34A production was completed in 1956, with T-34Bs being built until October 1957 and licensed B45 versions built in Canada (125 manufactured by Canadian Car and Foundry), Japan (173 built by Fuji Heavy Industries), and Argentina (75 by FMA) until 1958. Beechcraft delivered the last Model B45s in 1959. Total production of the Continental-engined versions in the US and abroad was 1,904 aircraft.

Model 73 Jet Mentor

In 1955 Beechcraft developed a jet-engined derivative, again as a private venture, and again in the hope of winning a contract from the US military. The **Model 73 Jet Mentor** shared many components with the piston-engined aircraft; major visual differences were the redesigned cockpit which was relocated further forward in the fuselage and the air intakes for the jet engine in the wing roots, supplying air to a single jet engine in the rear fuselage. The first flight of the Model 73, registered N134B, was on 18 December 1955. The Model 73 was evaluated by the USAF, which ordered the Cessna T-37, and the USN, which decided upon the Temco TT Pinto. The Model 73 was not put into production.

T-34C Turbo-Mentor

A T-34C Turbo-Mentor, which can be distinguished from the B (piston) model by the extended nose and exhaust stacks on either side behind the prop

After a production hiatus of almost 15 years, the **T-34C Turbo-Mentor** powered by a Pratt & Whitney Canada PT6A-25 turboprop engine was developed in 1973. Development proceeded at the behest of the USN, which supplied two T-34Bs for conversion. After re-engining with the PT6, the two aircraft were redesignated as **YT-34Cs**, the first of these flying with turboprop power for the first time on 21 September 1973. Mentor production re-started in 1975 for deliveries of **T-34Cs** to the USN and of the **T-34C-1** armed version for export customers in 1977, this version featuring four underwing hardpoints. The last Turbo-Mentor rolled off the production line in 1990.

Operational history

The first flight of the Model 45 was on 2 December 1948, by Beechcraft test pilot Vern Carstens. In 1950 the USAF ordered three **Model A45T** test aircraft, which were given the military designation YT-34. A long competition followed to determine a new trainer, and in 1953 the Air Force put the Model 45 into service as the T-34A Mentor, while the USN followed in May 1955 with the T-34B. The US Air Force began to replace the T-34A at the beginning of the 1960s, while the U.S. Navy kept the T-34B operational until the early 1970s. As of 2007, Mentors are still used by several air forces and navies.

From 1978, the T-34C Turbo-Mentor was the Argentine Naval Aviation basic trainer used by the 1st Naval Aviation Force (Training), alongside 15 T-34C-1 light attack aircraft forming the Fourth Naval Air Attack Squadron. During the 1982 Falklands War, four T-34C-1s were deployed to Port Stanley on 25 April 1982, primarily to be employed in a reconnaissance role. The main encounter with British forces occurred on 1 May 1982 when three Turbo-Mentors attacked a Royal Navy Westland Sea King helicopter in the area of Berkeley Sound but were intercepted by RN Sea Harriers flown by Lts Watson and Ward, with one of the T-34Cs being damaged by cannon fire from Ward's aircraft. The four T-34C-1 Turbo-Mentors continued to operate, flying a few reconnaissance missions, but were redeployed to Borbon Station where they were ultimately destroyed by the SAS Raid on Pebble Island on 15 May 1982. Although all four hulks remained on the island for a considerable length of time, eventually, 0729/(1-A)411 was recovered on 10 June 1983 and stored for future display at the Fleet Air Arm Museum.

Julie Clark in the T-34 "Free Spirit" c. 2006

In 2004, due to a series of crashes involving in-flight structural failure during simulated combat flights, the entire US civilian fleet of T-34s was grounded by the Federal Aviation Administration. The grounding has since been eased to a series of restrictions on the permitted flight envelope.

The T-34C is still used as the primary training aircraft for United States Navy and Marine Corps pilots. The T-34C is currently being replaced by the T-6 Texan II. NAS Pensacola has already completed the transition to the T-6 and one of three training squadrons at Whiting Field has also transitioned. The remaining two squadrons will be transitioned in 2011.

NASA Dryden Flight Research Center has operated two T-34C aircraft. The first was previously flown at the Glenn Research Center in Cleveland, Ohio, for propulsion experiments involving turboprop engines, and then came to Dryden as a chase aircraft in 1996. That aircraft was returned to the US Navy in 2002. Dryden obtained its second T-34C in early 2005 from the Navy's Air Warfare Center Aircraft Division at NAS Patuxent River, where it was due to be retired. At Dryden, the T-34C is primarily used for chasing remotely piloted unmanned air vehicles which fly slower than NASA's F-18's mission support aircraft can fly. It is also used for required pilot proficiency flying.

The United States Army received six ex-US Navy T-34C, used as test platforms and chase planes at Edwards Air Force Base and at Fort Bragg.

The Mentor is the aircraft used by the Lima Lima Flight Team and Dragon Flight, both civilian demonstration teams. It is also used by aerobatic pilot Julie Clark, who flies her T-34 "Free Spirit" (registration N134JC) at air shows.

Variants

YT-34
Prototype, three built.
T-34A
US Air Force trainer. Replaced by the Cessna T-37 around 1960 (450 built).
T-34B
US Navy trainer. Used until early 70s when it was replaced by the T-34C (423 built by Beechcraft).
YT-34C
Two T-34Bs were fitted with turboprop engines, and were used as T-34C prototypes.
T-34C Turbo-Mentor
Two-seat primary trainer, fitted with a turboprop engine.

30 - Beechcraft T-34 Mentor

T-34C-1
Equipped with hardpoints for training or light attack, able to carry 1,200 lb of weapons on four underwing pylons. The armament could include flares, incendiary bombs, rocket or gun pods and anti-tank missiles. Widely exported.

Turbo-Mentor 34C
Civilian version

Operators

Military operators

Military T-34 operators

A T-34A Mentor at the National Museum of the USAF

T-34C of the Ecuadorian Air Force

Beech T-34C Turbo Mentor operated by NASA

- **Algeria**
- **Argentina**
  - Argentine Air Force - T-34B
  - Argentine Naval Aviation - T-34C
- **Bolivia**
- **Canada**
  - Royal Canadian Air Force
- **Chile**
  - Chilean Air Force
  - Chilean Navy
  - Being replaced by the T-35 Pillán
- **Colombia**
- **Dominican Republic**
- **Ecuador**
  - Ecuadorian Air Force
  - Ecuadorian Navy
- **El Salvador**
- **France**
- **Gabon**
- **Indonesia**
  - Indonesian Air Force
- **Japan**
  - Japan Air Self-Defense Force
- **Mexico**
- **Morocco**
  - Royal Moroccan Air Force
- **Peru**
  - Peruvian Naval Aviation
- **Philippines**
  - Philippines Air Force
- **Republic of China**
- **Spain**
- **Turkey**
- **United States**
  - United States Air Force
  - United States Army
  - United States Navy
  - United States Marine Corps
  - United States Coast Guard
- **Uruguay**
  - Uruguayan Air Force
  - Uruguayan Navy
- **Venezuela**

Civil operators

- **Chile**
  - Club Aéreo de Santiago
- **Turkey**
  - Turkish Aeronautical Association
  - Istanbul Havacilik Kulubu
- **United States**
  - Dragon Flight
  - Lima Lima Flight Team
  - NASA
  - The San Diego Salute

Specifications (T-34C)

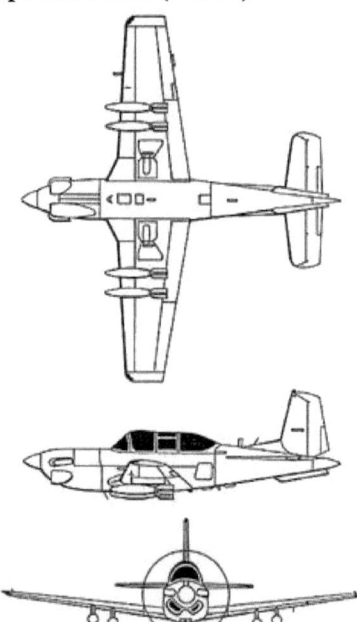

Data from Janes's All The World's Aircraft 1988-89

General characteristics

- **Crew:** Two
- **Length:** 28 ft 8½ in (8.75 m)
- **Wingspan:** 33 ft 3⅞ in (10.16 m)
- **Height:** 9 ft 7 in (2.92 m)
- **Wing area:** 179.6 ft² (16.69 m²)
- **Empty weight:** 2,960 lb (1,342 kg)
- **Max takeoff weight:** 4,300 lb

- (1,950 kg) (T-34C-1 weapons trainer - 5,500 lb (2,494 kg))
- **Powerplant:** 1× Pratt & Whitney Canada PT6A-25 turboprop, 715 shp (533 kW) (derated to 400 shp (298 kW))

Performance
- **Never exceed speed:** 280 knots (518 km/h, 322 mph) (IAS)
- **Cruise speed:** 214 knot (396 km/h, 246 mph) max cruise at 17,000 ft (5,180 m)
- **Stall speed:** 53 knots (98 km/h, 61 mph) flaps down, power off
- **Range:** 708 nmi (1,311 km, 814 mi) at 180 knots (333 km/h, 207 mph) and 20,000 ft (6,100 m)
- **Service ceiling:** 30,000 ft (9,145 m)
- **Rate of climb:** 1,480 ft/min (7.5 m/s)
- **g limit:** 6 positive, 3 negative

Armament
- **Hardpoints:** 4 with a capacity of 600 lb (272 kg) inner, 300 lb (136 kg) outer, 1,200 lb (544 kg) total

Source (edited): "http://en.wikipedia.org/wiki/Beechcraft_T-34_Mentor"

Bell UH-1N Twin Huey

The **Bell UH-1N Twin Huey** is a medium military helicopter that first flew in April, 1969. The UH-1N has a fifteen seat configuration, with one pilot and fourteen passengers. In cargo configuration the UH-1N has an internal capacity of 220 ft³ (6.23 m³). An external load of 5,000 lb (2,268 kg) can be carried by the UH-1N. The **CUH-1N** (later **CH-135**) Twin Huey was the original version, first ordered by the Canadian Forces.

Development

Based on the stretched fuselage Bell 205, the Bell 212 was originally developed for the Canadian Forces (CF) under the designation **CUH-1N Twin Huey**. Later the CF adopted a new designation system and the aircraft was re-designated as the **CH-135 Twin Huey**. The CF approved the development of the aircraft on 1 May 1968 and purchased 50 aircraft, with deliveries commencing in May 1971.

Canadian CH-135 Twin Hueys serving with the Multinational Force and Observers Sinai, Egypt 1989

The US military came very close to not procuring the Twin Huey. The purchase of the aircraft for US military use was opposed by the Chairman of the House Armed Services Committee at the time, L. Mendel Rivers. Rivers took this position because the aircraft powerplant, the Pratt & Whitney Canada PT6T was produced in Canada. The Canadian government had not supported US involvement in Vietnam and had opposed US policies in southeast Asia, as well as accepting US draft dodgers. Rivers was also concerned that procurement of the engines would result in a negative trade deficit situation with Canada. Congress only approved the purchase when it was assured that a US source would be found for the PT6T/T400 engines. As a result the United States military services ordered 294 Bell 212s under the designation UH-1N, with deliveries commencing in 1970.

Unlike in the Canadian Forces, in US service, the UH-1N retained the official name "Iroquois" from the single engined UH-1 variants, although US service personnel refer to the aircraft as a "Huey" or "Twin Huey".

The Bell 412 is a further development of the Bell 212, the major difference being the composite four-blade main rotor. The UH-1N has also been developed into the upgraded, four-blade UH-1Y.

Design

A USAF UH-1N during Exercise WOUNDED EAGLE '83

A Marine UH-1N sitting on the flight line at NAS Whiting Field, Florida, in 1982

32 - Bell UH-1N Twin Huey

U.S. Navy HH-1N from NAS China Lake at the Mojave Spaceport.

The UH-1N's main rotor is powered by a PT6T-3/T400 Turbo Twin Pac made up of two Pratt & Whitney Canada PT6 turboshaft power turbines driving a single output shaft. They are capable of producing up to 1,342 kW (1,800 shp). Should one engine fail the remaining engine can deliver 671 kW (900 shp) for 30 minutes or 571 kW (765 shp) enabling the UH-1N to maintain cruise performance at maximum weight.

The United States Marine Corps (USMC) modified a large number of their UH-1Ns with a Stability Control Augmentation System (SCAS) which provides servo inputs to the rotor head to help stabilize the aircraft during flight. This modification removed the gyroscopic "Stabilization Bar" on top of the main rotor head, instead relying on the computer system for stability.

Operational history

Military service

The United States Air Force employs UH-1Ns to fulfill its ICBM mission, providing a utility helicopter for transport between bases such as Minot AFB, Francis E. Warren AFB and Malmstrom AFB to missile launch sites in North Dakota, Montana, Wyoming, Nebraska, and Colorado. The UH-1N is also used by the 36th Rescue Flight (36 RQF) at Fairchild AFB, WA for conducting Search-and-Rescue (SAR) and medical evacuation missions.

During the 1982 Falklands War, the Argentine Air Force deployed two Bell 212 to Goose Green grass airstrip from where they performed general support duties including the recovery of many downed pilots. By the end of the hostilities both aircraft were still intact and both captured by the British.

USMC UH-1Ns were used by the USMC during its 2003 invasion of Iraq. UH-1Ns provided reconnaissance, and communications support to Marine ground troops. They were also called upon to provide close air support during heavy fighting in Nasiriyah.

Significant flights

On 6 March 1972, Hendrick V. Gorick of the United States Navy Antarctic Development Squadron Six (VXE-6) jumped at an altitude of 20,500 ft (6,248 m) from a UH-1N helicopter. In doing so he set a record for parachute jumping over the Antarctic continent.

Variants

U.S. variants
UH-1N Iroquois
Initial production model, used by the USAF, USN, and USMC. Over the years the primary operators, the USMC has developed a number of upgrades for the aircraft including improved avionics, defenses, and a FLIR turret. The USAF plans to replace their UH-1Ns with the Common Vertical Lift Support Platform to support the service's ICBM activities.
VH-1N
VIP transport configuration
HH-1N
SAR variant.
UH-1Y Venom
A UH-1N replacement and upgrade as part of the H-1 upgrade program for the USMC, designed to coincide with a similar upgrade for the AH-1W attack helicopter to AH-1Z Viper standard, with common engines and other major systems.

Canadian variants
CUH-1N Twin Huey
Original Canadian Armed Forces designation for the UH-1N utility transport helicopter.
CH-135 Twin Huey
Canadian version of the UH-1N. Canada purchased 50 CH-135s with deliveries starting in 1971. The aircraft were retired from the Canadian Forces starting in 1996 and struck off strength in December 1999. 41 of the surviving CH-135s were acquired by the US government in December 1999 and transferred to the National Army of Colombia and Colombian National Police. At least one CH-135 was destroyed in combat. 135135 was transferred to the Colombian National Police and flown by the Dirección Antinarcóticos (DIRAN). It was destroyed on the ground by FARC rebels on 18 January 2002, following an incident in which it was forced down by gunfire. Two CH-135s are on display in museums, one at the Canada Aviation Museum in Ottawa and one at the National Air Force Museum of Canada at CFB Trenton.

Italian-built variants

Agusta Bell AB 212 ASW of the Spanish Navy.

Agusta-Bell AB 212
Civil or military utility transport version. Built under license in Italy by Agusta.
Agusta-Bell AB 121EW
Electronic warfare version for Turkey.
Agusta-Bell AB 212ASW
Anti-submarine warfare, anti-shipping version of the AB 212 helicopter, built under license in Italy by Agusta. Operated by the Italian Navy, Hellenic Navy and Islamic Republic of Iran Navy, Greece, Iran, Italy, Peru, Spain, Turkey, and Venezuela.
The AB-212ASW is a Model 212 Twin Huey with a prominent radome above the cockpit. Early production had a dome-shaped radome, while later production had a flatter "drum" radome. A left side winch is used for dipping the Bendix ASQ-18 sonar. Other changes

include structural reinforcement for a gross weight of 11,197 lbs (5080 kg), ECM, shipboard deck tie-down attachments and corrosion protection. Armament is two Mk 44 or Mk 46 torpedoes or two depth charges in the ASW role and four AS.12 air-to-surface wire-guided missiles for the anti-shipping role.

Operators

Austrian UH-1N (Bell 212)

Canadian Coast Guard UH-1N (Bell 212)

Canadian CH-135 Twin Huey serving with 408 Tactical Helicopter Squadron 1985

AB.212 of Italian Air Force, airshow at Pratica di Mare AFB, Italy

A UH-1N helicopter, with Philippine Army officers aboard, prepares to land

The USAF's 20th Special Operations Squadron conducts a training exercise using a specially-painted UH-1N

United States Navy HH-1N Twin Huey, 2004

Angola
- Angolan Air Force operates Bell 212s.

Argentina
- Argentine Air Force operates Bell 212s from 1978.
- Argentine Army operates Bell 212s from 1976.

Austria
- Austrian Air Force operates Agusta-Bell 212s and Bell 212s from 1980.

Bangladesh
- Bangladesh Air Force operates Bell 212s.

Bahrain
- Royal Bahraini Air Force operates Agusta-Bell 212s.

Bolivia
- Bolivian Air Force operates Bell 212s.

Brunei
- Royal Brunei Air Force operates Bell 212s.

Canada
- Canadian Forces operated CH-135 version from 1972 to 1998.
  - 403 (Helicopter) Operational Training Squadron
  - 408 Tactical Helicopter Squadron
  - 422 Tactical Helicopter Squadron (disbanded 16 August 1980)
  - 424 Transport & Rescue Squadron
  - 427 Tactical Helicopter Squadron
  - 430 Tactical Helicopter Squadron (430e Escadron Tactique d'Hélicoptères)
  - 444 Combat Support Squadron
  - VU32 - Navy Utility Squadron
  - Aerospace Engineering Test Establishment
  - Base Flight Cold Lake
  - Base Rescue Goose Bay
  - Rotary Wing Aviation Unit, Canadian Contingent, Multinational Force and Observers, El Gorah Egypt, 1986-1990
- Canadian Coast Guard operates Bell 212s.

Colombia
- Colombian Air Force operates Agusta-Bell 212s.

- Colombian Army operates UH-1N and CH-135 versions.
- Colombian Navy operates Bell 212s.
- *Policía Nacional de Colombia* operates Bell 212s and CH-135s.

Croatia
- Special Operations Battalion operates Agusta Bell 212s.
- Croatian Police operates Agusta Bell 212s.

Ecuador
- *Fuerza Aérea Ecuatoriana* operates Bell 212s.

Gabon
- Gabonese Air Force

Germany
- Luftwaffe former operator, three helicopters only
- German Federal Police operates Bell 212s.

Greece
- Hellenic Air Force operates Agusta-Bell 212s.
- Hellenic Army operates Agusta-Bell 212s.
- Hellenic Navy operates Agusta-Bell 212ASW/EW variants.

Guatemala
- *Fuerza Aérea Guatemalteca* operates Bell 212s.

Guyana
- Guyana Defence Force operated Bell 212s from 1975 to 1990.

Iran
- Imperial Iranian Air Force operated Agusta-Bell 212s from 1978, Islamic Republic of Iran Air Force after 1979.
- Islamic Republic of Iran Navy operates Agusta-Bell 212ASW variants.

Iraq
- Iraqi Navy operated Agusta-Bell 212ASW variant between 1984 and 2003

Israel
- Israeli Air Force operated Bell 212s.

Italy
- *Aeronautica Militare* operates Agusta-Bell 212s.
- *Marina Militare* operates Agusta-Bell 212ASW variants.

Jamaica
- Jamaica Defence Force operated three Bell 212s from 1973 to 1999.

Japan
- Japan Coast Guard operates Bell 212s.

Lebanon
- Lebanese Air Force operated Agusta-Bell 212s, aircraft are stored currently.

Libya
- Libyan Air Force operates Bell 212s.

Malta
- Armed Forces of Malta operates Agusta-Bell 212s with mixed crews on SAR duties by an Italian Technical Assistance Mission.

Mexico
- Mexican Air Force operates Bell 212s.

Morocco
- Royal Moroccan Air Force operates Bell 212s.

Panama
- National Aeronaval Service

Peru
- *Fuerza de Aviación Naval* operates Agusta-Bell 212ASW variant.

Philippines
- Philippine Air Force operates Bell 212s.

Saudi Arabia
- Royal Saudi Air Force operates Agusta-Bell 212s.

Serbia
- Serbian Police

Singapore
- Republic of Singapore Air Force operated three Bell 212s for SAR missions. Helicopters were retired in 1985 and sold to Sri Lanka.

Somalia
- Somali Air Corps operated Agusta-Bell 212s.

South Korea
- Republic of Korea Air Force introduced Bell 212s in January 1971.

Spain
- Spanish Army has six Agusta-Bell 212s in use as of January 2010.
- Spanish Navy Air Arm operates 11 Agusta-Bell 212ASWs as of January 2010.

Sri Lanka
- Sri Lanka Air Force operates Bell 212s bought from Singapore.

Sudan
- Sudanese Air Force operates Agusta-Bell 212s.

Thailand
- Royal Thai Army
- Royal Thai Navy operates Bell 212s.

Tunisia
- Tunisian Air Force operates Bell 212s.

Turkey
- Turkish Army operates Agusta-Bell 212s.
- Turkish Navy operates Agusta-Bell 212ASW variant.

Uganda
- Uganda People's Defence Force operates Agusta-Bell 212s.

United Arab Emirates

United Kingdom
- Army Air Corps operates Bell 212s in Belize and Brunei.

United States
- United States Air Force
- United States Marine Corps
- United States Navy

Uruguay
- *Fuerza Aérea Uruguaya* operates Bell 212s.

Yemen
- Yemeni Air Force operates Agusta-Bell 212s.

Aircraft on display

Bell CH-135 Twin Huey in the Canada Aviation Museum

Bell UH-1N Twin Huey - page 35

- Air Mobility Command Museum, Dover AFB, Delaware, United States
- Canada Aviation Museum, Ottawa, Ontario, Canada
- Marine Corps Base Camp Pendleton, San Diego County, California, United States

Specifications (USMC UH-1N, as modified)

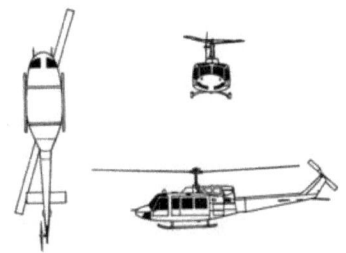

U.S. Navy HH-1N cockpit.

HH-1N rotor head.

Data from USMC UH-1N Fact Sheet, The International Directiory of Military Aircraft, 2002-2003

General characteristics
- **Crew:** 4 (Pilot, copilot, crew chief, gunner)
- **Capacity:** 6-8 combat-equipped troops, or equivalent cargo
- **Length:** 41 ft 8 in (12.69 m)
- **Rotor diameter:** 48 ft 0 in (14.6 m)
- **Height:** 14 ft 5 in (4.4 m)
- **Disc area:** 1,808 ft² (168.0 m²)
- **Empty weight:** 6,000 lb (2,721.5 kg)
- **Loaded weight:** 10,500 lb (4,762.7 kg)
- **Useful load:** 4500 lb (2038.0 kg)
- **Max takeoff weight:** 10,500 lb (4,762.7 kg)
- **Powerplant:** 2× Pratt & Whitney Canada T400-CP-400 turboshaft, 900 shp (671 kW), (total 1,250 shp) each

Performance
- **Maximum speed:** 120 knots (135 mph, 220 km/h)
- **Cruise speed:** 110 knots (126 mph, 207.3 km/h)
- **Range:** 248 nmi (286 mi, 460 km)
- **Service ceiling:** 17,300 ft (5,273 m)
- **Rate of climb:** 1,755 ft/min (8.9 m/s)
- **Power/mass:** hp/lb (W/kg)

Armament
- 2.75-inch rocket pods,
- GAU-16 .50 Cal. Machinegun,
- GAU-17 7.62mm minigun or M240 7.62mm lightweight machinegun

Gallery

CH-135 Twin Huey 135102 serving with the Multinational Force and Observers Sinai, Egypt, 1989.

CH-135 Twin Huey 135137 in the original blue-gray and green camouflage pattern worn by these aircraft prior to 1986/88.

CH-135 Twin Huey 135135 in the early-style SAR markings, 1988. This aircraft was serving with Base Rescue Goose Bay and had formerly been assigned to 424 Transport & Rescue Squadron, CFB Trenton.

CH-135 Twin Huey 135127 from Base Rescue Goose Bay in the later SAR scheme used after 1986/88.

CH-135 Twin Huey 135103 in special flight test markings. The aircraft was used by the Aerospace Engineering Test Establishment at CFB Cold Lake, 1987.

CH-135 Twin Huey 135103 after repainting in anti-IR olive and green scheme.

CH-135 Twin Huey badge worn by some Canadian Forces air and ground crew, 1980s

408 Tactical Helicopter Squadron UTTH Flight badge worn by CH-135 Twin Huey crews circa 1990. The badge is based on the shield of the province of Alberta
Source (edited): "http://en.wikipedia.org/wiki/Bell_UH-1N_Twin_Huey"

Bell UH-1 Iroquois

The **Bell UH-1 Iroquois** is a military helicopter powered by a single, turboshaft engine, with a two-bladed main rotor and tail rotor. The helicopter was developed by Bell Helicopter to meet the United States Army's requirement for a medical evacuation and utility helicopter in 1952, and first flew on 20 October 1956. Ordered into production in March 1960, the UH-1 was the first turbine-powered helicopter to enter production for the United States military, and more than 16,000 have been produced worldwide.

The first combat operation of the UH-1 was in the service of the U.S. Army during the Vietnam War. The original designation of *HU-1* led to the helicopter's nickname of *Huey*. In September 1962, the designation was changed to UH-1, but Huey remained in common use. Approximately 7,000 UH-1 aircraft saw service in Vietnam.

Development

A Bell XH-40, a prototype of the UH-1

In 1952, the Army identified a requirement for a new helicopter to serve as medical evacuation (MEDEVAC), instrument trainer and general utility aircraft. The Army determined that current helicopters were too large, underpowered, or were too complex to maintain easily. In November 1953, revised military requirements were submitted to the Department of the Army. Twenty companies submitted designs in their bid for the contract, including Bell Helicopter with the Model 204 and Kaman Aircraft with a turbine-powered version of the H-43. On 23 February 1955, the Army announced its decision, selecting Bell to build three copies of the Model 204 for evaluation, designated as the XH-40.

Model 204

Powered by a prototype Lycoming YT53-L-1 (LTC1B-1) engine producing 700 shp (520 kW), the XH-40 first flew on 20 October 1956, at Fort Worth, Texas, with Bell's chief test pilot, Floyd Carlson, at the controls. Two more prototypes were built in 1957, and the Army had previously ordered six YH-40 service test aircraft, even before the first prototype had flown. In March 1960, the Army awarded Bell a production contract for 100 aircraft, which was designated as the HU-1A and officially named *Iroquois*, after the native American nations.

The helicopter quickly developed a nickname derived from its designation of HU-1, which came to be pronounced as "Huey". The reference became so popular that Bell began casting the name on the helicopter's anti-torque pedals. The official U.S. Army name was almost never used in practice. After September 1962, the designation for all models was changed to UH-1 under a unified Department of Defense (DOD) designation system, but the nickname remained.

While glowing in praise for the helicopter's advances over piston-engined helicopters, the Army reports from the service tests of the YH-40 found it to be under-powered with the production T53-L-1A powerplant producing a maximum continuous 770 shaft horsepower (570 kilowatts). The Army indicated the need for improved, follow-on models even as the first UH-1As were being delivered. In response, Bell proposed the UH-1B, equipped with the Lycoming T53-L-5 engine producing 960 shp (720 kW) and a longer cabin that could accommodate seven passengers, or four stretchers and a medical attendant. Army testing of the UH-1B started in November 1960, with the first production aircraft delivered in March 1961.

Bell commenced development of the UH-1C in 1960, to correct aerodynamic deficiencies of the armed UH-1B. Bell fitted the UH-1C with a 1,100 shp (820 kW) T53-L-11 engine to provide the power needed to lift all weapons systems in use or under development. The Army would eventually refit all UH-1B aircraft with the same engine. A new rotor system was developed for the UH-1C to allow higher airspeeds and reduce the incidence of retreating blade stall during diving engagements. The improved rotor resulted in better maneuverability and a slight speed increase. The increased power and a larger diameter rotor required Bell's engineers to design a new tailboom for the UH-1C. The longer tailboom incorporated a wider chord vertical fin on the tail rotor pylon and larger synchronized elevators.

Bell also introduced a dual hydraulic control system for redundancy, and an improved inlet filter system for the dusty conditions found in southeast Asia. The UH-1C fuel capacity was increased to 242 US gallons (920 liters) and gross weight was raised to 9,500 lb (4,309 kg), giving a nominal useful load of 4,673 lb (2,120 kg). UH-1C production started in June 1966, with a total of 766 aircraft produced, including five for the Royal Australian Navy, designated "N9", and five for Norway.

Model 205

While earlier "short-body" Hueys were a success, the Army wanted a version that could carry more troops. Bell's solution was to stretch the HU-1B fuselage by 41 in (104 cm) and use the extra space to fit four seats next to the transmission, facing out. Seating capacity increased to 15, including crew. The enlarged cabin could also accommodate six stretchers and a medic, two more than the earlier models. In place of the earlier model's sliding side doors with a single window, larger doors were fitted which had two windows, plus a small hinged panel with an optional window, providing access to the cabin. The doors and hinged panels were quickly removable, allowing the Huey to be flown in a "doors off" configuration.

The Model 205 prototype flew on 16 August 1960. Seven pre-production/prototype aircraft were delivered and tested at Edwards AFB starting in March 1961. The 205 was initially equipped with a 44-foot (13.4 m) main rotor and a Lycoming T53-L-9 engine with 1,100 shp (820 kW). The rotor was lengthened to 48 feet (14.6 m) with a chord of 21 in (53 cm). The tailboom was also lengthened, in order to accommodate the longer rotor blades. Altogether, the modifications resulted in a gross weight capacity of 9,500 lb (4,309 kg). The Army ordered production of the 205 in 1963, produced with a T53-L-11 engine for its multi-fuel capability. The prototypes were designated as YUH-1D and the production aircraft was designated as the UH-1D.

In 1966, Bell installed the 1,400 shp (1,000 kW) Lycoming T53-L-13 engine to provide more power for the aircraft. The pitot tube was relocated from the nose to the roof of the cockpit, to prevent damage during landing. Production models in this configuration were designated as the UH-1H.

Marine Corps

In 1962, the United States Marines Corps held a competition to choose an assault support helicopter to replace the Cessna O-1 fixed-wing aircraft and the Kaman OH-43D helicopter. The winner was the UH-1B, which was already in service with the Army. The helicopter was designated the UH-1E and modified to meet Marine requirements. The major changes included the use of all-aluminum construction for corrosion resistance, radios compatible with Marine Corps ground frequencies, a rotor brake for shipboard use to stop the rotor quickly on shutdown and a roof-mounted rescue hoist.

The UH-1E was first flown on 7 October 1963, and deliveries commenced 21 February 1964, with 192 aircraft completed. Due to production line realities at Bell, the UH-1E was produced in two different versions, both with the same UH-1E designation. The first 34 built were essentially UH-1B airframes with the Lycoming T53-L-11 engine producing 1,100 shp (820 kW). When Bell switched production to the UH-1C, the UH-1E production benefited from the same changes. The Marine Corps later upgraded UH-1E engines to the Lycoming T53-L-13, which produced 1,400 shp (1,000 kW), after the Army introduced the UH-1M and upgraded their UH-1C helicopters to the same engine.

Air Force

The United States Air Force's (USAF) competition for a helicopter to be used for support on missile bases included a specific requirement to mandate the use of the General Electric T58 turboshaft as a powerplant. The Air Force had a large inventory of these engines on hand for its fleet of HH-3 Jolly Green Giant rescue helicopters and using the same engine for both helicopters would save costs. In response, Bell proposed an upgraded version of the 204B with the T58 engine. Because the T58 was mounted in front of the transmission on the S-61R, it had to be mounted "backwards" with its exhaust rerouted to the back of the aircraft.

On 7 June 1963, the Air Force named Bell Helicopter as the winner. Originally designated the H-48, it was later designated as the UH-1F. A TH-1F trainer was also built for the USAF, with the first TH-1F flown in January 1967, followed by delivery of 27 aircraft from April to July of that year. In Italy, Agusta produced a model similar to the UH-1F by re-engining the 204B with the 1,225 shp (914 kW) Rolls-Royce Gnome turboshaft and later the UH-1F's General Electric engine. The Italian version was exported to the military of the Netherlands, Austria, Sweden and Switzerland.

Twin engine variants

The single engine UH-1 variants were followed by the twin-engine UH-1N Twin Huey and later the UH-1Y Venom. Bell began development of the UH-1N for Canada in 1968. It changed to the more powerful Pratt & Whitney Canada PT6T twin-engine set. The U.S. also ordered the helicopter with the U.S. Air Force receiving it in 1970. Canada's military, the U.S. Marine Corps, and the U.S. Navy first received the model in 1971.

In 1996, the USMC began the H-1 upgrade program by awarding a contract to Bell Helicopter for developing the improved UH-1Y and AH-1Zs variants. The UH-1Y includes a lengthened cabin, four-blade rotor and two more powerful GE T700 engines. The UH-1Y entered service with the USMC in 2008.

Design

The UH-1 has a metal fuselage of semi-monocoque construction with tubular landing skids and two rotor blades on the main rotor. Early UH-1 models featured a single Lycoming T53 turboshaft engine in versions with power ratings from 700 shp (522 kW) to 1,400 shp (1,040 kW). Later UH-1 and related models would feature twin engines and four-blade rotors.

All aircraft in the UH-1 family have similar construction. The UH-1H is the most-produced version, and is representative of all types. The main structure consists of two longitudinal main beams that run under the passenger cabin to the nose and back to the tail boom attachment point. The main beams are separated by transverse bulkheads and provide the supporting structure for the cabin, landing gear, under-floor fuel tanks, transmission, engine and tail boom. The main beams are joined at the lift beam, a short aluminum girder structure that is attached to the transmission via a lift link on the top and the cargo hook on the bottom and is located at the aircraft's centre of gravity. The lift beams were changed to steel later in the UH-1H's life, due to cracking on high-time airframes. The semi-monocoque tail boom attaches to the fuselage with four bolts.

The UH-1H's dynamic components include the engine, transmission, rotor mast, main rotor blades, tail rotor driveshaft, and the 42-degree and 90-degree gearboxes. The transmission is of a planetary type and reduces the engine's output to 324 rpm at the main rotor. The two-bladed, semi-rigid rotor design, with pre-coned and under-slung blades, is a development of early Bell model designs, such as the Bell 47 with which it shares common design features, including a dampened stabilizer bar. The two-bladed system reduces storage space required for the aircraft, but at a cost of higher vibration levels. The two-bladed design is also responsible for the characteristic 'Huey thump' when the aircraft is in flight, which is particularly evident during descent and in turning flight. The tail rotor is driven from the main transmission, via the two directional gearboxes which provide a tail rotor speed approximately six times that of the main rotor to increase tail rotor effectiveness.

The UH-1H also features a synchronized elevator on the tail boom, which is linked to the cyclic control and allows a wider center of gravity range. The standard fuel system consists of five interconnected fuel tanks, three of which are mounted behind the transmission and two of which are under the cabin floor. The landing gear consists of two arched cross tubes joining the skid tubes. The skids have replaceable sacrificial skid shoes to prevent wear of the skid tubes themselves. Skis and inflatable floats may be fitted.

Internal seating is made up of two pilot seats and additional seating for up to 13 passengers or crew in the cabin. The maximum seating arrangement consists of a four-man bench seat facing rearwards behind the pilot seats, facing a five-man bench seat in front of the transmission structure, with two, two-man bench seats facing outwards from the transmission structure on either side of the aircraft. All passenger seats are constructed of aluminium tube frames with canvas material seats, and are quickly removable and reconfigurable. The cabin may also be configured with up to six stretchers, an internal rescue hoist, auxiliary fuel tanks, spotlights, or many other mission kits. Access to the cabin is via two aft-sliding doors and two small, forward-hinged panels. The doors and hinged panels may be removed for flight or the doors may be pinned open. Pilot access is via individual hinged doors.

While the five main fuel tanks are self-sealing, the UH-1H was not equipped with factory armour, although armoured pilot seats were available.

The UH-1H's dual controls are conventional for a helicopter and consist of a single hydraulic system boosting the cyclic stick, collective lever and anti-torque pedals. The collective levers have integral throttles, although these are not used to control rotor rpm, which is automatically governed, but are used for starting and shutting down the engine. The cyclic and collective control the main rotor pitch through torque tube linkages to the swash plate, while the anti-torque pedals change the pitch of the tail rotor via a tensioned cable arrangement. Some UH-1Hs have been modified to replace the tail rotor control cables with torque tubes similar to the UH-1N Twin Huey.

Aircraft markings

UH-1Hs used for ferrying VIPs into Panmunjom in the DMZ area between North and South Korea used three 12" wide Yellow stripes vertically over the fuselage. It signified unarmed aircraft carrying UNCMAC members.

Operational history

The UH-1 has been widely exported and remains in front line service in a number of countries.

U.S. Army

A rifle squad from the 1st Squadron, 9th Cavalry exiting from a UH-1D

The HU-1A (later redesignated UH-1A) first entered service with the 101st Airborne Division at Fort Campbell, Kentucky, the 82nd Airborne Division, and the 57th Medical Detachment. Although intended for evaluation only, the Army quickly pressed the new helicopter into operational service and Hueys with the 57th Medical Detachment arrived in Vietnam in March 1962.

The UH-1 has long been a symbol of US involvement in Southeast Asia in general and Vietnam in particular, and as a result of that conflict, has become one of the world's most recognized helicopters. In Vietnam primary missions included general support, air assault, cargo transport, aeromedical evacuation, search and rescue, electronic warfare, and later, ground attack. During the conflict, the craft was upgraded, notably to a larger version based on the Model 205. This version was initially designated the UH-1D and flew operationally from 1963.

Helicopters played an integral part in the U.S military's land and air operations. Here UH-1Ds airlift members of the 2nd Battalion, 14th Infantry Regiment from the Filhol Rubber Plantation area to a new staging area, in 1966

During service in the Vietnam War, the UH-1 was used for various purposes and various terms for each task abounded. UH-1s tasked with a ground attack or armed escort role were outfitted with rocket launchers, grenade launchers, and machine guns. As early as 1962, UH-1s were modified locally by the companies themselves, who fabricated their own mounting systems. These gunship UH-1s were commonly referred to as *Frogs* or *Hogs* if they carried rockets, and *Cobras* or simply *Guns* if they had guns. UH-1s tasked and configured for troop transport were often called *Slicks* due to an absence of weapons pods. Slicks did have door gunners, but were generally employed in the troop transport and medevac roles.

USS *Garrett County* (LST-786) at anchor in the Mekong Delta, South Vietnam, date unknown. On her deck are two Navy Helicopter Attack (Light) Squadron Three (HAL-3) "Seawolf" UH-1B Huey gunships from the squadrons Det Four or Det Six assigned to the ship.

UH-1s also flew hunter-killer teams with observation helicopters, namely the Bell OH-58A Kiowa and the Hughes OH-6 Cayuse (*Loach*).

Towards the end of the conflict, the UH-1 was tested with TOW missiles, and two UH-1B helicopters equipped with the XM26 Armament Subsystem were deployed to help counter the 1972 Easter Invasion. USAF Lieutenant James P. Fleming piloted a UH-1F on a 26 November 1968 mission that earned him the Medal of Honor.

UH-1 troop transports were designated by *Blue* teams, hence the nickname for troops carried in by these Hueys as the *Blues*. The reconnaissance or observation teams were *White* teams. The attack ships were called *Red* teams. Over the duration of the conflict the tactics used by the military evolved and teams were mixed for more effective results. *Purple* teams with one or two *Blue* slicks dropping off the troops, while a *Red* attack team provided protection until the troops could defend themselves. Another highly effective team was the *Pink* Recon/Attack team, which offered the capability of carrying out assaults upon areas where the enemy was known to be present but could not be pinpointed.

During the course of the war, the UH-1 went through several upgrades. The UH-1A, B, and C models (short fuselage, Bell 204) and the UH-1D and H models (stretched-fuselage, Bell 205) each had improved performance and load-carrying capabilities. The UH-1B and C performed the gunship, and some of the transport, duties in the early years of the Vietnam War. UH-1B/C gunships were replaced by the new AH-1 Cobra attack helicopter from 1967 to late 1968. The increasing intensity and sophistication of NVA anti-aircraft defenses made continued use of UH-1 gunships impractical, and after Vietnam the Cobra was adopted as the Army's main attack helicopter. Devotees of the UH-1 in the gunship role cite its ability to act as an impromptu dustoff if the need arose, as well as the superior observational capabilities of the larger Huey cockpit, which allowed return fire from door gunners to the rear and sides of the aircraft.

During the war 7,013 UH-1s served in Vietnam and of these 3,305 were destroyed. In total 1,074 Huey pilots were killed, along with 1,103 other crew members.

The US Army phased out the UH-1 with the introduction of the UH-60 Black Hawk, although the Army UH-1 Residual Fleet has around 700 UH-1s that were to be retained until 2015, primarily in support of Army Aviation training at Fort Rucker and in selected Army National Guard units. Army support for the craft was intended to end in 2004. In 2009, Army National Guard retirements of the UH-1 accelerated with the introduction of the UH-72 Lakota.

U.S. Air Force

VNAF UH-1H lands during a combat mission in Southeast Asia in 1970

In October 1965, the USAF 20th Helicopter Squadron was formed at Tan Son Nhut Air Base in South Vietnam, equipped initially with CH-3C helicopters. By June 1967 the UH-1F and UH-1P were also added to the unit's inventory, and by the end of the year the entire unit had shifted from Tan Son Nhut to Nakhon Phanom Royal Thai Air Force Base, with the CH-3s transferring to the 21st Helicopter Squadron. On 1 August 1968, the unit was redesignated the 20th Special Operations Squadron. The 20th SOS's UH-1s were known as the *Green Hornets*, stemming from their color, a primarily green two-tone camouflage (green and tan) was carried, and radio call-sign "hornet". The main role of these helicopters were to insert and extract reconnaissance teams, provide cover for such operations, conduct psychological warfare, and other support roles for covert operations especially in Laos and Cambodia during the so-called Secret War.

US Navy

The United States Navy began acquiring UH-1B helicopters from the Army and these aircraft were modified into gunships with special gun mounts and radar altimeters and were known as Seawolves in service with Navy Helicopter Attack (Light) (HA(L)-3). UH-1C helicopters were also acquired in the 1970s. The Seawolves worked as a team with Navy river patrol operations.

Australia

The Royal Australian Air Force also employed the UH-1H until 1989. Iroquois helicopters of RAAF No. 9 Squadron were deployed to South Vietnam in mid 1966 as part of the 1st Australian Task Force. In this role they were armed with single M60 doorguns. In 1969 four of No. 9 Squadron's helicopters were converted to gunships (known as 'Bushrangers'), armed with two fixed forward firing M134 7.62 mm minigun (one each side) and a 7 round rocket pod on each side. Aircrew were armed with twin M60 flexible mounts in each door. UH-1 helicopters were used in many roles including troop transport, medevac and Bushranger gunships for armed support.

Between 1982 and 1986 the Squadron contributed aircraft and aircrew to the Australian helicopter detachment which formed part of the Multinational Force and Observers peacekeeping force in the Sinai Peninsula, Egypt.

Some UH-1 were transferred to Australian Army Aviation after the RAAF ended their use in the 1980s.

El Salvador

During its civil war El Salvador received about 80 UH-1H and 24 UH-1M from the US, as part of the aid to fight the guerrillas between 1979 and 1992. These helicopters were heavily engaged in combat, supporting the army in fighting guerrillas throughout the country. As a result many were shot down. After the war only 20 UH-1H and 14 UH-1M survived, most of them scrapped a few years later.

These helicopters were operated by El Salvador Air Force, being at its time the biggest and most experienced combat helicopter force in Central and South America, fighting during 10 years and being trained by US Army in tactics developed during the Vietnam War. Gunship UH-1M helicopters used by El Salvador were modified to carry bombs instead of rocket pods. UH-1Hs were also used as improvised bombers.

Lebanon

During the battle of Nahr el-Bared camp in North Lebanon, the Lebanese army, lacking fixed-wing aircraft, modified the UH-1H allowing it to carry 500 lb (227 kg) Mark 82 bombs to strike militant positions. Each Huey was equipped on each side with special mounts engineered by the Lebanese army, to carry the high explosive bombs. (See Helicopter bombing.)

Rhodesia

Very late in the Rhodesian Bush War the Rhodesian Air Force was able to obtain and use eleven former Israeli Agusta-Bell 205As, known in service as *Cheetahs*. After much work these then formed No. 8 Sqn Rhodesian Air Force and took part as troop transports in the counter-insurgency fight. One was lost in combat in September 1979, when hit in Mozambique by a RPG. At least other three were lost. The survivors were put up for sale in 1990.

Argentina

UH-1Hs at Port Stanley Airport. These were transported to the islands by C-130H Hercules and did not have their rotors reattached yet

Nine Argentine Army Aviation UH-1Hs and two Argentine Air Force Bell 212 were included with the aircraft deployed during the Falklands War (Spanish: *Guerra de las Malvinas*). They performed general transport and SAR missions and were based at Port Stanley (BAM Puerto Argentino). Two of the Hueys were destroyed and, after the hostilities had ended, the balance were captured by the British. At least three of the aircraft were reused by the British ferrying supplies and troops but had to be painted with a distinct color to avoid misidentifications, until they were grounded.

656 Sqn, AAC and 820 NAS operated these captured UH-1s. The captured

UH-1H AE-409 is now in the Museum of Army Flying at AAC Middle Wallop. UH-1H AE-422 is in the Fleet Air Arm Museum, Yeovilton. One of these UH-1Hs was civil registered as G-HUEY in the UK and participated in a number of airshows and in the James Bond movie "The Living Daylights" (1987) as medevac.

Israel

The Israeli Air Force was another prominent operator of the UH-1, using it for over thirty years in various different conflicts against both the armies of Arab countries and Palestinian militants. Israel's first Hueys were UH-1Ds, delivered from the United States in October 1968 under arms shipments via the administration of Lyndon Johnson. Israel also acquired Italian UH-1s made by Augusta under license. In total, Israel acquired 64 UH-1s of different models.

The UH-1s were used throughout the 1970s and 1980s, first seeing action against Egypt during the War of Attrition. During the Yom Kippur War, UH-1s assisted in the transport of Israeli ground troops throughout the Sinai and Golan Heights against both Egyptian and Syrian troops. In an act of desperation, they were also used with other helicopters to spot Egyptian and Syrian surface to air missile batteries for fighter aircraft, a process that was quickly discontinued and never used again. Israeli UH-1s would go on to see their final combat in Lebanon, delivering Israeli troops and supplies in the fight against the PLO, Syria, and later Hezbollah.

Israel withdrew its UH-1s from service in 2002, after thirty three years of service. They were replaced by Sikorsky UH-60 Blackhawk helicopters given to Israel after complying with the United States and Britain for not retaliating against Iraqi Scud missile attacks. While some were passed on to pro-Israeli militias in Lebanon, eleven other UH-1Ds were reportedly sold to a Singapore based logging company but were, instead, delivered in October 1978 to the Rhodesian Air Force to skirt the UN endorsed embargo imposed during the Rhodesian Bush War.

Operation Enduring Freedom (2001-present)

UH-1Hs have been used by the United States Drug Enforcement Agency (DEA) in counter-narcotics raids in the ongoing conflict in Afghanistan. Operated by contractors, these Hueys provide transportation, surveillance, and air support for DEA FAST teams. Four UH-1Hs and two Mi-17s were used in a raid in July 2009 which led to the arrest of an Afghan Border Police commander.

Variant overview

U.S. Military variants

UH-1A Iroquois in flight.

- **XH-40**: The initial Bell 204 prototype. Three prototypes were built, equipped with the Lycoming XT-53-L-1 engine of 700 shp (520 kW).
- **YH-40**: Six aircraft for evaluation, as XH-40 with 12-inch (300 mm) cabin stretch and other modifications.
  - **Bell Model 533**: One YH-40BF rebuilt as a flight test bed with turbofan engines and wings.
- **HU-1A**: Initial Bell 204 production model, redesignated as the **UH-1A** in 1962. 182 built.
  - **TH-1A**: UH-1A with dual controls and blind-flying instruments, 14 conversions.
  - **XH-1A**: A single UH-1A was redesignated for grenade launcher testing in 1960.
- **HU-1B**: Upgraded HU-1A, various external and rotor improvements. Redesignated **UH-1B** in 1962. 1014 built plus four prototypes designated **YUH-1B**.
- **NUH-1B**: a single test aircraft, serial number 64-18261.
- **UH-1C**: UH-1B with improved engine, modified blades and rotor-head for better performance in the gunship role. 767 built.
- **YUH-1D**: Seven pre-production prototypes of the UH-1D.
- **UH-1D**: Initial Bell 205 production model (long fuselage version of the 204). Designed as a troop carrier to replace the CH-34 then in US Army service. 2008 built many later converted to UH-1H standard.
  - **HH-1D**: Army crash rescue variant of UH-1D.
- **UH-1E**: UH-1B/C for USMC with different avionics and equipment. 192 built.
  - **NUH-1E**: UH-1E configured for testing.
  - **TH-1E**: UH-1C configured for Marine Corps training. Twenty were built in 1965.
- **UH-1F**: UH-1B/C for USAF with General Electric T-58-GE-3 engine of 1,325 shp (988 kW). 120 built. Originally designated **H-48**.
  - **TH-1F**: Instrument and Rescue Trainer based on the UH-1F for the USAF. 26 built.

Base Rescue Moose Jaw CH-118 Iroquois helicopters at CFB Moose Jaw, 1982

- **UH-1H**: Improved UH-1D with a Lycoming T-53-L-13 engine of 1,400 shp (1,000 kW). 5435 built.
  - **CUH-1H**: Canadian Forces designation for the UH-1H utility transport helicopter. Redesignated **CH-118**. 10 built.
  - **EH-1H**: Twenty-two aircraft converted by installation of AN/ARQ-33 radio intercept and jamming equipment for Project

Quick Fix.
- **HH-1H**: SAR variant for the USAF with rescue hoist. 30 built.
- **JUH-1**: Five UH-1Hs converted to SOTAS battlefield surveillance configuration with belly-mounted airborne radar.
- **TH-1H**: Recently modified UH-1Hs for use as basic helicopter flight trainers by the USAF.
- **UH-1G**: Unofficial name applied locally to at least one armed UH-1H by Cambodia.

JGSDF UH-1J in Okadama STA, 2007

- **UH-1J**: An improved Japanese version of the UH-1H built under license in Japan by Fuji was locally given the designation UH-1J. Among improvements were an Allison T53-L-703 turboshaft engine providing 1,343 kW (1,800 shp), a vibration-reduction system, infrared countermeasures, and a night-vision-goggle (NVG) compatible cockpit.
- **HH-1K**: Purpose built SAR variant of the Model 204 for the US Navy with USN avionics and equipment. 27 built.
- **TH-1L**: Helicopter flight trainer based on the HH-1K for the USN. A total of 45 were built.
  - **UH-1L**: Utility variant of the TH-1L. Eight were built.
- **UH-1M**: Gunship specific UH-1C upgrade with Lycoming T-53-L-13 engine of 1,400 shp (1,000 kW).
- **UH-1N**: Initial Bell 212 production model, the Bell "Twin Pac" twin-engined Huey.
- **UH-1P**: UH-1F variant for USAF for special operations use and attack operations used solely by the USAF 20th Special Operations Squadron, "the Green Hornets".
- **EH-1U**: No more than 2 UH-1H aircraft modified for Multiple Target Electronic Warfare System (MULTEWS).
- **UH-1V**: Aeromedical evacuation, rescue version for the US Army.
- **EH-1X**: Ten Electronic warfare UH-1Hs converted under "Quick Fix IIA".
- **UH-1Y**: Upgraded variant developed from existing upgraded late model UH-1Ns, with additional emphasis on commonality with the AH-1Z.

Note: In U.S. service the G, J, Q, R, S, T, W and Z model designations are used by the AH-1. The UH-1 and AH-1 are considered members of the same H-1 series. The military does not use I (India) or O (Oscar) for aircraft designations to avoid confusion with "one" and "zero" respectively.

Other military variants
- **Bell 204**: Bell Helicopters company designation, covering aircraft from the XH-40, YH-40 prototypes to the UH-1A, UH-1B, UH-1C, UH-1E, UH-1F, HH-1K, UH-1L, UH-1P and UH-1M production aircraft.
  - **Agusta-Bell AB 204**: Military utility transport helicopter. Built under license in Italy by Agusta.
  - **Agusta-Bell AB 204AS**: Anti-submarine warfare, anti-shipping version of the AB 204 helicopter.
  - **Fuji-Bell 204B-2**: Military utility transport helicopter. Built under license in Japan by Fuji Heavy Industries. Used by the Japan Ground Self-Defense Force under the name **Hiyodori**.
- **Bell 205**: Bell Helicopters company designation of the UH-1D and UH-1H helicopters.
  - **Bell 205A-1**: Military utility transport helicopter version, initial version based on the UH-1H.
  - **Bell 205A-1A**: As 205A-1, but with armament hardpoints and military avionics. Produced specifically for Israeli contract.
  - **Agusta-Bell 205**: Military utility transport helicopter. Built under license in Italy by Agusta.
  - **AIDC UH-1H**: Military utility transport helicopter. Built under license in Taiwan by Aerospace Industrial Development Corporation.
- **Dornier UH-1D**: Military utility transport helicopter. Built under license in Germany by Dornier Flugzeugwerke.
  - **Fuji-Bell 205A-1**: Military utility transport helicopter. Built under licence in Japan by Fuji. Used by the Japanese Ground Self Defense Force under the designation **HU-1H**.
- **Bell 211 Huey Tug** With up-rated dynamic system and larger wide chord blades, the Bell 211 was offered for use as the US Army's prime artillery mover, but not taken up.
- **Bell Huey II**: A modified and re-engined UH-1H, significantly upgrading its performance, and its cost-effectiveness. Currently offered by Bell to all current military users of the type.
- **UH-1/T700 Ultra Huey**: Upgraded commercial version, fitted with a 1,400-kW (1900-shp) General Electric T700-GE-701C turboshaft engine.

Operators

Aircraft on display

A UH-1P on display

A UH-1H on display at Sun 'n Fun 2006. The aircraft is owned by a Vietnam War veteran's association

A UH-1 Huey of the Philippine Air Force on display at the Armed Forces of the Philippines Museum in Camp Aguinaldo

The UH-1 experienced a production number in the thousands (both short and long-frame types), and a large number exist in flyable condition in nations around the world. A large number of decommissioned and retired aircraft exist as "gate guards" to various military bases, in aviation museums, and other static-display sites. Examples include:

Canada
- Canadian CH-118 (UH-1H) 118101 at the National Air Force Museum of Canada, CFB Trenton, Ontario

Germany
- German Army UH-1D at the Deutsches Museum Flugwerft Schleissheim, Oberschleissheim

New Zealand
- UH-1 at the Army Museum New Zealand, Waiouru.

Norway
- UH-1B on static display at the Norwegian Aviation Museum in Bodø.

South Korea
- UH-1B on display at the War Memorial of Korea, Seoul, Republic of Korea

United Kingdom
- UH-1 at the American Air Force Hangar of the Imperial War Museum, Duxford.
- UH-1H at The Helicopter Museum, Weston super Mare.

United States
- The Bell UH-1H "Smokey III" that resides in the Steven F. Udvar-Hazy Center served four tours and over 2,500 hours in Vietnam.
- UH-1A located at the Intrepid Sea-Air-Space Museum in New York City.
- A fully refurbished UH-1 "Huey" is located in the Frontiers of Flight Museum in Dallas, Texas.
- The UH-1A formerly used as Command and Control aircraft for Gen William C. Westmoreland while he was commander of the 101st Airborne Division and Ft. Campbell, KY is located in front of 101st Airborne Division Headquarters.
- UH-1B on static display at the Ft. Campbell, Kentucky museum. Also, a UH-1H is displayed at main entrance of 101st Airborne Division barracks.
- UH-1M on display at the Texas Military Forces Museum at Camp Mabry, in Austin, Texas.
- UH-1H formerly assigned to the Illinois Army National Guard on static display at the Prairie Aviation Museum located at the Central Illinois Regional Airport in Bloomington, Illinois.
- UH-1C/M on display on a stand at the entrance of the Tennessee National Guard Training Center at the Smyrna Airport in Smyrna, Tennessee.
- UH-1s of various models on stands at the entrances of Fort Rucker, Alabama as well as at the Ft Rucker museum.
- The Heartland Museum of Military Vehicles near Lexington, Nebraska, has a UH-1 visible from Interstate 80 as it passes by the museum. The display includes a sculptural representation of the iconic 1975 rooftop evacuation of the U.S. embassy in Saigon, Vietnam.
- The Cole Land Transportation Museum in Bangor, Maine, has a UH-1D on static display as part of the Vietnam Memorial. The display is visible from Interstate 395.
- UH-1H on display, All Veterans Memorial, Emporia, Kansas.
- UH-1 on display, War Memorial Park, Hopkinsville, Kentucky.
- UH-1 on display, Greenup County War Memorial, near Flatwoods, Kentucky.
- One UH-1 on display at Barbers Point CGAS (John Rogers field) At the Vietnam aircraft museum.
- Two UH-1s on display at the Mississippi Armed Forces Museum, Camp Shelby, Hattiesburg, Mississippi, One aircraft is a Medevac UH-1 in a jungle diorama.
- Two UH-1s on display in the Minnesota Air National Guard Museum, Minneapolis-St. Paul International Airport, Minneapolis, Minnesota.
- UH-1, BuNo 60-3614, is on display on the flight deck of the USS Midway Museum aboard the USS *Midway* in San Diego, California
- UH-1H, 65-09889, is on display as "Rattler 26" at the Concho Valley Vietnam Veterans Memorial next to Mathis Field in San Angelo, Texas.
- 1964 UH-1H Iroquois Serial #64-13731 served with United States Army/ NC National Guard and is on display at Carolinas Aviation Museum in Charlotte, North Carolina.
- UH-1 on static display, SR 99E, Canby, Oregon.

Specifications (UH-1D)

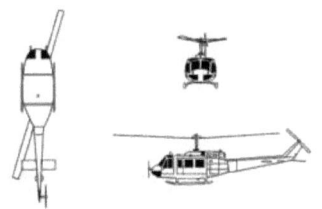

General characteristics
- **Crew:** 1-4
- **Capacity:** 3,880 lb including 14

troops, or 6 stretchers, or equivalent cargo
- **Length:** 57 ft 1 in (17.40 m) with rotors
- **Wingspan:** 48 ft 0 in (14.63 m)
- **Width:** 8 ft 7 in (2.62 m) (Fuselage)
- **Height:** 14 ft 5 in (4.39 m)
- **Empty weight:** 5,215 lb (2,365 kg)
- **Gross weight:** 9,040 lb (4,100 kg)
- **Max takeoff weight:** 9,500 lb (4,309 kg)
- **Powerplant:** 1 × Lycoming T53-L-11 turboshaft, 1,100 shp (820 kW)
- **Main rotor diameter:** 48 ft 0 in (14.63 m)

Performance
- **Maximum speed:** 135 mph (217 km/h; 117 kn)
- **Cruise speed:** 125 mph (109 kn; 201 km/h)
- **Range:** 315 mi (274 nmi; 507 km)
- **Service ceiling:** 19,390 ft (5,910 m) (Dependent on environmental factors such as weight, outside temp., etc)
- **Rate of climb:** 1,755 ft/min (8.92 m/s)
- **Power/mass:** 0.15 hp/lb (0.25 kW/kg)

Armament
Variable, but may include a combination of:
- 2× 7.62 mm M60 machine gun, or 2x 7.62 mm GAU-17/A machine gun
- 2× 7-round or 19-round 2.75 in (70 mm) rocket pods
- 2× 7.62 mm Rheinmetall MG3 (German Army and German Luftwaffe)
- 2× .303 Browning Mk II (Rhodesian, twin machine guns mounted on port side)

For information on US armament systems see:

Notable appearances in media
The image of American troops disembarking from a Huey has become an iconic image of the Vietnam War, and can be seen in many films, video games and television shows on the subject, as well as more modern settings. The UH-1 is seen in many films about the Vietnam War, including *The Green Berets*, *Platoon*, *Hamburger Hill*, *Apocalypse Now*, *Casualties of War*, and *Born on the Fourth of July*. It is prominently featured in *We Were Soldiers* as the main helicopter used by the U.S. Cavalry in the Battle of Ia Drang. Author Robert Mason recounts his career as a UH-1 "Slick" pilot in his memoir, *Chickenhawk*.

The 2002 journey of "Huey 091", displayed in the Smithsonian American History Museum, is outlined in the documentary *In the Shadow of the Blade*.
Source (edited): "http://en.wikipedia.org/wiki/Bell_UH-1_Iroquois"

Boeing 707

The **Boeing 707** is a four-engine narrow-body commercial passenger jet airliner developed by Boeing in the early 1950s. Its name is most commonly pronounced as "Seven Oh Seven". The first airline to operate the 707 was Pan American World Airways, inaugurating the type's first commercial flight on October 26, 1958. Boeing delivered a total of 1,011 Boeing 707s including a smaller, faster model of the aircraft that was marketed as the **Boeing 720**.

Although it was not the first commercial jet in service, the 707 was among the first to be commercially successful. Dominating passenger air transport in the 1960s, and remaining common throughout the 1970s, the 707 is generally credited with ushering in the Jet Age. It established Boeing as one of the largest makers of passenger aircraft, and led to the later series of aircraft with "7x7" designations.

Development

Model 367-80 origins
Boeing, during and immediately after World War II, was known for its military aircraft. The company had produced innovative and important bombers, from the B-17 Flying Fortress and B-29 Superfortress, to the jet-powered B-47 Stratojet and B-52 Stratofortress. The company's civil aviation department lagged far behind Douglas and other competitors, the only noteworthy airliners being the Boeing 314 Clipper and 307 Stratoliner. During 1949–1950, Boeing embarked on serious studies for a new jet transports, realizing that any design must have the potential to fulfill both the military and civil markets. At the time, aerial refueling was increasingly becoming a standard operational technique, with over 800 KC-97 Stratotankers being on order. With the advent of the jet age, a new tanker was required to meets the USAF's fleet of jet-powered bombers; this was where Boeing's new design would potentially win military orders.

Boeing studied numerous wing and engine configurations for its new transport/tanker, some of which were based on the B-47 and C-97, before settling on Model 367-80. The "Dash 80" took less than two years from project launch in 1952 to rollout on May 14, 1954, then first flew on July 15, 1954. It was powered by the Pratt & Whitney JT3C turbojet engine, which was the civilian version of the J57 used on many military aircraft of the day, including the F-100 fighter and the B-52 bomber.

The prototype was conceived as a proof of concept aircraft for both military and civilian use: the United States Air Force was the first customer for the design, using it as the KC-135 Stratotanker midair refueling platform. It was far from certain that the passenger 707 would be profitable. At the time, Boeing was making nearly all of its money from military contracts: its last passenger transport, the Boeing 377 Stratocruiser, had netted the company a $15 million loss before it was purchased by the Air Force as the KC-97 Stratotanker.

The 132-inch (3,350 mm) fuselage of the Dash 80 was only wide enough to fit two-plus-two seating (in the manner of the Stratocruiser). Answering customers demands and under Douglas competition, Boeing soon realized that this would not provide a viable payload, so decided to widen the fuselage to 144 in (3,660 mm), the same as the KC-135 Stratotanker, which would allow six-abreast seating — and the shared use of the KC-135's tooling. However, Douglas Aircraft had launched its DC-8 with a fuselage width of 147 in (3,730 mm). The airlines liked the extra space, and so Boeing was obliged to increase the 707's cabin width again, this time to 148 in (3,760 mm). This meant that little of the tooling that was made for the Dash 80 was usable for the 707. The extra cost meant the 707 did not become profitable until some years after it would have if these modifications had not been necessary.

Early production Boeing 707-329 of Sabena in April 1960 retaining the original short tail-fin and no ventral fin

Production and testing

The first flight of the first production 707-120 took place on December 20, 1957, and FAA certification followed on September 18, 1958. A number of changes were incorporated into the production models from the prototype. A Krueger flap was installed along the leading edge between the inner and outer engines on early 707-120 and -320 models.

Further developments

The initial standard model was the 707-120 with JT3C turbojet engines. Qantas ordered a shorter body version called the 707-138, which was a -120 that had six fuselage frames removed, three in front of the wings, three aft. The frames in the 707 were each 20 inches (500 mm) long, so this resulted in a net shortening of 10 ft (3 m) to 134 ft (41 m), 6 inches (41 m). Because the maximum takeoff weight remained the same 247,000 lb (112 t) as the -120, the 138 was able to fly the longer routes that Qantas needed. Braniff International Airways ordered the higher-thrust version with Pratt & Whitney JT4A engines, the 707-220. The final major derivative was the 707-320 which featured an extended-span wing and JT4A engines, while the 707-420 was the same as the -320 but with Rolls-Royce Conway turbofan engines. British certification requirements relating to engine-out go-arounds also forced Boeing to increase the height of the tail fin on all 707 variants, as well as add a ventral fin, which was retrofitted on earlier -120 and -220 aircraft. These modifications also aided in the mitigation of dutch roll by providing more yaw stability.

A Pakistan International Airlines Boeing 707 photographed in Germany, 1961

Though initially fitted with turbojet engines, the dominant engine for the Boeing 707 family was the Pratt & Whitney JT3D, a turbofan variant of the JT3C with lower fuel consumption as well as higher thrust. JT3D-engined 707s and 720s were denoted with a "B" suffix. While many 707-120Bs and 720Bs were conversions of existing JT3C-powered machines, 707-320Bs were only available as newly-built aircraft as they had a stronger structure to support a maximum take-off weight increased by 19,000 lb (8,600 kg), along with minor modifications to the wing. The 707-320B series enabled non-stop westbound flights from Europe to the US west coast.

The final 707 variant was the 707-320C, (C for "Convertible") which was fitted with a large fuselage door for cargo applications. This aircraft also had a significantly revised wing featuring three-section leading-edge flaps. This provided an additional improvement to takeoff and landing performance, and also allowed the ventral fin to be removed (although the taller fin was retained). 707-320Bs built after 1963 used the same wing as the -320C and were known as *707-320B Advanced* aircraft.

Production of the passenger 707 ended in 1978. In total, 1,010 707s were built for civil use, though many of these found their way to military service. The purpose-built military variants remained in production until 1991.

Traces of the 707 are still found in the 737, which uses a modified version of the 707's fuselage, as well as essentially the same external nose and cockpit configuration as the 707. These were also used on the previous Boeing 727, while the Boeing 757 also used the 707 fuselage cross-section. The Chinese government sponsored development of the Shanghai Y-10 during the 1970s, which was a near carbon-copy of the 707; however, this did not enter production.

Design

Wings

The 4 wheel landing gear bogies on a 707-120

The 707 wings are swept back at 35 degrees and, like all swept-wing aircraft, displayed an undesirable "Dutch roll" flying characteristic which manifested itself as an alternating yawing and rolling motion. Boeing already had considerable experience with this on the B-47 and B-52, and had developed the yaw damper system on the B-47 that would be applied to later swept wing configurations like the 707. However, many new 707 pilots had no experience with this phenomenon as they were transitioning from straight-wing propeller driven aircraft such as the Douglas DC-7 and Lockheed Constellation.

On one customer acceptance flight, where the yaw damper was turned off to familiarize the new pilots with flying techniques, a trainee pilot's actions violently exacerbated the Dutch Roll motion and caused three of the four engines to be torn from the wings. The plane, a brand new 707-227, *N7071*, destined for Braniff, crash landed on a river bed north of Seattle at Arlington, Washington, killing four of the eight occupants.

In his autobiography, test pilot Tex Johnston described a Dutch Roll incident he experienced as a passenger on an early commercial 707 flight. As the aircraft's movements did not cease and most of the passengers became ill, he suspected a misrigging of the directional autopilot (yaw damper). He went to the cockpit and found the crew unable to understand and resolve the situation. He introduced himself and relieved the ashen-faced captain who immediately left the cockpit feeling ill. Johnston disconnected the faulting autopilot and manually stabilized the plane "with two slight control movements".

Engines

View of number 1 (top left) and 2 (center) Pratt & Whitney JT3D jet engines on the port side of a British Caledonian Boeing 707-320B. The number 1 engine mount (top) is different from the other three engines.

The 707's used engine-driven turbocompressors to supply high-pressure air for pressurization. The engines could not supply sufficient bleed air for this purpose without a serious loss of thrust. On many commercial 707s the outer port (#1) engine mount is distinctly different from the other three, as this is the only engine not fitted with a turbocompressor. With engines 2 through 4 being fitted with TCs, they provide the triple redundancy required of the aircraft's cabin pressurization and air-conditioning system.

The P&W JT3D-3B engines are readily identifiable by the large gray secondary air inlet doors in the nose cowl. These doors are fully open (sucked in at the rear) during takeoff to provide additional air. When the engines are throttled back to cruise, the doors are shut.

Upgraded engines

Omega Air's 707-330C testbed for the 707RE program takes off from the Mojave Airport

Pratt & Whitney, in a joint venture with Seven Q Seven (SQS) and Omega Air, has developed the JT8D-219 as a re-engine powerplant for Boeing 707-based aircraft, calling their modified configuration a **707RE**. Northrop Grumman has selected the -219 to re-engine the United States Air Force's fleet of 19 E-8 Joint STARS aircraft, which will allow the J-STARS more time on station due to the engine's greater fuel efficiency. NATO also plans to re-engine their fleet of E-3 Sentry AWACS aircraft. The -219 is publicized as being half the cost of the competing 707 re-engine powerplant, the CFM International CFM56, and is 40 dB quieter than JT3D engines that are being replaced.

Operational history

The first commercial orders for the 707 came on October 13, 1955, when Pan Am committed to 20 707s and 25 Douglas DC-8s, a dramatic increase in passenger capacity over its existing fleet of propeller aircraft. The competition between the 707 and DC-8 was fierce. Several major airlines committed only to the DC-8, as Douglas Aircraft was a more established maker of passenger aircraft at the time. To stay competitive, Boeing made a late and costly decision to redesign and enlarge the 707's wing to help increase range and payload. The new version was numbered 707-320.

Conway-powered BOAC 707-436 at London Heathrow Airport in 1964.

Pan Am was the first airline to operate the 707; the aircraft's first commercial flight was from New York to Paris on October 26, 1958 with a fuel stop in Gander, Newfoundland. In December National Airlines operated the first U.S. domestic jet airline flights between New York/Idlewild and Miami, using 707s leased from Pan Am; American Airlines was the first domestic airline to fly its own jets, on January 25, 1959. TWA started domestic 707-131 flights in March and Continental Airlines started 707-124 flights in June; airlines which had only ordered the DC-8, such as United, Delta and Eastern, were left jetless until September and lost market share on transcontinental flights.

The 707 quickly became the most popular jetliner of its time. Its popularity led to rapid developments in airport terminals, runways, airline catering, baggage handling, reservations systems and other air transport infrastructure. The advent of the 707 also led to the upgrading of air traffic control systems to prevent interference with military jet operations.

As the 1960s drew to a close, the exponential growth in air travel led to the 707 being a victim of its own success. The 707 was now too small to handle the increased passenger densities on the routes for which it was designed. Stretching the fuselage was not a viable option because the installation of larger, more powerful engines would in turn need a larger undercarriage, which was not feasible given the design's limited ground clearance. Boeing's answer to the problem was the first twin aisle airliner — the Boeing 747. The 707's first-generation engine technology was also rapidly becoming obsolete in the areas of noise and fuel economy.

In 1982, during the Falklands War the Argentine Air Force extensively used civilian 707s for long-range maritime patrol, with some of them being intercepted and shepherded away by Royal Navy Sea Harriers, it also led to the conversion of British Nimrods to carry Sidewinder air-to-air missiles after a casual encounter.

Trans World Airlines flew the last scheduled 707 flight for passengers by a US carrier on October 30, 1983, although 707s remained in scheduled service by airlines from other nations for much longer. For example Middle East Airlines (MEA) of Lebanon flew 707s and 720s in front-line passenger service until the end of the 1990s. Since LADE of Argentina took its 707-320B from regular service in 2007, Saha Air Lines of Iran is the last airline to keep 707s in scheduled passenger service.

An ex-Qantas Boeing 707-138B, owned by John Travolta, repainted in vintage Qantas livery

In 1984, a Boeing 720 that was flown by remote control was intentionally crashed at Edwards AFB as a part of the FAA and NASA Controlled Impact Demonstration program. The test provided peak accelerations during a crash.

Operations of the 707 were threatened by the enactment of international noise regulations in 1985. Shannon Engineering of Seattle, Washington developed a hush kit with funding from Tracor, Inc, of Austin, Texas. By the late 1980s, 172 Boeing 707s had been equipped with the Quiet 707 package. Boeing acknowledged that more 707s were in service then than before the hush kit was available. Most remaining 707s are in freighter form, or as Business Jets.

Honeywell operated the last Boeing 720 in operation in the United States, flying out of Sky Harbor airport in Phoenix. The aircraft had been modified with an extra engine nacelle mounted on the right side of the fuselage to allow testing of a turbine engine at altitude, operating on special certification allowing it to be used for experimental use. This 720B was scrapped on June 21 and 22, 2008. Honeywell replaced their aircraft with a Boeing 757.

Pratt & Whitney Canada flew the last 720 until the end of its operational life in 2010. The final operational flight took place on September 29, 2010 with a decision still to come regarding whether it will be scrapped or placed in a museum. Pratt & Whitney Canada replaced their testbed with a Boeing 747SP.

Variants

Although certificated as Series 100s, 200s, 300s, etc. the different 707 variants are more commonly known as Series 120s, 220s, 320s, and so on where the "20" part of the designation is Boeing's "customer number" for its development aircraft.

367-80

The 367-80 (Dash-80) was the original prototype Boeing jet transport. Used to develop the KC-135 Stratotanker and the 707, it was fitted with four Pratt & Whitney JT3C engines, each producing 10,000 lbf (44.5 kN). First flight was 15 July 1954. Upon completion of initial test programs, it found use as a flying testbed for new technologies and for continuing improvements to the 707 series. Later fitted with Pratt & Whitney JT3D turbofans, it was retired to storage in Arizona. It is now preserved for public viewing at the Steven F. Udvar-Hazy Center of the Smithsonian National Air and Space Museum (NASM)'s annex near Washington Dulles International Airport.

707-120

Turkish Airlines

Boeing 707-123B cockpit

The **707-120** was the first production

707 variant. The variant featured a longer, wider fuselage and greater wingspan than the original Dash-80. A full set of rectangular cabin windows was included for the interior, which was capable of a seating 179 passengers. It was designed for transcontinental routes and often required a refuelling stop when used on the North Atlantic route. It was fitted with four Pratt and Whitney JT3C-6 turbojets, civilian versions of the military J57 model, which produced 12,500 lbf (55.6 kN) each, allowing a 247,000 lb (112,000 kg) takeoff gross weight. (Engines on American's 707s started at 13,000 lbf (58 kN) thrust, later increased to 13,500 lbf (60 kN) by increasing the turbine's allowed temperature.) First flight was on December 20, 1957. Major orders were the launch order for 20 **707-121** aircraft by Pan American and an American Airlines order for 30 **707-123** aircraft. The first revenue service of a 707 was on October 26, 1958. A total of 69 were built.

The **707-138** was based on the -120 but had a 10 ft (3.05 m) reduction to the rear fuselage and were capable of increased range. It was a variant for Qantas and included Boeing customer number of 38 for Qantas. A total of 13 -138s were built.

707-120B (VC-137B) wing, showing the new inboard leading edge from the 720. Also, note the British Airways Concorde G-BOAG to the side.

The **707-120B** was the first major upgrade to the design was a re-engining with JT3D-1 turbofans, which were quieter, more powerful, and more fuel-efficient, producing 17,000 lbf (75.6 kN) each, with the later JT3D-3 version giving 18,000 lbf (80 kN). The aircraft also received the wing modifications introduced on the 720. The tailplane was also enlarged on the -120B. A total of 72 of these were built, and many more were converted from 707-120 aircraft, including Qantas' aircraft, which became 707-138B aircraft upon conversion. The first flight of the -120B was on 22 June 1960.

707-220

The **707-220** was designed for hot and high operations with powerful Pratt & Whitney JT4A-3 turbojets, only five of these were produced, however only four were ultimately delivered with one being lost during a test flight. All were for Braniff International Airways and carried the model number **707-227**. This version was made obsolete by the arrival of the turbofan-powered 707-120B.

707-320

British Caledonian Boeing 707 shown at Glasgow Prestwick Airport, South Ayrshire, Scotland, c. 1972.

The **707-320 Intercontinental** is a stretched version of the turbojet-powered 707-120, initially powered by JT4A-3 or JT4A-5 turbojets producing 15,800 lbf (70,000 N) each. The interior allowed for up to 189 passengers due to an 80-inch (2,000 mm) fuselage stretch (from 138 ft 10 in (42.32 m) to 145 ft 6 in), with extensions to both the tail and horizontal stabilizer extending the aircraft's length further. while a longer wing carried more fuel, increasing range by 1,600 miles (2,600 km) and allowing the aircraft to operate as true transoceanic aircraft. The wing modifications included outboard and inboard inserts, as well as a kink in the trailing edge to add area inboard. Takeoff weight was increased to 302,000 lb (137,000 kg) initially, and to 311,000 lb (141,000 kg) and perhaps further as higher-rated JT4A's became available. First flight was on January 11, 1958, and 69 turbojet 707-320s were produced. No -320 Intercontinental models were re-engined with fan engines in civil use, but around year 2000 the Israeli Air Force re-engined two ex-Sabena -320 based military tankers.

The **707-320B** is a re-engined version undertaken in parallel with the -120B, using the same JT3D-3 turbofans and incorporating many of the same airframe upgrades as well. The wing was modified from the -320 by adding a second inboard kink, a dog-toothed leading edge, and triangular wingtips instead of the earlier blunt ones. These new wingtips increased overall wingspan by three feet. Takeoff gross weight was increased to 335,000 lb (152,000 kg). The 175 707-320B aircraft produced were all new-build, no original -320 models were converted to fan engines in civilian use.

The **707-320B Advanced** is a slightly improved version of the -320B aircraft, adding three-section leading-edge flaps. These reduced takeoff and landing speeds, and also altered the lift distribution of the wing, allowing the ventral fin found on earlier 707s to be removed. The same wing was also used on the 707-320C.

The **707-320C** has a convertible passenger–freight configuration which became the most widely produced variant of the 707. The 707-320C added a strengthened floor and a new cargo door to the -320B model. 335 of these variants were built, including a small number with uprated JT3D-7 engines and a takeoff gross weight of 336,000 lb (152,000 kg). Despite the convertible option, a number of these were delivered as pure freighters. One of the final orders was by the Iranian Government for 14 **707-3J9C** aircraft capable of VIP transportation, communication, and inflight refuelling tasks.

The **707-420** is a version of the 707-320 originally produced at specific request for BOAC and powered by Rolls-Royce Conway 508 turbofans, producing 17,500 lbf (77.8 kN) each.

Although BOAC were first to order the 707-320 delays in getting British certification meant that Lufthansa were the first to receive and operate the 707-320 in February 1960. A total of 37 were built to this configuration.

The **707-700** was a test aircraft used to study the feasibility of using CFM International's CFM56 powerplants on a 707 airframe and possibly retrofitting them to existing aircraft. After a testing in 1979, N707QT, the last commercial 707 airframe, was refitted to 707-320C configuration and delivered to the Moroccan Air Force as a tanker aircraft. (This purchase was considered a "civilian" order and not a military one.) Boeing abandoned the program, since they felt it would be a threat to the Boeing 757 program. The information gathered in the test led to the eventual retrofitting program of CFM56 engines to the USAF C-135/KC-135R models, and some military versions of the 707 also used the CFM56. Ironically the Douglas DC-8 "Super 70" series by Cammacorp did develop commercially, extending the life of DC-8 airframes in a stricter noise regulatory environment, so there are today more DC-8s in commercial service than there are 707s.

720

Boeing 720-048 of Aer Lingus-Irish International in 1965

The **720** was originally designated *707-020* but later changed for marketing reasons. It was a modification of the 707-120 designed for medium-range operation from shorter runways. It had four frames removed in front of the wing, and one aft, making it 8 feet 4 inches (2.54 m) shorter than the -120, and certified to a lower maximum takeoff weight. The wing modifications consisted of adding Krueger flaps outboard of the outboard engines to lower takeoff and landing speeds and thus shorten field length, and a thickened inboard section at the leading edge which had a slightly greater sweep. This modification increased the top speed over the -120, and was later available on the -120B and on -120s retrofitted to the B standard. This model had few sales but was still profitable due to the minimal R&D costs associated with modifying an existing type. At one point in the promotion stage to airlines it was known as the *717*, although this was the Boeing model designation of the KC-135 and remained unused for a commercial airliner until it was applied to the MD-95 following Boeing's merger with McDonnell Douglas. The 720 was used before the Boeing 727 replaced it in the market. Its first flight was on November 23, 1959, and 64 of the original version were built.

The **720B** was the turbofan-powered version of the 720, with JT3D-1-MC6 turbofans producing 17,000 lbf (75.6 kN) each. Takeoff gross weight was increased to 235,000 lb (107,000 kg). A total of 89 of these were built in addition to conversions of existing 720s. Boeing built a combined 154 of both 720 models from 1959 to 1967.

Military

USAF E-3 Sentry in flight

RAAF 707-368C at Perth International airport, Australia

Boeing 707s at AMARG being used for salvage parts for the KC-135s.

The militaries of the United States and other countries have used the civilian 707 aircraft in a variety of roles, and under different designations. (Note the 707 and U.S. Air Force's KC-135 were developed in parallel from the Boeing 367-80 prototype.) The Canadian Forces also operated Boeing 707 with designation CC-137 Husky (707-347C) from 1972 to 1997.

The VC-137C variant of the Stratoliner was a special-purpose design meant to serve as Air Force One, the secure transport for the President of The United States of America. These models were in operational use from 1962 to 1990. The two aircraft remain on display: SAM 26000 is at the National Museum of the United States Air Force near Dayton, Ohio and SAM 27000 is at the Ronald Reagan Presidential Library in Simi Valley, California.

717

Boeing 717 was the company designation for C-135 Stratolifter and KC-135 Stratotanker derivatives of the 367-80. The designation was later re-used in renaming the McDonnell Douglas MD-95 to Boeing 717 after the company was merged with Boeing.

Operators

In the 1980s, the USAF acquired around 250 used 707s to provide parts for the KC-135E Stratotanker program.

Although 707s are no longer employed by major airlines, as of March 2011, 43 aircraft were in use mainly with air cargo operators and air forces in Africa, Middle East and South America. Commercial operators of the Boeing 707 include Saha Airline, BETA Cargo, Enterprise World Airways, Libyan Airlines, Mid Express Tchad, Hewa Bora Airways and some other users with mostly stored aircraft. The Romanian Government uses a 707-320C as a Presidential Aircraft, being operated by Romavia. American actor John Travolta owns, and is qualified to fly as second in command, an ex-Qantas 707-138B, registration N707JT.

The list of customer codes used by Boeing to identify specific options and trim specified by customers was started with the 707, and has been maintained through all Boeing's models. Essentially the same system as used on the earlier Boeing 377, the code consisted of two digits affixed to the model number to identify the specific aircraft version. For example, Pan American Airlines was assigned code "21". Thus a 707-320B sold to Pan Am had the model number 707-321B. The number remained constant as further aircraft were purchased, thus when Pan American purchased the 747-100 it had the model number 747-121.

Accidents and incidents

As of May 2011, the 707 has been in a total of 170 hull-loss occurrences with 2,739 fatalities.

Notable accidents

- On October 19, 1959, a Boeing 707-227 crashed northeast of Arlington, Washington while on a training flight for Braniff International Airways. Four people were killed in the crash, and four survived.
- On February 15, 1961, Sabena Flight 548, 707-320, crashed while on approach to Brussels Airport, Belgium. A total of 73 people were killed, including the United States Figure Skating team.
- On March 1, 1962, American Airlines Flight 1, a 707-123B, crashed into Jamaica Bay after taking off from Idlewild Airport (now JFK Airport) while heading for Los Angeles International Airport. All 95 people on board died.
- On May 22, 1962, Continental Airlines Flight 11, 707-124, was destroyed by a bomb while en route from Chicago, Illinois, to Kansas City, Missouri. Everyone on board was killed.
- On June 3, 1962, Air France Flight 007, a 707-300, crashed while attempting to takeoff from Paris's Orly Airport. The crash killed 130 people aboard; two stewardesses survived. It was, at the time, the worst single-plane disaster.
- On June 22, 1962, Air France Flight 117, a 707, crashed into a hill in Guadalupe while attempting to land at Pointe-à-Pitre, killing all 113 aboard.
- On November 27, 1962: Varig flight 810, a Boeing 707-441 registration PP-VJB flying from Rio de Janeiro-Galeão to Lima, after initiating an overshoot procedure at the suggestion of the control tower because it was too high, proceeded to start another approach when it crashed into La Cruz peak, 8 miles away from Lima Airport. Possibly there was a misinterpretation of navigation instruments. All 97 passengers and crew aboard died.
- On February 12, 1963, Northwest Orient Airlines Flight 705, a 720B, suffered an in-flight break-up over the Florida Everglades approximately 12 minutes after leaving Miami, bound for Chicago. All 35 passengers and eight crew died. The cause of the crash was determined to be an unrecoverable loss of control due to severe turbulence.
- On December 8, 1963, Pan Am Flight 214, a 707-121, crashed outside Elkton, Maryland during a severe electrical storm, with a loss of all 81 passengers and crew. The Boeing 707-121, registered as N709PA, was on the final leg of a San Juan — Baltimore — Philadelphia flight.
- On May 20, 1965, Pakistan International Airlines Flight PK 705, a 720, crashed short of the runway at Cairo International Airport, killing 119 of the 125 people on board.
- On September 17, 1965, Pan Am Flight 292, 707-120B, crashed into the side of a mountain in a storm on the island of Montserrat killing all 30 passengers and crew on board.
- On January 24, 1966, Air India Flight 101, a 707-437, crashed into Glacier des Bossons on the SW face of Mont Blanc in the French Alps. All 106 passengers and 11 crew were killed.
- On March 6, 1966, BOAC Flight 911, a 707-436 en route from Tokyo to Hong Kong, encountered clear air turbulence close to Mount Fuji; the sudden violent gusting caused the vertical stabilizer to detach from the aircraft, following which the aircraft entered an uncontrolled dive. The 707 progressively broke up as a result of aerodynamic over-stressing of the airframe, then struck the ground near the foot of the mountain. All those on board died.
- On April 8, 1968, BOAC Flight 712, a 707-465, suffered engine failure on takeoff from London Heathrow Airport followed by an engine fire. The plane made an emergency landing back at the airport, but an explosion in the port wing caused the plane to catch fire. Four passengers and a flight attendant were killed and 122 escaped.
- On April 20, 1968, South African Airways Flight 228 crashed shortly after takeoff from Windhoek, Namibia. The crew used a flap retraction sequence from the 707-B series on newly-delivered 707-C, which retracted the flaps in larger increments than desirable for that stage of the flight, leading to a loss of lift at 600 ft (180 m) above

ground level. The inquiry blamed the crew for not observing their flight instruments when they had no visual reference.
- On December, 12 1968, Pan Am Flight 217, a 707, en route to Caracas, Venezuela, crashed into the Caribbean Sea. All 51 passengers and crew on board died. City lights may have caused an optical illusion that affected the pilots.
- On July 11, 1973, Varig Flight 820, a 707 registered PP-VJZ, on scheduled airline service from Galeão Airport, Rio de Janeiro, Brazil to Orly Airport, Paris, France made an emergency landing in a field in the Orly community due to smoke in the cabin. The fire, smoke and crash resulted in 123 deaths, with 11 survivors (10 crew, one passenger).
- On July 22, 1973, Pan Am Flight 816, a 707-321C, crashed shortly after takeoff at Papeete, Tahiti resulting in 78 deaths.
- On November 3, 1973, Pan Am Flight 160, a 707-321C, crashed on approach to Boston-Logan. Smoke in the cockpit caused the pilots to lose control. Three people were killed in the hull-loss accident.
- On April 22, 1974, Pan Am Flight 812, a 707-321B, crashed into a mountain while preparing for landing after a 4 hour 20 minutes flight from Hong Kong to Denpasar, Bali, Indonesia. All 107 people on board were killed.
- On August 3, 1975, a chartered 707-321C crashed into a mountain while preparing to land at Agadir-Inezgane Airport. All 188 passengers and crew on board were killed. The 1975 Agadir Morocco Air Disaster has the highest death toll of any crash involving a 707.
- On January 1, 1976, Middle East Airlines Flight 438, a 720B, was destroyed en-route from Beirut to Dubai by a bomb in the forward cargo hold. All 66 passengers and 15 crew were killed.
- On April 20, 1978, Korean Air Lines Flight 902, a 707, was hit by a missile fired from a Soviet Sukhoi Su-15 interceptor after it had entered Soviet airspace. This caused a rapid decompression of the fuselage which killed two passengers. The 707 made an emergency landing on a frozen lake near Murmansk, USSR.
- On January 30, 1979, a Varig cargo 707-323C, registration PP-VLU crashed while flying from Tokyo to Rio de Janeiro. Causes are unknown since the wreck was never found.
- On October 13, 1983, a Bolivian cargo 707 crashed in Santa Cruz, Bolivia killing 91 (of whom 88 were killed on the ground when the aircraft crashed into a practice football game).
- On January 3, 1987, Varig Flight 797, a 707-379C, crashed when making a return to Abidjan, Côte d'Ivoire after one of its engines failed. One person survived out of the 51 people onboard.
- On November 29, 1987, Korean Air Flight 858, a 707-3B5C, exploded over the Andaman Sea, in the Indian Ocean in a terrorist attack with a bomb placed by North Korean agents. All 115 people on board died.
- On February 8, 1989, Independent Air Flight 1851, a Boeing 707, crashed into a hill on approach to Santa Maria, Azores. All 144 people on board were killed. Wreckage remains at the site to this day.
- On January 25, 1990, Avianca Flight 52, a 707-321B, crashed after running out of fuel in Long Island, New York. The 707 was delayed numerous times because of heavy fog in New York. A total of 73 people died.
- On October 29, 1991, a 707 of the Royal Australian Air Force stalled and crashed into the sea off East Sale, Victoria. All five crew on board died.
- On October 23, 1996, a 707 belonging to the Argentinian Air Force crashed on takeoff roll after failing to achieve required takeoff speed (V) at Buenos Aires International Airport (EZE).
- On September 21, 2000, the 707 belonging to the Government of Togo coming from Valencia Airport, Spain en route to Lomé-Tokoin Airport, Togo, experienced a cockpit fire approximately 200 km/125 miles from Niamey, Niger, and crash landed at Hamani Diori Airport, Niger. None of the 10 people aboard was killed but the aircraft was destroyed by subsequent fire.
- On July 4, 2002, a 707-123B on a Gomair flight from N'Djamena Airport, Chad to Brazzaville-Maya Maya Airport, Rep. of Congo carrying a mixed load of cargo and passengers crashed. It experienced technical problems and diverted to Bangui, Central African Republic. On landing approach it descended too quickly and made ground-contact in a suburb. It subsequently bounced and broke up. Of the 30 people on board, 28 died in the accident.
- On October 23, 2004, a BETA Cargo 707 on a Cargo flight from Manaus-Eduardo Gomes International Airport, Brazil to São Paulo-Guarulhos International Airport, Brazil aborted takeoff from Manaus due to a "loud noise". The aircraft afterwards started tilting to the right. It appeared the landing gear ruptured the right wing. The 37-year old aircraft (registration PP-BSE) was written-off.
- On March 19, 2005, a Cargo Plus Aviation-owned 707-300 freighter on a wet-lease to Ethiopian Airlines crashed into Lake Victoria on approach to Runway 35 at Entebbe, Uganda on the lake's northern shore. The 31-year-old 707 freighter was on approach to Runway 35 during its second attempt to land. Its right wing clipped an outcrop on approach and it began to break up. The accident happened in heavy rain. The aircraft broke up, but the crew of five survived.
- On 20 April 2005, Saha Air Lines Flight 171, a 707-3J9C, registration EP-SHE, flying from Kish Island, crashed on landing at Mehrabad Air-

port, Tehran following an unstabilized approach with a higher than recommended airspeed. Gear and/or a tyre failed after touchdown and the flight overran the far end of the runway. Of the 12 crew and 157 passengers, three passengers were killed, reportedly falling into the river after evacuation.
- On 21 October 2009, Azza Transport Flight 2241, a 707-320, crashed shortly after takeoff from Sharjah International Airport, United Arab Emirates. The flight was carrying cargo only and all six crew members were killed.
- On 18 May 2011, a Boeing 707 tanker operated by Omega Aerial Refueling Services crashed on take-off from Naval Air Station Point Mugu, California, United States and was burnt out. All three crew survived.

Aircraft on display

Ex-Qantas Boeing 707-138B VH-XBA undergoing taxi tests at Sydney International Airport prior to its delivery to the Qantas Founders Outback Museum

Retired South African Air Force Boeing 707-328C at the South African Air Force Museum, Pretoria

- *N70700* Model 367-80 (Prototype) previously at the Museum of Flight, Seattle, Washington; now at Steven F. Udvar-Hazy Center, Washington, D.C.
- *N714PA* Model 707-321 (msn. 17592, no. 13) The nose section of this former Pan American aircraft is on display at the New England Air Museum at Bradley International Airport (KBDL), Windsor Locks, CT.
- *VH-XBA* Model 707-138B (No. 29) one of the first 707s exported, and the first civilian jet registered in Australia (to airline Qantas in 1959), is on display at the Qantas Founders Outback Museum in Longreach, Queensland, Australia.
- *4X-BYD* Model 707-131(F), (No. 34) ex-Israel Air Force is on display at the Israeli Air Force Museum near Hatzerim, Israel.
- *58-6971* Model 707-153B (VC-137B) (msn. 17926, no. 40) USAF VIP transport on display at Davis–Monthan Air Force Base, Tucson, AZ.
- *N3951A* Model 707-123B (msn. 17647, no. 53) Nose section of former American Airlines aircraft (N7520A) on display at Auto Technik Museum Sinsheim, Germany.
- *00-SGA* Model 707-329 (msn. 17623, no. 78) The forward fuselage section of Sabena's first Boeing 707 is preserved at the Royal Army & Military Museum in Brussels, Belgium.
- *N99WT* Model 707-321 (msn. 17606, no. 107) Former Pan American aircraft (N728PA) is used as the Club 707 restaurant near Manila, Philippines.
- *4X-JYW* Model 707-328 (msn. 173617, no. 110)) Former Air France (F-BHSE) aircraft sold to the Israel Air Force, aircraft on display at the Israel Air Force Museum, Beersheba - Hatzerim (LLHB).
- *D-AFHG* Model 707-430 (msn. 17720, no. 115) Former Lufthansa airliner on display at Hamburg Airport (HAM/EDDH).
- *4X-JYG* Model 720-023B (msn. 18013, no. 120) Former American Airlines (N7527A) aircraft sold to the Israel Air Force, aircraft on display at the Israel Air Force Museum, Beersheba - Hatzerim (LLHB).
- *F-BHSL* Model 707-328 (msn. 17919, no. 153) Front fuselage of former Air France aircraft preserved at the French Air and Space Museum (Musée de l'Air et de l'Espace), Paris, France
- *VN-A304* Model 707-344 (msn. 17929, no. 154) Former Hang Khong Vietnam Airlines aircraft, originally delivered to South African Airways as ZS-CKD is complete but in poor condition in a park in Saigon, Vietnam.
- *D-ABOF* Model 707-430 (msn. 17721, no. 162) Nose section of former Lufthansa aircraft preserved at the Deutsches Museum, Munich, Germany.
- *G-APFJ* Model 707-436 (msn. 17711, no. 163) Front fuselage of former BOAC/British Airways aircraft is on display at the National Museum of Flight, East Fortune, Scotland.
- *4X-ATA* Model 707-458 (msn 18070, no. 205) The nose section of first Boeing 707 delivered to El Al is on display at the Cradle of Aviation Museum in Garden City, NY. The aircraft was formerly on display on board the Intrepid Sea-Air-Space Museum.
- *18351* Model 720-047B (msn. 18351, no. 211) Taiwan Air Force VIP aircraft on display at Kangshan AFB, Taiwan.
- *TY-BBW* Model 707-321 (msn. 18084, no. 212 Former Pan American N758PA - on display in Wetteren, Belgium, in the colors of the Republique Populaire du Benin VIP aircraft.
- *N93143* Model 720-047B (msn. 18063, no. 213) Nose section of former Western Airlines on display at the Pima Air and Space Museum, Tucson, AZ.
- *N130KR* Model 707-458 (msn. 18071, no. 216) Former El Al (4X-

ATB) aircraft restored in 1960s Lufthansa markings with fictitious registration D-ABOC at Berlin - Tegel (TXL/EDDT).
- *CC-CCG* Model 707-330B (msn. 18642, no. 233) This ex-Lufthansa and LAN Chile is undergoing restoration at Santiago - Los Cerillos, Chile (ULC/SCTI) and will be repainted in the Chilean airline's 1960s scheme.
- *HK-749* Model 720-030B (msn. 18248, no. 258) Airframe preserved at Museo de los Ninos, Bogota, Colombia.
- *7O-ACJ* Model 707-348C (msn. 18737, no. 377) Fuselage of former Yemen Airlines used as a restaurant in Damascus, Syria. The aircraft was originally delivered to Aer Lingus as EI-AMW.
- *AP-AXL* Model 720-047B (msn. 18818, no. 390) ex-Pakistan International Airlines aircraft after being hijacked for 13 days in 1981, it was withdrawn from service, and is now displayed at PIA Planetarium Karachi.
- *EP-IRJ* Model 707-321B (msn. 18958, no. 475) Former Iran Air aircraft originally delivered to Pan American as N416PA is currently the Air Restaurant at Mehrabad Airport, Tehran.
- *F-BLCD* Model 707-328B (no. 471) is on display at the Musée de l'Air et de l'Espace, Paris, France.
- *1419* Model 707-328C (no. 763) ex-South African Air Force is on display at the South African Air Force Museum - Swartkops Air Force Base, Pretoria.
- *9T-MSS* Model 707-382B (msn. 19969, no. 751) Former TAP Air Portugal (CS-TBD) - nose section restored and on display at the Sintra Air Museum.
- *N893PA* Model 707-321B (msn. 20030, no. 791) Former CAAC aircraft originally delivered to Pan American is preserved at Tianjin, China.
- *HZ-HM2* Model 707-386C (msn. 21081, no. 903) Saudi Air Force VIP aircraft painted in the current Saudia color scheme. Del. 1975, reg. HZ-HM1. Entire aircraft preserved at Saudi Air Force Museum, Riyadh, Saudi Arabia.
- Unknown Boeing 707 forward fuselage painted in the colors of Air Force One at Presidential Park, Williamsburg, VA.

Sources:

Notable appearances in media

The 707 is mentioned in the songs "Boeing Boeing 707" by Roger Miller; "Jet Airliner" performed by the Steve Miller Band and written by Paul Pena; and "Early Morning Rain", written by Gordon Lightfoot and popularized by artists such as Elvis Presley, Bob Dylan, and Peter, Paul and Mary.

The aircraft has had major roles in the *Airport* and *Airplane* films, and has been alluded to in both television and theatrical movies.

Source (edited): "http://en.wikipedia.org/wiki/Boeing_707"

Boeing CH-47 Chinook

The **Boeing CH-47 Chinook** is a twin-engine, tandem rotor heavy-lift helicopter. Its top speed of 170 knots (196 mph, 315 km/h) was faster than contemporary utility and attack helicopters of the 1960s. It is one of the few aircraft of that era, such as the C-130 Hercules and the UH-1 Iroquois, that is still in production and front line service with over 1,179 built to date. Its primary roles include troop movement, artillery emplacement and battlefield resupply. It has a wide loading ramp at the rear of the fuselage and three external-cargo hooks.

The Chinook was designed and initially produced by Boeing Vertol in the early 1960s. The helicopter is now produced by Boeing Rotorcraft Systems. Chinooks have been sold to 16 nations with the US Army and the Royal Air Force (see Boeing Chinook (UK variants)) being the largest users. The CH-47 is among the heaviest lifting Western helicopters.

Design and development

Early development

In late 1956, the Department of the Army announced plans to replace the CH-37 Mojave, which was powered by piston engines, with a new, turbine-powered helicopter. Turbine engines were also a key design feature of the smaller UH-1 "Huey" utility helicopter. Following a design competition, in September 1958, a joint Army-Air Force source selection board recommended that the Army procure the Vertol medium transport helicopter. However, funding for full-scale development was not then available, and the Army vacillated on its design requirements. Some in the Army aviation corps thought that the new helicopter should be a light tactical transport aimed at taking over the missions of the old piston-engined H-21 and H-34 helicopters, and consequently capable of carrying about fifteen troops (one squad). Another faction in the Army aviation corps thought that the new helicopter should be much larger to be able to airlift a large artillery piece, and have enough internal space to carry the new MGM-31 "Pershing" Missile System.

HC-1B in flight being tested and evaluated.

Vertol began work on a new tandem-rotor helicopter designated Vertol Model 107 or V-107 in 1957. In June 1958, the US Army awarded a contract to Vertol for the aircraft under the

YHC-1A designation. The YHC-1A had a capacity for 20 troops. Three were tested by the Army to derive engineering and operational data. However, the YHC-1A was considered by most of the Army users to be too heavy for the assault role and too light for the transport role. The decision was made to procure a heavier transport helicopter and at the same time upgrade the UH-1 "Huey" as a tactical troop transport. The YHC-1A would be improved and adopted by the Marines as the CH-46 Sea Knight in 1962. The Army then ordered the larger Model 114 under the designation HC-1B. The pre-production Boeing Vertol YCH-1B made its initial hovering flight on September 21, 1961. In 1962 the HC-1B was redesignated the **CH-47A** under the 1962 United States Tri-Service aircraft designation system.

A CH-47 in a training exercise with US Navy Special Warfare, in July 2008

The name "Chinook" alludes to the Chinook people of the Pacific Northwest. The CH-47 is powered by two turboshaft engines, mounted on each side of the helicopter's rear end and connected to the rotors by driveshafts. Initial models were fitted with engines of 2,200 horsepower. The counter-rotating rotors eliminate the need for an antitorque vertical rotor, allowing all power to be used for lift and thrust. The ability to adjust lift in either rotor makes it less sensitive to changes in the center of gravity, important for the cargo lifting role. If one engine fails, the other can drive both rotors. The "sizing" of the Chinook was directly related to the growth of the Huey and the Army's tacticians' insistence that initial air assaults be built around the squad. The Army pushed for both the Huey and the Chinook, and this focus was responsible for the acceleration of its air mobility effort.

Improved and later versions

A CH-47F practicing the Pinnacle maneuver whereby soldiers are deposited without the helicopter ever landing.

Improved and more powerful versions of the CH-47 have been developed since the helicopter entered service. The US Army's first major design leap was the now-common CH-47D, which entered service in 1982. Improvements from the CH-47C included upgraded engines, composite rotor blades, a redesigned cockpit to reduce pilot workload, improved and redundant electrical systems, an advanced flight control system and improved avionics. The latest mainstream generation is the CH-47F, which features several major upgrades to reduce maintenance, digitized flight controls, and is powered by two 4,733-horsepower Honeywell engines.

A commercial model of the Chinook, the **Boeing-Vertol Model 234**, is used worldwide for logging, construction, fighting forest fires, and supporting petroleum extraction operations. On 15 December 2006, the Columbia Helicopters company of the Salem, Oregon, metropolitan area, purchased the Type Certificate of the Model 234 from Boeing. The Chinook has also been licensed to be built by companies outside of the United States, such as Elicotteri Meridionali (now AgustaWestland) in Italy, Kawasaki in Japan, and a company in the United Kingdom.

Operational history

Vietnam War

US troops board CH-47 Chinooks and UH-1 Hueys during Operation Crazy Horse, Vietnam, 1966.

The Army finally settled on the larger Chinook as its standard medium transport helicopter and as of February 1966, 161 aircraft had been delivered to the Army. The 1st Cavalry Division had brought their organic Chinook battalion with them when they arrived in 1965 and a separate aviation medium helicopter company, the 147th, had arrived in Vietnam on 29 November 1965. This latter company was initially placed in direct support of the 1st Infantry Division.

The most spectacular mission in Vietnam for the Chinook was the placing of artillery batteries in perilous mountain positions inaccessible by any other means, and then keeping them resupplied with large quantities of ammunition. The 1st Cavalry Division found that its Chinooks were limited to 7,000 pounds payload when operating in the mountains, but could carry an additional 1,000 pounds when operating near the coast. The early Chinook design was limited by its rotor system which did not permit full use of the installed power, and users were anxious for an improved version which would upgrade this system.

Troops unload from a CH-47 helicopter in the Cay Giep Mountains, Vietnam, 1967.

As with any new piece of equipment, the Chinook presented a major problem of "customer education". Commanders and crew chiefs had to be constantly alert that eager soldiers did not overload the temptingly large cargo compartment. It would be some time before troops would be experts at using sling loads. The Chinook soon proved to be such an invaluable aircraft for artillery movement and heavy logistics that it was seldom used as an assault troop carrier. Some of the Chinook fleet were used for casualty evacuation, due to the very heavy demand for the helicopters they were usually overburdened with wounded. Perhaps the most cost effective use of the Chinook was the recovery of other downed aircraft.

The Chinooks were generally armed with a single 7.62 millimeter M60 machine gun on a pintle mount on either side of the machine for self-defense, with stops fitted to keep the gunners from firing into the rotor blades. Dust filters were also added to improve engine reliability. At its peak employment in Vietnam, there were 22 Chinook units in operation.

Of the nearly 750 Chinooks in the US and Republic of Vietnam fleets, about 200 were lost in combat or wartime operational accidents. US Army supplied Chinooks to the Australian Task Force as required.

Iran-Iraq war

During the 1970s, the United States and Iran had a strong relationship, in which the Iranian armed forces began to use many American military aircraft, most notably the F-14 Tomcat, as part of a modernisation programme. After an agreement signed between Boeing and Elicotteri Meridionali, the Imperial Iranian Air Force purchased 20 Elicotteri Meridionali-built CH-47Cs in 1971. The Imperial Iranian Army Aviation purchased 70 CH-47Cs from Elicotteri Meridionali during the period of 1972–1976. In late 1978, Iran placed an order for an additional 50 helicopters with Elicotteri Meridionali, but that order was canceled immediately after the revolution. Despite the arms embargo on place upon Iran, they have managed to keep their fleet operational.

In the 1978 Iranian Chinook shootdown, four Iranian CH-47C Chinooks penetrated 15–20 km into Soviet airspace in the Turkimenistan Military District. They were intercepted by a MiG-23M which shot down one Chinook, killing eight crew members, and forced a second one to land. Chinooks were used in efforts by the Imperial Iranian loyalist forces to resist the 1979 Iranian revolution. During the war with Iraq, Iran made heavy use of its US-bought equipment, and lost at least 8 Chinooks during the 1980–1988 period; most notably during a clash on 15 July 1983, where an Iraqi Mirage F-1 destroyed three Iranian CH-47s transporting troops to the front line.

Falklands War

The Chinook was used both by Argentina and the United Kingdom during the Falklands War in 1982. The Argentine Air Force and the Argentine Army deployed four CH-47C (two each) which were widely used in general transport duties. Of the Army's airframes one was destroyed on ground by a Harrier while the other was captured (and reused after the war) by the British. Both Air Force helicopters returned to Argentina and remained in service until 2002.

Iraq and Afghanistan

Soldiers wait for pickup from two Chinooks in Afghanistan, 2008.

Approximately 163 CH-47Ds served in Kuwait and Iraq during Operations Desert Shield and Desert Storm in 1990–91.

The CH-47D has been seen wide use in Operation Enduring Freedom in Afghanistan and Operation Iraqi Freedom in Iraq. The Chinook is being used in air assault missions, inserting troops into fire bases and later bringing food, water, and ammunition. It is also the casualty evacuation (casevac) aircraft of choice in the British Army. In today's usage it is typically escorted by attack helicopters such as the AH-64 Apache for protection. Its tandem rotor design and lift capacity have been found to be particularly useful in the mountainous terrain of Afghanistan where high altitudes and temperatures limit the use of the UH-60 Black Hawk. The CH-47F is being fielded by more units such as the 101st Combat Aviation Brigade and 4th Combat Aviation Brigade in the U.S. Army as it continues to operate in Afghanistan.

The Chinooks of several nations have participated in the Afghanistan War, including aircraft from Britain, Italy, the Netherlands, Spain, Canada, and Australia. Despite the age of the Chinook, it is still in heavy demand, in part due its proven versatility and ability to operate in demanding environments such as Afghanistan.

Japan

Three CH-47 Chinooks were used to cool Reactors 3 and 4 of the Fukushima Nuclear power-plant with sea water after the 9.0 earthquake in 2011. To protect the crew from the heightened radiation levels, lead plates were attached to the floor.

Variants

A view of the Chinook's interior

HC-1B

The pre-1962 designation for Model 114 development aircraft that would be re-designated CH-47 Chinook.

CH-47A

The all-weather, medium-lift CH-47A Chinook was powered initially by Lycoming T55-L-5 engines rated at 2,200 horsepower (1,640 kW) but then replaced by the T55-L-7 rated at 2,650 hp (1,980 kW) engines or T55-L-7C engines rated at 2,850 hp (2,130 kW). The CH-47A had a maximum gross weight of 33,000 pounds (15,000 kg). Initial delivery of the CH-47A Chinook to the US Army was in August 1962. A total of 349 were built.

ACH-47A

The ACH-47A was originally known as the Armed/Armored CH-47A (or A/ACH-47A). It was officially designated ACH-47A by US Army *Attack Cargo Helicopter* and unofficially *Guns A Go-Go*. Four CH-47A helicopters were converted to gunships by Boeing Vertol in late 1965. Three were assigned to the 53rd Aviation Detachment in South Vietnam for testing, with the remaining one retained in the US for weapons testing. By 1966, the 53rd was redesignated the 1st Aviation Detachment (Provisional) and attached to the 228th Assault Support Helicopter Battalion of the 1st Cavalry Division (Airmobile). By 1968, only one gunship remained, and logistical concerns prevented more conversions. It was returned to the United States, and the program stopped.

The ACH-47A carried five M60D 7.62x51 mm machine guns or M2HB .50 caliber machine guns, provided by the XM32 and XM33 armament subsystems, two M24A1 20 mm cannons, two XM159B/XM159C 19-Tube 2.75 in rocket launchers or sometimes two M18/M18A1 7.62×51 mm gun pods, and a single M75 40 mm grenade launcher in the XM5/M5 armament subsystem (more commonly seen on the UH-1 series of helicopters). The surviving aircraft, Easy Money, has been restored and is on display at Redstone Arsenal, Alabama.

CH-47B

The CH-47B was an interim solution while Boeing worked on a more substantially improved CH-47C. CH-47B was powered by two Lycoming T55-L-7C 2,850 shp (2,130 kW) engines. It featured a blunted rear rotor pylon, redesigned asymmetrical rotor blades, and strakes along the rear ramp and fuselage to improve flying characteristics. It could be equipped with two door-mounted M60D 7.62 mm NATO machine guns on the M24 armament subsystem and a ramp-mounted M60D using the M41 armament subsystem. Some CH-47 "bombers" were equipped to drop tear gas or napalm from the rear cargo ramp onto NLF (aka Việt Cộng) bunkers. The CH-47 could be equipped with a hoist and cargo hook. The Chinook proved especially valuable in "Pipe Smoke" aircraft recovery missions. The "Hook" recovered about 12,000 aircraft valued at over $3.6 billion during the war. 108 built.

CH-47C

The CH-47C featured more powerful engines and transmissions. Three versions of the "C model" were built. The first had Lycoming T55-L-7C engines delivering 2,850 shp (2,130 kW). The "Super C" included Lycoming T55-L-11 engines delivering 3,750 shp (2,800 kW), an upgraded maximum gross weight of 46,000 lb (21,000 kg) and a pitch stability augmentation system (PSAS). Due to difficulties with the T55-L-11 engines, which were hurriedly brought to war to increase payload, they were temporarily removed from the "Super C" prior to 1970 and the very reliable Lycoming T55-L-7C's were installed until the L-11 engine difficulties could be quantified and corrected. This L-7C engine configuration was affectionately referred to as the "baby C" although it was still a Super C. It distinguished itself from the "C" in that it had PSAS and an uprated maximum gross weight. The CH-47 A, B, and all variants of the C were not able to receive certification from the FAA for civil use due to the non-redundant hydraulic flight boost system drive. A redesign of the hydraulic boost system drive was incorporated in the CH-47D which allowed that model to achieve FAA certification as the Boeing Model 234. 233 CH-47Cs were built.

The CH-47A, B, and all versions of the C saw wide use during the Vietnam war. They replaced the H-21 Shawnee in the combat assault support role.

The Royal Air Force variant of the CH-47C is known as the Chinook HC1. The export version of the CH-47C Chinook for the Italian Army was designated "CH-47C Plus".

CH-47D

CH-47D of the Spanish Army in 2009

The CH-47D model was originally powered by two T55-L-712 engines, but most are now fitted with the T55-GA-714A. Models CH-47A, CH-47B, and CH-47C, all used the same airframe, but later models featured upgraded engines. With its triple-hook cargo system, the CH-47D can carry heavy payloads internally and up to 26,000 pounds (for example, bulldozers and 40-foot / 12 m containers) externally, at speeds over 155 mph (250 km/h). The aircraft's top cruising speed is 163 mph (142 knots). The D-model was first introduced into service in 1979. In air assault operations, it often serves as the principal mover of the 155 mm M198 howitzer, 30 rounds of ammunition, and an 11-man crew. Like most US Army helicopters, the Chinook has advanced avionics and electronics, including the Global Positioning System.

Nearly all of the Army production CH-47D models were conversions from previous US Army A, B, and C models with a total of 472 converted into D-models. The last US Army D-model built was delivered to the US Army Reserve, located at Fort Hood, Texas, in early 2002.

The Royal Air Force versions of the CH-47D are known as the Chinook HC2 and HC2A. While the CH-47SD (also known as the "Super D") is a modified variant of the CH-47D, with extended range fuel tanks and higher payload carrying capacity; the CH-47SD is currently in use by the Republic of Singapore Air Force, Hellenic Army and the Republic of China Army. The CH-47DG is an upgraded version of the CH-47C for Greece.

In 2008, Canada purchased 6 CH-47Ds for use with the Canadian Helicopter Force Afghanistan from the United States for $252 million. The helicopters were transferred to the Canadian Forces on 30 December 2008.

MH-47D

A US MH-47D stands ready to receive medical supplies in Feyzabad, Afghanistan.

The MH-47D variant was developed for special forces operations and has in-flight refueling capability, a fast-rope rappelling system and other upgrades. The MH-47D was used by US Army 160th Special Operations Aviation Regiment. 12 MH-47D helicopters were produced. 6 were conversions from CH-47A models and 6 were conversions from CH-47C models.

MH-47E

The current model used by US Army Special Operations is the MH-47E. Beginning with the E model prototype manufactured in 1991, there were a total of 26 Special Operations Aircraft produced. All aircraft were assigned to 2–160th SOAR(A) "Nightstalkers", home based at Fort Campbell Kentucky. E models were conversions from existing CH-47C model airframes. The MH-47E has similar capabilities as the MH-47D, but includes an increased fuel capacity similar to the CH-47SD and terrain following/terrain avoidance radar.

In 1995, the Royal Air Force ordered eight Chinook HC3s, effectively a low cost version of the MH-47E for the special forces operations role. They were delivered in 2001 but never entered operational service due to technical issues with their avionics fit, unique to the HC3. In 2008, work started to downgrade the HC3s to HC2 standard, to enable them to enter service.

CH-47F

Soldiers prepare to board a CH-47F at the National Training Center, Fort Irwin, Calif. in November 2007

The CH-47F, an upgraded D model, first flew in 2001. The first production model was rolled out on June 15, 2006 at the Boeing facility in Ridley Park, Pennsylvania, and had its maiden flight on October 23, 2006. The CH-47F was designed to extend the service life of the Chinook class beyond 2030. Among its upgrades are new 4,868 shaft horsepower Honeywell engines, improved avionics, and an upgraded airframe with larger single-piece sections to reduce part count and need for fasteners. The new milled construction will reduce vibrations, eliminate points of joint flexing, and reduce the need for inspections and repairs, and reduce maintenance costs. It is also expected to increase service life. The CH-47F can fly at speeds of over 175 mph (282 km/h) with a payload of more than 21,000 lb (9,530 kg). The improved avionics include a Rockwell Collins Common Avionics Architecture System (CAAS) cockpit, and BAE Systems' Digital Advanced Flight Control System (DAFCS).

Boeing has delivered 48 F-model helicopters to the United States Army; on 26 August 2008, Boeing announced that the Army has signed a five-year contract, worth over $4.8 billion for 191 more, plus 24 options. In February 2007, the Netherlands were the first international customer to order the F model; six helicopters were ordered to expand their current fleet to 17. These helicopters will be equipped with an upgraded version of the Honeywell Avionics Control Management System (ACMS) cockpit. The Netherlands also plans to upgrade its current 11 CH-47Ds to the CH-47F configuration. On 10 August 2009, Canada signed a contract to purchase 15 CH-47Fs for delivery in 2013–14, entering service with the Canadian Forces after its planned withdrawal from combat operations in Afghanistan. They will be based at CFB Petawawa.

On 15 December 2009, the British government announced its Future Helicopter Strategy including the purchase of 24 new CH-47F Chinooks to be delivered from 2012. Australia ordered seven CH-47Fs in March 2010. These aircraft are to replace the Australian Army's six CH-47Ds between 2014 and 2017.

MH-47G

MH-47G Chinook, during the aircraft's rollout ceremony 6 May 2007 at Boeing

The MH-47G Special Operations Aviation (SOA) version is currently being delivered to the US Army. It is similar to the MH-47E, but features a more sophisticated avionics including a digital Common Avionics Architecture System (CAAS). The CAAS is common glass cockpit used by different helicopters such as MH-60K/Ls, CH-53E/Ks, and ARH-70As. The MH-47G will also incorporate all of the new sections of the CH-47F.

Based on operational experience in Afghanistan, the CH-47 was found to be an effective substitute for the UH-60 Black Hawk as an assault helicopter. With its larger payload, range, and higher operating speed, one Chinook can replace up to five UH-60s in this role as an air assault transport.

The new modernization program will improve MH-47D and MH-47E Special Operations Chinooks to the MH-47G design specs. A total of 25 MH-47E and 11 MH-47D aircraft were upgraded by the end of 2003. In 2002 the army announced plans to expand the Special Operations Aviation Regiment. The expansion would add 12 additional MH-47G helicopters. On February 10, 2011, Leaders and employees from the H-47 program gathered for a ceremony at Boeing's helicopter facility in Ridley Township, PA., to commemorate the delivery of the final MH-47G Chinook to U.S. Army Special Operations Command.

CH-47J

CH-47JA of the Japan Ground Self-Defense Force, during the USAF Yokota Air Base Friendship Festival, 22 August 2009.

The CH-47J is a medium-transport helicopter for the Japan Ground Self-Defense Force (JGSDF), and the Japan Air Self-Defense Force (JASDF). The differences between the CH-47J and the CH-47D are the engine, rotor brake and avionics. To use it by the general transportation, SAR and disaster activity like U.S. forces. The CH-47JA, introduced in 1993, is a long range version of the CH-47J, fitted with enlarged fuel tank, an AAQ-16 FLIR in a turret under the nose, and a partial glass cockpit. Both versions are built under license in Japan by Kawasaki Heavy Industries, who produced 61 aircraft by April 2001.

The Japan Defense Agency ordered 54 aircraft of which 39 were for the JGSDF and 15 were for the JASDF. Boeing supplied flyable aircraft, to which Kawasaki added full avionics, interior, and final paint. The CH-47J model Chinook (N7425H) made its first flight in January 1986, and it was sent to Kawasaki in April. Boeing began deliverering five CH-47J kits in September 1985 for assembly at Kawasaki.

HH-47

On 9 November 2006, the HH-47, a new variant of the Chinook based on the MH-47G, was selected by the US Air Force as the winner of the Combat Search and Rescue (CSAR-X) competition. Four development HH-47s were to be built, with the first of 141 production aircraft planned to enter service in 2012. However, in February 2007 the contract award was protested and the GAO ordered the CSAR-X project to be re-bid.

In February 2010, the US Air Force announced plans to replace aging HH-60G helicopters. The Air Force is deferring secondary combat search and rescue requirements that called for a larger helicopter.

Other export models

The HH-47D is a search and rescue version for the Republic of Korea Air Force.

Eight CH-47C Chinooks were delivered to the Canadian Forces in 1974. The Chinooks were in Canadian service from 1974 to 1991; they were designated "CH-147". These aircraft were subsequently sold to the Netherlands and are now operated by the Royal Netherlands Air Force as CH-47Ds. Additional orders are expected from Italy. Plans are to upgrade the current fleet of CH-47Ds to the F-model standard and eventually enlarge the fleet to 20 aircraft, pending funding.

Civilian models

Model 234 C-FHFB (cn MJ005) during inspection at Columbia Helicopters helipad adjacent to Aurora State Airport. Aircraft under lease to Helifor. Formerly G-BISN with British Airways.

- **Model 234LR (long range)**: Commercial transport helicopter. The Model 234LR can be fitted out as an all-passenger, all-cargo, or cargo/passenger transport helicopter.
- **Model 234ER (extended range)**: Commercial transport version.
- **Model MLR (multi-purpose long range)**: Commercial transport version.
- **Model 234UT (utility transport)**: Utility transport helicopter.

Boeing CH-47 Chinook - page 59

- **Model 414**: The Model 414 is the international export version of the CH-47D. It is also known as the **CH-47D International Chinook**.

Derivatives

In 1969, work on the experimental Model 347 was begun. It was a CH-47A with a lengthened fuselage, four-blade rotors, detachable wings mounted on top of the fuselage and other changes. It first flew on 27 May 1970 and was evaluated for a few years.

In 1973, the Army contracted Boeing to design a "Heavy Lift Helicopter" (HLH), designated XCH-62A. It appeared to be a scaled-up CH-47 without a conventional body, in a configuration similar to the S-64 Skycrane (CH-54 Tarhe), but the project was canceled in 1975. The program was restarted for test flights in the 1980s and was again not funded by Congress. The scaled up model of the HLH was scrapped at the end of 2005 at Fort Rucker, Alabama.

Operators

Military operators

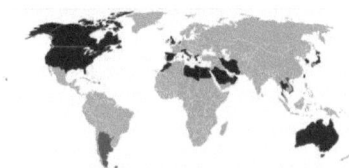

Military CH-47 Chinook Operators (former operators in red)

A CH-47 lifts an F-15 to a training installation at Creech Air Force Base

 Australia
 Canada
 Egypt
 Greece
 Iran
 Italy
 Japan
 Libya
 Morocco
 Netherlands
 Republic of China (Taiwan)
 Saudi Arabia
 Singapore
 South Korea
 Spain
 Thailand
 Turkey
14 CH-47s requested
 United Kingdom
see Boeing Chinook (UK variants)
 United Arab Emirates
 United States
 Vietnam
captured ex-USAF Chinook CH-47A

Civilian operators

Boeing 234 flying in Civil Aviation Administration of China. Demonstration aircraft.

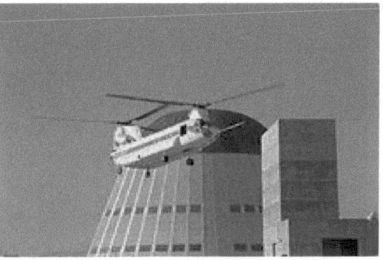

NASA CH-47B used as an in-flight simulator. Former US Army 66-19138

 Canada
- Helifor Canada Corp (under lease from Columbia Helicopters)

 Republic of China (Taiwan)
- Taiwan National Fire Administration (currently operates three 234s)

 People's Republic of China
- *Civil Aviation Administration of China* (one month demonstration period)

 Ecuador
- Icaro Air (under lease from Columbia Helicopters)

 Norway
- *CHC Helikopter Service (formerly Helikopter Services)*

 United Kingdom
- *British Airways Helicopters*
- *British International Helicopters*

 United States
- Columbia Helicopters (currently operates seven 234s)
- *Era Aviation*
- *NASA* (August 14, 1979 – September 20, 1989)

- *Trump Airlines*

Former civil operators are marked by italics

Notable accidents and incidents

- On September 11, 1982, at an airshow in Mannheim, Germany a United States Army Chinook (serial number 74-22292) carrying parachutists crashed, killing 46 people. The crash was later found to be caused by an accumulation of ground walnut shells that had been used to clean the machinery.
- On November 6, 1986, a British International Helicopters Chinook crashed on approach to Sumburgh Airport, Shetland Islands resulting in the loss of 45 lives and the withdrawal of the Chinook from crew servicing flights in the North Sea.
- Major Marie Therese Rossi Cayton was the first American woman to fly in combat during Desert Storm in 1991. She was killed when her Chinook helicopter crashed on 1 March 1991.
- On 29 May 2001 a ROK Army CH-47D installing a sculpture onto Olympic Bridge in Seoul, South Korea failed to unlatch the sculpture. The helicopter's rotors struck the monument; then the fuselage hit and broke into two. One section crashed onto the bridge in flames and the other fell into the river. All three crew members on board died.

Specifications (CH-47D)

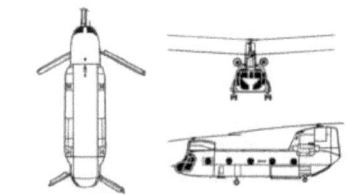

Turboshaft engine on the rear of a CH-47

M240 machine gun emplacement on the loading ramp, as well as another partly visible on the right shoulder window

Data from Boeing CH-47D/F, Army Chinook file, International Directory

General characteristics

- **Crew:** 3 (pilot, copilot, flight engineer)
- **Capacity:**
  - 33–55 troops *or*
  - 24 litters and 3 attendants *or*
  - 28,000 lb (12,700 kg) cargo
- **Length:** 98 ft 10 in (30.1 m)
- **Rotor diameter:** 60 ft 0 in (18.3 m)
- **Height:** 18 ft 11 in (5.7 m)
- **Disc area:** 5,600 ft (2,800 ft per rotor disc) (260 m)
- **Empty weight:** 23,400 lb (10,185 kg)
- **Loaded weight:** 26,680 lb (12,100 kg)
- **Max takeoff weight:** 50,000 lb (22,680 kg)
- **Powerplant:** 2× Lycoming T55-GA-712 turboshaft, 3,750 hp (2,796 kW) each

Performance

- **Maximum speed:** 170 knots (196 mph, 315 km/h)
- **Cruise speed:** 130 kt (137 mph, 220 km/h)
- **Range:** 400 nmi (450 mi, 741 km)
- **Ferry range:** 1,216 nmi (1,400 mi, 2,252 km)
- **Service ceiling:** 18,500 ft (5,640 m)
- **Rate of climb:** 1,522 ft/min (10.1 m/s)
- **Disc loading:** 9.5 lb/ft (47 kg/m)
- **Power/mass:** 0.28 hp/lb (460 W/kg)

Armament

- up to 3 pintle mounted medium machine guns (1 on loading ramp and 2 at shoulder windows), generally 7.62 mm (0.308 in) M240/FN MAG machine guns

Avionics

- Rockwell CAAS (MH-47G/CH-47F)

Source (edited): "http://en.wikipedia.org/wiki/Boeing_CH-47_Chinook"

Boeing Chinook (UK variants)

The **Boeing Chinook** is a tandem rotor helicopter operated by the Royal Air Force. A series of variants based on the United States Army's Boeing CH-47 Chinook, the RAF Chinook fleet is the largest outside of the United States. RAF Chinooks have seen extensive service including fighting in the Falklands War, peace-keeping commitments in the Balkans, and action in the Iraq and Afghanistan wars.

The Chinook HC2 aircraft, normally based at RAF Odiham, provides heavy-lift support and transport across all branches of the British armed forces, and is supported by the smaller, medium-lift helicopters such as the AgustaWestland Merlin HC3 and the Westland Puma HC1, based at RAF Benson and RAF Aldergrove.

Design and development

Chinook HC1

In March 1967 an order was placed for fifteen Chinook HC1s, standing for *Helicopter, Cargo Mark 1*, for the Royal Air Force to replace the Bristol Belvedere. This original HC1 variant was to be based on the CH-47B but the order was cancelled in a review of defence spending in November 1967,

UK Chinook procurement ambitions were revived in 1978 with an announced requirement for a new heavy-lift helicopter to replace the Westland Wessex. Thirty Chinooks were ordered at a price of US$200 million. These helicopters, comparable to the CH-47C with Lycoming T55-L-11E engines, were again designated Chinook HC1, and entered service in December 1980. Eight more HC1s were delivered from 1984 to 1986 with the CH-47D's Lycoming T55-L-712 turboshafts.

The replacement of the HC1's metal rotor blades with aluminium and glass fibre composite rotor blades saw these aircraft designated **Chinook HC1B**. All surviving aircraft were later returned to Boeing and updated to the Chinook HC2 standard for further service within the RAF.

Chinook HC2

RAF Chinook HC2 in 2009

The US Army's next generation Chinook, the CH-47D, entered service in 1982. Improvements from the CH-47C included upgraded engines, composite rotor blades, a redesigned cockpit to reduce pilot workload, redundant and improved electrical systems, an advanced flight control system (FCS) and improved avionics. The RAF returned their original HC1s to Boeing for upgrading to CH-47D standard, the first of which returned to the UK in 1993.

Three additional HC2 Chinooks were ordered with delivery beginning in 1995. Another six were ordered in 1995 under the **Chinook HC2A** designation; the main difference between these and the standard HC2 was the strengthening of the front fuselage to allow the fitting of an aerial refueling probe in future.

One Argentine CH-47C was captured during the Falklands War, and used by the RAF as a training aid. The rear fuselage was later used to repair a crashed RAF Chinook in 2003.

In 2006, the retirement dates for the HC2 and HC2A fleets were scheduled for 2015 and 2025 respectively, however if planned upgrades were made both types could expect to be flying until 2040.

Chinook HC3

Edward Leigh, then Chairman of the Public Accounts Committee.

Eight Chinook HC3s were ordered in 1995 as dedicated special forces helicopters. The HC3s were to be effectively low-cost variants of the US Army's special forces Chinook, the MH-47E. The HC3s would include improved range, night vision sensors and navigation capability. The eight aircraft were to cost £259 million and the forecast in-service date was November 1998. Although delivered in 2001, they could not be given airworthiness certificates because it was not possible to certify the avionics software to UK military standards. This was a result of poor risk analysis and crucial requirements being omitted from the procurement contract. *The Times* claimed that the Ministry of Defence planned to perform software integration itself, without Boeing's involvement, in order to reduce costs. Due to the lack of certification, the helicopters were only permitted to fly in visual meteorological conditions. They were subsequently stored in climate controlled hangars.

After protracted negotiations to allow them to enter service, *Air Forces Monthly* reported in November 2006 that the Defence Aviation Repair Agency would likely receive a contract to install the Thales "TopDeck" avionics system on the Chinook HC3s. However, the Ministry of Defence announced in March 2007 that this so-called "Fix to Field" programme would be cancelled, and instead it would revert the helicopters' avionics to Chinook HC2/2A specification. The programme was estimated to cost £50-60 million. In June 2008, the National Audit Office issued a scathing attack on the MoD's handling of the affair, calling it a "gold standard cock-up", with the whole programme likely to cost a total of £500 million by the time the helicopters enter service. On 6 July 2009 the first of the eight modified Chinook HC3s made its first test flight at MoD Boscombe Down as part of the flight testing and evaluation phase of the HC3 "reversion" program.

Chinook HC4 / HC5 / HC6

A programme to upgrade 46 Chinook HC2, HC2A and HC3 helicopters was initiated in December 2008. Called *Project Julius*, it includes new digital flight deck avionics based on the Thales TopDeck avionics suite, comprising new multifunction displays, a digital moving map display and an electronic flight bag, installation of a nose-mounted FLIR detector, and upgrading the engines to the more powerful T55-714 standard. Upgraded HC2, HC2A and HC3 aircraft will be redesignated HC4, HC4A and HC5 respectively, and deliveries are expected to commence in 2011. The first conversion, a Chinook HC4, first flew on 9 December 2010.

The Chinook HC6 designation has been assigned to the 24 (later reduced to 12) CH-47F Chinooks ordered in 2009. These will have Boeing digital flight-control systems and are expected to be delivered during 2012 and 2013.

Operational history

RAF Chinook at Camp Davis in 1996

RAF Chinooks have been widely deployed in support of British military engagements, serving their first wartime role in Operation Corporate, the Falklands War, in 1982. Chinooks were used in Operation Granby in the 1991 Gulf War, attached to large peace-keeping commitments in the Balkans, the continued British presence in Afghanistan, and in Operation Telic in the 2003 Iraq War. They provide routine supply and support missions to the British military, notably in Operation Banner in Northern Ireland. The helicopter has also been of use in military humanitarian missions and the extraction of civilians from warzones, such as the evacuation of Sierra Leone in 2000, and the evacuation from Lebanon in 2006.

During the Falklands War, Chinooks were deployed by both the British and Argentinian forces. In April 1982 Chinooks were loaded aboard the container ship MV *Atlantic Conveyor* bound for the Falkland Islands, to spearhead the British landings there. When the *Atlantic Conveyor* was attacked and sunk on 25 May 1982 by an Argentine Navy Dassault Super Étendard that had fired an Exocet sea-skimming missile one of these chinooks, *Bravo November*, was airborne on a task at the time, picking up freight from HMS *Glasgow*. It thus avoided the ship's destruction, assisted in the evacuation of the ship, and later landed on the aircraft carrier HMS *Hermes*, gaining the nickname "The Survivor". Owing to the rapid spread of fire and smoke aboard the *Atlantic Conveyor* after the Exocet strike, it was not possible to fly any of the helicopters that remained on the ship's deck.

This was not the only incident of note in the Falklands, a single Argentinian Chinook was captured intact by British Army forces. RAF Chinooks were part of an estimated force of 40 helicopters in the British task force, alongside Westland Sea King and Westland Wessex helicopters. Post-war, two Chinooks were operated by No. 78 Squadron as part of the Falklands Garrison; this was reduced to a single helicopter in the mid-1990s and the type was eventually withdrawn from the Falklands in 2006 in order to free up resources and craft for operations in Afghanistan.

RAF Chinook HC2 in 2008

The Chinook became a vital transit tool during the 1991 Gulf War in Iraq. They were used for moving troops into the region at the start of the conflict; a Chinook was used on 22 January 1991 to transport an SAS patrol on the infamous Bravo Two Zero mission. In the aftermath of the conflict as many as nine British Chinooks delivered food and supplies to thousands of Kurdish refugees from Iraq.

On 6 June 1999, two Chinooks of No. 27 Squadron left base at RAF Odiham in Hampshire, carrying paratroopers to join NATO forces serving in the Balkans; six more arrived the following week in Kosovo to support operations such as casualty evacuations and transporting vital supplies. On 12 June 1999, waves of Chinooks, escorted by Westland Lynx and American AH-64 Apache attack helicopters, were used to rapidly deploy British infantry forces into Kosovo as apart of NATO's first phase of deployment. On 10 August 1999 hundreds of Chinooks around the world, including those used by the British armed forces, were grounded due to cracking discovered in the landing gear of a British helicopter during routine inspection.

In May 2000, several Chinook helicopters airlifted British and European Union citizens out of Freetown in Sierra Leone in an evacuation due to regional instability. In September 2000 Chinooks were being used to evacuate casualties from fighting in Freetown to RFA *Sir Percivale*, a support ship docked there. In July 2006, 3 Chinook helicopters of No. 27 Squadron deployed to RAF Akrotiri in Cyprus to evacuate British citizens from Lebanon; the squadron also flew the EU foreign affairs representative Javier Solana to Beirut at the start of the crisis. Members of the SAS and SBS units were deployed via Chinooks into Lebanon to locate and make contact with British citizens.

View out of a Chinook flying over Helmand province, Afghanistan in 2007

Chinook helicopters have been relied upon heavily to support the British forces in Afghanistan continuously since the start of the war in Afghanistan in 2001; Operation Snipe saw the helicopters used to assist the 1,000 British Commandos sweeping a region of southeathern Afghanistan. Due to the threat of IEDs scattered throughout the terrain by insurgents, transport helicopters have become highly valued and demanded units in this style of warfare. By April 2006 six Chinooks have been deployed by C-17 transport planes to Kandahar in Southern Afghanistan, in support of Operation Herrick. Two RAF Chinooks were lost in August 2009 during combat operations with the Taliban, one of which was brought down by enemy fire, in spite of warnings months before of Taliban plans to attack the helicopters.

The continued operation of the fleet was made more cost effective when maintaince and support regimes were altered in 2006-7. On 15 December

2009 the British government announced its Future Helicopter Strategy including the purchase of 24 new build Chinooks, 22 to expand the force and 2 to replace losses in Afghanistan, to be delivered to the Royal Air Force from 2012. The number of additional Chinooks was cut to 12 the October 2010 defence review, however. This will bring the total fleet size to 60 aircraft; currently the RAF has 48 Chinooks in inventory.

One Chinook in particular, identified as serial *ZA718* (Boeing construction number B-849) and also known by its original squadron code "Bravo November", has come to widespread public recognition due to its remarkable service record. It has seen action in every major operation involving the RAF in the helicopter's 25-year service life, including the Falkland Islands, Lebanon, Germany, Northern Ireland, Iraq, and Afghanistan.

Variants
Chinook HC1
New-build aircraft for the RAF based on the CH-47C, 41 built.
Chinook HC1B
Modification of the 41 HC1s with metal rotor blades, survivors converted to HC2.
Chinook HC2
Conversion by Boeing of 32 surviving HC1Bs to CH-47D standard, and 3 new build-aircraft
Chinook HC2A
Similar to the HC2 with strengthened fuselage using milled structure manufacturing techniques, six built.
Chinook HC3
Special forces variant based on the CH-47SD, 8 built.
Chinook HC4/HC4A
HC2/HC2A aircraft with upgraded engines and avionics under *Project Julius*. 46 conversions planned.
Chinook HC5
HC3 aircraft with upgraded avionics under *Project Julius*.
Chinook HC6
New-build Chinooks ordered in 2009, expected to be delivered 2012-2013 (currently under review). Originally 24, later reduced to 12 aircraft.

Operators
Three RAF squadrons operate Chinook helicopters, No. 7 Squadron, No. 18 Squadron and No. 27 Squadron, all of which are based at RAF Odiham in Hampshire, England. The day-to-day maintenance of Nos. 18 and 27 Squadron aircraft is carried out by a joint ground crew known as the ExCES (Expeditionary Chinook Engineering Squadron).

When deployed, the detachment of Nos. 18 and 27 Squadron aircrew and ExCES groundcrew is known as No. 1310 Flight. The RAF has a total of 48 Chinooks in inventory as of late August 2009.

Notable incidents and accidents
- On 13 May 1986, Chinook HC1 *ZA715* crashed in bad weather in the Falkland Islands. The helicopter, with four crew and 12 troops, crashed into a hill 4 miles from its destination. With rescuers hampered by blizzards, the personnel were recovered but one crew member had died shortly after the crash, and the co-pilot and a soldier died on the way to hospital. The board of enquiry concluded that the crew had become disorientated due to "whiteout" conditions.
- On 27 February 1987, Chinook HC1 *ZA721* crashed in the Falkland Islands on a test flight following servicing. After leaving RAF Mount Pleasant, the helicopter was at a normal cruising speed and an altitude of between 300 and 700 feet when it nosed down and crashed into the ground about 6 kilometres southeast of the airfield; it was destroyed by a subsequent fire. The board of enquiry was unable to determine the exact cause but it may have been the forward-swivelling upper boost actuator jamming. All seven on board, three crew and four technicians, were killed.
- On 6 May 1988, Chinook HC1 *ZA672* hit a pier at Hannover Airport while taxiing into position in a confined space. Its front rotor struck the underside of Pier 10, causing the helicopter to rear up vertically and then fall on its side. A fire started at the rear of the fuselage and soon spread. Three crew members were killed and one had major injuries; the Chinook was destroyed.
- On 2 June 1994, Chinook HC2 *ZD576* crashed on the Mull of Kintyre, Scotland, killing all 25 passengers and all four crew members; the cause is disputed.
- On 19 August 2009, the Ministry of Defence announced that a Chinook made an emergency landing following an RPG strike and subsequent engine fire after a cargo drop-off just north of Sangin in Helmand Province, Afghanistan. The Chinook flew two kilometres to a safe area before landing. None of the crew sustained any injuries and all evacuated the aircraft before they were rescued by a second Chinook on the same sortie. The damaged aircraft was then destroyed by coalition air strikes to prevent it falling into the hands of the Taliban.
- On 30 August 2009, the loss of another Chinook was announced. The helicopter made a hard landing while on operations near Sangin, Helmand province. It suffered damage to the undercarriage, nose and front rotor, but the crew and 15 soldiers on board were unharmed. According to the Ministry of Defence due to the location of the crash it was not possible to safely recover the aircraft and it was destroyed with explosives deliberately. The cause of the hard landing is being investigated, although it is not thought to have been shot down.

Data from Royal Air Force.

General characteristics
- **Crew:** 3–4 (pilot, copilot, one or two air loadmasters depending on aircraft role)
- **Length:** 30.1 m (98 ft 9 in)
- **Rotor diameter:** 18.3 m (60 ft 0 in)
- **Height:** 5.7 m (18 ft 8 in)
- **Empty weight:** 10,185 kg (22,450 lb)
- **Loaded weight:** 12,100 kg

(26,680 lb)
- **Max takeoff weight:** 22,680 kg (50,000 lb)
- **Powerplant:** 2× Honeywell T55-GA-712 turboshaft, 2,800 kW (3,750 hp) each

Performance
- **Maximum speed:** 295 km/h (183 mph)
- **Service ceiling:** 2,590 m (18,500 ft)
- **Rate of climb:** 10.1 m/s (1,980 ft/min)

Armament
- 2× M134 Miniguns and 1× M60 machine gun

Source (edited): "http://en.wikipedia.org/wiki/Boeing_Chinook_(UK_variants)"

British Aerospace 125

The **British Aerospace 125** is a twin-engined mid-size corporate jet, with newer variants now marketed as the Hawker 800. It was known as the **Hawker Siddeley HS.125** until 1977. It was also used by the British Royal Air Force as a navigation trainer (as the **Hawker Siddeley Dominie T1**) until January 2011, and was used by the United States Air Force as a calibration aircraft (as the **C-29**).

Development

In 1961, de Havilland began working on a revolutionary small business jet, the **DH.125 Jet Dragon**, intended to replace the piston engined de Havilland Dove business aircraft and light transport. The DH.125 design was for a low-winged monoplane with a pressurised fuselage accommodating two pilots and six passengers. It was powered by two Bristol Siddeley Viper turbojets mounted on the rear fuselage. The slightly swept wing employed large slotted flaps and airbrakes to allow operation from small airfields. The first of two prototypes flew on 13 August 1962, with the second following on 12 December that year. The first production aircraft, longer and with a greater wingspan than the two prototypes, flew on 12 February 1963, with the first delivery to a customer on 10 September 1964.

The aircraft went through many designation changes during its service life. Hawker Siddeley had bought de Havilland the year before project start, but the old legacy brand and the "DH" designation was used throughout development. After the jet achieved full production, the name was finally changed to "HS.125". When Hawker Siddeley Aircraft merged with the British Aircraft Corporation to form British Aerospace in 1977, the name changed to **BAe 125**.

Then, when British Aerospace sold its Business Jets Division to Raytheon in 1993, the jet acquired the name **Raytheon Hawker**. The fuselage, wings and tail-fin are to this day fully assembled and partially equipped (primary and secondary flight controls) in Airbus UK's Broughton plant, on the outskirts of Chester, sub-assemblies are produced in Airbus UK's Buckley (Bwcle in Welsh) site. All these assembled components are then shipped to Wichita, Kansas in the United States, to where final assembly was transferred in 1996.

Over 1,000 aircraft have been built.

Variants

BAe 125 CC3 of No. 32 Squadron, RAF.

Raytheon Hawker 800

- **DH.125 Series 1** - first version, powered by 3,000 lbf (13 kN) Viper 20 or 520 engines. Nine built, including two prototypes (43 ft 6 in (13.26 m) long, 44 ft (13.41 m) span) and seven production aircraft (47 ft 5 in (14.56 m) long, 47 ft (14.33 m) long.
- **DH.125 Series 1A/1B** - upgraded Bristol Siddeley Viper 521 or 522 engines with 3,100 lbf (14 kN) of thrust each, and five cabin windows instead of six. Series 1A for US FAA certification (62 built), Series 1B for sale elsewhere (13 built).
- **HS.125 Series 2** - navigation trainer for Royal Air Force, known in service as the **Dominie T.Mk.1** - (Rolls Royce Viper 301)
- **HS.125 Series 3** - upgraded engines
- **HS.125 Series 400** - upgraded engines
  - **HS.125 CC1** - Series 400 liaison aircraft for Royal Air Force
- **HS.125 Series 600** - 3 ft 1 in (0.94 m) fuselage stretch to increase capacity to 14 passengers
  - **HS.125 CC2** - Series 600 liaison aircraft for Royal Air Force
- **HS.125 Series 700** - Honeywell TFE731-3RH turbofan engines with 3,720 lbf (16.5 kN) of thrust each, first flight 19 June 1976
  - **BAe 125 CC3** - Series 700 liaison aircraft for Royal Air Force
- **HS.125 Protector** - Series 700-based maritime patrol aircraft with a search radar and cameras
- **BAe 125 Series 800** - increased wingspan, streamlined nose, tail fin extension, increased fuel capacity, first corporate jet to feature an EFIS cockpit, upgraded engines, first flight 26 May 1983
- **Hawker 800** - BAe 125-800 after 1993
- **Hawker 800XP** - TFE731-5BR1H turbofan engines with 4,660 lbf (20.7 kN) of thrust each
- **Hawker 800SP and 800XP2** - New

designation for 800A/B and 800XP aircraft when upgraded with aftermarket winglets
- **Hawker 850XP** - 800XP with factory installed winglets and interior updates
- **Hawker 900XP** - 850XP with Honeywell TFE731-50R turbofan engines for increased hot/high performance and longer range
- **Hawker 750** - 800XP with a lightweight interior and heated baggage compartment in place of the ventral fuel tank
- **C-29A** - Series 800 for US military designed to replace the Lockheed C-140A, used by the Air Force to accomplish the combat flight inspection and navigation mission (C-FIN) at US airbases around the world, participated in Operation Desert Shield and Operation Desert Storm during the First Persian Gulf War.
- **U-125** - Series 800-based flight inspection aircraft for Japan (similar to C-29A)
- **U-125A** - Series 800-based search and rescue aircraft for Japan
- **BAe 125 Series 1000** - intercontinental version of the Series 800, 2 ft 9 in (0.84 m) fuselage stretch to increase capacity to 15, increased fuel capacity, Pratt & Whitney Canada PW-305 turbofans with 5,200 lbf (23 kN) thrust each, first flight 16 June 1990, 52 built
- **Hawker 1000** - BAe 125-1000 after 1993
- **Handley Page HP.130** - A 1965 proposal with boundary layer control wings (not built). It was to be powered by two Bristol Siddeley Viper 520s of 3,000 lbf (13 kN) thrust with a projected Maximum speed of Mach 0.8. This conversion was for laminar-flow research purposes.

Operators

Civil operators

Private operators, air taxi, shared ownership and corporate charter operators worldwide.

Australia
- Qantas - Two HS.125 Series 3s were used for crew training. The aircraft were in service from 1965 to 1972.

Canada
- Air Georgian - 1 HS.125 in service operated on behalf of Air Canada

Kuwait
- Government of Kuwait - Former operator

Nigeria
- Associated Aviation - 2 HS. 125 Series 700 are in use.

China
- Deerjet, Hainan Airlines - 4 Hawker 800XP, 2 Hawker 850XP and 1 Hawker 900XP are in service in Deerjet based at Beijing. Deerjet is a branch of Hainan Airlines(HNA)
- Shanghai Airlines - 1 Hawker 800XP is in service in Shanghai Airlines based at Shanghai.

Pakistan
- Royal Airlines - 1 Hawker Siddeley HS 125 (Passenger) V.I.P

Military operators

Argentina
- Argentine Naval Aviation operated one VIP. See also Escuadrón Fénix

Biafra
- Biafran Air Force operated one aircraft.

Brazil
- Brazilian Air Force

Botswana
- Botswana Defence Force Air Wing

Ireland
- Irish Air Corps

Japan
- Japan Air Self-Defense Force

Malawi
- Military of Malawi

Malaysia
- Royal Malaysian Air Force

Nicaragua
- National Guard (Nicaragua)

Nigeria
- Nigerian Air Force

Saudi Arabia
- Royal Saudi Air Force

South Africa
- South African Air Force
  - No. 21 Squadron SAAF

United Kingdom
- Royal Air Force
  - No. 32 Squadron RAF
  - No. 55(R) Squadron RAF (Dominie T1)

United States
- United States Air Force

Accidents and incidents

- On 22 November 1966, de Havilland DH.125 N235KC of Florida Commuter Airlines crashed into the sea 7.3 kilometres (3.9 nmi) off Grand Bahama International Airport, Freeport, Bahamas during an illegal flight from Miami, Florida.
- In July 1967, Air Hanson HS125 (G-ASNU) carrying former Congolese president Moise Tshombe was hijacked and taken to Algeria.
- On 23 December 1967 a Hawker Siddeley HS 125 (registration: G-AVGW) of Court Line crashed shortly after taking off from Luton Airport, killing both pilots. The aircraft had been on a training flight. The crash occurred when the crew simulated an engine failure on takeoff. The HS 125 lost height rapidly and hit the roof of the nearby Vauxhall Motors factory. This resulted in a post-crash fire.
- On 26 May 1971, three Mercurius HS-125 aircraft belonging to the South African Air Force flew into Devil's Peak, Cape Town, while practising for a flypast for the 10th anniversary of the republic.
- On 20 November 1975, a British Aerospace BAe 125 overran the runway at Dunsfold Aerodrome after a bird strike on take off. The aircraft hit a car and stopped in a field, killing six people in the car and one crew member out of nine passengers and crew.
- On 8 September 1987: a Brazilian Air Force Hawker Siddeley HS.125 registration FAB-2129 crashed upon take-off from Carajás. All nine occupants died.
- On 7 August 1988, a BAe-125

owned by the Botswana Government was carrying the President of Botswana, J.K. Quett Masire, and his staff to a meeting in Luanda. An Angolan MiG-23 Flogger pilot fired two R-60 (AA-8 Aphid) missiles at the plane. One missile hit the no. 2 engine, causing it to fall off the aircraft. The second missile then hit the falling engine. The crew was able to make a succesful emergency landing on a bush strip at Cutio Bie.
- On March 16, 1991 a Hawker Siddeley charter aircraft carrying band members for Reba McEntire crashed into the side of Otay Mountain. The accident occurred shortly after take off from a municipal airport outside of San Diego, California. All eight band members aboard plus two pilots were killed in the crash believed to have been caused by poor visibility.
- On 3 January 2006, Russian aircraft (AVCOM - Moscow) crashed in Kharkiv, Ukraine into the Komsomolsk lake, 3 people died (crew).
- On 31 July 2008, East Coast Jets Flight 81 crashed on approach to an airport in Owatonna, Minnesota killing all 8 passengers and crew.
- On 26 October 2009, S-Air Flight 9607, operated by BAe 125 RA-02807 crashed on approach to Minsk International Airport. All three crew and both passengers were killed.

Specifications (HS 125 Series 600)

Data from Jane's All The World's Aircraft 1976–77

General characteristics
- **Crew:** 2
- **Capacity:** 8 passengers (normal layout), 14 passengers in high density layout
- **Length:** 50 ft 6 in (15.39 m)
- **Wingspan:** 47 ft 0 in (14.33 m)
- **Height:** 17 ft 3 in (5.26 m)
- **Wing area:** 353.0 ft² (32.8 m²)
- **Empty weight:** 12,530 lb (5,683 kg)
- **Max takeoff weight:** 25,000 lb (11,340 kg)
- **Powerplant:** 2 × Rolls-Royce Viper 601-22 turbojets, 3,750 lbf (16.7 kN) each

Performance
- **Maximum speed:** 522 mph (454 knot, 840 km/h) at 28,000 ft (8,500 m) (Max cruise)
- **Cruise speed:** 464 mph (403 knot, 747 km/h) at 39,000 ft (11,900 m) (Econ cruise)
- **Stall speed:** 96 mph (83 knots, 155 km/h) (flaps down)
- **Range:** 1,796 mi (1,560 nmi, 2,891 km) max fuel and payload
- **Service ceiling:** 41,000 ft (12,500 m)
- **Rate of climb:** 4,900 ft/min (24.9 m/s)

Source (edited): "http://en.wikipedia.org/wiki/British_Aerospace_125"

British Aerospace Sea Harrier

The **British Aerospace Sea Harrier** is a naval VTOL/STOVL jet fighter, reconnaissance and attack aircraft, a development of the Hawker Siddeley Harrier. It first entered service with the Royal Navy in April 1980 as the **Sea Harrier FRS1** and became informally known as the "*Shar*". Unusual in an era in which most naval and land-based air superiority fighters were large and supersonic, the principal role of the subsonic Sea Harrier was air defence from Royal Navy aircraft carriers.

The Sea Harrier served in the Falklands War, both of the Gulf Wars, and the Balkans conflicts; on all occasions it mainly operated from aircraft carriers positioned within the conflict zone. Its usage in the Falklands War was its most high profile and important success, where it was the only fixed-wing fighter available to protect the British Task Force. The Sea Harriers shot down 20 enemy aircraft during the conflict with one loss to enemy ground fire. They were also used to launch ground attacks in the same manner as the Harriers operated by the Royal Air Force.

The Sea Harrier was marketed for sales abroad, but by 1983 India was the only operator other than Britain after sales to Argentina and Australia were unsuccessful. A second, updated version for the Royal Navy was made in 1993 as the **Sea Harrier FA2**, improving its air to air abilities and weapons compatibilities, along with a more powerful engine; this version continued manufacture until 1998. The aircraft was withdrawn early from Royal Navy service in March 2006 and replaced in the short term by the Harrier GR9, now itself retired, although the intended long term replacement is Lockheed Martin's F-35 Lightning II. The Sea Harrier is in active use in the Indian Navy, although it will eventually be replaced by the Mikoyan MiG-29K.

Development

In the post-war era the Royal Navy began contracting in parallel with the breakup of the British Empire overseas and the emergence of the Commonwealth; reducing the importance and coverage feeding the need for a larger navy. By 1960 the last battleship, HMS *Vanguard*, was retired from the Navy, having been in service for less than fifteen years. Perhaps the biggest sign of the new trend towards naval austerity came in 1966, when the planned CVA-01 class of large aircraft carriers destined for the Royal Navy were cancelled; apparently ending the Navy's involvement in fixed-wing carrier aviation as World War II era carriers were slowly retired one by one. During this time requirements within the Royal Navy began to form for a Vertical and/or Short Take-Off and Landing (V/STOL) carrier-based interceptor to replace the de Havilland Sea Vixen. Afterward the first V/STOL tests on a ship began with a Hawker Siddeley P. 1127 landing on HMS *Ark Royal* in 1963.

A second concept for the future of

naval aviation emerged in the early 1970s as the first of a new class of "through deck cruisers" was planned. These were very carefully and politically designated as cruisers to deliberately avoid the term "aircraft carrier", in order to increase the chances of funding from a hostile political climate against expensive capital ships, they were considerably smaller than the previously sought CVA-01. These ships were ordered as the *Invincible* class in 1973, and are now popularly recognised as aircraft carriers. Almost immediately upon their construction, a ski-jump was added to the end of the 170-metre deck, enabling the carriers to effectively operate a small number of V/STOL jets. The Royal Air Force's Hawker Siddeley Harrier GR1s had entered service in April 1969. A navalised variant of the Harrier was developed by Hawker Siddeley to serve on the upcoming ships, this became the Sea Harrier. In 1975 the Royal Navy ordered 24 Sea Harrier *FRS.1* (standing for 'Fighter, Reconnaissance, Strike') aircraft, the first of which entered service in 1978. During this time Hawker Siddeley became part of British Aerospace through a merger in 1977. By the time the prototype Sea Harrier was flown at Dunsfold on 20 August 1978 the order had been increased to 34. The Sea Harrier was declared operational in 1981 onboard the first *Invincible* class ship HMS *Invincible*, and further aircraft joined the aging HMS *Hermes* aircraft carrier later that year.

Following their key role in the Falklands War, several lessons were learned from the aircraft's performance which led to approval for an upgrade of the fleet to *FRS.2* (later known as *FA2*) standard to be given in 1984. The first flight of the prototype took place on September 1988 and a contract was signed for 29 upgraded aircraft in December that year. In 1990 the Navy ordered 18 new-build FA2s, at a unit cost of around £12 million, four further upgraded aircraft were ordered in 1994. The first aircraft was delivered on 2 April 1993.

Design

Sea Harrier FA2 ZA195 (upgrade) vector thrust nozzle - distinguishing feature of the jump jet

The Sea Harrier is a subsonic aircraft designed to fill strike, reconnaissance and fighter roles. It features a single Pegasus turbofan engine with two intakes and four vectorable nozzles. It has two landing gear on the fuselage and two outrigger landing gear on the wings. The Sea Harrier is equipped with four wing and three fuselage pylons for carrying weapons and external fuel tanks. Use of the ski jump allowed the aircraft to take off with a heavier loadout than otherwise possible.

The Sea Harrier was largely based on the Harrier GR3, but was modified to have a raised cockpit with a "bubble" canopy for greater visibility, and an extended forward fuselage to accommodate the Ferranti Blue Fox radar. Parts were changed to use corrosion resistant alloys or coatings were added to protect against the marine environment. After the Falklands War, the Sea Harrier was fitted with the new anti-ship Sea Eagle missile.

The Sea Harrier FA2 featured the Blue Vixen radar, which was described as one of the most advanced pulse doppler radar systems in the world; the Blue Fox radar was seen be some critics as having comparatively low performance for what was available at the time of procurement. The Blue Vixen formed the basis for development of the Eurofighter Typhoon's CAPTOR radar. The Sea Harrier FA2 also carried the AIM-120 AMRAAM missile, the first UK aircraft to be provided with this capability. An upgraded model of the Pegasus engine, the Pegasus Mk 106, was used in the Sea Harrier FA2; in response to the threat of radar-based anti aircraft weapons electronic countermeasures were added. Other improvements included an increase to the air-to-air weapons load, look-down radar, increased range, and improved cockpit displays.

The cockpit in the Sea Harrier includes a conventional centre stick arrangement and left-hand throttle. In addition to normal flight controls, the Harrier has a lever for controlling the direction of the four vectorable nozzles. The nozzles point rearward with the lever in the forward position for horizontal flight. With the lever back, the nozzles point downward for vertical takeoff or landing. The usefulness of the vertical landing capability of the Sea Harrier was demonstrated in an unintended incident on 6 June 1983, when Sub Lieutenant Ian Watson lost contact with the aircraft carrier *HMS Illustrious* and had to land on the foredeck of the Spanish cargo ship Alraigo.

In 2005, although already timetabled to be retired, a Sea Harrier was modified with an 'Autoland' system to allow the fighter to perform a safe vertical landing without any pilot interaction. Despite the pitching of a ship posing a natural problem, the system was designed to be aware of such data, and successfully performed a landing at sea in May 2005.

Operational history

Entry into service

The first three Sea Harriers were a development batch and were used for clearance trials. The first production aircraft was delivered to RNAS Yeovilton in 1979 to form an Intensive Flying Trials Unit (also known as 700A Naval Air Squadron). In March 1980 the Intensive Flying Trials Unit became 899 Naval Air Squadron and would act as the landborne headquarters unit for the type. The first operational squadron 800 Naval Air Squadron was also formed in March 1980 initially to operate from HMS *Invincible* before it transferred to HMS *Hermes*. In January 1981 a second operation squadron 801 Naval Air

Squadron was formed to operate from HMS *Invincible*.

Falklands War

Sea Harrier at RNAS Yeovilton. The glossy metallic blue paint scheme seen here was altered to a duller one en route.

Sea Harriers took part in the Falklands War of 1982, flying from the aircraft carriers HMS *Invincible* and HMS *Hermes*. The Sea Harriers performed the primary air defence role with a secondary role of ground attack. The RAF Harrier GR3 provided the main ground attack force, a total of 28 Sea Harriers and 14 Harrier GR3s were deployed in the theatre. The Sea Harrier squadrons shot down 20 Argentine aircraft in air-to-air combat with no air-to-air losses, although two Sea Harriers were lost to ground fire and four to accidents. Out of the total Argentine air losses, 28% were shot down by Harriers.

A number of factors contributed to the failure of the Argentinian fighters to shoot down a Sea Harrier. Although the Mirage III and Dagger jets were considerably faster, the Sea Harrier was considerably more manoeuvrable. Tactics such as such as the 'Viff' (Vectored in Forward Flight) using the nozzles normally used for vertical flight for braking and other directions proved decisive in dogfights. Moreover, the Harrier employed the latest AIM-9L Sidewinder missiles and the Blue Fox radar. The British pilots had superior air-combat training, one manifestation of which was that they thought they noticed Argentinian pilots occasionally releasing weapons outside of their operating parameters. This is now thought to have been Mirages releasing external fuel tanks rather than weapons, and turning away from conflict with the Sea Harrier. This later reduced their capability to fight an effective campaign against the Sea Harrier due to reduced range and lack of external fuel tanks.

800 NAS Sea Harrier FRS1 from HMS *Illustrious* in low-visibility paint scheme.

British aircraft received fighter control from warships in San Carlos Water, although its effectiveness was limited by their being stationed close to the islands, which severely limited the effectiveness of their radar. The differences in tactics and training between 800 Squadron and 801 Squadron has been a point of criticism, suggesting that the losses of several ships were preventable had Sea Harriers from *HMS Hermes* been used more effectively.

Both sides' aircraft were operating in adverse conditions. Argentine aircraft were forced to operate from the mainland because airfields on the Falklands were only suited for propellor-driven transports. In addition, fears partly aroused by the bombing of Port Stanley airport by a British Vulcan bomber added to the Argentinians' decision to operate them from afar. As most Argentine aircraft lacked in-flight refuelling capability, they were forced to operate at the limit of their range. The Sea Harriers also had limited fuel reserves due to the tactical decision to station the British carriers out of Exocet missile range and the dispersal of the fleet. The result was that an Argentine aircraft could only allow five minutes over the islands to search and attack an objective, while a Sea Harrier could stay near to 30 minutes waiting in the Argentine approach corridors and provide Combat Air Patrol coverage for up to an hour.

The Sea Harriers were outnumbered by the available Argentinian aircraft, and were on occasion decoyed away by the activities of the *Escuadrón Fénix* or civilian jet aircraft used by the Argentine Air Force. They had to operate without a fleet early warning system such as AWACS that would have been available to a full NATO fleet in which the Royal Navy had expected to operate, which was a significant weakness in the operational environment. However, it is now known that Chile did provide early radar warning to the Task Force. The result was that the Sea Harriers could not establish complete air superiority and prevent Argentine attacks during day or night, nor could they completely stop the daily C-130 Hercules transports' night flights to the islands. A combined six Sea Harriers were lost to either enemy fire, accidents or mechanical failure during the war. The total aggregate loss rate for both the Harriers and Sea Harriers on strike operations was 2.3%.

Operations in the 1990s

The Sea Harrier participated in the Gulf War in 1991, attacking Iraqi military ground targets and escorting other aircraft in and out of the zone. The hot climate of the region hindered the effectiveness and availability of the aircraft. Afterwards Sea Harriers maintained no fly zones established over southern Iraq.

British Aerospace Sea Harrier FA2 of the Royal Navy on the flight deck of the HMS *Invincible*

The Sea Harrier saw action in war again when was deployed by the United Kingdom in the 1991–1995 conflict in Bosnia, part of Yugoslav wars. It launched raids on Serb forces and provided airsupport for the international taskforce units conducting operations Deny Flight and Deliberate Force against Army of Republika Srpska. On 16 April 1994 a Sea Harrier of the 801

Naval Air Squadron operating from the aircraft carrier HMS *Ark Royal* was brought down by a SAM fired by Army of Republika Srpska while attempting to bomb two Serbian tanks. The pilot, Lieutenant Nick Richardson ejected and landed in the territory controlled by friendly Bosnian Muslims.

It was used again in 1999 NATO campaign against Federal Republic of Yugoslavia in Operation Allied Force, Sea Harriers operating from HMS *Invincible* patrolled the airspace frequently to keep Yugoslavian MiGs on the ground. They were also deployed to Sierra Leone onboard HMS *Illustrious* in 2000, which was itself part of a Royal Navy convoy to supply and reinforce British intervention forces in the region.

Royal Navy retirement

A Sea Harrier FA2 on display at the National Maritime Museum in May 2006

The Sea Harrier was withdrawn from service in 2006 and the last remaining aircraft from 801 Naval Air Squadron were decommissioned on 29 March 2006. The plans for retirement were announced in 2002 by the Ministry of Defence. The aircraft's replacement, the F-35 Lightning II, was originally due in 2012, the MoD arguing that significant expenditure would be required to upgrade the fleet for only six years of service; By March 2010 the F-35's introduction had been pushed back to 2016 at the earliest, with the price doubled. The decision to retire the Sea Harrier early has been criticised by some officers within the military.

Both versions of Harrier experienced reduced engine performance (Pegasus Mk 106 in FA2 - Mk 105 in GR7) in the higher ambient temperatures of the Middle East, which restricted the weight of payload that the Harrier could return to the carrier in 'vertical' recoveries. This was due to the safety factors associated with aircraft "land-on" weights. The natural option - to install higher-rated Pegasus engines - would not be as straightforward as the Harrier GR7 upgrade and would likely be an expensive and slow process. Furthermore, the Sea Harriers were subject to a generally more hostile environment than land-based Harriers, with corrosive salt spray a particular problem. A number of aircraft were retained by the School of Flight Deck Operations at RNAS *Culdrose*, in theory these could be regenerated.

The Royal Navy's Fleet Air Arm will continue to share the other component of Joint Force Harrier, the Harrier GR7 and the upgraded Harrier GR9 with the RAF, with the two front-line squadrons, 800 NAS re-commissioned in 6 April and 801 NAS are expected to reform in 2007 both using the GR9 by 2007. The projected purchase of around 150 F-35s will be split between the two services and they will operate from the Royal Navy's Future Carrier (CVF).

Indian Navy

Indian Navy's Sea Harriers fly along side U.S. Navy's F/A-18F Super Hornet during Malabar 2007.

India purchased 30 Sea Harriers in 1983, using 25 of these for operational flying and the remaining to train pilots. A further ten Sea Harriers were purchased in November 1985. Sea Harriers in Indian service operated from the aircraft carriers INS *Vikrant* (ex-HMS *Hercules*) and INS *Viraat* (ex-HMS *Hermes*). There have been a significant number of accidents involving the Sea Harrier; this accident rate has caused more than half the fleet to be lost with only 11 fighters remaining in service. Following a crash in August 2009, all Sea Harriers were temporarily grounded for inspection. Since the beginning of operational service in the Indian Navy, seven pilots have died in 17 crashes involving the Sea Harrier, usually during routine sorties.

The Indian Navy is in the process of upgrading up to fifteen Sea Harriers in collaboration with Israel by installing the Elta EL/M-2032 radar and the Rafael 'Derby' medium range air to air missile. This will enable the Sea Harrier to remain in Indian service until beyond 2012, and also see limited service off the new carriers it will acquire by that time frame. Although India plans to ultimately supplement and replace the Sea Harrier with Russian MiG-29K carrier fighters, the Indian Navy expressed interest in acquiring up to eight of the Royal Navy's retired Sea Harrier FA2s in order to maintain their operational Sea Harrier fleet, which consists of 13 Pegasus 104-powered Sea Harrier FRS51s. The deal excluded ongoing support from both BAE Systems and Rolls Royce. The sale would not have transferred the Sea Harrier FA2's Blue Vixen radar, the radar warning receiver or AMRAAM capability. Certain US software would also have been deleted from the aircraft prior to shipment. By 13 October 2006 it had been reported that the deal had not materialised due to the cost of re-equipping the airframes.

Variants

A Sea Harrier FRS 1 on HMS Invincible

British Aerospace Sea Harrier

Sea Harrier FRS51. of the Indian Navy taking off from INS Viraat

Sea Harrier FRS1
57 FRS1s were delivered between 1978 and 1988; most survivors converted to Sea Harrier FA2 specifications from 1988.

Harrier T4N
The Harrier T4N is a two-seat naval version of the Harrier T2, used by the Royal Navy for land-based pilot conversion training towards the Sea Harrier FRS1.

Sea Harrier Mk51
Single-seat fighter, reconnaissance and attack aircraft made for the Indian Navy, similar to the British FRS1. Unlike the FRS1 Sea Harrier, it is fitted with Matra R550 Magic air-to-air missiles.

Harrier T60
Export version of the T4N two-seat training version for the Indian Navy.

Sea Harrier FA2
Upgrade of FRS1 fleet in 1988, featuring the Blue Vixen Pulse-Doppler radar and the AIM-120 AMRAAM missile.

Harrier T8
Seven Harrier T4s two-seat trainers updated with Sea Harrier FA2 instrumentation.

Operators
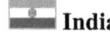 **India**
- Indian Navy
  - Indian Naval Air Squadron 300 'White Tigers'

Former operators
United Kingdom
- Fleet Air Arm
  - 800 Naval Air Squadron - disbanded 2006
  - 801 Naval Air Squadron - disbanded 2006
  - 809 Naval Air Squadron - disbanded 1982
  - 899 Naval Air Squadron - disbanded 2006

Survivors

Sea Harrier FA2 ZE694 at the Midland Air Museum

United Kingdom
- Sea Harrier FA2 ZE694, Midland Air Museum, Coventry.
- Two Sea Harriers, Sea Harrier FRS1 XZ493/001/N and Sea Harrier FA2 (XZ499) are on display at the Fleet Air Arm Museum at Yeovilton.

United States
- Sea Harrier FA2 serial number XZ439, Hawker-Siddeley build number 912002 Nalls Aviation St Mary's County, Maryland.
- A single Sea Harrier is privately owned and flying. The Sea Harrier FA2 was purchased for $1.5M from the RN in 2006 by Art Nalls who spent the next two years restoring it to flying condition. In December 2007 it suffered a hard landing while undergoing testing at Naval Air Station Patuxent River and damage had to be repaired. The aircraft made its first public appearance at an air show in Culpeper, Virginia in October 2008.

Specifications (Sea Harrier FA2)
Data from Bull, Donald Spick

General characteristics
- **Crew:** 1
- **Length:** 46 ft 6 in (14.2 m)
- **Wingspan:** 25 ft 3 in (7.6 m)
- **Height:** 12 ft 2 in (3.71 m)
- **Wing area:** 201.1 ft² (18.68 m²)
- **Empty weight:** 14,052 lb (6,374 kg)
- **Max takeoff weight:** 26,200 lb (11,900 kg)
- **Powerplant:** 1 × Rolls-Royce Pegasus turbofan, 21,500 lbf (95.64 kN)

Performance
- **Maximum speed:** 635 knots (735 mph, 1,182 km/h)
- **Combat radius:** 540 nmi (620 mi, 1,000 km)
- **Ferry range:** 1,740 nmi (2,000 mi, 3,600 km)
- **Service ceiling:** 51,000 ft (16,000 m)
- **Rate of climb:** 50,000 ft/min (250 m/s)

Armament
- **Guns:** 2× 30 mm (1.18 in) ADEN cannon pods under the fuselage, with 130 rounds each
- **Hardpoints:** 4× under-wing pylon stations, and 1 fuselage pylon on centerline plus 2 attach points for gun pods with a total capability of 8,000 lb (3,630 kg) of payload.
- **Rockets:** 4× Matra rocket pods with 18 SNEB 68 mm rockets each
- **Missiles:** **Air-to-air missiles:
  - AIM-9 Sidewinder
  - AIM-120 AMRAAM
  - R550 Magic (Sea Harrier FRS51)
  - Air-to-surface missile:
    - ALARM Anti-radiation missile (ARM)
    - Martel missile ARM
  - Anti-ship missiles:
    - Sea Eagle
- **Bombs:** A variety of unguided iron bombs (including 3 kg and 14 kg practice bombs) *or* WE.177 nuclear bomb (until 1992 on RN Sea Harriers)
- **Others:**
  - reconnaissance pods *or*
  - 2× auxiliary drop tanks for ferry flight or extended range/loitering time

Avionics
- Blue Vixen radar

Notable appearances in media
The Harrier's unique characteristics have led to it being featured a number of films and video games.
Source (edited): "http://en.wikipedia.org/wiki/British_Aerospace_Sea_Har-

rier"

Dassault-Breguet Super Étendard

The **Dassault-Breguet Super Étendard** (French for "battle flag") is a French carrier-borne strike fighter aircraft designed for service with the French Navy. The aircraft entered service in June 1978 and was first used in combat by Argentina during the 1982 Falklands War.

Design and development

The Super Étendard is a development of the earlier Étendard IVM that was originally to have been replaced by a navalised version of the SEPECAT Jaguar (the Jaguar M), until this plan was stalled by political problems, together with problems with operating the Jaguar aboard ships, including the inability to land back on a carrier after an engine failure. Instead, Dassault proposed an improved version of the Étendard IVM, with a more powerful engine, a new wing and improved avionics. This proposal was accepted by the French Navy in 1973 as the Super Étendard.

The Super Étendard is a small, single-engined, mid-winged aircraft with an all-metal structure. Both the wings and tailplane are swept, with the folding wings having a sweepback of about 45 degrees, while the aircraft is powered by a non-afterburning SNECMA Atar 9K-50 turbojet with a rating of 49 kN (11,025 lbf). It is fitted with a Thomson-CSF Agave radar, closely integrated with the new air-launched version of Aérospatiale's anti-shipping missile, the AM 39 Exocet, which forms the main anti-ship armament of the aircraft. French Étendards could also carry tactical nuclear weapons.

The first of three prototypes, a IVM modified with the new engine and some of the new avionics, made its maiden flight on 28 October 1974. The French Navy initially ordered 60 of the new model, with options for a further 20, but budget cuts lead to only 71 being purchased in the end, with deliveries starting in June 1978, while the Argentinian Navy ordered a further 14. Production was completed in 1983.

Operational history

Argentina

2nd Sqd insignia

The Argentine Naval Aviation decided to buy 14 Super Étendards in 1980, after the United States put an arms embargo in place—due to the Dirty War—and refused to supply spare parts for their A-4Q Skyhawks. Assigned to 2nd Naval Air Fighter/Attack Squadron, Argentine pilots used French flight trainers between November 1980 and August 1981 in France, but at the time of the Falklands War, they had received only 45 hours of actual flight time in the aircraft. Between August and November 1981, five Super Étendards and five Exocets were shipped to Argentina. All five of the missiles were used during the conflict, with one missile hitting the British destroyer HMS *Sheffield* and two the merchant aircraft transporter *Atlantic Conveyor*. Two missiles were used in each of those attacks.

Touch and go on USS *Ronald Reagan*

The fifth missile was launched in an attack intended to strike against the British aircraft carrier HMS *Invincible* but the attacking aircraft failed to find their target. (A sixth Exocet, which was fired from an improvised land based launcher failed to acquire a target, but the seventh missile hit and the warhead detonated causing casualties and damage to HMS *Glamorgan*. This launcher was designed by Argentine technicians.)

Once the conflict was over, Super Etendards performed qualifications on aircraft carrier ARA 25 de Mayo until the ship's final retirement From 2001, qualifications are made on Brazilian Navy carrier São Paulo and/or touch-and-go on US Navy carriers during Gringo-Gaucho maneuvers when they are in transit within Argentine coastal waters.

As of 2010, Argentine Super Étendards are still in service and French co-operation to upgrade the aircraft was announced.

France

Deliveries of the Super Étendard to the French Navy started in 1978, with the first squadron, *Flotille 11F* becoming operational in February 1979. In total, three operational squadrons and a training unit were equipped with the Super Étendard.

The first operational missions took place in Lebanon during Operation Olifant. On 22 September 1983, French Navy Super Étendards operating from the aircraft carrier *Foch* bombed and destroyed Syrian forces positions after a few artillery rounds were fired at the French peace keepers. On 17 November 1983, the same airplanes attacked and destroyed an Islamic Amal training camp in Baalbeck after a terrorist attack on French paratroopers in Beirut.

72 - Dassault-Breguet Super Étendard

Launch from *Charles de Gaulle*

France's Super Étendards were modified to carry the ramjet powered Air-Sol Moyenne Portée air-launched nuclear missile. From 1991, the original Étendard IVMs were withdrawn from French service, (although the reconnaissance version of the Étendard IV, the IVP remained in service until July 2000) and the Super Étendards underwent a series of upgrades throughout the 1990s to better suit them to modern warfare. These modifications included a new Thomson-CSF Anemone radar, with nearly twice the range of the previous Agave radar, the ability to carry and target the latest generation of laser-guided bombs and missiles, improved self defence ECM systems and the ability to carry a reconnaissance pod. These uprated aircraft, designated **Super Étendard Modernisé** (SEM) participated in NATO's *Allied Force* operations over Serbia in 1999, flying over 400 combat missions with 73% of the assigned objectives destroyed : the best performance of all the air forces involved in the missions over Serbia. The SEM also flew strike missions in Operation Enduring Freedom.

Mission Héraclès starting 21 November 2001 saw the deployment of the *Charles de Gaulle* and its Super Étendard in Afghanistan. Operation Anaconda, starting on 2 March 2002 saw extensive use of the Super Étendard in support of French and allied ground troops. Super Étendard's returned to operations over Afghanistan in 2007 and 2008. One of their main roles was to carry laser designation pods to illuminate targets for Dassault Rafales.

In March 2011, Étendards were deployed as a part of Task Force 473, during France's Opération Harmattan in support of UN resolution 1973 during the Libyan conflict. They were paired again with Dassault Rafales on interdiction missions.

All Super Étendards are expected to be retired from French service by 2015, to be replaced from 2006 onwards with Dassault's Rafale M.

Iraq

Five Super Étendards were loaned to Iraq in 1983 while the country waited for deliveries of Agave equipped Dassault Mirage F1s capable of launching Exocet missiles that had been ordered, arriving in Iraq on 8 October 1983. These aircraft used Exocets with some success against shipping (particularly tankers) sailing to and from Iranian ports, 51 attacks in total in the Persian Gulf before being returned to France in 1985. At least two were shot down during the spring and summer of 1984 by Iranian F-14s, while Iran claims to have shot down a third one. Of the two aircraft destroyed one was indeed shot down, the other was only damaged but crashed whilst trying to return to base. Only three aircraft were returned to France.

Operators

Argentine Navy's Super Étendard

Argentina
- Argentine Naval Aviation received 14 aircraft, eleven are still in service.

France
- Aviation Navale received 71 aircraft, all are to be replaced by the Rafale M by 2015.

Iraq
- Iraqi Air Force was lent five French aircraft between 1983 and 1985. Only three returned. The other two were lost during the Iran-Iraq war

Argentina
- 1 August 1989, 0760 3-A-210. Pilot Lt Carlos Manchinelli died.
- 11 December 1989, 0762 3-A-212. Engine stopped. Pilot Lt Félix Médici ejected safely.
- 29 May 1993, 0754 3-A-203 . Pilot Lt Sergio Marquez died.

France
- On 27 May 1982, a Super Étendard crashed off the coast of Toulon; the pilot was killed.
- In September 1986, a Super Étendard crashed into the Mediterranean Sea; the pilot ejected.
- During the night of 2 April 1987, a Super Étendard disappeared during a training flight north of the Île Vierge lighthouse off the northwestern coast of Brittany. Neither the aircraft nor the pilot were found.
- In July 1987, a Super Étendard crashed in a forest in Ille-et-Vilaine; the pilot ejected.
- During the night of 17 July 1988, Super Étendard 54 crashed during a carrier landing on the French aircraft carrier *Clemenceau*; the pilot was killed.
- On 31 May 1990, a Super Étendard pilot ejected 110 km off the coast of Hyères. He was rescued by a Dauphin helicopter from the French Navy's squadron 23S
- On 27 March 1994, Super Étendard 5 from the French Navy's flotilla 11F crashed in the Adriatic Sea; the pilot was rescued from the water by a helicopter from squadron 23S.
- On 26 January 1996, a Super Étendard crashed off the coast of La Ciotat; the pilot ejected.
- On 14 April 2004, Super Étendard Modernisé 35 from the French Navy's flotilla 17F missed a landing on the French aircraft carrier Charles De Gaulle, crashing on the runway; the pilot was unharmed.
- On 7 December 2005, Super Étendard Modernisé 45 from the French Navy's flotilla 11F (registered F-XCKA) was lost at sea in the Gulf of Ajaccio after its

engine ingested a bird. The pilot ejected and was only mildly injured.
- On 21 March 2006, a bird shattered the canopy of Super Étendard Modernisé 3 from the French Navy's flotilla 11F, over Pontorson. The pilot made a forced landing in a field in Dinard.
- On August 24, 2006, around 18:30 (local time), Super Étendard Modernisé 43 from the French Navy's flotilla 11F landed hard at BAN Landivisiau and was damaged; there were no injuries.
- On 21 March 2008, a Super Étendard Modernisé from the French Navy's flotilla 17F was lost at sea south of Cavalaire-sur-Mer during a training flight. The pilot ejected safely.
- On 1 October 2008, at 17:10 (local time), two Super Étendards Modernisés (numbers 38 and 49) from the French Navy's flotilla 11F collided over the bay of Lannion, about 27 km north of Morlaix. They were conducting a training flight originating from BAN Landivisiau. Both pilots ejected, but only one was rescued alive. The minesweeper *Lyre* (M648) was not able to locate the wreckage in over 60 m of water, and the rescue attempts for the second downed pilot (lieutenant de vaisseau Sébastien Lhéritier) were called off the next day at noon. On October 17, wreckage and the missing pilot's body were found 20 km north of Île de Batz with the assistance of robotic submersibles.

Specifications

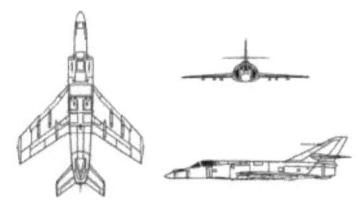

Data from Jane's All The World's Aircraft 1982-83

General characteristics
- **Crew:** 1
- **Length:** 14.31 m (45 ft 11½ in)
- **Wingspan:** 9.60 m (31 ft 6 in)
- **Height:** 3.86 m (12 ft 8 in)
- **Wing area:** 28.4 m² (306.7 ft²)
- **Empty weight:** 6,500 kg (14,330 lb)
- **Max takeoff weight:** 12,000 kg (26,455 lb)
- **Powerplant:** 1 × SNECMA Atar 8K-50 turbojet, 49.0 kN (11,025 lbf)

Performance
- **Maximum speed:** 1,180 km/h (637 knots, 733 mph) at low level
- **Range:** 1,820 km (983 nmi, 1,130 mi)
- **Combat radius:** 850 km (460 nmi, 530 mi) with one AM39 Exocet missile one wing pylon and one drop tank on opposite pylon, hi-lo-hi profile
- **Service ceiling:** 13,700 m (44,900 ft)
- **Rate of climb:** 100 m/s (19,700 ft/min)
- **Wing loading:** 423 kg/m² (86.3 lb/ft²)
- **Thrust/weight:** 0.42

Armament
- **Guns:** 2× 30 mm (1.18 in) DEFA 552 cannons with 125 rounds per gun
- **Hardpoints:** 4× underwing and 2× under-fuselage with a capacity of 2,100 kg (4,600 lb) maximum
- **Rockets:** 4× Matra rocket pods with 18× SNEB 68 mm rockets each
- **Missiles:**
  - 1× AM-39 Exocets Anti-shipping missile *or*
  - 1× Air-Sol Moyenne Portée nuclear armed missile *or*
  - 2× AS-30L *or*
  - 2× Matra Magic Air-to-air missile
- **Bombs:** Conventional unguided or laser-guided bombs, provision for 1 × AN-52 free-fall nuclear bomb, provision for "buddy" air refuelling pod

Source (edited): "http://en.wikipedia.org/wiki/Dassault-Breguet_Super_%C3%89tendard"

Dassault Mirage 5

The **Dassault Mirage 5** is a supersonic attack aircraft designed in France by Dassault Aviation during the 1960s, and manufactured in France and a number of other countries. It was derived from Dassault's popular Mirage III fighter, and spawned several variants of its own.

Design and development

Early development
The **Mirage 5** grew out of a request to Dassault from the Israeli Air Force. Since the weather over the Middle East is clear and sunny most of the time, the Israelis suggested removing avionics, normally located behind the cockpit, from the standard Mirage IIIE to reduce cost and maintenance, and replacing them with more fuel storage for attack missions. In September 1966, the Israelis placed an order for 50 units of the new aircraft.

Mirage 5

French Air Force Mirage-5F.

The first Mirage 5 flew on 19 May 1967. It looked much like the Mirage III, except it had a long slender nose that extended the aircraft's length by about half a metre, and made it arguably the most elegant of the Mirage delta series. A pitot tube was distinctively moved from the tip of the nose to below the nose in the majority of Mirage 5 variants.

The Mirage 5 retained the IIIE's twin DEFA guns, but added two additional pylons, for a total of seven. Maximum warload was 4,000 kg (8,800 lb). Provision for the SEPR rocket engine was deleted.

Rising tensions in the Middle East led French President Charles de Gaulle to embargo the Israeli Mirage 5s on 3 June 1967. The Mirages continued to roll off the production line, even though they were embargoed, and by 1968 the batch was complete and the Israelis had provided final payments.

In late 1969, the Israelis, who had pilots in France testing the aircraft, requested that the aircraft be transferred to Corsica, in theory to allow them to continue flight training during the winter. The French government became suspicious when the Israelis also tried to obtain long-range fuel tanks and cancelled the move.

The Israelis finally gave up trying to get the aircraft and accepted a refund. Later however, cooperation with France resumed outside the public's eye and Israel received 50 **Mirage 5s** in crates from AdA, while Ada took over the 50 aircraft originally intended for Israel, as **Mirage 5Fs**. The aircraft were delivered between May 1971 and February 1974 and assembled by Israeli technicians. Officially, Israel claimed to have built the aircraft after obtaining complete blueprints, naming them **Nesher**.

Like the Mirage IIIE, the Mirage 5 was popular with export customers, with different export variants fitted with a wide range of different avionics. While the Mirage 5 had been originally oriented to the clear-weather attack role, with some avionic fits it was refocused to the air-combat mission. As electronic systems became more compact and powerful, it was possible to provide the Mirage 5 with increased capability, even though the rear avionics bay had been deleted, therefore in some sub-versions, Dassault finished up with a "reinvented" Mirage IIIE.

Reconnaissance and two-seat versions of the Mirage 5 were sold, with the designation **Mirage 5R**, and **Mirage 5D** respectively. However, a little consideration of the differences between a Mirage III and a Mirage 5 quickly shows that these designations were simply for marketing purposes. There was no clear dividing line between the configuration of a Mirage III reconnaissance or trainer version and that of a Mirage 5 equivalent, and were one and the same in many cases.

A Mirage 5 of the Belgian Air Component parked at an airbase on 15 May 1978 during exercise *Tactical Air Meet '78*.

The Mirage 5 was sold to Abu Dhabi, Belgium, Colombia, Egypt, Gabon, Libya, Pakistan, Peru, Venezuela, and Zaire, with the usual list of subvariant designations and variations in kit. The Belgian aircraft were fitted with mostly US avionics, and Egyptian aircraft fitted with the MS2 attack avionics system from the Dassault-Dornier Alpha Jet.

In 1978 and 1980 Israel sold a total of 35 of their **Neshers** plus 4 Nesher trainer aircraft (Nesher Ts) to Argentina where they were locally known first as **Daggers** and after their last upgrade as **Fingers**. The Argentines lost two IIIEA and 11 Daggers during the Falklands War in 1982, and as a measure of solidarity the Peruvians transferred 10 of their Mirage 5s to Argentina, under the name **Mirage Mara** to help make good their losses.

Chile incorporated some Mirage 5s under name **Mirage Elkan**.

A total of 582 Mirage 5s were built, including 51 Israeli Neshers.

Mirage 50

The Atar 09K-50 engine, however, was still a good idea, and fit of this engine led to the next Mirage variant, the **Mirage 50**, during the 1970s. The uprated engine gave the Mirage 50 better take-off and climb characteristics than its predecessors. While the Mirage 50 also incorporated new avionics, such as a Cyrano IV radar system, it did not prove popular in export sales, as the first-generation Mirage series was becoming obsolete.

Chile ordered a quantity of Mirage 50s, receiving both new production as well as updated Armee de l'Air Mirage 5s. The Chilean aircraft were later modernized along the lines of the IAI Kfir as the ENAER Pantera. The Pantera incorporates fixed canards and other aerodynamic improvements, as well as advanced avionics. These aircraft have an extended nose to accommodate some of the new systems.

In 1990, Dassault upgraded a batch of Venezuelan Mirage IIIEs and 5s to the Mirage 50 spec, with the upgrades designated **Mirage 50M**.

Mirage 5 ROSE

A Mirage 5 ROSE fighter taxiing during flight operations at a Pakistan Air Force airbase. The FLIR sensor housing under the cockpit can be clearly seen. Parked in the background is a JF-17 fighter.

Project ROSE (Retrofit Of Strike Element) was an upgrade programme launched by the Pakistan Air Force to upgrade old Dassault Mirage III and Mirage 5 aircraft with modern avionics. In the first phases of the project, 33 ex-Australian Mirage III fighters were upgraded and designated *ROSE I*. The PAF then procured surplus Mirage 5F fighters in the late 1990s from the French Air Force in two batches. 20

fighters from the first batch were upgraded with new cockpits, navigation/attack suites, defensive aids systems and a forward-looking infra-red (FLIR) sensor under the aircraft's nose/cockpit, being designated ROSE II. The cockpits included new MFDs, HUDs, HOTAS controls, radar altimeters and RWRs. 14 Mirage 5F fighters from the second batch were upgraded similarly but with newer systems and designated ROSE III. The FLIR sensors allow the Mirage 5 ROSE fighters to specialise in the night-time attack role.

Variants

- **Mirage 5** : Single-seat radarless ground-attack fighter aircraft.
  - **Mirage 5AD** : Export version of Mirage 5 for Abu Dhabi, UAE; 12 built.
  - **Mirage 5EAD** : Single-seat radar-equipped fighter-bomber version for Abu Dhabi, UAE. 14 built.
  - **Mirage 5BA** : Single-seat version of the Mirage 5 for Belgium, fitted with mainly US avionics; 63 built, 62 under license by SABCA.
  - **Mirage 5COA** : Export version of the Mirage 5 for Colombia. 14 built. Remaining aircraft upgraded by IAI with canards and new avionics.
  - **Mirage 5D** : Export single-seat ground attack aircraft of the Mirage 5 for Libya; 53 built.
  - **Mirage 5DE** : Single-seat radar-equipped fighter-bomber version for Libya.
  - **Mirage 5F** : Single-seat ground-attack fighter aircraft for the French Air Force. 50 ex-Israeli Mirage 5Js. Eight aircraft withdrawn for conversion to Mirage 50C for Chile, with eight new-build 5Fs built as replacements.
  - **Mirage 5G** : Export version of the Mirage 5 for Gabon. Three built.
  - **Mirage 5G-2** : Four upgraded aircraft for Gabon, two of which were upgraded 5G and two undelivered ex-Zaire 5M.
- **Mirage 5J** : 50 aircraft were ordered by Israel, but the order was later embargoed by the French government. The were delivered instead to the French Air Force as the **Mirage 5F**.
- **Mirage 5M** : Export version of the Mirage 5 for Zaire; 14 built, of which only 8 delivered to Zaire owing to funding shortages.
- **Mirage 5MA Elkan** : Upgraded Mirage 5BA aircraft sold to Chile.
- **Mirage 5P** : Export version of the Mirage 5 for Peru; 22 built.
- **Mirage 5P Mara** : Upgraded Mirage 5P aircraft for Argentina.
- **Mirage 5P3** : Upgraded aircraft for Peru; 10 built.
- **Mirage 5P4** : Upgraded aircraft for Peru; two built new plus upgraded older aircraft.
- **Mirage 5PA** : Single seat radarless version of the Mirage 5 for Pakistan. 28 built.
- **Mirage 5PA2** : New build radar equipped aircraft for Pakistan, fitted with Cyrano IV radar. 28 built.
- **Mirage 5PA3** : New build radar-equipped anti-shipping aircraft for Pakistan, fitted with an Agave radar for compatibility with Exocet anti-ship missile.
- **Mirage 5SDE** : Single-seat radar-equipped fighter-bomber version for Egypt, equivalent to Mirage IIIE; 54 built.
- **Mirage 5E2** : Upgraded radarless attack version for Egypt. 16 built.
- **Mirage 5V** : Single seat ground attack aircraft 5 for Venezuela; six built. Survivors rebuilt to Mirage 50EV standard.
- **Mirage 5R** : Single-seat reconnaissance aircraft.
  - **Mirage 5BR** : Reconnaissance version of 5BA for Belgium; 27 built, 23 in Belgium.
  - **Mirage 5COR** : Export version of the Mirage 5R for Colombia; two built.
  - **Mirage 5DR** : Export version of the Mirage 5R for Libya; 10 built.
  - **Mirage 5RAD** : Export version of the Mirage 5R for Abu Dhabi, UAE; three built.
  - **Mirage 5SDR** : Export version of the Mirage 5R for Egypt; six built.
- **Mirage 5Dx** : Two-seat training version.
  - **Mirage 5BD** : Two-seat trainer version of 5BA for Belgium; 16 built, 15 built locally.
  - **Mirage 5COD** : Two seat trainer for Colombia. Two built. Ugraded with canards and new avionics.
  - **Mirage 5DAD** : Two-seat trainer for Abu Dhabi, UAE. Three built.
  - **Mirage 5DD** : Two seat trainer for Libya; 15 built.
  - **Mirage 5DG** : Two-seat trainer for Gabon; four built, two delivered 1978 and two in 1984.
  - **Mirage 5DM** : Two seat trainer for Zaire; three built, all of which were delivered.
  - **Mirage 5DP** : Two seat trainer for Peru; four delivered.
  - **Mirage 5DP3** : Updated trainer for Peru. Two new build plus upgrade of remaining 5DPs.
  - **Mirage 5DPA2** : Two seat trainer version of 5 for Pakistan; two built.
  - **Mirage 5MD Elkan** : Upgraded Mirage 5BD aircraft sold to Chile.
  - **Mirage 5SDD** : Two seat trainer for Egypt; six built.
- **Mirage 50** : Single-seat multi-role fighter-bomber, ground-attack aircraft, powered by more powerful 49.2 kN (11,055 lbf) dry, 70.6 kN (15,870 lbf) with reheat Atar 9K-50 engine. Available with or without radar.
  - **Mirage 50C** : New build radar equipped Mirage 50 for Chile; six built.
  - **Mirage 50FC** : Eight re-engined Mirage 5F aircraft sold to Chile.
  - **Mirage 50DC** : Two-seat training version for Chile. Three built, two with lower powered

Atar 9C-3 engine.
- **Mirage 50CN Pantera**: Mirage 50C and 50FC aircraft upgraded by ENAER with help from the Israeli company IAI for Chile with canards, revised, Kfir style nose and new avionics; 13 50C and FC upgraded plus two 50DC trainers.
- **Mirage 50EV**: Upgraded Mirage 5V aircraft for Venezuela, with Atar 9K-50 engine, canards and updated avionics (including radar). Six new-build aircraft, three upgraded ex-Zaire 5M, plus six upgraded remaining IIIEV and 5Vs.
- **Mirage 50DV**: Upgraded Mirage IIIDV/5DV aircraft for Venezuela, similar standard to 50EV. One new build plus two upgrades.

Operators

- United Arab Emirates (Abu Dhabi, retired and sold to Pakistan)
- Argentina (from Peru and IAI Nesher from Israel)
- Belgium (retired in 1993, 25 Mirage 5M Elkans sold to Chile)
- Chile (retired in 2006-2007)
- Colombia (retired)
- Ecuador (donated by Venezuela)
- Egypt
- France (retired)
- Gabon
- Israel (IAI Nesher, retired, some sold to Argentina)
- Libya (retired, sold to Pakistan)
- Pakistan (scheduled to be replaced with JF-17 in 2015)
- Peru (12 remaining aircraft retired from inventory on 14 June 2008)
- Venezuela (retired)
- Zaire (retired)

Specifications (Mirage 5F)

Data from Encyclopedia of World Military Aircraft

General characteristics

- **Crew:** 1
- **Length:** 15.55 m (51 ft 0¼ in)
- **Wingspan:** 8.22 m (26 ft 11⅝ in)
- **Height:** 4.50 m (14 ft 9 in)
- **Wing area:** 35.00 m² (376.8 ft²)
- **Empty weight:** 7,150 kg (15,763 lb)
- **Max takeoff weight:** 13,700 kg (30,203 lb)
- **Powerplant:** 1 × SNECMA Atar 09C turbojet
  - **Dry thrust:** 41.97 kN (9,436 lbf)
  - **Thrust with afterburner:** 60.80 kN (13,688 lbf)

Performance

- **Maximum speed:** Mach 2.2 (2,350 km/h, 1,268 knots, 1,460 mph) at 12,000 m (39,400 ft)
- **Cruise speed:** 956 km/h (516 knots, 594 mph)
- **Combat radius:** 1,250 km (675 nmi, 777 mi) hi-lo-hi profile, payload two 400 kg bomb and max external fuel
- **Ferry range:** 4,000 km (2,158 nmi, 2,485 mi)
- **Service ceiling:** 18,000 m (59,055 ft)
- **Rate of climb:** 186 m/s (36,600 ft/min)

Armament

- **Guns:** 2× 30 mm (1.18 in) DEFA 552 cannons with 125 rounds per gun
- **Rockets:** 2× Matra JL-100 drop tank/rocket pack, each with 19× SNEB 68 mm rockets and 66 US gallons (250 liters) of fuel
- **Missiles:** 2× AIM-9 Sidewinders OR Matra R550 Magics
- **Bombs:** 8,800 lb (4,000 kg) of payload on five external hardpoints, including a variety of bombs, reconnaissance pods or Drop tanks

Source (edited): "http://en.wikipedia.org/wiki/Dassault_Mirage_5"

Dassault Mirage III

The **Mirage III** (French pronunciation: [miʁaʒ]) is a supersonic fighter aircraft designed by Dassault Aviation during the late 1950s, and manufactured both in France and a number of other countries. It was a successful fighter aircraft, being sold to many air forces around the world and remaining in production for over a decade. Some of the world's smaller air forces still fly Mirage IIIs or variants as front-line equipment today.

Development

Cockpit of a Mirage III simulator of the Swiss Air Force.

The Mirage III family grew out of French government studies began in 1952 that led in early 1953 to a specification for a lightweight, all-weather interceptor capable of climbing to 18,000 m (59,040 ft) in six minutes and able to reach Mach 1.3 in level flight.

Dassault's response to the specification was the Mystère-Delta 550, a diminutive and sleek jet that was to be powered by twin Armstrong Siddeley MD30R Viper afterburning turbojets, each with thrust of 9.61 kN (2,160 lb). A SEPR liquid-fuel rocket motor was to provide additional burst thrust of 14.7 kN (3,300 lb). The aircraft had a tailless delta configuration, with a 5% chord (ratio of airfoil thickness to length) and 60 degree sweep.

The tailless delta configuration has a number of limitations. The lack of a horizontal stabilizer meant flaps cannot be used, resulting in a long takeoff run and a high landing speed. The delta wing itself limits maneuverability; and suffers from buffeting at low altitude, due to the large wing area and resulting low wing loading. However, the delta is a simple and pleasing design, easily built and robust, capable of high speed in a straight line, and with plenty of space in the wing for fuel storage.

The first prototype of the Mystere-Delta, without afterburning engine or rocket motor and with an unusually large vertical stabiliser, flew on 25 June 1955. After some redesign, reduction of the fin to more rational size, installation of afterburners and rocket motor, and renaming to **Mirage I**, in late 1955, the prototype attained Mach 1.3 in level flight without rocket assist, and Mach 1.6 with the rocket.

However, the small size of the Mirage I restricted its armament to a single air-to-air missile, and even before this time it had been prudently decided the aircraft was simply too tiny to carry a useful warload. After trials, the Mirage I prototype was eventually scrapped.

Dassault then considered a somewhat bigger version, the **Mirage II**, with a pair of Turbomeca Gabizo turbojets, but no aircraft of this configuration was ever built. The Mirage II was bypassed for a much more ambitious design that was 30% heavier than the Mirage I and was powered by the new SNECMA Atar afterburning turbojet with thrust of 43.2 kN (9,700 lb). The Atar was an axial flow turbojet, derived from the German World War II BMW 003 design.

The new fighter design was named the **Mirage III**. It incorporated the new area ruling concept, where changes to the cross section of an aircraft were made as gradual as possible, resulting in the famous "wasp waist" configuration of many supersonic fighters. Like the Mirage I, the Mirage III had provision for a SEPR rocket engine.

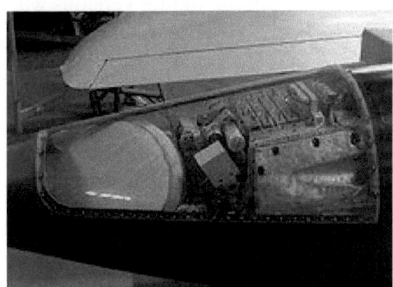

Cutaway view of the Cyrano radar system

The prototype Mirage III flew on 17 November 1956, and attained a speed of Mach 1.52 on its seventh flight. The prototype was then fitted with the SEPR rocket engine and with manually-operated intake half-cone shock diffusers, known as *souris* ("mice"), which were moved forward as speed increased to reduce inlet turbulence. The Mirage III attained a speed of Mach 1.8 in September 1957.

The success of the Mirage III prototype resulted in an order for 10 pre-production **Mirage IIIAs**. These were almost two meters longer than the Mirage III prototype, had a wing with 17.3% more area, a chord reduced to 4.5%, and an Atar 09B turbojet with afterburning thrust of 58.9 kN (13,230 lb). The SEPR rocket engine was retained, and the aircraft were fitted with Thomson-CSF Cyrano Ibis air intercept radar, operational avionics, and a drag chute to shorten landing roll.

The first Mirage IIIA flew in May 1958, and eventually was clocked at Mach 2.2, making it the first European aircraft to exceed Mach 2 in level flight. The tenth IIIA was rolled out in December 1959. One was fitted with a Rolls-Royce Avon 67 engine with thrust of 71.1 kN (16,000 lb) as a test model for Australian evaluation, with the name "Mirage IIIO". This variant flew in February 1961, but the Avon powerplant was not adopted.

The belly of a Mirage III

Mirage IIIC and Mirage IIIB

The first major production model of the Mirage series, the **Mirage IIIC**, first flew in October 1960. The IIIC was largely similar to the IIIA, though a little under a half meter longer and brought up to full operational fit. The IIIC was a single-seat interceptor, with an Atar 09B turbojet engine, featuring an "eyelet" style variable exhaust.

The Mirage IIIC was armed with twin 30 mm DEFA revolver-type cannon, fitted in the belly with the gun ports under the air intake. Early Mirage IIIC production had three stores pylons, one under the fuselage and one under each wing, but another outboard pylon was quickly added to each wing, for a total of five. The outboard pylon was intended to carry a AIM-9 Sidewinder air-to-air missile (AAM), later replaced by Matra Magic.

Although provision for the rocket engine was retained, by this time the day of the high-altitude bomber seemed to be over, and the SEPR rocket engine was rarely or never fitted in practice. In the first place, it required removal of the aircraft's cannon, and in the second, apparently it had a reputation for setting the aircraft on fire. The space for the rocket engine was used for additional fuel, and the rocket nozzle was replaced by a ventral fin at first, and an airfield arresting assembly later.

A total of 95 Mirage IIICs were obtained by the AdA, with initial operational deliveries in July 1961. The Mirage IIIC remained in service with the AdA until 1988.

The French Armée de l'Air (AdA) also ordered a two-seat **Mirage IIIB** operational trainer, which first flew in October 1959. The fuselage was stretched about a meter (3 ft 3.5 in) and both cannons were removed to accommodate the second seat. The IIIB had no radar, and provision for the SEPR rocket was deleted, although it could carry external stores. The AdA ordered 63 Mirage IIIBs (including the prototype), including five **Mirage IIIB-1** trials aircraft, ten **Mirage IIIB-2(RV)** inflight refueling trainers with dummy nose probes, used for training Mirage IVA bomber pilots, and 20 **Mirage IIIBE**s, with the engine and some other features of the multi-role Mirage IIIE. One Mirage IIIB was fitted with a fly-by-wire flight control system in the mid-1970s and redesignated **Mirage IIIB-SV** (*Stabilité Variable*); this aircraft was used as a testbed for the system in the later Mirage 2000.

Mirage IIIE

While the Mirage IIIC was being put into production, Dassault was also considering a multirole/strike variant of the aircraft, which eventually materialized as the **Mirage IIIE**. The first of three prototypes flew on 1 April 1961.

The Mirage IIIE differed from the IIIC interceptor most obviously in having a 30 cm (11.8 in) forward fuselage extension to increase the size of the avionics bay behind the cockpit. The stretch also helped increase fuel capacity, as the Mirage IIIC had marginal range and improvements were needed. The stretch was small and hard to notice, but the clue is that the bottom edge of the canopy on a Mirage IIIE ends directly above the top lip of the air intake, while on the IIIC it ends visibly back of the lip.

Many Mirage IIIE variants were also fitted with a Marconi continuous-wave Doppler navigation radar radome on the bottom of the fuselage, under the cockpit. However, while no IIICs had this feature, it was not universal on all variants of the IIIE. A similar inconsistent variation in Mirage fighter versions was the presence or absence of an HF antenna that was fitted as a forward extension to the vertical tailplane. On some Mirages, the leading edge of the tailplane was a straight line, while on those with the HF antenna the leading edge had a sloping extension forward. The extension appears to have been generally standard on production Mirage IIIAs and Mirage IIICs, but only appeared in some of the export versions of the Mirage IIIE.

The IIIE featured Thomson-CSF Cyrano II dual mode air / ground radar; a radar warning receiver (RWR) system with the antennas mounted in the vertical tailplane; and an Atar 09C engine, with a petal-style variable exhaust.

The first production Mirage IIIE was delivered to the AdA in January 1964, and a total of 192 were eventually delivered to that service.

Total production of the Mirage IIIE, including exports, was substantially larger than that of the Mirage IIIC, including exports, totaling 523 aircraft. In the mid-1960s one Mirage IIIE was fitted with the improved SNECMA Atar 09K-6 turbojet for trials, and given the confusing designation of **Mirage IIIC2**.

Nose of a Mirage IIIR: thinner than the fighter version, this nose has several glass apertures for medium-format cameras.

Mirage IIIR

A number of reconnaissance variants were built under the general designation of **Mirage IIIR**. These aircraft had a Mirage IIIE airframe; Mirage IIIC avionics; a camera nose and unsurprisingly no radar; and retained the twin DEFA cannon and external stores capability. The camera nose accommodated up to five OMERA cameras.

The AdA obtained 50 production Mirage IIIRs, not including two prototypes. The Mirage IIIR preceded the Mirage IIIE in operational introduction. The AdA also obtained 20 improved **Mirage IIIRD** reconnaissance variants, essentially a Mirage IIIR with an extra panoramic camera in the most forward nose position, and the Doppler radar and other avionics from the Mirage IIIE.

Exports and license production

Exports

The largest export customers for Mirage IIICs built in France were Israel and

South Africa as the **Mirage IIICZ**. Some export customers obtained the Mirage IIIB, with designations only changed to provide a country code. Such as the **Mirage IIIDA** for Argentina, **Mirage IIIDBR** and **Mirage IIIDBR-2** for Brazil. **Mirage IIIBJ** for Israel, **Mirage IIIDL** for Lebanon, **Mirage IIIDP** for Pakistan, **Mirage IIIBZ** and **Mirage IIIDZ** and **Mirage IIID2Z** for South Africa, **Mirage IIIDE** for Spain and **Mirage IIIDV** for Venezuela.

After the outstanding Israeli success with the Mirage IIIC, scoring kills against Syrian Mikoyan-Gurevich MiG-17s and MiG-21 aircraft and then achieving a formidable victory against Egypt, Jordan, and Syria in the Six-Day War of June 1967, the Mirage III's reputation was greatly enhanced. The "combat-proven" image and low cost made it a popular export success.

Mirage IIIC of the Argentinian Air Force

A good number of IIIEs were built for export as well, being purchased in small quantities by Argentina as the **Mirage IIIEA** and **Mirage IIIEBR-2** Brazil as the **Mirage IIIEBR**, Lebanon as the **Mirage IIIEL**, Pakistan as the **Mirage IIIEP**, South Africa as the **Mirage IIIEZ**, Spain as the **Mirage IIIEE**, and Venezuela as the **Mirage IIIEV**, with a list of subvariant designations, with minor variations in equipment fit. Dassault believed the customer was always right, and was happy to accommodate changes in equipment fit as customer needs and budget required. Pakistani **Mirage 5PA3**, for example, were fitted with Thomson-CSF Agave radar with capability of guiding the Exocet anti-ship missile.

Some customers obtained the two-seat Mirage IIIBE under the general designation **Mirage IIID**, though the trainers were generally similar to the Mirage IIIBE except for minor changes in equipment fit. In some cases they *were* identical, since two surplus AdA Mirage IIIBEs were sold to Brazil under the designation **Mirage IIIBBR**, and three were similarly sold to Egypt under the designation **Mirage 5SDD**. New-build exports of this type included aircraft sold to Abu Dhabi, Argentina, Brazil, Chile, Colombia, Egypt, Gabon, Libya, Pakistan, Peru, Spain, Venezuela, and Zaire.

Export versions of the Mirage IIIR were built for Pakistan as the **Mirage IIIRP** and South Africa as the **Mirage IIIRZ**, and **Mirage IIIR2Z** with an Atar 9K-50 jet engine. Export versions of the IIIR recce aircraft were purchased by Abu Dhabi, Belgium, Colombia, Egypt, Libya, Pakistan, and South Africa. Some export Mirage IIIRDs were fitted with British Vinten cameras, not OMERA cameras. Most of the Belgian aircraft were built locally.

Israel

The IDF/AF purchased three models of the Mirage III:
- 70 Mirage IIICJ single-seat fighters, received between April 1962 and July 1964.
- Two Mirage IIIRJ single-seat photo-reconnaissance aircraft, received in March 1964.
- Four Mirage IIIBJ two-seat combat trainers, three received in 1966 and one in 1968.

The Israeli AF Mirage III fleet went through several modifications during their service life.

Over the demilitarized zone on the Israeli side of the border with Syria, a total of six MiGs were shot down the first day Mirages fought the MiGs. In the Six-Day war, except for 12 Mirages (four in the air and eight on the ground), left behind to guard Israel from Arab bombers, all the Mirages were fitted with bombs, and sent to attack the Arab air bases. However the Mirage's performance as a bomber was limited. During the following days Mirages performed as fighters, and out of a total of 58 Arab planes shot down in air combat during the war, 48 were accounted for by Mirages.

In the 1973 Yom Kippur war, the Mirage performed in air to air operations only.

Argentina

License production

The Mirage IIIE was also built under license in Australia, Belgium and Switzerland.

Australia

Australian Mirage IIIO (top) and Mirage IIID (bottom) in 1980. These aircraft are now operated by the Pakistan Air Force

An Australian Mirage III-D in 1988

While an experimental Rolls-Royce Avon-powered version did not enter production, the Australian government decided that the Royal Australian Air Force (RAAF) would receive the IIIE, albeit a variant assembled by the Government Aircraft Factory (GAF) in Fishermans Bend, Melbourne from Australian-made components, under the designation **Mirage IIIO**. The major difference between the IIIE and the IIIO was the avionics installed. The other major Australian aircraft manufacturer at the time, the Commonwealth Aircraft Corporation (CAC), also in Melbourne, built the SNECMA Atar engine.

GAF produced three variants: the **Mirage IIIO(F)**, which was an interceptor, the Mirage **IIIO(A)**, a surface attack aircraft and the twin seat **Mirage IIIO(D)**, a fighter lead-in trainer. Dassault produced two sample IIIO(F) aircraft, with the first flying in March 1963. GAF completed 48 IIIO(F), 50 IIIO(A) and 16 IIIO(D) aircraft.

All the surviving Mirage IIIO(F) aircraft were converted to IIIO(A) standard between 1967 and 1979. The Mirage was finally withdrawn from RAAF service in 1988, and 50 surviving examples were sold to Pakistan in 1990.

Several examples are preserved in museums around Australia, and at least one is currently under restoration to airworthy condition.

Belgium

In 1968, the Belgian government ordered 106 Mirage 5s from Dassault to re-equip No 3 Wing at Bierset air base. All aircraft but the first one were to be license-built by SABCA in Belgium. Component production at the SABCA Haren plant near Brussels was followed by assembly at the SABCA plant at Gosselies airfield, near Charleroi. The ATAR engines were produced by FN Moteurs at this company's Liège plant. SABCA production included three versions: Mirage 5BA for the ground attack role, Mirage 5BR for the reconnaissance role and Mirage 5BD for training and conversion.

By the end of the 1980s, a MIRage Safety Improvement Program (MIRSIP) was agreed to by parliament, calling for 20 low-time Mirages to be upgraded. Initial plans included a new more powerful engine, but this idea was abandoned to limit cost. The upgrade eventually included a new state of the art cockpit, a new ejection seat, and canards to improve takeoff performance and overall maneuverability. A new government canceled MIRSIP however. SABCA, having a watertight contract for MIRSIP, was allowed to complete the update of the 20 aircraft. After completion, the Belgian government sold all 20 at a loss to Chile.

Switzerland

In 1961, Switzerland bought a single Mirage IIIC from France. This Mirage IIIC was used as development aircraft. The Swiss Mirages was built in Switzerland by F+W Emmen (today RUAG) (the federal government aircraft factory in Emmen) as the Mirage IIIS. As did Australia, one French-made aircraft was bought in preparation for license production. Cost overruns during the production led to the so-called "Mirage affair" . In all, 36 Mirage IIIS interceptors were built with strengthened wings, airframe, and undercarriage. The Swiss Air Force required performance comparable to those of carrier based planes. The airframes were reinforced so the aircraft could be moved by lifting them over other aircraft with a crane. The caverns in the mountains offer very little space to maneuver around parked aircraft. Also, the strengthened frames allowed for JATO assisted takeoffs. The main differences to the standard Mirage IIIE were as follows:

- New wiring of avionics with U.S. electronics
- Changed cockpit design with gray instead of black panels
- New U.S. radar, TARAN-18 from Hughes
- Use of HM-55S "Falcon" (Swiss designation of the from SAAB in Licence built Robot 27 (Rb27) which is similar to the Hughes AIM-26 "Falcon")
- Radar warning receiver (RWR) on both wingtips and on the back of the rudder
- Strengthened structure for use of JATO-Rockets
- Retractable nosecone for storing in mountain cavern
- Lengthened nosewheel for storing in mountain cavern
- Four lifting points for moving aircraft in mountain cavern with a crane
- Bay at the fin with a SEPR rocket engine to double the velocity for short time or climb to 20 000 m (60 000 ft)
- US TRACOR AN/ALE-40 chaff/flare dispenser at the back under the end of the engine (fitted with the upgrade 1988)
- Canards designed and produced by RUAG Aerospace(fitted with the upgrade 1988)
- New Martin-Baker ejection-seat (fitted with the upgrade 1988)

The Swiss Mirages are equipped with RWS, chaff & flare dispensers. Avionics differed as well, with the most prominent difference being that the Thomson-CSF Cyrano II radar was replaced by Hughes TARAN-18 system, giving the Mirage IIIS compatibility with the Hughes AIM-4 Falcon AAM. Also the Mirage IIIS had the wiring to carry a Swiss-built nuclear bomb or French nuclear bomb. The Swiss nuclear bomb was stopped in the preproduction stage and Switzerland did not purchase the French-made bomb. The Mirage IIIS had an integral fuel tank under the aft belly; this fuel tank could be removed and replaced with an adapter of the same shape. This adapter housed a SEPR rocket engine with its liquid fuel tanks. With the SEPR rocket, the Mirage IIIS easily reached altitudes of 20,000 m. The rocket fuel was very hazardous and highly toxic, so the SEPR rocket was not used very often. The Mirage IIIRS could also carry a photo-reconnaissance centerline pod and an integral fuel tank under the aft belly; this carried a smaller fuel load but allowed a back looking film camera to be added. In the early 1990s, the 30 surviving Swiss Mirage IIIS interceptors were put through an upgrade program, which included fitting them with fixed canards and updated avionics. The Mirage IIIS were phased out of service in 1999. The remaining Mirage IIIRS, BS and DS were taken out of service in 2003.

Variants

M.D.550 Mystere-Delta

Single-seat delta-wing interceptor-fighter prototype, fitted with a delta vertical tail surface, equipped with a retractable tricycle landing gear, powered by two 980-kg (2,160-lb) thrust M.D.30 (Armstrong Siddeley Viper) turbojet engines; one built.

Mirage I
Revised first prototype, fitted with a swept vertical tail surface, powered by two M.D.30R turbojet engines, also fitted with a 1500-kg (3,307-lb) thrust SEPR auxiliary rocket motor.

Mirage II
Single-seat delta-wing interceptor-fighter prototype, larger version of the Mirage I, powered by two Turbomeca Gabizo turbojet engines; one built.

Mirage III-001
Prototype, powered by a 4490-kg (9,900-lb) thrust Atar 101G2 turbojet engine, also fitted with a SEPR auxiliary rocket motor; one built.

Mirage IIIA
Pre-production aircraft, powered by a 6.000 kg (13,228 lb) thrust Atar 9B turbojet engine, also fitted with an auxiliary rocket motor; ten built for the French Air Force.

Mirage IIIB
Two-seat tandem trainer aircraft, fitted with one piece canopy, also fitted with radio beacon equipment, lacks radar; 59 built for the French Air Force.
- **Mirage IIIB-1** : Trials aircraft.
- **Mirage IIIB-2(RV)** : Inflight refuelling training aircraft.
- **Mirage IIIBE** : Two-seat training aircraft for the French Air Force, similar to the Mirage IIID; 20 built.
- **Mirage IIIBJ** : Export version of the Mirage IIIB for Israeli Air Force; five built.
- **Mirage IIIBL** : Export version of the Mirage IIIB for Lebanese Air Force.
- **Mirage IIIBS** : Export version of the Mirage IIIB for the Swiss Air Force; four built.
- **Mirage IIIBZ** : Export version of the Mirage IIIB for the South African Air Force; three built.

Mirage IIIC
Single-seat all-weather interceptor-fighter aircraft, equipped with a Cyrano I radar, powered by a 6000-kg (13,228-lb) thrust Atar 9B-3 turbojet engine, fitted with an auxiliary rocket motor in the rear fuselage, armed with two 30 mm cannons, plus one Matra R530 and two AIM-9 Sidewinder air-to-air missiles; 95 built for the French Air Force.
- **Mirage IIIC-2** : One aircraft fitted with an Atar 9K-6 turbojet engine.
- **Mirage IIICJ** : Export version of the Mirage IIIC for the Israeli Air Force; 72 built.
- **Mirage IIICS** : One evaluation and test aircraft for the Swiss Air Force; one built.
- **Mirage IIICZ** : Export version of the Mirage IIIC for the South African Air Force; 16 built.

Mirage IIID
Two-seat trainer version of the Mirage IIIE.
- **Mirage IIID** : Two-seat training aircraft for the RAAF. Built under licence in Australia; 16 built.
- **Mirage IIIDA** : Export version of the Mirage IIID for the Argentine Air Force; four built.
- **Mirage IIIDBR** : Export version of the Mirage IIID for the Brazilian Air Force; four built.
- **Mirage IIIDRR-2** : Refurbished and updated aircraft for the Brazilian Air Force. Two ex-French aircraft sold to Brazil in 1988.
- **Mirage IIIDE** : Export version of the Mirage IIID for the Spanish Air Force; six built.
- **Mirage IIIDL** : Export version of the Mirage IIID for the Lebanese Air Force; two built.
- **Mirage IIIDP** : Export version of the Mirage IIID for the Pakistan Air Force; five built.
- **Mirage IIIDS** : Export version of the Mirage IIID for the Swiss Air Force; two built.
- **Mirage IIIDV** : Export version of the Mirage IIID for the Venezuelan Air Force; three built.
- **Mirage IIIDZ** : Export version of the Mirage IIID for the South African Air Force; three built.
- **Mirage IIID2Z** : Export version of the Mirage IIID for the South African Air Force, fitted with an Atar 9K-50 turbojet engine; 11 built.

Mirage IIIE
Single-seat all-weather fighter-bomber, strike aircraft, powered by an 60.80 kN (13,668-lb) thrust Atar 9C-3 turbojet engine, fitted with a Cyrano II radar and a avionics bay behind the cockpit, equipped with a Doppler radar and a TACAN navigation system; 183 built for the French Air Force.
- **Mirage IIIEA** : Export version of the Mirage IIIE for the Argentine Air Force; 17 built.
- **Mirage IIIEBR** : Export version of the Mirage IIIE for the Brazilian Air Force; 16 built.
- **Mirage IIIEBR-2** : Refurbished and updated aircraft for the Brazilian Air Force. Four ex-French aircraft sold to Brazil in 1988.
- **Mirage IIIEE** : Export version of the Mirage IIIE for the Spanish Air Force; 24 built.
- **Mirage IIIEL** : Export version of the Mirage IIIE for the Lebanese Air Force; 10 built.
- **Mirage IIIEP** : Export version of the Mirage IIIE for the Pakistan Air Force; 18 built.
- **Mirage IIIEV** : Export version of the Mirage IIIE for the Venezuelan Air Force; seven built.
- **Mirage IIIEZ** : Export version of the Mirage IIIE for the South African Air Force; 17 built.

Mirage IIIO
Single-seat all-weather fighter-bomber aircraft for the Royal Australian Air Force. Built under licence in Australia; 100 built.

Mirage IIIR
Single-seat all-weather reconnaissance aircraft, fitted with five cameras and an infra-red package. 50 built for the French Air Force.
- **Mirage IIIRD** : Single-seat all-weather reconnaissance aircraft for the French Air Force, equipped with a Doppler navigation radar; 20 built.
- **Mirage IIIRJ** : Single-seat all-weather econniassance aircraft of the Israeli Air Force. Two Mirage IIICZs converted into reconnaissance aircraft.
- **Mirage IIIRP** : Export version of the Mirage IIIR for the Pakistan Air

Force; 13 built.
- **Mirage IIIRS**: Export version of the Mirage IIIR for the Swiss Air Force; 18 built.
- **Mirage IIIRZ**: Export version of the Mirage IIIR for the South African Air Force; four built.
- **Mirage IIIR2Z**: Export version of the Mirage IIIR for the South African Air Force, fitted with an Atar 9K-50 turbojet engine; four built.

Mirage IIIS
Single-seat all-weather interceptor fighter aircraft for the Swiss Air Force, fitted with a Hughes TARAN 18 radar and fire-control system, armed with AIM-4 Falcon and Sidewinder air-to-air missiles. Built under licence in Switzerland; 36 built.

Mirage IIIT
One aircraft converted into an engine testbed, it was fitted with a 9000-kg (19,482-lb) SNECMA TF-106 turbofan engine.

Mirage IIIX
Proposed version, announced in 1982, fitted with updated avionics and fly-by-wire controls, powered by an Atar 9K-50 turbojet engine. Original designation of the Mirage 3NG.

Derivatives

Mirage 5/Mirage 50

The next major variant, the **Mirage 5**, grew out of a request to Dassault from the Israeli Air Force. The first Mirage 5 flew on 19 May 1967. It looked much like the Mirage III, except it had a long slender nose that extended the aircraft's length by about half a metre. The Mirage 5 itself led directly to the Israeli Nesher, either through a Mossad (Israeli intelligence) intelligence operation or through covert cooperation with AdA (Armée de l'Air — the French Air Force), depending upon which story is accepted. (See details in the **Nesher** article.) In either case, the design gave rise to the Kfir, which can be considered a direct descendant of the **Mirage III**.

Milan

In 1968, Dassault, in cooperation with the Swiss, began work on a Mirage update known as the *Milan* ("Kite"). The main feature of the Milan was a pair of pop out foreplanes in the nose, which were referred to as "moustaches". The moustaches were intended to provide better take-off performance and low-speed control for the attack role.

The three initial prototypes were converted from existing Mirage fighters and had non-retractable canards "moustaches". One of these prototypes was nicknamed "Asterix", after the internationally popular French cartoon character, a tough little Gallic warrior with a huge moustache.

A fully equipped prototype rebuilt from a **Mirage IIIR** flew in May 1970, and was powered by the uprated SNECMA Atar 09K-50 engine, with 70.6 kN (15,900 lb) afterburning thrust, following the evaluation of an earlier model of this new series on the one-off **Mirage IIIC2**. The Milan also had updated avionics, including a laser designator and rangefinder in the nose. A second fully equipped prototype was produced for Swiss evaluation as the **Milan S**.

The canards did provide significant handling benefits, but they had drawbacks. They blocked the pilot's forward view to an extent, and set up turbulence in the engine intakes. The Milan concept was abandoned in 1972, while work continued on achieving the same goals with canards.

Mirage 3NG

Mirage III fitted with canards

Following the development of the Mirage 50, Dassault had experimented with yet another derivative of the original Mirage series, named the **Mirage 3NG** (*Nouvelle Génération*, next generation). Like the Milan and Mirage 50, the 3NG was powered by the Atar 9K-50 engine. The prototype, a conversion of a Mirage IIIR, flew in December 1982.

The 3NG had a modified delta wing with leading-edge root extensions, plus a pair of fixed canards fitted above and behind the air intakes. The canards provided a degree of turbulent airflow over the wing to make the aircraft more unstable and so more maneuverable.

Avionics were completely modernized, leveraging off the development effort for the next-generation Mirage 2000 fighter. The Mirage 3NG used a fly-by-wire system to allow control over the aircraft's instabilities, and featured an advanced nav/attack system; new multimode radar; and a laser rangefinder system. The uprated engine and aerodynamics gave the Mirage 3NG impressive performance. The type never went into production, but to an extent the 3NG was a demonstrator for various technologies that could be and were featured in upgrades to existing Mirage IIIs and Mirage Vs.

After 1989, enhancements derived from the 3NG were incorporated into Brazilian Mirage IIIEs, as well as into four ex-*Armée de l'Air* Mirage IIIEs that were transferred to Brazil in 1988. In 1989, Dassault offered a similar upgrade refit of ex-AdA Mirage IIIEs under the designation **Mirage IIIEX**, featuring canards, a fixed in-flight refueling probe, a longer nose, new avionics, and other refinements.

A total of 1,422 Mirage III/5/50 aircraft of all types were built by Dassault. There were a few unbuilt variants:
- A **Mirage IIIK** that was powered by a Rolls-Royce Spey turbofan was offered to the British Royal Air Force.
- The **Mirage IIIM** was a carrier-based variant, with catapult spool and arresting hook, for operation with the French *Aéronavale*.
- The **Mirage IIIW** was a lightweight fighter version, proposed for a US competition, with Dassault partnered with Boeing. The aircraft would have been produced by Boeing, but it lost to the Northrop F-5 Freedom

Fighter.

Balzac / Mirage IIIV

One of the offshoots of the Mirage III/5/50 fighter family tree was the **Mirage IIIV** vertical take-off and landing (VTOL) fighter. ("IIIV" is read "three-vee," not "three-five"). This aircraft featured eight small vertical lift jets straddling the main engine. The Mirage IIIV was built in response to a mid-1960s NATO specification for a VTOL strike fighter.

French Mirage IIIR

Mirage III ROSE

Project ROSE (Retrofit Of Strike Element) was an upgrade programme launched by the Pakistan Air Force to upgrade old Dassault Mirage III and Mirage 5 aircraft with modern avionics. In the early 1990s the PAF procured 50 ex-Australian Mirage III fighters, 33 of which were selected after an inspection to undergo upgrades. In the first phases of Project ROSE the ex-Australian Mirage III fighters were fitted with new defensive systems and cockpits, which included new HUDs, MFDs, RWRs, HOTAS controls, radar altimeters and navigation/attack systems. They were also fitted with the FIAR Grifo M3 multi-mode radar and designated *ROSE I*. Around 34 Mirage 5 attack fighters also underwent upgrades designated *ROSE II* and *ROSE III* before Project ROSE was cancelled. The Mirage III/5 ROSE fighters are expected to remain in service with the PAF until replacement in the mid-2010s.

Mirage IIICJ in Israeli Air Force museum (13 victory markings)

Operators

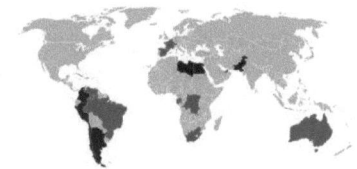

Map of Mirage III/V operators (former operators in red)

- Abu Dhabi (retired)
- Argentina
- Australia (retired 1988, 50 sold to Pakistan)
- Belgium (retired)
- Brazil 20/8 MirageIIIE/D (retired 2005)
- Chile (retired 2006)
- Colombia
- Colombian Air Force (retired 2010)
- Egypt (retired)
- France (retired)
- Gabon
- Israel (retired)
- Lebanon (sold to Pakistan in 2000)
- Libya
- Pakistan
- Peru (retired 2007)
- South Africa (retired 2008)
- Spain (retired in 1991, sold to Pakistan in 1992)
- Switzerland (retired)
- Venezuela (retired 2007)
- Zaire

Specifications (Mirage IIIE)

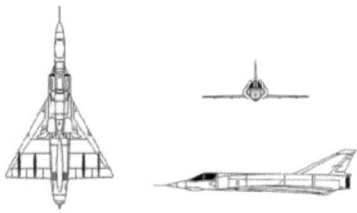

General characteristics
- **Crew:** 1
- **Length:** 15 m (49 ft 3.5 in)
- **Wingspan:** 8.22 m (26 ft 11 in)
- **Height:** 4.5 m (14 ft 9 in)
- **Wing area:** 34.85 m² (375 ft²)
- **Empty weight:** 7,050 kg (15,600 lb)
- **Max takeoff weight:** 13,500 kg (29,700 lb)
- **Powerplant:** × SNECMA Atar 09C turbojet

Performance
- **Maximum speed:** Mach 2.2 (2,350 km/h, 1,460 mph)
- **Range:** 2,400 km (1,300 NM, 1,500 mi)
- **Service ceiling:** 17,000 m (56,000 ft)
- **Rate of climb:** 83.3 m/s (16,400 ft/min)
- **Wing loading:** 387 kg/m² (79 lb/ft²)

Armament
- **Guns:** 2× 30 mm (1.18 in) DEFA 552 cannons with 125 rounds per gun
- **Rockets:** 2× Matra JL-100 drop tank/rocket pack, each with 19× SNEB 68 mm rockets and 66 US gallons (250 liters) of fuel
- **Missiles:** 2× AIM-9 Sidewinders OR Matra R550 Magics plus 1× Matra R530, 2× AM-39 Exocet anti-ship missiles
- **Bombs:** 4,000 kg (8,800 lb) of payload on five external hardpoints, including a variety of bombs, reconnaissance pods or Drop tanks; French Air Force IIIEs through 1991, equipped for AN-52 nuclear bomb.

Mirage III C

Mirage III E

Notable appearances in media
The Mirage fighter aircraft series is featured in the popular French comic *Tanguy et Laverdure*. The stories were made into the 1967–1969 French TV series *Les Chevaliers du Ciel*, and a French feature film *Les Chevaliers du ciel* (international title *Skyfighters*) in 2005, in which the Mirage 2000 is flown instead.

Source (edited): "http://en.wikipedia.org/wiki/Dassault_Mirage_III"

Douglas A-4 Skyhawk

The **Douglas A-4 Skyhawk** is a carrier-capable ground-attack aircraft designed for the United States Navy and United States Marine Corps. The delta winged, single-engined Skyhawk was designed and produced by Douglas Aircraft Company, and later McDonnell Douglas. It was originally designated the **A4D** under the U.S. Navy's pre-1962 designation system.

Skyhawks played key roles in the Vietnam War, the Yom Kippur War, and the Falklands War. Fifty years after the aircraft's first flight, some of the nearly 3,000 produced remain in service with several air arms around the world, including with the Brazilian Navy's aircraft carrier, *São Paulo*.

Design and development
The Skyhawk was designed by Douglas Aircraft's Ed Heinemann in response to a U.S. Navy call for a jet-powered attack aircraft to replace the older AD Skyraider. Heinemann opted for a design that would minimize its size, weight, and complexity. The result was an aircraft that weighed only half of the Navy's weight specification. It had a wing so compact that it did not need to be folded for carrier stowage. The diminutive Skyhawk soon received the nicknames "Scooter", "Kiddiecar", "Bantam Bomber", "Tinker Toy Bomber", and, on account of its nimble performance, "Heinemann's Hot-Rod".

The XA4D-1 prototype in 1954

The aircraft is of conventional post-World War II design, with a low-mounted delta wing, tricycle undercarriage, and a single turbojet engine in the rear fuselage, with two air intakes on the fuselage sides. The tail is of cruciform design, with the horizontal stabilizer mounted above the fuselage. Armament consisted of two 20 mm (.79 in caliber) Colt Mk 12 cannons, one in each wing root, with 200 rpg, plus a large variety of bombs, rockets, and missiles carried on a hardpoint under the fuselage centerline and hardpoints under each wing (originally one per wing, later two).

The second production A4D-1

The choice of a delta wing, for example, combined speed and maneuverability with a large fuel capacity and small overall size, thus not requiring folding wings, albeit at the expense of cruising efficiency. The leading edge slats were designed to drop automatically at the appropriate speed by gravity and air pressure, saving weight and space by omitting actuation motors and switches. Similarly the main undercarriage did not penetrate the main wing spar, designed so that when retracted only the wheel itself was inside the wing and the undercarriage struts were housed in a fairing below the wing. The wing structure itself could be lighter with the same overall strength and the absence of a wing folding mechanism further reduced weight. This is the opposite of what can often happen in aircraft design where a small weight increase in one area leads to a compounding increase in weight in other areas to compensate, leading to the need for more powerful, heavier engines and so on in a vicious circle.

A4D-2 refueling a F8U-1P

The A-4 pioneered the concept of "buddy" air-to-air refueling. This allows the aircraft to supply others of the same type, eliminating the need of dedicated tanker aircraft—a particular advantage for small air arms or when operating in remote locations. This allows for greatly improved operational flexibility and reassurance against the loss or malfunction of tanker aircraft, though this procedure reduces the effective combat force on board the carrier. A designated supply A-4 would mount a center-mounted "buddy store", a large external fuel tank with a hose reel in the aft section and an extensible drogue refueling bucket. This aircraft was fueled up without armament and launched first. Attack aircraft would be armed to the maximum and given as much fuel as was allowable by maximum takeoff weight limits, far less than a full tank. Once airborne, they would then proceed to top off their fuel tanks from the tanker using the A-4's fixed refueling probe on the starboard side of the aircraft nose. They could then sortie with both full armament and fuel loads. While rarely used in U.S. service since the KA-3 Skywarrior tanker became available, the F/A-18E/F Super Hornet includes this capability.

Thermal cockpit shield for nuclear weapons' delivery.

The A-4 was also designed to be able to make an emergency landing, in the event of a hydraulic failure, on the two drop tanks nearly always carried by these aircraft. Such landings resulted in only minor damage to the nose of the aircraft which could be repaired in less than an hour.

The Navy issued a contract for the type on 12 June 1952, and the first prototype first flew from Edwards Air Force Base, California on 22 June 1954. Deliveries to Navy and Marine Corps squadrons (to VA-72 and VMA-224 respectively) commenced in late 1956.

The Skyhawk remained in production until 1979, with 2,960 aircraft built, including 555 two-seat trainers. The last production A-4, an A-4M issued to a Marine squadron (VMA-223) had the flags of all nations who had operated the A-4 series aircraft painted on the fuselage sides.

Operational history

United States

The Skyhawk proved to be a relatively common United States Navy aircraft export of the postwar era. Due to its small size, it could be operated from the older, smaller World War II-era aircraft carriers still used by many smaller navies during the 1960s. These older ships were often unable to accommodate newer Navy fighters such as the F-4 Phantom II and F-8 Crusader, which were faster and more capable than the A-4, but significantly larger and heavier than older naval fighters.

The Navy operated the A-4 in both Regular Navy and Naval Reserve light attack squadrons (VA). Although the A-4's use as a training and adversary aircraft would continue well into the 1990s, the Navy began removing the aircraft from its front line attack squadrons in 1967, with the last ones (Super Foxes of VA-55/212/164) being retired in 1976.

A US Navy TA-4J Skyhawk of TW-3 on the deck of USS *Lexington*, 1989

The Marine Corps would not take the U.S. Navy's replacement warplane, the A-7 Corsair II, instead keeping Skyhawks in service with both Regular Marine Corps and Marine Corps Reserve attack squadrons (VMA), and ordering the new A-4M model. The last USMC Skyhawk was delivered in 1979, and they were used until the mid-1980s before they were replaced by the equally small, but more versatile STOVL AV-8 Harrier II.

VMA-131, Marine Aircraft Group 49 (the Diamondbacks) retired its last four OA-4Ms on 22 June 1994. Lieutenant Colonel George "Eagle" Lake III (CO), Major John "Baja" Rufo (XO), Captain Dave "Yoda" Hurston, and Major Mike "Struts" Volland flew a final official USMC A-4 sortie during the A-4 Standdown Ceremony. Trainer versions of the Skyhawk remained in Navy service, however, finding a new lease on life with the advent of "adversary training", where the nimble A-4 was used as a stand-in for the Mikoyan-Gurevich MiG-17 in dissimilar air combat training (DACT). It served in that role at "Top Gun" until 1999.

The A-4's nimble performance also made it suitable to replace the F-4 Phantom II when the Navy downsized its aircraft for the Blue Angels demonstration team, until F/A-18 Hornets were available in the 1980s. The last U.S. Navy Skyhawks, TA-4J models belonging to the composite squadron VC-8, remained in military use for target-towing, and as adversary aircraft, for combat training at Naval Station Roosevelt Roads. These aircraft were officially retired on 3 May 2003.

Skyhawks were well-loved by their crews for being tough and agile. These attributes, along with their low purchase and operating cost as well as easy maintenance, have contributed to the popularity of the A-4 with American and international armed forces. Besides the United States, at least three other nations have used A-4 Skyhawks in combat (Argentina, Israel, and Kuwait).

Vietnam War era

VA-146 A-4Cs over the Gulf of Tonkin in August 1964. USS *Kearsarge* (CV-33) steams below.

Skyhawks were the Navy's primary light bomber used over North Vietnam during the early years of the Vietnam War while the USAF was flying the supersonic F-105 Thunderchief; they were later supplanted by the A-7 Corsair II in the Navy light bomber role. Skyhawks carried out some of the first air strikes by the US during the conflict, and a Marine Skyhawk is believed to have dropped the last American bombs on the country. Notable naval aviators who flew the Skyhawk included Lieutenant Commanders Everett Alvarez Jr. and John McCain, and Commander James Stockdale. On 1 May 1967, an A-4C Skyhawk piloted by Lieutenant Commander Theodore R. Swartz of VA-76 aboard the carrier USS *Bon Homme Richard*, shot down a North Vietnamese Air Force MiG-17 with an unguided Zuni rocket as the Skyhawk's only air-to-air victory of the Vietnam war.

From 1956 on, Navy Skyhawks were the first aircraft to be deployed outside of the U.S. armed with the AIM-9 Sidewinder. On strike missions, which was the Skyhawk's normal role, the air-to-air armament was for self defensive purposes.

In the early-to-mid 1960s, standard US Navy A-4B Skyhawk squadrons were assigned to provide daytime fighter protection for ASW aircraft operating from some *Essex* class US anti-submarine warfare carriers, these aircraft retained their ground- and sea-attack capabilities. The A-4B model did not have an air-to-air radar, and it required visual identification of targets and guidance from either ships in the fleet or an airborne E-1 Tracer AEW aircraft. Lightweight and safer to land on smaller decks, Skyhawks would later also play a similar role flying from Australian, Argentinean, and Brazilian upgraded World War II surplus light ASW carriers, which were also unable to operate most large modern fighters. Primary air-to-air armament consisted of the internal 20 mm (.79 in) Colt cannons and ability to carry an AIM-9 Sidewinder missile on both underwing hardpoints, later additions of two more underwing hardpoints on some aircraft made for a total capacity of four AAMs.

The first combat loss of an A-4 occurred on 5 August 1964, when Lieutenant junior grade Alvarez, of VA-144 aboard the USS *Constellation*, was shot down while attacking enemy torpedo boats in North Vietnam. Alvarez safely ejected after being hit by anti-aircraft artillery (AAA) fire, and became the first US Naval POW of the war; he was released as a POW on 12 February 1973. The last A-4 loss in the Vietnam War occurred on 26 September 1972, when USMC pilot Captain James P. Walsh, USMC of VMA-211, flying from his land base at Bien Hoa Air Base, South Vietnam, was hit by ground fire near An Loc. An Loc was one of the few remaining hotly contested areas during this time period, and Captain Walsh was providing close air support (CAS) for ground troops in contact (land battle/fire fight) when his A-4 was hit, catching fire, forcing him to eject. Rescue units were sent, but the SAR helicopter was damaged by enemy ground fire, and forced to withdraw. Captain Walsh, after safely ejecting, had landed within NVA (North Vietnamese Army) positions, and had become a POW as soon as his feet had touched the ground. Captain Walsh was the last US Marine to be taken prisoner during the war, and was released as a POW on 12 February 1973.

Although the first A-4Es were flown in Vietnam in early 1965, the A-4Cs continued to be used until late 1970. The Seabees of MCB-10 went ashore on 7 May 1965. On 1 June 1965, the Chu Lai Short Airfield for Tactical Support (SATS) was officially opened with the arrival of eight A-4 Skyhawks from Cubi Point, Philippine Islands.The group landed with the aid of arresting cables, refueled and took off with the aid of JATO, with fuel and bombs to support Marine combat units. The Skyhawks were from Marine Attack Squadron VMA-223 and VMA-311. <

Armed A-4Fs on the USS *Hancock* in 1972

On 29 July 1967, the aircraft carrier USS *Forrestal* was conducting combat operations in the Gulf of Tonkin during the Vietnam War. A Zuni rocket misfired, knocking off an external tank on an A-4. Fuel from the leaking tank caught fire, creating a massive conflagration that burned for hours, killing 134 sailors, and injuring 161. (See 1967 USS *Forrestal* fire.)

During the war, 362 A-4/TA-4F Skyhawks were lost to all causes. The US Navy lost 271 A-4s, the US Marine Corps lost 81 A-4s and 10 TA-4Fs. A total of 32 A-4s were lost to surface-to-air missiles (SAMs), and one A-4 was lost in aerial combat to a MiG-17 on 25 April 1967.

Training/Adversary role

The A-4 Skyhawk was introduced to a training role in the two-seat TA-4J configuration replacing the TF-9J Cougar as the advanced jet trainer The TA-4J served as the advanced jet trainer in white and orange markings for decades until being replaced by the T-45 Goshawk. Additional TA-4J Skyhawks were assigned to Instrument Training RAGs at all the Navy master jet bases under RCVW-12 and RCVW-4. The Instrument RAGs initially provided jet transition training for Naval Aviators during the time period when Naval Aviation still had a great number of propeller-driven aircraft and also provided annual instrument training and check rides for Naval Aviators. The assigned TA-4J models were installed with collapsible hoods so the aviator under training had to demonstrate instrument flying skills without any outside reference. These units were VF-126 at NAS Miramar, VA-127 (later VFA-127) at NAS Lemoore, VF-43 at NAS Oceana and VA-45 (later VF-45) at NAS Cecil Field until its later move to NAS Key West.

VFC-13 adversary A-4Fs at NAS Fallon in 1993.

Additional single-seat A-4 Skyhawks were also assigned to composite squadrons (VC) worldwide to provide training and other services to deployed units. These included VC-1 at NAS Barber's Point, VC-7 at NAS Miramar, VC-5 at NAS Cubi Point, the Philippines, VC-8 at NS Roosevelt Roads, Puerto Rico, VC-10 at NAVBASE Guantánamo Bay, Cuba, and Naval Reserve squadrons VC-12 (later VFC-12) at NAS Oceana and VC-13 (later VFC-13) at NAS Miramar.

With renewed emphasis on Air Combat Maneuvering (ACM) training brought on with the establishment of the Navy Fighter Weapons School (*TOPGUN*) in 1969, the availability of A-4 Skyhawks in both the Instrument RAGs and Composite Squadrons at the master jet bases presented a ready resource of the nimble Skyhawks that had become the TOPGUN preferred surrogate for the MiG-17. At the time, the F-4 Phantom was just beginning to be exploited to its full potential as a fighter and had not performed as well as expected against the smaller North Vietnamese MiG-17 and MiG-21 opponents. TOPGUN introduced the notion of dissimilar air combat training (DACT) using the A-4E in the stripped Mongoose configuration with fixed slats.

The small size of the Skyhawk and superb low speed handling in the hands of a well trained aviator made it ideal to teach fleet aviators the finer points of DACT. The squadrons eventually began to display vivid threat type paint schemes signifying their transition into the primary role of Adversary training. To better perform the Adversary role, single-seat A-4E and F models were introduced into the role, but the ultimate adversary Skyhawk was the Super Fox, which was equipped with the uprated J52-P-408 engine. This variant had entered service in 1974 with VA-55/VA-164/VA-212 on the final USS Hancock cruise and had been the variant that the Blue Angels had selected in 1973.

The surplus of former USMC Skyhawks resulted in A-4M versions being used by both VF-126 and TOPGUN. Even though the A-4 was augmented by the F-5E, F-21 (Kfir), F-16, and F/A-18 in the Adversary role, the A-4 remained a viable threat surrogate until it was retired by VF-43 in 1993 and shortly thereafter by VFC-12. The last A-4 fleet operators were VC-8, which retired its Skyhawks in 2003.

The A-4M was also operated by the Operations Maintenance Detachment(OMD) in an Adversary role based at Naval Air Station Dallas for the Naval Air Reserve. Many of the aviators that flew the 4 jets were attached to NAS Dallas, including the Commanding Officer. The aircraft were instrumental in training and development of Air Combat Maneuvers(ACM) for VF-201 and VF-202. The unit also completed several missions involving target towing to NAS Key West, NAS Kingsville, TX, and deployments to NAS Miramar, CA and NAS Fallon, NV for adversary support. The detachment was under the operational command of the Commander Fleet Logistics Support Wing(CFLSW) based at NAS Dallas.

Israel

An Israeli A-4N.

In the late 1960s and 1970s, Israeli Air Force Skyhawks were the primary ground attack aircraft in the War of Attrition and the Yom Kippur War. They cost only ¼ what a Phantom II cost and carried more bombs and had longer range than the air superiority fighters they replaced. In May 1970, an Israeli Skyhawk piloted by Col. Ezra Dotan shot down two MiG-17s over south Lebanon (one with unguided rockets, the other with 30mm cannon fire) even though the Skyhawk's heads up display has no "air to air mode". The Skyhawks bore the brunt of losses to sophisticated SA-6 Gainful missile batteries.

During the 1982 Lebanon War an Israeli A-4 piloted by Aharon Ahiaz was shot down over Lebanon on 6 June 1982. Israel claimed this was one of its only two fixed wing aircraft shot down over the Beqaa Valley during the air battle of 6 June 1982 to 11 June 1982 where 150 aircraft took part. The Skyhawks have been replaced by F-16s but are still used for pilot training. In October 2008, it was decided due to maintenance issues that the A-4 fleet would be grounded and replaced. Some of Israel's A-4 later were exported to Indonesia.

Argentina

Argentina was not only the first foreign user of the Skyhawk but also one of the largest with nearly 130 A-4s delivered since 1965. The Argentine Air Force received 25 A-4Bs in 1966 and another 25 in 1970, all refurbished in the United

States by Lockheed Service Co. prior to their delivery as **A-4P**, although they were still locally known as *A-4B*. They had three weapon pylons and served in the 5th Air Brigade (Spanish: *V Brigada Aérea*). In 1976, 25 A-4Cs were ordered to replace the F-86 Sabres still in service in the 4th Air Brigade (Spanish: *IV Brigada Aérea*). They were received *as is* and refurbished to flight status by the Air Force technicians at Río Cuarto, Cordoba. The C model had five weapon pylons and could use AAM AIM-9B Sidewinders.

The Argentine Naval Aviation also bought the Skyhawk known as **A-4Q** in the form of 16 A-4B plus two for spare parts, modified with five weapon pylons and to carry AIM-9B Sidewinders. They were received in 1971 to replace F9F Panther and F9F Cougar in use from the aircraft carrier ARA *Veinticinco de Mayo* by the 3rd Fighter/Attack Squadron (Spanish: *3ra Escuadrilla Aeronaval de Caza y Ataque*).

The United States placed an embargo of spare parts in 1977 due to the Dirty War backing the Humphrey-Kennedy amendment to the Foreign Assistance Act of 1976, the Carter administration placed an embargo on the sale of arms and spare parts to Argentina and on the training of its military personnel (which was lifted in the 1990s under Carlos Menem's presidency when Argentina became a Major non-NATO ally). Ejection seats did not work and there were many other mechanical faults. In spite of this, A-4s still served well in the 1982 Falklands War where they achieved some success against the Royal Navy.

Falklands War

An Argentine A-4C being refueled shortly before its loss on 9 May 1982.

During the 1982 Falklands War, Argentina deployed 48 Skyhawk warplanes (26 A-4B, 12 A-4C and 10 A-4 aircraft). Armed with unguided bombs and lacking any electronic or missile self-defense, Argentine Air Force Skyhawks sank the Type 42 Destroyer HMS *Coventry* and the Type 21 Frigate HMS *Antelope* as well as inflicting heavy damage on several others: the RFA *Sir Galahad* (1966) (which was subsequently scuttled as a war grave), the Type 42 HMS *Glasgow*, the Leander Class Frigate HMS *Argonaut*, the Type 22 Frigate HMS *Broadsword*, and the RFA *Sir Tristram*. Argentine Navy A-4Qs, flying from Río Grande, Tierra del Fuego naval air station, also played a role in the bombing attacks against British ships, destroying the Type 21 HMS *Ardent*.

In all, 22 Skyhawks (10 A-4Ps, nine A-4Cs, and three A-4Qs) were lost to all causes in the six weeks-long war (according to other sources, 23 Skyhawks were lost: 10 A-4Bs, 9 A-4Cs and four A-4Qs). These losses included eight to British Sea Harriers, seven to ship-launched surface-to-air missiles, four to ground-launched surface-to-air missiles and anti-aircraft fire (including one to "friendly-fire"), and three to crashes.

After the war, Argentine Air Force A-4Ps and A-4Cs survivors were upgraded under the *Halcon* program with 30 mm (1.2 in) DEFA cannons, air-to-air missiles, and other minor details, and merged into the 5th Air Brigade. All of these were withdrawn from service in 1999, and they were replaced with 36 of the much improved OA/A-4AR Fightinghawk. Several TA-4J and A-4E airframes were also delivered under the A-4AR program mainly for spare parts use.

In 1983, the United States vetoed the delivery by Israel of 24 A-4Hs for the Argentine Navy as the A-4Q replacement. The A-4Qs were finally retired in 1988.

Kuwait

Kuwaiti A-4KUs on the flight line in 1991

More recently, Kuwaiti Air Force Skyhawks fought in 1991 during Operation Desert Storm. When Iraq invaded Kuwait, the available Skyhawks flew attack missions against the advancing Iraqi forces from deserted roads after their bases were overrun. A total of 24 of the 29 A-4KUs that remained in service with Kuwait (from 36 delivered in the 1970s) escaped to Saudi Arabia. The escaped Skyhawks (along with escaped Mirage F1s) operated as the Free Kuwait Air Force, flying 1,361 sorties during the liberation of Kuwait. Twenty-three A-4s survived the conflict and the Iraqi invasion, with only one being destroyed in combat. The remaining Kuwaiti Skyhawks were later sold to Brazil, where they currently serve aboard the aircraft carrier NAe *São Paulo*.

Variants

Brazilian Navy AF-1 (A-4KU)

Douglas A-4 Skyhawk - page 89

VA-81 A4D-2 on the USS *Forrestal* in 1962.

TA-4F Skyhawk of VA-164 aboard the aircraft carrier USS *Hancock* in the early 1970s

OA-4M of MAG-32 in 1990

A-4C landing on the USS *Kitty Hawk* in 1966.

A4-G of VF-805 takes a wire aboard HMAS *Melbourne* in 1980

Brazilian Navy A-4BR

Republic of Singapore Air Force A-4SU Super Skyhawk

Naval Reserve A-4L of VA-203

Gate guardian A-4Q at Mar del Plata

RNZAF A-4K

A-4M of VMA-322

A-4B in the Intrepid Sea-Air-Space Museum

Prototypes
- **XA4D-1**: Prototype
- **YA4D-1** (**YA-4A**, later **A-4A**): Flight test prototypes and pre-production aircraft.

A-4A
- **A4D-1** (**A-4A**): Initial production version, 166 built

A-4B

- **A4D-2 (A-4B)**: Strengthened aircraft and added air-to-air refueling capabilities, improved navigation and flight control systems, provision for AGM-12 Bullpup missile, 542 built.
- **A-4P**: Remanufactured A-4Bs sold to Argentine Air Force known as A-4B by the Argentines.
- **A-4Q**: Remanufactured A-4Bs sold to Argentine Navy.
- **A-4S**: 50 A-4Bs remanufactured for Republic of Singapore Air Force.
- **TA-4S**: seven trainer versions of the above. Different from most TA-4 trainers with a common cockpit for the student and instructor pilot, these were essentially rebuilt with a 28 in (710 mm) fuselage plug inserted into the front fuselage and a separate bulged cockpit (giving better all round visibility) for the instructor seated behind the student pilot.
- **TA-4S-1**: eight trainer versions of the above. These were designated as **TA-4S-1** to set it apart from the earlier batch of seven airframes.
- *A4D-3: Proposed advanced avionics version, none built.*

A-4C

- **A4D-2N (A-4C)**: Night/adverse weather version of A4D-2, with AN/APG-53A radar, autopilot, LABS low-altitude bombing system. Wright J65-W-20 engine with 8,200 lbf (36 kN) of takeoff thrust, 638 built.
- **A-4L**: 100 A-4Cs remanufactured for Marine Corps Reserves and Navy Reserve squadrons. Fitted with A-4F avionics (including the fuselage "hump") but retaining J-65 engine and three-pylon wing.
- **A-4S-1**: 50 A-4Cs remanufactured for Republic of Singapore Air Force.
- **ST Aerospace A-4SU Super Skyhawk**: extensively modified and updated version of the A-4S, exclusively for the Republic of Singapore Air Force (RSAF), fitted with a General Electric F404 non-afterburning turbofan engine, and modernized electronics.
- **TA-4SU Super Skyhawk**: extensively modified and updated version of the TA-4S & TA-4S-1 to TA-4SU standard.
- **A-4PTM**: 40 A-4Cs and A-4Ls refurbished for Royal Malaysian Air Force, incorporating many A-4M features (**PTM** stands for **Peculiar to Malaysia**).
- **TA-4PTM**: Small number of trainer versions of above (**PTM** stands for **Peculiar to Malaysia**).
- *A4D-4: Long-range version with new wings cancelled; A-4D designation skipped to prevent confusion with A4D*

A-4E

- **A4D-5 (A-4E)**: Major upgrade, including new Pratt & Whitney J52-P-6A engine with 8,400 lbf (37 kN) of thrust, strengthened airframe with two more weapon pylons (for a total of five), improved avionics, with TACAN, Doppler navigation radar, radar altimeter, toss-bombing computer, and AJB-3A low-altitude bombing system. Many later upgraded with J52-P-8 engine with 9,300 lbf (41 kN) thrust; 499 built.
- **TA-4E**: two A-4Es modified as prototypes of a trainer version.
- *A4D-6: Proposed version, none built.*

A-4F

- **A-4F**: Refinement of A-4E with extra avionics housed in a hump on the fuselage spine (this feature later retrofitted to A-4Es and some A-4Cs) and more powerful J52-P-8A engine with 9,300 lbf (41 kN) of thrust, later upgraded in service to J52-P-408 with 11,200 lbf (50 kN), 147 built. Some served with Blue Angels acrobatic team from 1973 to 1986.
- **TA-4F**: Conversion trainer - standard A-4F with extra seat for an instructor, 241 built.
- **OA-4M**: 23 TA-4Fs modified for Forward Air Control duties for the USMC.
- **EA-4F**: four TA-4Fs converted for ECM training.
- **TA-4J**: Dedicated trainer version based on A-4F, but lacking weapons systems, and with down-rated engine, 277 built new, and most TA-4Fs were later converted to this configuration.
- **A-4G**: eight aircraft built new for the Royal Australian Navy with minor variations from the A-4F; in particular, they were not fitted with the avionics "hump". Subsequently, eight more A-4Fs were modified to this standard for the RAN. Significantly the A-4G were modified to carry four underwing Sidewinder AIM-9B missiles increasing their Fleet Defense capability.
- **TA-4G**: two trainer versions of the A-4G built new, and two more modified from TA-4Fs.
- **A-4H**: 90 aircraft for the Israeli Air Force based on the A-4F. Used 30 mm (1.18 in) DEFA cannon with 150 rpg in place of US 20 mm (.79 in) guns. Later, some A-4Es later locally modified to this standard. Subsequently modified with extended jetpipes as protection against heat-seeking missiles.
- **TA-4H**: 25 trainer versions of the above. These remain in service, and are being refurbished with new avionics and systems for service till at least 2010.
- **A-4K**: 10 aircraft for Royal New Zealand Air Force. In the 1990s, these were upgraded under Project KAHU with new radar and avionics, provision for AGM-65 Maverick, AIM-9 Sidewinder, and GBU-16 Paveway II laser-guided bomb. The RNZAF also rebuilt an A-4C and 10 A-4Gs to A4K standard.
- **TA-4K**: four trainer versions of the above. A fifth was later assembled in NZ from spare parts.

A-4M Skyhawk II

- **A-4M**: Dedicated Marine version with improved avionics and more powerful J52-P-408a engine with 11,200 lbf (50 kN) thrust, enlarged cockpit, IFF system. Later fitted with Hughes AN/ASB-19 Angle Rate Bombing System (ARBS) with TV and laser spot tracker, 158 built.
- **A-4N**: 117 modified A-4Ms for the Israeli Air Force.

- **A-4KU**: 30 modified A-4Ms for the Kuwaiti Air Force. Brazil purchased 20 of these second-hand and redesignated them **AF-1**. Now used by the Brazilian Navy on carrier duty.
  - **TA-4KU**: three trainer versions of the above. Brazil purchased some of these second-hand and redesignated them **AF-1A**.
- **A-4AR Fightinghawk**: 36 A-4Ms refurbished for Argentina.
- **TA-4R**: Refurbished two-seat training version for Argentina.
- **A-4Y**: Provisional designation for A-4Ms modified with the ARBS. Designation never adopted by the US Navy or Marine Corps.

Operators

Argentina
- Argentine Air Force - as fighter and fighter trainer

Brazil
- Brazilian Navy - naval fighter

Singapore
- Republic of Singapore Air Force - retired from frontline duty in 2006, currently being used for Advance Jet Training (AJT) based at BA 120 Cazaux airbase in France.

Aircraft on display

Argentina
- Argentine Air Force A-4B C-233 BuNo 147714 (painted as A-4C C-301), IV Air Brigade Mendoza
- Argentine Air Force A-4C C-302 BuNo 148438, Malvinas Museum, Olivia Córdoba
- Argentine Air Force A-4B C-231 BuNo 142748, V Air Brigade, Villa Reynolds, San Luis
- Argentine Air Force A-4B and A-4C at National Aeronautics Museum
- Argentine Air Force/Navy A-4 (spares?) painted as Navy A-4Q 0667/3-A-312, Naval Museum Tigre
- Argentine Air Force A-4B C-232 BuNo 142749 painted as C-222, Museo Santa Romana, San Luis
- Argentine Air Force A-4F (spares) BuNo 154173 painted as (fake) A-4AR C-937, Museo Santa Romana
- Argentine Air Force (spares) TA-4J BuNo 158126 + A-4M tail painted as (fake) OA-4AR C-938, Museo Santa Romana
- Argentine Navy A-4Q - 0655/3-A-302 BuNo 144882 Argentine Naval Aviation Museum
- Argentine Navy A-4Q - 0657/3-A-304 BuNo 144915 Navy HQ, Buenos Aires
- Argentine Navy A-4Q - 0661/3-A-308 BuNo 144898 (painted as 3-A-314) Mar del Plata

Australia
- A-4 – Australia's Museum of Flight at HMAS *Albatross* in Nowra, New South Wales

Japan
- USMC OA-4M - MCAS Iwakuni

New Zealand
- Early US model converted to A4K standard – Royal New Zealand Air Force Museum in Christchurch

United States
- Douglas A-4C Skyhawk (A-4D-2N)U. S. Navy, 8/26/75,12624, BuAer 148314 Combat missions during Vietnam War aboard USS Enterprise, 10/65-6/66: Iron Hand missions to suppress SAM radars; USS Bonhome Richard, Mar-Jun 1967; USS Independence Mediterranean cruise 5/68, National Air and Space Museum, Washington, D.C. http://www.nasm.si.edu/collections/artifact.cfm?id=A19760757000
- US Navy A-4 Skyhawk from USS Oriskany on display at village green as part of USS Oriskany tribute, Oriskany, NY.
- Tail # 2777 Marine A-4 at Nashua NH traccon station on Northeastern Blvd. on outside display behind a security checkpoint; unknown condition.
- US Navy BuNo 158716 - Combat Air Museum, Topeka, Kansas
- US Navy A-4B Skyhawk - San Diego Air & Space Museum, San Diego, California
- US Navy A-4E Skyhawk BuNo 49996 - Evergreen Aviation Museum, McMinnville, Oregon
- US Navy A-4F Skyhawk BuNo 155036- Accomac County Airport, Accomac, Virginia
- US Navy A-4L Skyhawk BuNo 149532 - Castle Air Museum, Atwater, California
- US Navy A-4B Skyhawk – Intrepid Sea-Air-Space Museum, New York, New York
- Four former Blue Angel Skyhawks hung from atrium in "diamond" formation - National Museum of Naval Aviation, Pensacola, Florida.
- USMC BuNo 151194 - Pacific Coast Air Museum, Santa Rosa, California
- New England Air Museum, Windsor Locks, Connecticut
- Entrance to former Naval Air Station South Weymouth off Rte18 in Mass. Former USMC Skyhawk #2940 of VMA-322.
- A-4B (upgraded from an A-4A) BuNo 142200 that was on display since 1969 at the main (north) gate of the former Alameda Naval Air Station in California, blown off its pylon Feb 2008 by storm winds, is undergoing restoration and is scheduled to be back on display June 2011, repainted in the original VA-113 markings it wore fresh out the Douglas factory door in Apr 1957.
- An A-4C Skyhawk is on on display on the flight deck of the USS *Yorktown* (CV-10), at the Patriot's Point Naval and Maritime Museum in Mount Pleasant, South Carolina.
- USMC A-4M *160036* is on display at the Prairie Aviation Museum in Bloomington, Illinois.
- USMC A-4M on display at Marine Corps Air Ground Combat Center Twentynine Palms, Twentynine Palms, California.
- Carolinas Aviation Museum Douglas 1956 A4D-1 Skyhawk BuNo 142226 - US Marines 156th of 2960 built
- The Flying Leatherneck Aviation Museum located at MCAS Miramar has three Skyhawks on display; USMC A-4M BuNo 160264, USMC A-4C BuNo 148492, and an USMC TA-4J BuNo 158467.
- USN A-4F is on display on the deck of the USS Midway Museum in San

Diego Bay, BuNo 154977
- USN A-4 on display on the roof of Nauticus, in Blue Angels livery
- A-4 on display at Oregon Air & Space Museum at Mahlon Sweet Airport in Eugene, OR

Specifications (A-4F Skyhawk)

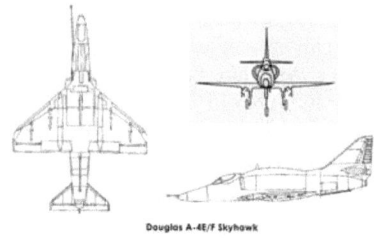

Douglas A-4E/F Skyhawk

Data from globalsecurity.org

General characteristics
- **Crew:** 1 (2 in OA-4F, TA-4F, TA-4J)
- **Length:** 40 ft 3 in (12.22 m)
- **Wingspan:** 26 ft 6 in (8.38 m)
- **Height:** 15 ft (4.57 m)
- **Wing area:** 259 ft² (24.15 m²)
- **Airfoil:** NACA 0008-1.1-25 root, NACA 0005-0.825-50 tip
- **Empty weight:** 10,450 lb (4,750 kg)
- **Loaded weight:** 18,300 lb (8,318 kg)
- **Max takeoff weight:** 24,500 lb (11,136 kg)
- **Powerplant:** 1 × Pratt & Whitney J52-P8A turbojet, 9,300 lbf (41 kN)

Performance
- **Maximum speed:** 585 kn (673 mph, 1,077 km/h)
- **Range:** 1,700 nmi (2,000 mi, 3,220 km)
- **Combat radius:** 625 nmi, 1,158 km/h ()
- **Service ceiling:** 42,250 ft (12,880 m)
- **Rate of climb:** 8,440 ft/min (43 m/s)
- **Wing loading:** 70.7 lb/ft² (344.4 kg/m²)
- **Thrust/weight:** 0.51
- **g-limit:** -3/+8 g

Armament
- **Guns:** 2× 20 mm (0.79 in) Colt Mk 12 cannon, 100 rounds/gun
- **Hardpoints:** 4× under-wing & 1× under-fuselage pylon stations holding up to 9,900 lb (4,490 kg) of payload
- **Rockets:**
  - 4× LAU-10 rocket pods (each with 4× 127 mm Mk 32 Zuni rockets)
- **Missiles:**
  - Air-to-air missiles:
    - 4× AIM-9 Sidewinder
  - Air-to-surface missiles:
    - 2× AGM-12 Bullpup
    - 2× AGM-45 Shrike anti-radiation missile
    - 2× AGM-62 Walleye TV-guided glide bomb
    - 2× AGM-65 Maverick
- **Bombs:**
  - 6× Rockeye-II Mark 20 Cluster Bomb Unit (CBU)
  - 6× Rockeye Mark 7/APAM-59 CBU
  - Mark 80 series of unguided bombs (including 3 kg and 14 kg practice bombs)
  - B57 nuclear bomb
  - B61 nuclear bomb
- **Others:**
  - up to 3× 370 US gallons (1,400 L) *Sargent Fletcher* drop tanks (pylon stations 2, 3, 4 are wet plumbed) for ferry flight/extended range/loitering time

Avionics
- Bendix AN/APN-141 Low altitude radar altimeter (refitted to C and E, standard in the F)
- Stewart-Warner AN/APQ-145 Mapping & Ranging radar (mounted on A-4F, also found on A-4E/N/S/SU)

Notable appearances in media

Source (edited): "http://en.wikipedia.org/wiki/Douglas_A-4_Skyhawk"

Embraer EMB 110 Bandeirante

The **Embraer EMB 110 Bandeirante** is a general purpose 15-21 passenger twin-turboprop light transport aircraft suitable for military and civil duties. It is manufactured by the Brazilian corporation, Embraer.

Bandeirante (**English:** pioneer) was the name given to the Portuguese settlers and pioneers who expanded the limits of the Portuguese Empire, language and culture in Brazil by progressively moving in and then settling from the early coastal settlements towards the inner, then unknown and uncharted zones of the vast continent.

Design and development

The EMB 110 was designed by the French engineer Max Holste following the specifications of the IPD-6504 program set by the Brazilian Ministry of Aeronautics in 1965.

The goal was to create a general purpose aircraft, suitable for both civilian and military roles with a low operational cost and high reliability. On this measure, the EMB 110 has succeeded.

The first prototype, with the military designation **YC-95**, was flown on 26 October 1968. Two more prototypes were built, and an order placed for 80 production aircraft, by now known as the Bandeirante for the Brazilian Air Force with the newly formed aircraft company Embraer.

The Bandeirante received its Brazilian airworthiness certificate at the end of 1972.

Further development of the EMB 110 was halted by the manufacturer in order to shift focus to the larger, faster, and pressurized 30-seat EMB 120 Brasilia.

On Dec 15, 2010, the Brazilian Air Force first flew an upgraded EMB 110 equipped with modern avionics equipment. Designated as the C/P-95, the aircraft has had several new systems installed by Israeli firm Elbit Systems' Brazilian subsidiary, Aeroeletronica. The Brazilian Air Force has an active fleet of 96 EMB-110s.

Operational history

Deliveries started to the Brazilian Air Force in February 1973. The passenger model first flew on 9 August 1972 and entered commercial service on 16 April

1973 with the now defunct Brazilian airline company Transbrasil.

Over the next 21 years Embraer built 494 aircraft in numerous configurations for a variety of roles including:

EMB 110B

EMB 110P1 operated by Manaus Aerotáxi

- **YC-95** or **EMB 100** - Prototype, powered by two 550 shp (410 kW) Pratt & Whitney Canada PT6A-20 turboprop engines. Three built.
- **EMB 110** Initial production version, powered by 680 shp (507 kW) PT6A-27 engines - Twelve seat military transport for the Brazilian Air Force, who designate it the **C-95**. 60 built.
- **EMB 110A** - Radio calibration version for the Brazilian Air Force (**EC-95**). Three built.
- **EC-95B** - Calibration version for the Brazilian Air Force.
- **EMB 110B** - Aerial survey, aerial photography version. Seven built, six as **R-95** for the Brazilian Air Force.
- **EMB 110C** - The first commercial model, similar to C-95, a 15-seat passenger version.
- **EMB 110C(N)** - Three navalised EMB 110Cs sold to the Chilean Navy.
- **EMB 110E** Executive version of EMB 110C. Six to eight seats.
  - **EMB 110E(J)** Modified version of EMB 110E.
- **EMB 110K** Stretched version with 0.85 m (2 ft 9½ in) fuselage plug and 750 shp (560 kW) PT6A-34 engines and fitted with ventral fin.
  - **EMB 110K1** - Cargo transport version for the Brazilian Air Force, with cargo door in rear fuselage. 20 built, designated **C-95A**.
- **EMB 110P** Dedicated commuter version of EMB 110C for Brazilian airlines, powered by PT6A-27 or -34 engines.
- **EMB 110P1** - Quick change civil cargo/passenger transport version based on EMB 110K1, with same rear cargo door.

EMB 110P2 in 1980

- **EMB 110P2** - Dedicated civil passenger version of EMB 110P1, without cargo door.
- **EMB 111A** - Maritime patrol version for the Brazilian Air Force. The aircraft also has the Brazilian Air Force designation **P-95 Bandeirulha**. Two were leased to the Argentine Navy during the Falklands War due to the retirement of their last SP-2H Neptune and until the introduction of modified L-188 Electras.
- **P-95B** -
- **EMB 111AN** - Six maritime patrol aircraft sold to the Chilean Navy.
- **C-95B** - Quick change cargo/passenger version for the Brazilian Air Force.
- **EMB 110P1 SAR** - Search and rescue version.
- EMB 110P/A - 18 seat passenger version, intended for export.
- EMB 110P1/A - Mixed passenger/freight version with enlarged cargo door.
- **EMB 110P1/41** - Cargo/passenger transport aircraft.
- **EMB 110P1K/110K** - Military version.
- **C-95C** - The Brazilian Air Force version of the EMB 110P2.
- **EMB 110P2**
- **EMB 110P2/A** - Modifications for airline commuter role, seating up to 21 passengers.
- **EMB 110P2/41** - 21-seat pressurised commuter airliner.
- **EMB 110S1** - Geophysical survey version.
- **SC-95** - Search and rescue version for the Brazilian Air Force.
- **XC-95** - Rain research version for the Brazilian Air Force.
- **C/P-95** - Updated version with modernised avionics.

Production was halted in 1990, as the EMB 110 had been superseded by the increasingly popular EMB120.

Operators

Civil Operators

In August 2008 a total of 122 EMB 110 aircraft (all variants) remained in airline service worldwide with some 45 airlines. Major operators include:

Australia
- Aeropelican (1)
- King Island Airlines (1)

Brazil
- Abaeté Linhas Aéreas (6)
- Manaus Aerotáxi
- Táxi Aéreo Weiss

Canada
- Aeropro (2)
- Air Creebec (3)
- Kenn Borek Air (4)

Cook Islands
- Air Rarotonga (3)

Cuba
- Aerocaribbean (4)

Curaçao
- Insel Air (3)

Guatemala
- Transportes Aéreos Guatemaltecos (4)

United Kingdom
- SkyDrift Air Charter (1)
- Air UK

Honduras
- CM Airlines

Ireland
- Ryanair (1)

United States
- Agape Flights (1)
- AirNow (9)
- Air Sunshine (2)
- Royal Air Fraight (5)
- Spacial Aviation Systems (4)
- Tropical Air Transport (1)

Venezuela
- Rutaca (5)

Iran
- Payam Air (5)

Military Operators
- EMB 100

Angola

Brazil
Brazilian Air Force

Chile

Gabon

Senegal
- EMB 110

Brazil
Brazilian Air Force

Cape Verde

Chile

Colombia

Gabon

Uruguay
- EMB 111

Argentina
Argentine Navy - leased by naval aviation during the Falklands War

Brazil
Brazilian Air Force - Being replaced by Lockheed P-3 Orion

Chile
Chilean Navy

Specifications (EMB 110P1A/41)
Data from Jane's All The World's Aircraft 1988–89

General characteristics
- **Crew:** 2
- **Capacity:** 18 passengers
- **Length:** 15.10 m (49 ft 6½ in)
- **Wingspan:** 15.33 m (50 ft 3½ in)
- **Height:** 4.92 m (16 ft 1¾ in)
- **Wing area:** 29.10 m² (313.2 ft²)
- **Airfoil:** NACA 23016(mod) at root, NACA 23012 (mod) at tip
- **Aspect ratio:** 8.1:1
- **Empty weight:** 3,393 kg (7,480 lb)
- **Max takeoff weight:** 5,900 kg (13,010 lb)
- **Powerplant:** 2× Pratt & Whitney Canada PT6A-34 turboprop engines, 559 kW (750 shp) each

Performance
- **Cruise speed:** 341 km/h (184 knots, 212 mph) - econ cruise at 3,050 m (10,000 ft)
- **Range:** 1,964 km (1,060 nm, 1,220 mi)
- **Service ceiling:** 6,550 m (21,500 ft)
- **Rate of climb:** 1.9 m/s (370 ft/min)

Incidents and accidents
- 27 February 1975: a VASP Embraer EMB 110 Bandeirante registration PP-SBE operating a flight from São Paulo-Congonhas to Bauru crashed after take-off from Congonhas. All 2 crew members and 13 passengers died.
- 23 April 1977: Brazilian Air Force, an Embraer C-95 Bandeirante registration FAB-2169 crashed upon landing at Natal Air Force Base.
- 3 June 1977: Brazilian Air Force, an Embraer C-95 Bandeirante registration FAB-2157 crashed after take-off from Natal Air Force Base. All 18 occupants died.
- 08 February 1979: a TAM Airlines Embraer EMB 110 Bandeirante registration PT-SBB operating a flight from Bauru to São Paulo-Congonhas, while on initial climb from Bauru, struck trees and crashed into flames. All 2 crew and 16 passengers died.
- 18 April 1984: two Votec Embraer EMB 110 Bandeirante registrations PT-GJZ and PT-GKL collided on air, while on approach to land at Imperatriz. PT-GJZ was flying from São Luís to Imperatriz and crashed on ground killing all its 18 passengers and crew died. PT-GKL was flying from Belém-Val de Cães to Imperatriz and its pilot was able to make an emergency landing on Tocantins river. One passenger of its 17 passenger and crew died.
- 7 October 1986: TAM Airlines, an Embraer EMB 110C Bandeirante registration PP-SBH flying from Campo Grande to Araçatuba struck the ground just short of the runway threshold after missing the approach at Araçatuba Airport twice. Seven crew and passengers died.
- 1 March 1988: Comair Flight 206, using an Embraer 110, crashed in Johannesburg, killing all 17 occupants.
- 14 November 1988: Oy Wasawings Ab flight to Seinäjoki crashed during landing in Ilmajoki, Finland. 6 deaths, 6 injured.
- 20 September 1990: an Embraer EMB110P1 Bandeirante registration PT-FAW belonging to the Government of Pernambuco, flying from Fernando de Noronha to Recife, crashed into the sea shortly after take-off. All 12 crew and passengers died.
- 11 November 1991: a Nordeste Embraer EMB110P1 Bandeirante registration PT-SCU, flying from Recife to Salvador da Bahia, during on initial climb had an engine failure followed by fire. The aircraft crashed on populated area. All 15 occupants of the aircraft and 2 persons on the ground died.
- 3 February 1992: Nordeste, an Embraer EMB 110 Bandeirante registration PT-TBB en route from Salvador da Bahia to Guanambi, descended below minimum levels in bad weather and crashed on a hill hidden by clouds near Caetité. All 12 passengers and crew aboard died.
- 13 January 1993: A Titan Airways cargo flight crashed into a hill near Sellafield, enroute from London Southend Airport to Glasgow International Airport. The flight used *G-ZAPE*, a 110P, and both pilots were killed in the crash.

- 26 October 1993: A Brazilian Air Force patrol P-95 (Embraer EMB 111 Bandeirante Patrulha) registration FAB-2290 that departed from Canoas Air Force Base crashed into the ocean near Angra dos Reis while flying in bad weather conditions. All crew of 3 died.
- 19 July 1994: Alas Chiricanas Flight 00901 Panamanian domestic airline ALAS, registration HP-1202AC using an Embraer 110P1, the aircraft crashed after a bomb exploded in the cabin killing 21, twelve Jewish businessmen were among the passengers.
- 24 May 1995 G-OEAA, an Embraer EMB-110-P1 operated by UK domestic airline Knight Air flight between Leeds and Aberdeen entered a steeply descending spiral dive, broke up in flight and crashed into farmland at Dunkeswick Moor near Leeds. All 12 occupants were killed. The probable cause of the accident was the failure of one or both artificial horizon instruments. There was no standby artificial horizon installed (as there was no airworthiness requirement for one on this aircraft) and the accident report concluded that this left the crew without a single instrument available for assured attitude reference or simple means of determining which flight instruments had failed. The aircraft entered a spiral dive from which the pilot, who was likely to have become spatially disoriented, was unable to recover.
- 17 November 1996: Brazilian Air Force, an Embraer P-95 Bandeirante registration FAB-7102 flying from Salvador da Bahia Air Force Base to Natal Air Force Base had an accident in the vicinity of Caruaru. Four Brazilian Air Force Bandeirantes were flying on formation from Salvador to Natal when the tail of FAB-7102 was struck by the propeller of another aircraft. Control of the aircraft was lost and it crashed. All 9 occupants died.
- 26 December 2002: Brazilian Air Force, an Embraer EMB 110 Bandeirante registration FAB-2292 en route from São Paulo-Campo de Marte to Florianópolis Air Force Base, crashed while trying to carry out an emergency landing at Curitiba-Afonso Pena. Reportedly, both engines had quit. The airplane had taken off with insufficient fuel on board to complete the flight to Florianópolis. Three passengers and crew of the 16 aboard died.
- 7 February 2009 An Embraer 110, operated by Manaus Aerotáxi, registration PT-SEA, flying a domestic route in Brazil from Coari to Manaus (Amazonas) struggled in bad weather conditions and crashed 80 km from Manaus killing 24 passengers. 4 survivors were reported.

Source (edited): "http://en.wikipedia.org/wiki/Embraer_EMB_110_Bandeirante"

English Electric Canberra

The **English Electric Canberra** is a first-generation jet-powered light bomber manufactured in large numbers through the 1950s. The Canberra could fly at a higher altitude than any other bomber through the 1950s and set a world altitude record of 70,310 ft (21,430m) in 1957. Due to its ability to evade early interceptors and providing a significant performance advancement over piston-engined bombers then common, the Canberra was a popular export product and served in many nations.

In addition to being a tactical nuclear strike aircraft; the Canberra proved to be highly adaptable, serving in such varied roles for tactical bombing, photographic, electronic, and reconnaissance in conventional warfare. Canberras served in the Vietnam War, the Falklands War, the Indo-Pakistani Wars, and numerous African conflicts. In several wars, both of the opposing forces had Canberras in their air forces. The Canberra was retired by its first operator, the Royal Air Force, in 23 June 2006, 57 years after its first flight; a few remain in service, performing meteorological work for NASA.

Development

Background

The Canberra had its origins in a 1944 Air Ministry requirement for a successor to the de Havilland Mosquito: a high-altitude, high-speed bomber with no defensive armament. Several British aircraft manufacturers submitted proposals. Among the companies shortlisted to proceed with development studies was English Electric, a well-established industrial manufacturer with very little aircraft experience, though when a desperate need for bombers had arisen during the early years of the Second World War, English Electric had begun to build the Handley-Page Hampden under licence.

Canberra B2 WH649 of the RAF 139 Squadron

In 1944 Westland Aircraft's technical director and chief designer W. E. W. Petter prepared a design study for a twin-engined fighter bomber, the P.1056, based on two fuselage mounted Metrovick F.2/4 "Beryl" engines. The authorities doubted its suitability for operations from unprepared fields and at low altitude but could see its potential as a bomber design; numerous manufacturers refused to take on the design. Petter left Westland to join the English Electric company in December 1944, where he was encouraged to develop his design, EE formed its own in-house aircraft design team in the following year.

The aircraft was named *Canberra* after the capital of Australia by Sir George Nelson, chairman of English Electric, as Australia was the first export customer for the aircraft. The Canberra had a simple design, looking like a scaled-up Gloster Meteor with a shoulder wing. The fuselage was circular in cross section, tapered at both ends and, cockpit aside, entirely without protrusions; the line of the large, low-aspect ratio wings was broken only by the tubular engine nacelles.

Although jet powered, the Canberra design philosophy was very much in the Mosquito mould, providing room for a substantial bomb load, fitting two of the most powerful engines available, and wrapping it in the smallest, most aerodynamic package possible. Rather than devote space and weight to defensive armament which historically could not overcome purpose-designed fighter aircraft, the Canberra was designed to fly fast and high enough to avoid air-to-air combat entirely.

Prototypes and first flights

The first Canberra B2 prototype, VX165.

In May 1945, a contract was signed. The subsequent Air Ministry specification B.3/45 requested production of four prototypes. Construction began in early 1946, but due to post-war military reduction the first aircraft did not fly until 13 May 1949. In the interim, the Air Ministry had already ordered 132 production aircraft in bomber, reconnaissance, and training variants. The prototype proved vice-free and required only a few modifications. A new glazed nose had to be fitted to accommodate a bomb-aimer because the advanced H2S Mk9 bombing radar was not ready for production, the engines were upgraded to more powerful Avon R.A.3s, and the distinctive teardrop-shaped fuel tanks were fitted under the wingtips.

The resultant aircraft, designated the Canberra B2, first flew on 21 April 1950, and entered squadron service with Royal Air Force (RAF) No. 101 Squadron in May 1951. In a testament to the aircraft's benign handling characteristics, the transition program consisted of only 20 hours in the Gloster Meteor and three hours in the dual-control Canberra trainer. With a maximum speed of 470 kt (871 km/h), a standard service ceiling of 48,000 ft (14,600 m), and the ability to carry a 3.6 tonne payload, the Canberra was an instant success. It was built in 27 versions that equipped 35 RAF squadrons, and were exported to Australia, Argentina, Chile, Ecuador, Ethiopia, France, India, New Zealand, Pakistan, Peru, Rhodesia, South Africa, Sweden, Venezuela and West Germany.

Photo-reconnaissance and conversion roles

The strategic reconnaissance role within the Royal Air Force had been carried out by the de Havilland Mosquito; in 1946 the Air Ministry issued Specification PR.31/46 as a jet-powered replacement for the Mosquito. To meet the requirement, the B2 design was modified by adding a 14-inch bay forward of the wing behind the cockpit to house seven cameras. It also had an additional fuel tank in the forward part of the bomb bay and only needed a two-man crew. The prototype, designated PR3, first flew on 19 March 1950, followed by the first of 35 production aircraft on the 31 July 1952. It entered service in December 1952 when No. 540 Squadron RAF began to convert from the Mosquito PR.34.

To enable crews to convert to flying the Canberra, a trainer version was developed to meet Air Ministry Specification T2/49. The prototype designated T4 first flew on 12 June 1951. It was the same basic design as the B2 apart from the introduction of side-by-side seating for the pilot and the instructor and the replacement of the glazed nose with a solid nose. The first production T4 flew on 20 September 1953 and the variant entered service with No. 231 Operational Conversion Unit RAF in early 1954. As well as the operational conversion unit, all the B2-equipped bomber squadrons received at least one T4 for training.

Manufacturing abroad

Martin EB-57B

In the United States, where the US Air Force needed to replace the B-26 Invader, 403 Canberras were manufactured under licence by Martin as the B-57 Canberra in several versions. While these were initially almost exactly the same as the English Electric pattern aircraft apart from the tandem crew seating, later models featured a series of substantial modifications. In Australia, the Government Aircraft Factory (GAF) built 48 for the Royal Australian Air Force, broadly similar to the British B2 but with a modified leading edge, increased fuel capacity and room for three starter cartridges, although in practice all three cartridges would sometimes fire, leading to the triple starter units being loaded singly.

In the United Kingdom, the demand for Canberras exceeded English Electric's ability to supply airframes, and so Handley Page, Avro and Short Brothers manufactured them under licence. 901 Canberras were manufactured in the UK, making total worldwide Canberra production 1,352 (including 403 made in the USA and 48 in Australia).

Design

Manufacturer's brochure, 1957.

The Canberra is mostly a metal aircraft,

only the forward portion of the fin being of wooden construction and covered with plywood. The fuselage is of semi-monocoque construction with a pressurised nose compartment. Each crew member has a Martin-Baker ejection seat except in the B(I)8 and its export versions where the navigator has to rely on a conventional escape hatch and parachute. The fuselage contains two bomb-bays with conventional clamshell doors (a rotating door was implemented on the Martin-built B-57 Canberra). The wing is of single-spar construction, the spar passing through the fuselage. Outboard of the engine nacelles the wing has a leading-edge sweep of 4° and trailing-edge sweep of -14°. Controls are conventional with ailerons, four-section flaps, and airbrakes on top and bottom surfaces of the wings.

Thrust was provided by a pair of 30 kN axial flow Rolls-Royce Avon turbojets. The manufacturer specified that cordite Coffman engine starters should be used to trigger the starter motor and activate the engine. An improvised method of starting the engine using compressed air was heavily discouraged by Rolls-Royce, but some operators successfully operated the Canberra's engines in such a manner, the benefit being significant cost savings over cartridges.

It was designed for a crew of two under a fighter-style canopy but delays in the development of the intended automatic radar bombsight resulted in the addition of a bomb aimer's position in the nose. Wingspan and length were almost identical at just under 20 metres, maximum takeoff weight a little under 25 tonnes. In part due to its range limitation of just 2,000 miles, and its inability to carry the early, bulky nuclear bombs, the Canberra became more of a tactical bomber than a strategic one. In some cases, Canberras stationed across the far reaches of the former British Empire were not made nuclear capable until as late as 1957.

The Canberra could deploy many conventional weapons, typical weapons used were 250-pound, 500-pound, and 1000-pound bombs, the total bomb load could weigh up to 10,000-pounds. Operators such as Rhodesia developed their own weapons such as anti-personnel bomblets, the *Alpha bomb*, to make the aircraft more effective in the operator's own operating context. Weapons such as anti-personnel flechette strikes were tested successfully from the Canberra, but not put into practice due to international agreements.

Due to the use of a new alloy, DTD683, the undercarriages of the Canberra suffered from stress corrosion, which caused them to decay within a few years. The extreme hazard posed of undercarriages collapsing during landings, especially if the aircraft were carrying nuclear weapons, led the RAF to institute regular inspections, at first using radiography before moving to more effective and reliable ultrasound technology.

Operational history

Royal Air Force

Canberra PR3 of No. 540 Squadron RAF at London Heathrow in June 1953

RAF Canberra TT18 painted to represent a Canberra B20 of the RAAF, owned by the Temora Aviation Museum's

The Canberra B2 started to enter service with 101 Squadron in January 1951, with 101 Squadron being fully equipped by May, and a further squadron, No. 9 Squadron equipping by the end of the year. The production of the Canberra was accelerated as a result of the outbreak of the Korean War, orders for the aircraft increased and outpaced production capacity, as the aircraft was designated as a *"super priority"*. A further five squadrons were able to be equipped with the Canberra by the end of 1952; however, production in the 1951–52 period had only been half of the level planned, due to shortages in skilled manpower, material, and suitable machine tools.

The Canberra replaced Mosquitos, Lincolns and Washingtons as front line bombers, showing a drastically improved performance, proving to be effectively immune from interception during air defence exercises until the arrival of the Hawker Hunter. The Canberra also replaced the RAF's Mosquitos in the reconnaissance role, with the Canberra PR3 entering service in December 1952.

The improved Canberra B6, with more powerful engines and more fuel, started to supplement the B2s in the UK based squadrons of Bomber Command from June 1954, when they replaced 101 Squadrons B2s. This freed up older B2s to allow Canberra squadrons to form overseas, with bomber and reconnaissance Canberra wings forming in RAF Germany and on Cyprus, with squadrons also being deployed to the Far East.

The Canberra allegedly executed a 1953 reconnaissance flight over the Soviet rocket launch and development site at Kapustin Yar, although the UK government has never admitted the existence of such a flight. Further reconnaissance flights are alleged to have taken place along, and over, the borders of the Soviet Union in 1954 under the code name *Project Robin*, using the Canberra B2 *WH726*. The USAF also used the Canberra for reconnaissance flights, however the aircraft were no longer required after June 1956, the introduction of the US Lockheed U-2 purpose-built reconnaissance aircraft; *Project Robin* was then terminated.

The Vickers Valiant entered service in 1955, capable of carrying much heavier weapon loads (including the Blue Danube atomic bomb) over longer ranges than the Canberra. This led to the Bomber Command force of Canberras equipped for high-level conventional bombing to be gradually phased out. This did not mean the end of the Canberra in front line service, however, as it proved suitable for the low-level strike and ground attack role, and versions dedicated to this role were brought into service. The interim B(I)6, converted from the B6 by adding provision for a pack of four 20 mm cannon in the rear bomb bay and underwing pylons for bombs and rockets, entered service in 1955, with the definitive, new build B(I)8, which added a new forward fuselage with a fighter-style canopy for the pilot, entering service in January 1956.

An important role for the new low-level force was tactical nuclear strike, using the Low Altitude Bombing System (LABS) to allow a nuclear bomb to be delivered from low level while allowing the bomber to escape the blast of the weapon. RAF Germany's force of four squadrons equipped with the B(I)6 and B(I)8 were equipped to carry US-owned Mark 7 nuclear bombs, while three squadrons based on Cyprus and one at Singapore were armed with British-owned Red Beard nuclear weapons.

RAF photo-reconnaissance Canberra PR9; the pilot is standing by the aircraft nose below the offset "fighter" style canopy.

Bomber Command retired the last of its Canberras on 11 September 1961, but the Germany, Cyprus and Singapore based squadrons continued in the nuclear strike role. The Cyprus based squadrons and one of the RAF Germany squadrons disbanded in 1969, with the Singapore based unit followed in 1970. The three remaining RAF Germany units, which by now had replaced the old Mark 7 bombs with newer (but still US-owned) B43 nuclear bombs, remained operational until 1972, the last Canberra bombers in RAF service.

The RAF continued to operate the Canberra after 1972, employing it for reconnaissance (with Squadrons equipped with PR7s and PR9s being based at RAF Wyton in the UK and RAF Luqa in Malta. The PR9s were fitted with special LOROP (Long-Range Optical Photography) cameras, reportedly based on those used by the Lockheed U-2, to allow high-altitude of targets deep into Eastern Europe while flying along the inner German border, as well as infrared linescan cameras for low level night reconnaissance. The RAF used Canberras to search for hidden arms dumps using false-colour photography during Operation Motorman in July 1972, when the British Army retook Irish republican held "no go areas" in Belfast and Derry. Canberras were used for reconnaissance over Bosnia during the war during the 1990s, where they were used to locate mass graves and during the Kosovo War in 1999. They were also operated from Uganda during the First Congo War, where they were used to search for refugees. Small numbers of specially equipped Canberras were also used for Signals Intelligence, being operated by 192 Squadron and then 51 Squadron from 1953 to 1976.

The PR9 variant remained in service with No. 39 (1 PRU) Squadron until July 2006 for strategic reconnaissance and photographic mapping, seeing service in the 2003 invasion of Iraq and, up to June 2006, in Afghanistan. During a ceremony to mark the standing down of 39 (1 PRU) Squadron at RAF Marham on 28 July 2006, a flypast by a Canberra PR9 on its last ever sortie was conducted.

Royal Australian Air Force

Shortly after the end of the Second World War, the Australian government began reorganising the armed forces. The Royal Australian Air Force (RAAF) developed Plan "D" for its postwar structure, built around the concept of a small, agile air arm employing leading edge technology. The RAAF decided to acquire the Canberra to replace or complement the Avro Lincoln, though fears were raised that the new design was not especially advanced. While Australia never introduced nuclear weapons into service, the Canberra's ability to carry such a payload was a factor in its acquisition; Australia's planned force of 48 Canberras, with the potential for being nuclear-armed, was viewed as far more potent and deterring than the entire RAAF's wartime forces of 254 heavy bombers. The first Australian-built Canberra first flew on 29 May 1953 at Avalon and was delivered to the RAAF for service trials a few weeks later. The Canberra entered Australian service in December 1953.

Canberra Mk 20 (A84-235) in RAAF No. 2 Squadron livery.

From July 1950 to July 1960, during the Malayan Emergency, Canberras from Australia, New Zealand and the UK were deployed into the Malaysia to fight against Communist Guerillas. In 1964, the RAAF deployed a squadron of Canberras to participate in the Vietnam War. The unit, No. 2 Squadron, was later commended for its performance by the United States Air Force. The Canberras were typically operated in the low-level bombing role. They were withdrawn from Vietnam in 1971, two of the aircraft having been lost in combat.

As early as 1954, Australia recognised that the Canberra was becoming outdated, and evaluated aircraft such as the Avro Vulcan and Handley-Page

Victor as potential replacements. The Canberra was incapable of providing adequate coverage of Indonesia from Australian bases, and was evaluated as having a "very low" chance of survival if it encounted modern fighters like the MiG-17. Political pressure for a Canberra replacement rose to a head in 1962. Australia evaluated the BAC TSR-2, Dassault Mirage IV, McDonnell Douglas F-4 Phantom II and North American A-5 Vigilante, and initially appeared to favour the TSR-2, but chose to procure the General Dynamics F-111C in October 1963. Due in part to delays in the delivery of the F-111Cs, the Canberra continued to be used by Australia for a total of 29 years before its retirement in June 1982.

Indian Air Force

The Canberra was the backbone of the Indian Air Force (IAF) for bombing raids and photo reconnaissance for many decades. Negotiations to acquire the Canberra as a replacement for the short-lived and obsolete Consolidated B-24 Liberator bombers then being used by India began in 1954. During the extended negotiations between Britain and India, the Soviet Union is alleged to have offered their own jet bomber, the Ilyushin Il-28, at a significantly lower price than that asked for the Canberra; however by April 1956 the Indian government was in favour of the purchase. In January 1957 India placed a large order for the Canberra; a total of 54 B(I)58 bombers, eight PR57 photo reconnaissance aircraft, and six T4 training aircraft were ordered, deliveries began in the summer of that same year. 12 more Canberras were ordered in September 1957, as many as 30 more may have also been purchased by 1962.

First used in combat by the IAF in 1962, the Canberra was employed during the UN campaign against the breakaway Republic of Katanga in Africa. During the Indo-Pakistani Wars of the 1960s and 1970s, the Canberra was used by both sides. One of the worst combat loss incidents occurred on 1 September 1965, four Indian Canberras were shot down by Pakistani fighters. The most audacious use of the bomber was in the *"Raid on Badin"* during the Second Kashmir War, when the Indian Air Force sent in the Canberra to attack a critical Pakistani radar post in West Pakistan. The raid was a complete success, the radars in Badin having been badly damaged by the bombing and put out of commission. A later raid by the IAF was attempted on Peshawar Air base with the aim of destroying, amongst other targets, several Pakistani B-57 bombers, American-built Canberras. Due to poor visibility, a road outside of the base was bombed, instead of the runway where the parked PAF B-57 bombers were located.

During the Indo-Pakistani War of 1971, Indian Canberras flew a strategically important sortie against the Karachi oil tanks, this had the effect of helping the Indian Navy in their own operations, a series of missile boat attacks against the Pakistani coast. On 21 May 1999, prior to the commencement of the Kargil War, the Indian Air Force Air HQ assigned a Canberra PR57 aircraft on a photographic mission near the LOC (Line of Control), where it took a severe blow from a FIM-92 Stinger infrared homing missile on the starboard engine; although it was left with only one operational engine, the aircraft successfully returned to base.

The entire Indian Air Force Canberra fleet was grounded and then retired following the crash of an IAF Canberra in December 2005. After 50 years of service, the Canberra was finally retired by the IAF on 11 May 2007.

Africa

SAAF Canberra B12 with inertial navigation and special sensors package over Transvaal.

During the Suez Crisis the RAF employed around 100 Canberras, flying conventional bombing and reconnaissance missions from airfields in both Malta and Cyprus. A total of 278 Canberra sorties were flown, dropping 1,439 1000 lb (450 kg) bombs; however low-level strikes by smaller fighters were judged to be more effective than the night time bombing operations performed by both the Canberra and the Vickers Valiant. In addition, many of the bombs, intended to hit Egyptian airfields, missed their targets, failing to do much damage to the Egyptian Air Force or to badly effect enemy morale. While interception of the Canberra was within the capabilities of Egypt's MiG-15s and MiG-17s, as shown by the interception of Canberras by MiG-15s prior to the Anglo-French invasion, these did not result in any losses. The only Canberra shot down during the Suez campaign was a PR7 shot down by a Syrian Gloster Meteor fighter on 6 November 1956, the last day of the war.

The Federation of Rhodesia and Nyasaland considered the Canberra an important objective to holding greater diplomatic sway in the African continent, and ongoing negotiations over the Baghdad treaty, and a step towards decolonisation. The Suez Crisis caused a delay in the sale, but in August 1957 18 Canberras had been earmarked to be refurbished and transferred from the RAF to the Royal Rhodesian Air Force (RRAF). Both Rhodesia and South Africa used Canberras in their respective Bush Wars; numerous aircraft were lost in the conflicts. Rhodesian Canberras carried out attacks on Mozambique, often armed with cluster bombs, more limited raids on Zambia, and an attack upon a terrorist base in Angola. Ethiopian Canberras were used against Eritrea and again against Somalia during the 1970s.

Europe

The Swedish Air Force purchased two Canberras from the RAF in 1960 and had these modified to T11s by Boulton Paul. The aircraft were secretly modified in Sweden as espionage aircraft for eavesdropping on primarily Soviet, Polish and East German military radio transmissions, although this was not publicly admitted until 10 years later. The Canberras were given the designation Tp 52, and taken into service as "testing aircraft", until they were replaced by two Tp 85 Caravelles in 1971.

South America

B-108 on its last mission

The Argentine Air Force received 10 B62 and two T64 trainers at the beginning of the 1970s. During the 1982 Falklands War, eight of them were deployed to Trelew, a distance of 670 miles (1,080 km) from the islands, to avoid congestion on the closer southern airfields. They were within operating range of the British task force, but the Canberra was judged to be a limited threat due to its poor manoeuvrability compared with the Sea Harriers on air defence duties. On 1 May 1982, during an attack on the British ships sailing towards the islands by several Israeli-made Daggers and a sole Canberra, the bomber, along with at least one of the Daggers, was shot down by the responding Sea Harriers for no losses on the British side. Following this engagement, Argentina stopped using the Canberra on such missions.

Nonetheless, from 1 May to 14 June 1982, the Argentine Canberras made 54 sorties; 36 of them bombing missions, of which 22 were at night against ground troops. Two aircraft were lost in combat, one to a Sea Harrier using an AIM-9L Sidewinder Air-to-air missile on 1 May 1982, and another to a Sea Dart missile on 13 June fired by HMS *Cardiff*. This latter aircraft was the last Argentine aircraft to be lost in combat during the Falklands War. Argentina retired its last Canberras in April 2000.

Peruvian Air Force Canberras flew combat sorties against Ecuadorian positions during the Cenepa War in 1995. On 6 February 1995, a Canberra Mk.68 disappeared over the operations zone; the aircraft had apparently struck a hill in poor weather conditions. Peru retired its Canberras in June 2008.

Development and trials aircraft

A former Canberra D14 used for development and trials work

A number of Canberras were used by English Electric for development work and trials on new equipment. It was also used by government establishments such as the Royal Aircraft Establishment and the Royal Radar Establishment. The Canberra proved to be a useful platform for such work and was used by a number of British tests and trials establishments. As well as those operated by English Electric a number of engine manufacturers were also loaned Canberras as engine test beds; Armstrong Siddeley for the Sapphire, Bristol Siddeley for the Olympus, de Havilland Engine Company for the Gyron Junior turbojet and Rolls-Royce Limited for the Avon. Ferranti used four different Canberra B2s for avionics development work.

WV787 a Canberra B2 with a modified nose used for trials and development work. On display at the Newark Air Museum in 2006

One example is *WV787* which was built as a Canberra B2 in 1952, it was loaned to Armstrong Siddeley and was fitted with Armstrong Siddeley Sapphire engines. It was later transferred to Ferranti for trials for the Blackburn Buccaneer radar and fitted with a B(I)8 type nose and a Buccaneer style radome. It next was moved to the Aeroplane and Armament Experimental Establishment where it was modified to be used as a water-spray tanker aircraft for de-icing trials. It would fly in front of the aircraft being tested which would fly into the artificial cloud created by the sprayed water to induce icing. It was retired in 1984 and later preserved at the Newark Air Museum and is a National Benchmark airframe on the National Aviation Heritage Register.

Flight records set by Canberras

- 21 January 1951 - first non-stop unrefuelled transatlantic crossing by a jet.
- 26 August 1952 - the prototype B5 made the first double transatlantic crossing by a jet, with a total time of 10 hr 3 min.
- 4 May 1953 - Canberra B2 *WD952*, fitted with Rolls-Royce Olympus engines set a world altitude record - 63,668 ft (19,406 m)
- 29 August 1955 - altitude record - 65,889 ft (20,083 m)
- 28 August 1957 - altitude record - 70,310 ft (21,430 m): Canberra B2 (*WK163*) with a Napier *Double Scorpion* rocket motor.

Variants

Argentine Air Force Canberra Mk.62 at Museo Nacional de Aeronáutica in Buenos Aires

See B-57 Canberra article for the US-built variants.

English Electric A.1
Company designation for the first four aircraft before being named Canberra.

Canberra B1
Prototypes for type development work and research at first known by the company designation A1, four built.

Canberra B2
First production version, crew increased to three with addition of bomb aimer, Avon R.A.3 engines with 6,500 lbf (28.91 kN) of thrust, wingtip fuel tanks. 418 built by English Electric (208), Avro (75), Handley Page (75) and Short Brothers & Harland (60) including eight for export (Australia, United States and Venezuela).

Canberra PR3
Photo-reconnaissance version of B2, it had a 14 inch section added to the fuselage to house the camera bay, internal fuel was increased and flat panel in the nose was removed. Needed only two crew. The prototype was flown on 19 March 1950 and the variant entered service in 1953.

Canberra T4
First trainer variant with dual controls and a crew of three.

Canberra B5
Prototype of second-generation Canberra with fuel tanks in the wings and Avon R.A.7 engines with 7,490 lbf (33.32 kN) of thrust, one built.

Canberra B6
Production version based on B5 with a 1 ft (0.3 m) fuselage stretch, 106 built by English Electric (57) and Short Brothers & Harland (49), includes 12 for export.

Canberra B6(RC)
RC = Radio Countermeasures (also known as B6(Mod) or PR16) - Specialist ELINT version with enlarged nose and Blue Shadow Side Looking Airborne Radar (SLAR). Only four produced, extended nose.

Canberra B(I)6
Interim interdictor version for the RAF pending delivery of the B(I)8. Based on B6 with a detachable ventral pack housing four 20 mm Hispano cannon for strafing; also had provision for two wing hard points. 22 produced.

Canberra PR7
Photo-reconnaissance version based on B6, had similar equipment to the PR3 but had the uprated Avon 109 engines of the B6 and increased internal fuel capacity, 74 built.

Canberra B(I)8
Third-generation Canberra derived from B6 as an interdictor. Fitted with a new forward fuselage with teardrop canopy on the port side, and Navigator station forward of pilot (early marks had the navigator behind the pilot. Provision for a ventral pack similar to the B(I)6 with 4 x 20 mm Hispano cannon, one external hardpoint under each wing for up to 1,000 lb (454 kg) of bombs or unguided rockets, LABS (Low-Altitude Bombing System) for delivery of nuclear bombs. Prototype converted from the only B5 and first flown 23 July 1954, 72 built including 17 for export and two converted from B2s.

Preserved PR9 XH135 at Kemble Airport. Note the offset pilot's canopy. The navigator sits inside the nose section

Canberra PR9
Photo-reconnaissance version based on B(I)8 with fuselage stretched to 68 ft (27.72 m), wingspan increased by 4 ft (1.22 m), and Avon R.A.27 (Avon 206) engines with 10,030 lbf (44.6 kN) of thrust. Had the offset canopy of the B(I)8 with a hinged nose to allow fitment of an ejection seat for the navigator. A total of 23 built by Short Brothers & Harland with three transferred to Chile after the Falklands War.

Canberra U10 (later designated D10)
Remote-controlled target drones converted from B2. 18 converted.

Canberra T11
Nine B2s converted to trainers for pilots and navigators of all-weather interceptors to operate the Airborne Intercept radar, crew of four.

Canberra B(I)12
Canberra B(I)8 bombers built for New Zealand and South Africa.

Canberra T13
Training version of the T4 for New Zealand, one built new and one conversion from T4.

Canberra U14 (later designated D14)
Remote-controlled target drones converted from the B2 for Royal Navy. Six converted.

Canberra B15
Upgraded B6 for use in the Far and Near East with underwing hardpoints for 1,000 lb (454 kg) bombs or rockets. New avionics and fitting of three cameras, 39 conversions.

Canberra B16
Similar to B15 for use in Germany and fitted with Blue Shadow, 19 conversions

Canberra T17
Electronic warfare training variant used to train surface-based radar and missile operators and airborne fighter and Airborne Early Warning crews in handling jamming (including chaff dropping) aircraft. 24 conversions from B2 with extended nose for sensors.

Canberra T17A
Updated version of the T17 with improved navigation aids, a spectrum analyser in place of the previously-fitted AN/APR-20, and a powerful communications jammer.

Canberra TT18
Target tug conversion of B2 for the Royal Navy, 22 conversions.

Canberra T19
T11 with radar removed as silent target.

Canberra B20
B2 with additional fuel tanks in the wings, licence-built in Australia.

Canberra T21
Trainers converted from B2 and B20.

Canberra T22
Conversion of the PR7 for Royal Navy's Fleet Requirement and Air Direction Unit, used for training Buccaneer navigators.

Canberra Mk.52
Refurbished B2 bombers sold to Ethiopia.

Canberra Mk.56
Refurbished B(I)6 bombers sold to Peru.

Canberra PR57
Tropicalized PR7 for India.

Canberra B(I)58
Tropicalized B(I)8 for India.

Canberra Mk.62
10 refurbished B2 bombers sold to Argentina.

Canberra Mk.64
2 refurbished T4 trainers sold to Argentina.

Canberra Mk.66
10 refurbished B(I)6 bombers sold to India.

Canberra Mk.67
2 refurbished PR7s sold to India.

Canberra Mk.68
1 refurbished B(I)8 bomber sold to Peru.

Canberra B92
1 modified B2 for Argentina, not delivered and embargoed in 1982.

Canberra T94
1 modified T4 for Argentina, not delivered and embargoed in 1982.

Short SC.9
1 Canberra PR9 rebuilt by Shorts fitted with an AI.23 radar, plus IR installation in the nose for Red Top air-to-air missile trials. Continued in use for radar missile development work.

Short SD.1
1 Canberra PR3 modified to carry two Short SD.2 variants of the Beech AQM-37A high-speed target missiles for trials by the Royal Aircraft Establishment.

Operators

Canberra (dark blue) and B-57 (light blue) operators

One of two Canberras operated by the Luftwaffe at the museum at Gatow Airport

Wreckage of a crashed Indian Air Force Canberra in Agra, India on 19 December 2005.

Argentina
- Argentine Air Force purchased 10 refurbished ex-RAF B2s and 2 T4s (redesignated B62 and B64 respectively in 1967. Two further aircraft were ordered in 1981 but were not delivered owing to the Falklands War.

Australia
- Royal Australian Air Force (58)
  - No. 1 Squadron RAAF
  - No. 2 Squadron RAAF
  - No. 6 Squadron RAAF
  - No. 1 Operational Conversion Unit RAAF
  - Aircraft Research and Development Unit RAAF

Chile
- Chilean Air Force (3)

Ecuador
- Ecuadorian Air Force (6) Six new-build B2 variants delivered in 1955.

Ethiopia
- Ethiopian Air Force (4)

France
- French Air Force (6)
  - *Centre d'Essais en Vol*
  - *Centre du Tir et de Bombardement*

Germany
- Luftwaffe (3)

India
- Indian Air Force (107)

New Zealand
- Royal New Zealand Air Force (31)
  - No. 14 Squadron RNZAF
  - No. 75 Squadron RNZAF

Peru
- Peruvian Air Force (60)

Rhodesia
- Royal Rhodesian Air Force (20)

South Africa
- South African Air Force (9)

Sweden
- Swedish Air Force(2)

United Kingdom
- Royal Air Force (782)
- Royal Navy Fleet Air Arm (69)
  - 728B NAS - RNAS Hal Far, Malta
  - Fleet Requirements Unit (FRU)
  - Fleet Requirements and Aircraft Direction Unit (FRADU)
- Royal Aircraft Establishment/DERA (2), RAE Bedford & DERA Llanbder

United States
- United States Air Force (two only for B-57 development)

Venezuela
- Venezuelan Air Force (46)

Zimbabwe
- Air Force of Zimbabwe

Survivors

Several ex-RAF machines and RB-57s remain flying in the US for research and mapping work. About 10 airworthy Canberras are in private hands today, and are flown at air displays. The Temora Aviation Museum, in Australia, has a former RAF Canberra which it acquired in 2001. The aircraft was fully restored to airworthiness and painted to represent the Canberras flown by the Royal Australian Air Force 2 Squadron during the Vietnam war. It is Australia's only airworthy Canberra. The only Canberras, albeit US variants, remaining in active service are two American-built B-57s operated by NASA for high altitude research.

At least two Canberras retired from the Argentine Air Force have been preserved in Argentina:
- B Mk.62 *B-102* (ex-RAF *WJ713*). Retired in 1998, and assigned to "Museo Nacional de Malvinas", Oliva, province of Córdoba.
- B Mk.62 *B-105*. On display at Mar del Plata Air Base, province of Buenos Aires.

Specifications (Canberra B6)

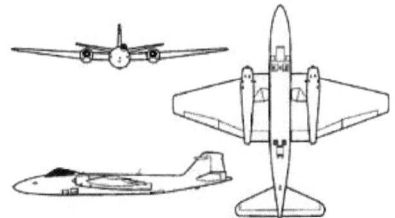

Data from Combat Aircraft Recognition

General characteristics
- **Crew:** 3
- **Length:** 65 ft 6 in (19.96 m)
- **Wingspan:** 64 ft 0 in (19.51 m)
- **Height:** 15 ft 8 in (4.77 m)
- **Wing area:** 960 ft² (89.19 m²)
- **Empty weight:** 21,650 lb (9,820 kg)
- **Loaded weight:** 46,000 lb (20,865 kg)
- **Max takeoff weight:** 55,000 lb (24,948 kg)
- **Powerplant:** 2 × Rolls-Royce Avon R.A.7 Mk.109 turbojets, 7,400 lbf (36 kN) each

Performance
- **Maximum speed:** Mach 0.88 (580 mph, 933 km/h) at 40,000 ft (12,192 m)
- **Combat radius:** 810 mi (700 nm, 1,300 km)
- **Ferry range:** 3,380 mi (2,940 nm, 5,440 km)
- **Service ceiling:** 48,000 ft (15,000 m)
- **Rate of climb:** 3,400 ft/min (17 m/s)
- **Wing loading:** 48 lb/ft² (234 kg/m²)
- **Thrust/weight:** 0.32

Armament
- **Guns:** 4× 20 mm Hispano Mk.V cannons mounted in rear bomb bay (500 rounds/gun), *Or* 2× 0.30 in (7.62 mm) machine gun pods
- **Rockets:** 2× unguided rocket pods with 37× 2 in (51 mm) rockets, *Or* 2× Matra rocket pods with 18× SNEB 68 mm rockets each
- **Missiles:** A variety of missiles can be carried according to mission requirements, e.g: 2× AS-30L air-to-surface missiles
- **Bombs:** Total of 8,000 lb (3,628 kg) of payload can be mounted inside the internal bomb bay and on two underwing hardpoints, with the ability to carry a variety of bombs. Typically, the internal bomb bay can hold up to 9× 500 lb (227 kg) bombs, *Or* 6× 1,000 lb (454 kg) bombs, *Or* 1× 4,000 lb (1,814 kg) bomb; while the pylons can hold 4× 500 lb (227 kg) bombs, *Or* 2× 1,000 lb (454 kg) bombs.
- **Nuclear Weapons:** in addition to conventional ordnance, the Canberra was also type-approved for tactical nuclear weapons delivery, including the Mk 7, B28 (Mod 2, 70 kiloton) and B57 (as part of a joint program with the United States) plus Red Beard and the WE.177A (Mod A, 10 kiloton) nuclear bombs. All nuclear weapons were carried internally.

Source (edited): "http://en.wikipedia.org/wiki/English_Electric_Canberra"

FMA IA 58 Pucará

The **FMA IA 58 Pucará** (Quechua: *Fortress*) is an Argentine ground-attack and counter-insurgency (COIN) aircraft. It is a low-wing two-turboprop-engined all-metal monoplane with retractable landing gear, manufactured by the Fábrica Militar de Aviones.

Development
Development began in August 1966, with the construction of an unpowered test vehicle. The first prototype, called **AX-2 Delfin**, first flew on 20 August 1969, powered by 674-kW (904-shp) Garrett TPE331I/U-303 turboprops. The IA-58 was designed to be able to operate from small front-line airfields. It has a tandem cockpit arrangement; the crew of two is seated under the upward opening clamshell canopy on Martin-Baker Mk 6AP6A zero/zero ejection seats. Dual controls are provided for the crew. In the following prototypes, and the production models that followed, the engines were switched to Turbomeca Astazou XVIG turboprops. The first production model first flew on 8 November 1974, and deliveries began in early 1976.

Operational history
The first units were delivered in 1975 to the Argentine Air Force (Spanish: *Fuerza Aérea Argentina*, FAA), 3rd Air Brigade (Spanish: *III Brigada Aérea*) in northern Reconquista, Santa Fe province.

1982 Falklands war

Cosford Pucara

The Pucara in Duxford

A-528 (8769M) at Flixton Air Museum

Helmet of pilot shot down by small arms fire from 2 PARA during the Falklands War

By the time of the Falklands War (Spanish: *Guerra de las Malvinas*), almost 100 airframes have been delivered and the unit was deployed south to perform coastal surveillance from airfields in Patagonia. It was the only aircraft available in substantial numbers for deployment on the islands as the runway at Port Stanley Airport was not long enough for FAA Skyhawks and Mirages to be deployed.

Most aircraft used in combat were armed with unguided bombs, 2.75 inch rocket pods, or 7.62 mm machine gun pods. *Pucarás* operated from Port Stanley airport and two small grass improvised airfields at Goose Green and Pebble Island. They were used in the reconnaissance and light-attack role.

Three *Pucarás* were destroyed and one of their pilots killed at Goose Green by cluster bombs dropped by 800 NAS Sea Harriers on 1 May 1982. Six more were destroyed in the SAS Raid on Pebble Island on 15 May 1982.

On 21 May a *Pucará* was lost to a Stinger SAM fired by D Squadron SAS (the first Stinger launched in combat) and another to 30 mm cannon rounds from Cmdr Nigel "Sharkey" Ward's RN Sea Harrier, the latter after leading a successful two-aircraft raid on a shed allegedly used as an observation post by British forces. The other *Pucará*, piloted by Lt. Micheloud, made good its escape after being chased by Lt. Cmdr. Alan Craig's Sea Harrier. Major Tomba, the pilot of the aircraft shotdown by Cmdr Ward, survived the ejection and was recovered by friendly forces.

Two *Pucarás* shot down a Royal Marines Scout helicopter with 7.62 mm machine gun fire on 28 May, while it was on a casualty evacuation mission during the battle of Goose Green. This was the only confirmed Argentine air-to-air victory of the war. One of these *Pucarás* crashed into Blue Mountain on the return flight to Port Stanley and was destroyed—the body of the pilot (Lt. Gimenez) was not found until 1986, and was buried with military honours at Port Darwin by his family, the first Argentine relatives to visit the Falklands since the end of the war.

Also on the 28 May 2 Para shot down a Pucará with small arms fire after it launched rockets on British troops (without causing any casualties), during the Battle of Goose Green. Lt Cruzado ejected and became POW.

Captured aircraft

After the Argentine surrender eleven *Pucarás* (four of them in flying condition) were captured by British forces. Six were taken back to the United Kingdom, as follows:

- A-515 (ZD485) – Royal Air Force Museum Cosford.
- A-517 – Privately owned. Possibly shipped to the Channel Islands.
- A-522 (8768M) – North East Aircraft Museum (on loan from the Fleet Air Arm Museum, Yeovilton).
- A-528 (8769M) – Norfolk and Suffolk Aviation Museum (on loan from Museum of Army Flying, Middle Wallop).
- A-533 (ZD486) – Boscombe Down Aviation Collection (Cockpit Section only).
- A-549 (ZD487) – Imperial War Museum Duxford.

Sri Lankan Civil War

Some *Pucarás* were used in Sri Lanka counter-insurgency operations from 1993 to 1999; three were destroyed during combat sorties.

Upgrades

On May 1982, at the peak of the Falklands war, the Argentine Air Force, in collaboration with the Navy, outfitted a prototype, AX-04, with pylons to mount Mark 13 torpedoes. The aim was its possible production as torpedo-carrying aircraft to enhance the anti-ship capabilities of the Argentine air forces. Several trials were performed off Puerto Madryn, over Golfo Nuevo, but the war was over before the technicians could evaluate the feasibility of the project.

In the 1990s the FAA *Pucarás* received several minor upgrades, known as '*IA-58D*'. As of 2010 they remain in service with the 3rd Air Brigade, and with the Uruguayan Air Force.

In 2007 an IA-58 of the Fuerza Aérea Argentina was converted to carry a modified engine operating on soy-derived bio-jet fuel. The project, financed and directed by the Argentine Government (*Secretaría de Ciencia Tecnología e Innovación Productiva de la Nación*), made Argentina the second nation in the world to propel an aircraft with biojet fuel. The project intends to make the FAA less reliant on fossil fuels.

Variants

- **AX-02 Delfin**: Prototype.

- **AX-04**: A torpedo-carrying prototype.
- **IA-58A Pucará**: Two-seat counter-insurgency, close-support, attack aircraft. Main production version.
- **IA-58B Pucará Bravo**: One prototype aircraft, with advanced avionics and armed with two 30-mm DEFA cannons.
- **IA-58C Pucará Charlie**: One single-seat prototype aircraft.
- **IA-58D Pucará Delta**: Upgraded IA-58A with minor revisions
- **IA-66**: One prototype aircraft, powered by two 1,000-ehp (746-kW) Garrett TPE331-11-601W turboprop engines.

Military operators

Current Operators

Argentina
- Argentine Air Force

Uruguay
- Uruguayan Air Force

Former Operators

Colombia
- Colombian Air Force

Sri Lanka
- Sri Lanka Air Force (1993–1999, 2 shot down, 1 crashed, 1 retired)

Specifications

Data from

General characteristics
- **Crew:** 2
- **Capacity:** 2
- **Length:** 14.25 m (46 ft 9 in)
- **Wingspan:** 14.5 m (47 ft 6 in)
- **Height:** 5.36 m (17 ft 7 in)
- **Wing area:** 30.3 m² (326.16 ft²)
- **Empty weight:** 4,020 kg (8,862 lb)
- **Gross weight:** 6,800 kg (14,991 lb)
- **Powerplant:** 2 × Turbomeca Astazou XVIG turboprops, 729 kW (978 hp) each each

Performance
- **Maximum speed:** 500 km/h (310 mph)
- **Cruising speed:** 430 km/h (267 mph)
- **Range:** 3,710 km (2,305 miles)
- **Service ceiling:** 10,000 m (31,800 ft)

Armament
- 2 × 20 mm Hispano-Suiza HS.804 autocannons
- 4 × 7.62 mm FM M2-20 machine guns
- 3 × hardpoints for up to 1,500 kg (3,300 lb) of gun pods, bombs, rockets, mines, or torpedoes

Source (edited): "http://en.wikipedia.org/wiki/FMA_IA_58_Pucar%C3%A1"

Fokker F27 Friendship

The **Fokker F27 Friendship** is a turboprop airliner designed and built by the Dutch aircraft manufacturer Fokker.

Design and development

Design of the Fokker F27 started in the 1950s as a replacement to the successful Douglas DC-3 airliner. The manufacturer evaluated a number of different configurations before finally deciding on a high-wing twin Rolls-Royce Dart engine layout with a pressurised cabin for 28 passengers.

The first prototype, registered PH-NIV, first flew on November 24, 1955. The second prototype and initial production machines were 0.9 m (3 ft) longer, addressing the first aircraft's slightly tail-heavy handling and also providing space for four more passengers, bringing the total to 32. These aircraft also used the more powerful Dart Mk 528 engine.

Production

Aer Lingus was the first airline to operate the F27 Friendship

Braathens SAFE F27 Friendship in August 1964

The first production model, the F27-100, was delivered to Aer Lingus in November 1958. Other early Friendship customers included Braathens SAFE, Luxair, Ansett, Trans Australia Airlines and Turkish Airlines.

In 1956, Fokker signed a licensing deal with the US aircraft manufacturer Fairchild for the latter to construct the F27 in the USA. The first U.S.-built aircraft flew on April 12, 1958. Fairchild also independently developed a stretched version, called the FH-227. Most sales by Fairchild were made in the North American market.

At the end of the Fokker F27's production in 1987, 586 units had been built (plus another 207 F-27s and FH-227s in the USA by Fairchild), more than any other western European civil turboprop airliner.

Many aircraft have been modified from passenger service to cargo or express-package freighter roles and remain in service in 2009. The last major user of the F27 in the United States was Fedex Express, as cargo "feeder" aircraft. These were retired and replaced by ATR42 and ATR72 aircraft by the end of 2009, with the last of the aircraft being donated to Hickory Aviation Museum.

In the early 1980s, Fokker developed a successor to the Friendship, the Fokker 50. Although based on the F27-500 airframe, the Fokker 50 is virtually a new aircraft with Pratt & Whitney Canada engines and modern systems. Its general performance and passenger comfort were improved over the F27.

Variants

F27-300M Troopship

- **F27-100** - was the first production model; 44 passengers.
- **F27-200** - uses the Dart Mk 532 engine.
- **F27-300 Combiplane** - Civil passenger/cargo aircraft.
- **F27-300M Troopship** - Military transport version for Royal Netherlands Air Force.
- **F27-400** - "Combi" passenger/cargo aircraft, with two Rolls-Royce Dart 7 turboprop engines and large cargo door.
- **F27-400M** - Military version for US Army with designation **C-31A Troopship**.
- **F27-500** - The most ubiquitous Fokker F27 model the -500, had a 1.5 m (4 ft 11 in) longer fuselage, a return to the Dart Mk 528 engine, and accommodation for up to 52 passengers. It first flew in November 1967.
- **F27-500M** - Military version.
- **F27-500F** - A version of the -500 for Australia with smaller front and rear doors.
- **F27-600** - Quick change cargo/passenger version of -200 with large cargo door.
- **F27-700** - A F27-100 with a large cargo door.
- **F27 200-MAR** - Unarmed maritime reconnaissance version.
- **F27 Maritime Enforcer** - Armed maritime reconnaissance version.
- **FH-227** - Fairchild Hiller stretched version.

Operators

Map of F27 operators. Light blue indicates civilian use. Dark blue indicates civilian and military use. Red indicates military use.

- Algeria
- Angola
- Argentina
- Australia
- Bangladesh
- Biafra
- Bolivia
- Brazil
- Côte d'Ivoire
- Cuba
- Denmark
- England
- Finland
- Ghana
- Guatemala
- Honduras
- India
- Indonesia
- Iran
- Iceland
- Italy
- Luxembourg
- Mexico
- Myanmar
- Netherlands
- Norway
- New Zealand
- Nigeria
- Pakistan
- Panama
- Peru
- Philippines
- Senegal
- Spain
- Sudan
- Sweden
- Thailand
- Turkey
- United States
- Uruguay
- Yemen

Notable accidents

- TAA Fokker Friendship disaster - June 10, 1960 Mackay, Queensland, Australia: 29 fatalities - this is still the deadliest civilian Australian aircraft accident in history. The investigation was not able to determine a probable cause of this accident.
- Pakistan International Airlines Flight 631 crashed on December 8, 1972 Multan, Pakistan: 26 fatalities.
- On September 15, 1978, a Philippine Air Force F-27 crashed due to windshear. 15 of the 24 people on board were killed, as well as 17 people on the ground.
- On May 26, 1980, a Nigerian Air Force F-27 crashed due to a thunderstorm, killing all 30 people on board. The aircraft was carrying a delegation of military and government officials on a diplomatic mission.
- On August 4, 1984, a Biman Bangladesh Airlines flight from Chittagong crashed in the swamps near Shahjalal International Airport. All 45 passengers and 4 crew of the F27 died. The flight was piloted by Kaniz Fatema Roksana, the country's first female commercial pilot.
- On December 8, 1987, the Alianza Lima air disaster in which a Naval F27 that was transporting the Alianza Lima football club crashed in Lima, Peru, killing the whole team.
- On October 19, 1988, thirty-four died in a Vayudoot F27 crash near Guwahati, India.
- On February 12, 1990, a TAM Air-

lines Fokker F27 registration PT-LCG operating a flight from São Paulo-Congonhas to Bauru, due to faulty approach procedures touched down at Bauru 775m past the runway threshold. The pilot was unable to initiate a go around procedure and went past the end of the runway hitting a car that was passing on a road nearby. One crew member and 2 occupants of the car died.
- November 11, 2002, a Laoag Air F27 crashed into Manila Bay, killing 20 people.
- On February 20, 2003, a military F27 crashed in northwestern Pakistan killing Pakistan Air Force Chief, Air Chief Marshal Mushaf Ali Mir, his wife and 15 others.
- Pakistan International Airlines Flight 688 carrying 45 people crashed 2–3 minutes after take off from Multan airport on July 10, 2006. There were no survivors. Engine fire was suspected as the cause of the crash.
- On April 6, 2009, an Indonesian Air Force F27 crashed in Bandung, Indonesia killing all 24 occupants on board. The cause of the incident was said to be heavy rain. The plane reportedly crashed into a hangar during its landing procedure and killed all on board. The casualties include: 6 crews, an instructor and 17 special forces trainee personnel

Specifications (F27 500)

F27 Rolls Royce Dart

Data from
General characteristics
- **Crew:** Two or three
- **Capacity:** 48-56 passengers
- **Length:** 25.06 m (82 ft 2½ in)
- **Wingspan:** 29.00 m (95 ft 1¾ in)
- **Height:** 8.72 m (28 ft 7¼ in)
- **Wing area:** 70.0 m² (754 ft²)
- **Empty weight:** 11,204 kg (24,650 lb)
- **Max takeoff weight:** 19,773 kg (43,500 lb)
- **Powerplant:** 2× Rolls-Royce Dart Mk.532-7 turboprop engines, 1,678 kW (2,250 eshp) each

Performance
- **Cruise speed:** 518 km/h (280 kn, 322 mph) at 20,000 ft (6,100 m)
- **Range:** 1,826 km (986 nmi, 1,135 mi)
- **Rate of climb:** 7.37 m/s (1,450 ft/min)

Source (edited): "http://en.wikipedia.org/wiki/Fokker_F27_Friendship"

Fokker F28 Fellowship

The **Fokker F28 Fellowship** is a short range jet airliner designed and built by defunct Dutch aircraft manufacturer Fokker.

Design and development
Announced by Fokker in April 1962, production was a collaboration between a number of European companies, namely Fokker, MBB of West Germany, Fokker-VFW (also of Germany), and Short Brothers of the United Kingdom. There was also government money invested in the project, with the Dutch government providing 50% of Fokker's stake and the West German government having 60% of the 35% German stake.

Projected at first to transport 50 passengers to 1,650 km (1,025 mi), the plane was later designed to have 60-65 seats. On the design sheet, the F28 was originally to mount Bristol Siddeley BS.75 turbofans, but the prototype flew with the lighter Rolls-Royce "Spey Junior", a simplified version of the Rolls-Royce Spey.

The F28 was similar in design to the BAC 1-11 and DC-9, as it had a T-tail and the engines at the rear of the fuselage. The aircraft had wings with a slight crescent angle of sweep with ailerons at the tip, simple flaps, and five-section liftdumper only operated after landing to dump the lift. The leading edge was fixed and was anti-iced by bleed air from the engines. The tail cone could split and be hydraulically opened to the sides to act as a variable air brake - also used on the contemporaneous Blackburn Buccaneer. This design was also copied and used on the HS-146, which became the BAe-146. It had a retractable tricycle landing gear.

In terms of responsibility for production, Fokker designed and built the nose section, centre fuselage and inner wing; MBB/Fokker-VFW constructed the forward fuselage, rear fuselage and tail assembly; and Shorts designed and built the outer wings.

Final assembly of the Fokker F28 was at Schiphol Airport in the Netherlands.

Operational history

F28-2000 prototype.

The F28-1000 prototype, registered PH-JHG, first flew on May 9, 1967 (exactly one month later than the famous Boeing 737). German certification was achieved on February 24, 1969. The first order was from German airline LTU, but the first revenue-earning

Fokker F28 Fellowship

flight was by Braathens on March 28, 1969 who operated five F28s.

Montenegro Airlines Fokker F28 landing at Karlovy Vary International Airport

The F28 with an extended fuselage was named F28-2000 and could seat up to 79 passengers instead of the 65 seats on the F28-1000. The prototype for this model was a converted F28-1000 prototype, and first flew on April 28, 1971. The models F28-6000 and F28-5000 were modified F28-2000 and F28-1000 respectively, with slats, greater wingspan, and more powerful and silent engines as the main features. The F28-6000 and F28-5000 were not a commercial success; only two F28-6000 and no F28-5000 were built. After being used by Fokker for a time, the F28-6000 were sold to Air Mauritanie, but not before they were converted to F28-2000s.

The most successful F28 was the F28-4000, which debuted on October 20, 1976 with the one of the world's largest Fokker operators, Linjeflyg. This version was powered by quieter Spey 555-15H engines, and had an increased seating capacity (up to 85 passengers), a larger wingspan with reinforced wings, a new cockpit and a new "wide-look" interior featuring enclosed overhead lockers and a less 'tubular' look. The F28-3000, the runner-up for the F28-1000, featured the same improvements as the F28-4000.

F28s of Ansett Transport Industries' Western Australian intrastate airline, MacRobertson Miller Airlines of Western Australia, flew the longest non-stop F28 route in the world, from Perth to Kununurra, in Western Australia - a distance of about 2,240 km (1,392 mi). MMA'a F28s also had the highest utilisation rates at the time, flying over 8 hours per day.

By the time production ended in 1987, 241 airframes had been built.

Variants

Data from

- F.28 Mk 1000 - First variant derived from the third prototype, with a maximum capacity of 65 passengers in a high-density configuration. The Mk 1000 had a length of 27.40 m. It was powered by two Rolls-Royce RB.183-2 Mk.555-15 each with 43.8 kN (9,850 lbf) of thrust. Maximum weight at take-off was 28,123 kg (62,001 lb).
- F.28 Mk 1000C - All-cargo, passenger/cargo version derived from Mk 1000 with a port-side cargo door.
- F.28 Mk 2000 - It first flew on April 28, 1971, being certified on August 30, 1972. This variant had a fuselage 2.21 m longer than the Mk 1000, with a passenger capacity of 79 in high-density single-class configuration. It began revenue service with Nigeria Airways in October 1972. Ten were built.

Dash-3000 variant in VIP configuration from the Colombian Air Force

- F.28 Mk 3000 - With the shorter fuselage of Mk 1000, it was one of the more successful variants, with greater structural strength and increased fuel capacity. It began revenue service with Garuda Airlines.
- F.28 Mk 4000 - The first prototype appeared on October 20, 1976 and had the longer fuselage of the Mk 2000 with a passenger capacity of 85. Wingspan was increased by 1.57 m and more powerful Rolls-Royce RB183 "Spey" Mk555-15P of 44 kN (9,901 lbf) thrust. It began service with Linjeflyg (Sweden) at the end of 1976.
- F.28 Mk 5000 - Derived from the Mk 6000, was to combine the shorter fuselage of the Mk 3000 and an increased wingspan. Slats were to be added to the wings and more powerful Rolls-Royce "Spey" Mk555-15H engines were to be used. Although expected to be an excellent plane to operate in short runways due to its superior power, it was finally not built and the project was abandoned.
- F.28 Mk 6000 - It first flew on September 27, 1973 and had the longer fuselage of the Mk 2000/4000 with an increased wingspan and the Slats. It was certified in October 1975.
- F.28 Mk 6600 - Proposed version. Not built.

Accidents and incidents

According to , the Fokker F28 has an average fatal incident rate of 1.67 per million flights.:

- Braathens Flight 239 - December 23, 1972, (Asker, suburb to Oslo, Norway): 40 fatalities. First fatal crash with a Fokker Fellowship.
- Turkish Airlines - January 26, 1974, (Izmir, Turkey): 66 fatalities. the aircraft crashed down 100m away from the airfield during takeoff.
- Turkish Airlines - January 30, 1975, (Marmara sea,near to Istanbul, Turkey): 41 fatalities. Crashed into the Sea of Marmara while attempting to land.
- Garuda Indonesia Airways Flight 150- 24 September 1975 near Palembang, Indonesia): 26 fatalities. crashed on approach in fog killing 25 people out of 61 passengers and crew. 1 person was killed on the ground.
- Garuda Indonesia Airways- July 11, 1979. 61 fatalities. Crashed into Mount Sibayak while on approach to Polonia International Airport. There

was bad weather at the time of the crash.
- Turkish Airlines - December 23, 1979, (Ankara, Turkey): 39 fatalities. Because of turbulence.
- NLM Cityhopper Flight 431 - October 6, 1981 (Moerdijk, North Brabant, Netherlands): 17 fatalities, the aircraft flew into a tornado which broke off one of the wings which led to a mid-air break up.
- Garuda Indonesia Domestic Flight - March 20, 1982, runway overrun at Tanjung Karang-Branti Airport in bad weather, 27 fatalities.
- Air Ontario Flight 1363 - March 10, 1989 (Dryden, Ontario, Canada): 24 fatalities. Due to various factors including snow, ice and lack of use of anti-icing measures.
- USAir Flight 405 - March 22, 1992 (Queens, New York, United States): 27 fatalities. Due to ice buildup on the wings, pilot error and improper deicing procedures at LaGuardia airport
- Iran Asseman Airlines Flight 746 - October 12, 1994 (near Natanz, Iran): 66 fatalities.
- Biman Bangladesh Flight 609 - December 22, 1997 (Sylhet, Bangladesh): No fatalities, CFIT onto a rice field approx 1 mile from runway. Aviation-Safety.net report
- TANS Peru Flight 222 - January 9, 2003: None of the 46 passengers aboard the Fokker F-28 survived after the aircraft hit a mountain near Chachapoyas, Peru
- Biman Bangladesh parked at Shahjalal International Airport - April 22, 2003 Aviation-Safety.net report
- Biman Bangladesh Flight 601 - October 8, 2004 (Sylhet, Bangladesh): No fatalities, overran runway on landing. Pictures at AirDisaster.com - Aviation-Safety.net report
- Icaro Air Flight 504 crashed during take off at Quito's Mariscal Sucre Airport No deaths, or injuries occurred.

More complete list of incidents at AirDisaster.com

Operators

In August 2006 a total of 92 Fokker F28 aircraft (all variants) remained in airline service. Major operators included: Garuda Indonesia (62 in total, the largest F-28 fleet in the world), MacRobertson Miller Airlines, Ansett Group Australia (more than 15), Toumaï Air Tchad (1), AirQuarius Aviation (3), SkyLink Arabia (1), Satena (1), Gatari Air Service (5), Montenegro Airlines (5), LADE - Lineas Aéreas del Estado (1),Aerolineas Argentinas operated 3 1000 series and one 4000 series, all scrapped by the end of the nineties, Pelita Air(5), AirQuarius Aviation (4) and Merpati Nusantara Airlines (1). Some 22 airlines operated smaller numbers of the type.

Military Operators

COAN (ARA) F-28 at Comandante Espora airbase

- Argentina
  - Argentine Air Force
  - Argentine Navy - Argentine Naval Aviation
- Cambodia
- Côte d'Ivoire
- Colombia
- Ecuador
- Gabon
- Ghana
- Indonesia
- Malaysia
- Netherlands
(Dutch Royal Flight)
- Peru
- Philippines
(Domestic Presidential Flights).The aircraft was named "Kalayaan"
- Tanzania
- Togo

Specifications
Data from
Source (edited): "http://en.wikipedia.org/wiki/Fokker_F28_Fellowship"

Grumman S-2 Tracker

The **Grumman S-2 Tracker** (previously **S2F** prior to 1962) was the first purpose-built, single airframe anti-submarine warfare (ASW) aircraft to enter service with the US Navy.

Its predecessor, Grumman's AF-2 Guardian was the first purpose-built aircraft system for ASW, using two airframes, one with the detection gear, and the other with the weapons.

Design and development

Grumman's design (model **G-89**) was for a large high-wing monoplane with twin Wright Cyclone radial engines. Both the two prototypes **XS2F-1** and 15 production aircraft, **S2F-1** were ordered at the same time, on 30 June 1950. First flight was 4 December 1952, and production aircraft entered service, with VS-26, in February 1954.

Follow-on versions included the **WF Tracer** and **TF Trader**, which became the Grumman E-1 Tracer and Grumman C-1 Trader in the tri-service designation standardization of 1962. The S-2 carried the nickname "Stoof" (S-two-F) throughout its military career; and the E-1 Tracer variant with the large overhead radome was called the "stoof with a roof.".

Grumman produced 1,185 Trackers. Another 99 aircraft carrying the **CS2F** designation were manufactured in Canada under license by de Havilland Canada. U.S.-built versions of the Tracker were sold to various nations, including Australia, Japan, Turkey and Taiwan.

Operational history

US Navy S-2 *Tracker* on the port catapult of USS *Lexington* (CVS-16) ready for take-off, 22 January 1963

The Tracker was eventually superseded for U.S. military use by the Lockheed S-3 Viking, the last USN Tracker squadron (VS-37 with S-2G models) was disestablished in 1976. The last Navy S-2 was withdrawn from service on 29 August 1976. A number live on as firefighting aircraft, however. Trackers continued to provide excellent service with the naval forces of other countries for years after the U.S. discontinued them. For example, the Royal Australian Navy continued to use Trackers as front line ASW assets until the mid 1980s.

Argentina

Argentine S-2T Turbo Tracker

The Argentine Naval Aviation received seven S-2A in 1962, six S-2E in 1978 and three S-2G in 1990s. They were used from both aircraft carriers, the ARA *Independencia* and the ARA *25 de Mayo* and used in the COD (US-2A conversions), Maritime Patrol and ASW roles. They were extensively used in the 1982 Falklands War, first from the *25 de Mayo*, from where they detected the British Task Force and then from the mainland when the carrier return to port after the sinking of the ARA *General Belgrano* cruiser. In the 1990s, six remaining airframes where refurbished by Israel Aerospace Industries with turboprop engines as S-2T Turbo Trackers. As of 2010, with the retirement of Argentina's only aircraft carrier, the Trackers are annually deployed on board Brazilian Navy NAe *São Paulo* during joint exercises ARAEX and TEMPEREX and with US Navy's aircraft carriers during Gringo-Gaucho maneuvers.

Australia

Australian Tracker *845* "in the chocks" prepares to launch from HMAS *Melbourne*, 1979

Between 1967 and 1984 the Royal Australian Navy operated two Squadrons of S-2E and S-2G variants, based at NAS Nowra (HMAS *Albatross*). These were VS-816 front line squadron, which embarked in the *Majestic* class aircraft carrier HMAS *Melbourne*, as part of the 21st Carrier Air Group whenever that ship was deployed; and VC-851 training squadron.

During approximately 17 years of operation of the Tracker, the RAN lost only one S-2 during aircraft operations due to an accident at sea on 10 February 1975. However, on 4 December 1976 a deliberately lit fire in a hangar at Nowra destroyed or badly damaged a large proportion of the RAN's complement of Trackers. These were subsequently replaced with ex-USN aircraft. The replacement aircraft were all S-2Gs, including the original aircraft modified by the USN to that status. This saw the introduction of AQA-7 acoustic gear into RAN service and all RAN operational Trackers were subsequently modified to this standard.

Brazil

The Brazilian Air Force used Trackers. They operated from the aircraft carrier NAeL *Minas Gerais*. Both S-2A and S-2E were used (respectively as P-16A and P-16E) at the end of its service in Brazilian Air Force, one S-2T was used as a possible upgrade, but due the high costs it was canceled.

Canada

Canadian Forces CP-121 Tracker from VU-33 folds its wings while taxiing at CFB Moose Jaw in 1982

In 1954, de Havilland Canada entered into a contract to build Trackers under license to replace the outmoded TBM-3E Avengers being used by the Royal

Canadian Navy. A total of 99 Canadian-built Trackers would enter service starting in 1956. From 1957 onwards, these aircraft operated from the newly-deployed aircraft carrier HMCS *Bonaventure* and various shore bases. All the Canadian Trackers were built to the earlier "A" model airframe design with a length of 42 feet (12.80 m) (c.f. 43' 6" for later model Trackers) in order to fit in the *Bonnie's* hangar. In 1960, 17 active-duty CS2F-1 aircraft were transferred to the Royal Netherlands Navy. In 1964, a pair of CS2F-1 aircraft were stripped of armament and ASW electronics, converted to transports, and subsequently used for carrier onboard delivery. The CS2F-1, -2, and -3 were redesignated as the CP-121 Mk.1, Mk. 2, and Mk. 3 respectively following the unification of Canadian forces in 1968.

After *Bonaventure* was decommissioned in 1970, all remaining Canadian Trackers were transferred to shore bases. This limited their usefulness for ASW patrols, and between 1974 and 1981, all but 20 were gradually placed in storage and the remainder were stripped of their ASW gear. The remaining active-duty Trackers served until 1990 doing fisheries protection and maritime patrol duties. A handful of Trackers were kept in flying condition until the late 1990s but were no longer used for active service.

A single Grumman-built S2F-1, serial number X-500, was sold to the RCN before Canadian production commenced. It was initially used for quality control purposes during Canadian production, and was later given a new RCN serial number, upgraded to CS2F-1 standards, and used to train RCN ground and maintenance personnel. This aircraft was placed in storage in 1972 and was undergoing restoration in March 2008.

Japan

Japan Maritime Self-Defense Force S2F-1 at Kanoya Air Base.

The Japan Maritime Self-Defense Force received 50 S2F-1 in 1957 from US, and operated until 1984. After being received, six S2F-1 were reconfigured into four S2F-U and two S2F-C variants. The S2F-1 is nicknamed *Aotaka(あおたか, Blue Hawk)*.

Netherlands

Dutch Grumman S-2 *Tracker*

The Royal Netherlands Navy, (Netherlands Naval Aviation Service) received in 1960 17 CS2F-1 aircraft formerly used by the Royal Canadian Navy. These aircraft were operated from land bases as well as from the light carrier Karel Doorman until a fire in 1968 took that ship out of Dutch service.

Peru

Peruvian Navy S-2E Trackers

The Peruvian Navy operated with S-2E and S-2G from 1975 until 1989, they were assigned to Naval Aviation Squadron N°12 (Escuadron Aeronaval N°12). A total of 12 S-2Es were bought from the US Navy in 1975 and 4 S-2G in 1983.

Taiwan

Grumman received a contract for the conversion of 32 S-2T Trackers (from 25 S-2Es and 7 S-2Gs) in service with the Republic of China Air Force in late 1980s. Only 27 were ultimately converted due to a shortage of parts supplied by Grumman resulting in the use of remaining conversion kits as spare parts. The 27 S-2Ts were transferred to the ROC Navy Aviation Command on 1 July 1999 and while the ROCN continues to operate the type, less than half of the fleet is in operational condition, will be replaced by 12 rebuilt P-3C from US Navy.

The conversion involved: two Garrett/Honeywell TPE-331-15AW turboprop engines, each rated at 1,227 kW (1,645 shp), with four-blade propellers. The upgrade also included new mission equipment of AN/AQS-92F digital sonobuoy processor, A/NARR-84 99-channel sonobuoy receiver, Litton AN/APS-504 radar, AN/ASQ-504 MAD and AN/AAS-40 FLIR. The new turboprop engines resulted in a payload increase of 500 kg. Usually carries depth charges, Mk. 44, and Mk 46 lightweight ASW homing torpedoes.

The Turkish Navy received a number of S-2A Trackers under the MAP program and operated them from the Cengiz Topel Naval Air Base starting in the 1960s. These were later retired and replaced with S-2Es, which remained in service until 1994. Turkish Trackers were retired after a series of accidents caused by the advanced age and fatigue of the airframes.

Uruguay

The Uruguayan Navy received the first three S-2A Trackers on 10 April 1965 at the Capitan Curbelo Navy Base. On 15 September 1982, one S-2G arrived. On 2 February 1983, another two S-2Gs arrived. By September 2004, the remaining Uruguayan Trackers were not in flight condition.

Civilian use

In the late 1980s and early '90s Conair Aviation of Abbotsford, British Columbia, Canada took possession of retired U.S. and Canadian Trackers and converted them into **Firecats**, with a retardant tank replacing the torpedo bay. The Firecats were made in two variants, a piston engine Firecat and a turboprop-powered Turbo Firecat.

Variants

XS2F-1
Two prototype anti-submarine warfare aircraft powered by 1,450 hp R-1820-76WA engines.

YS2F-1
Designation of the first 15 production aircraft used for development, redesignated YS-2A in 1962.

S2F-1
Initial production variant with two 1,525 hp R-1820-82WA engines, redesignated S-2A in 1962, 740 built.

S2F-1T
Trainer conversion of S2F-1, redesignated TS-2A in 1962.

S2F-1U
Utility conversion of S2F-1, redesignated US-2A in 1962.

S2F-1S
S2F-1 conversion with Julie/Jezebel detection equipment, redesignated S-2B in 1962. Survivors converted to US-2B after removal of ASW gear.

S2F-1S1
S2F-1S fitted with updated Julie/Jezebel equipment, redesignated S-2F in 1962.

S2F-2
As S2F-1 with asymmetrical (port-side) extension of bomb bay, slightly enlarged tail surfaces, 77 built, most redesignated S-2C in 1962.

S2F-2P
Photo reconnaissance conversion of S2F-2, redesignated RS-2C in 1962.

S2F-2U
Utility conversion of S2F-2/S-2C, redesignated US-2C in 1962. Some were used as target tugs.

S2F-3
Enlarged forward fuselage, enlarged tail surfaces, additional fuel capacity, and enlarged engine nacelles bays for 32 sonobouoys, redesignated S-2D in 1962, 100 built.

S2F-3S
As S2F-3 but with Julie/Jezebel equipment, redesignated S-2E in 1962, 252 built.

YS-2A
YS2F-1 redesignated in 1962.

S-2A
S2F-1 redesignated in 1962.

TS-2A
S2F-1T training version redesignated in 1962 and 207 conversion from S-2A.

US-2A
S-2A converted as light transports/target tugs, 51 conversions.

S-2B
S2F-1S redesignated in 1962.

US-2B
Utility and target tug conversions of S-2A and S-2B; most S-2Bs were converted and 66 S-2As.

S-2C
S2F-2 redesignated in 1962.

RS-2C
S2F-2P photo-reconnaissance version redesignated in 1962.

US-2C
S2F-2U utility version redesignated in 1962.

S-2D
S2F-3 redesignated in 1962.

YAS-2D/AS-2D
Proposed self-contained night attack aircraft to be developed under Operation Shed Light; none produced.

ES-2D
Electronic trainer conversion of the S-2D.

US-2S
Utility conversion of the S-2D.

S-2E
S2F-3S redesignated in 1962.

S-2F
S2F-1S1 redesignated in 1962.

US-2F
Transport conversion of S-2F.

S-2G
S-2E conversions with updated electronics.

CS2F-1
Initial production run of anti-submarine warfare aircraft for Canada based on S2F-1. A total of 42 built by De Havilland Canada.

CS2F-2
Improved version of CS2F-1 with Litton Industries tactical navigation equipment. A total of 57 were built by De Havilland Canada.

CS2F-3
New designation given to 43 CS2F-2 aircraft upgraded with additional electronics.

CP-121
New designation given to all CS2F-1, -2, and -3 aircraft following unification of Canadian military in 1968.

Military S-2T Turbo Tracker For Argentina
6 upgraded S-2E turboprop engines conversion by IAI in 1990s for the Argentine Navy.

Military S-2T Turbo Tracker For Taiwan
27 out of 32 upgraded S-2E and S-2G turboprop engines conversion by Northrop Grumman in 1990s for then Taiwan/ROC Air Force, now operates by Taiwan/ROC Navy aviation.

S-2T Turbo Tracker
Civil conversion

S-2AT
Civil firefighter conversion.

S-2ET

CDF S-2F3AT Turbine Tracker landing at Fox Field, Lancaster, California, while fighting the North Fire.

Civil conversion.

Marsh S-2F3AT Turbo Tracker
Turboprop conversion, powered by two Garrett TPE331 engines; A total of 22 are operated by the CDF.

Conair Firecat or Turbo Firecat
Civil conversion as a single-seat firefighting aircraft.

• For the crew trainer/transport

version based on the Tracker refer to Grumman C-1 Trader
- For the Airborne Early Warning version based on the Trader refer to Grumman E-1 Tracer

Operators

Military operators

Argentine *Tracker* operating from NAe *São Paulo*

View from an Australian *Tracker* on final approach to Australian aircraft carrier HMAS *Melbourne*

Tracker *848* about to take the wire aboard HMAS *Melbourne*, 1980

Canadian-made CS2F-2 *Tracker*

CDF S-2T on the Sawtooth Complex fire, 2006

French *Sécurité Civile* S-2FT Tracker used for fire-fighting duties

Argentina
- Argentine Naval Aviation

Australia
- Royal Australian Navy

Brazil
- Brazilian Air Force

Canada
- Royal Canadian Navy
- Canadian Forces

Italy
- Italian Air Force

Japan
- Japan Maritime Self-Defense Force

South Korea
- Republic of Korea Navy

Netherlands
- Royal Netherlands Navy

Peru
- Peruvian Navy

Republic of China (Taiwan)
- Republic of China Navy Taiwan currently operates 26 S-2T, not all operational (upgrade from S-2E and S-2G, will be replaced by 12 rebuilt P-3C Orions from US Navy).

Thailand
- Air Division of the Royal Thai Navy

Turkey
- Turkish Navy Aerial Wing

United States
- United States Navy operated their Trackers between 1954 and 1976.
- United States Marine Corps operated some Trackers.

Uruguay
- Uruguayan Navy

Venezuela
- Venezuelan Navy

Civil operators

Many retired *Trackers* were sold to private owners for fire-fighting duties. Some were rebuilt and re-engined with turboprop engines.

Canada
- Conair Group Inc. received TS-2A/Conair Firecat (G-89).
- Saskatchewan Environment received TS-2A/Conair Firecat (G-89).

France
- Sécurité Civile received US-2A/Conair Turbo Firecat (G-89).

Netherlands
- KLM - Royal Dutch Airlines operated S-2 Tracker (G-89/G-121/S2F) - ex-Dutch Navy Tracker was used by KLM to train their mechanics.

United States
- California Department of Forestry & Fire Protection received S-2F3AT Turbo Tracker (G-121)
- Hemet Valley Flying Service received TS-2A(FF) Tracker (G-89)
- Marsh Aviation received S-2A(FF) Tracker (G-89)
- Sis-Q Flying Service received TS-2A Tracker (G-89/S2F-1T)

- Aero Union, in addition to being an operator, Aero Union developed the prototype S-2 tankers for the State of California in 1973.

Aircraft on display

- CP-121 Tracker Canadian Air and Space Museum, Toronto, Ontario, Canada.
- CP-121 Tracker Shearwater Aviation Museum, Halifax, Nova Scotia, Canada.
- S2-E Tracker, s/n 151627, on the flight deck of the USS *Yorktown* (CV-10) at the Patriot's Point Naval and Maritime Museum in Charleston, SC.
- CP-121 Tracker, s/n 121176, Atlantic Canada Aviation Museum
- S2F-1, s/n 136431, on display at Cavanaugh Flight Museum, Addison, Texas.
- CS2F-2 Tracker, RCN s/n 1577 (construction number 76), on display at Canadian Warplane Heritage Museum in Hamilton, Ontario, Canada
- S2 Tracker, on the restoration area of the hangar bay at the USS *Hornet* (CV-12) Museum in Alameda, CA.
- One S2A Tracker and one S2E Tracker, on display at the Brazilian Air Force Aerospace Museum, Rio de Janeiro, Brazil.
- S-2 Tracker, on display at the War Memorial of Korea, Seoul, Republic of Korea
- A S2F-1 is displayed in Kanoya Air Base, Kanoya, Kagoshima.
- US-2A Tracker c/n 173 Argentine Naval Aviation 0510/6-G-52 at Naval Aviation Museum, Bahía Blanca
- S-2A Tracker 133160 C/N 131 Queensland Air Museum, Caloundra, Queensland, Australia

Specifications (S-2F)

Data from Canada Aviation and Space Museum

General characteristics

- **Crew:** four (two pilots, two detection systems operators)
- **Length:** 43 ft 6 in (13.26 m)
- **Wingspan:** 72 ft 7 in (22.12 m)
- **Height:** 17 ft 6 in (5.33 m)
- **Wing area:** 485 ft² (45.06 m²)
- **Empty weight:** 18,315 lb (8,310 kg)
- **Loaded weight:** 23,435 lb (10,630 kg)
- **Max takeoff weight:** 26,147 lb (11,860 kg)
- **Powerplant:** 2× Wright R-1820-82WA radial engines, 1,525 hp (kW) each

Performance

- **Maximum speed:** 280 mph (450 km/h) at sea level
- **Cruise speed:** 150 mph (240 km/h)
- **Range:** 1,350 mi (2,170 km) or 9 hours endurance
- **Service ceiling:** 22,000 ft (6,700 m)

Armament

- 4,800 lb (2,200 kg) of payload could be carried in the internal bomb bay and on 6× under-wing hardpoints
- Torpedoes: Mk. 41, Mk. 43, Mk. 34, or Mk. 44
- Depth charges: Mk. 54 or naval mines

Source (edited): "http://en.wikipedia.org/wiki/Grumman_S-2_Tracker"

Handley Page Victor

The **Handley Page Victor** was a British jet bomber aircraft produced by the Handley Page Aircraft Company during the Cold War. It was the third and final of the *V-bombers* that provided Britain's nuclear deterrent. The other two V-bombers were the Avro Vulcan and the Vickers Valiant. Some aircraft were modified for strategic reconnaissance role using both cameras and radar. After the Royal Navy assumed the nuclear deterrence mission using submarine-launched Polaris missiles in 1969 many surviving bombers were converted into aerial refuelling tankers. The last Victor was retired from service on 15 October 1993.

Design and development

Origins

Following the end of the Second World War, the British Air Ministry drew up its requirements for bombers to replace the piston-engined heavy bombers such as the Avro Lancaster and the new Avro Lincoln which equipped RAF Bomber Command. Its first ideas, which formed Operational Requirement OR.230 were for a long-range jet bomber, capable of carrying a 10,000 lb (4,500 kg) bomb load to a distance of 2,000 nmi (2,300 mi, 3,700 km) at a height of 50,000 ft (15,000 m) and a cruise speed of 575 mph (925 km/h). Responses were received from Short Brothers, Bristol, and Handley Page, but the Air Ministry realised that creating an aircraft to meet these stringent requirements would be technically demanding and would be so expensive that it could only be purchased in small numbers. As a result, realising that the majority of likely targets would not require such a long range, a less demanding specification for a medium-range bomber, Air Ministry Specification B.35/46 was issued. This demanded the ability to carry the same 10,000 lb bomb-load to a target 1,500 nmi (1,725 mi, 2,800 km) away at a height of 45,000–50,000 ft (13,700–15,200 m) at a speed of 575 mph. The weapons load was to include a 10,000 lb "Special gravity bomb" (i.e. a free-fall nuclear weapon), or over shorter ranges 20,000 lb (9,100 kg) of conventional bombs. No defensive weapons were to be carried, the aircraft relying on its speed and height to avoid opposing fighters.

HP.80

Handley Page's design in response to B.35/46 was given the internal designation of HP.80. To achieve the required performance, the HP.80 was given a crescent wing developed by Handley Page's aerodynamicist Dr. Gustav Lachmann and his deputy, Godfrey Lee. The sweep and chord of the wing decrease in three distinct steps from the root to the tip, to ensure a constant limiting Mach number across the entire wing and consequently a high cruise speed.

The HP.80 and Avro's Type 698 were chosen as the best two of the proposed designs to B.35/46, and orders for two prototypes of each were placed. It was recognised, however, that there were many unknowns associated with both designs, and an order was also placed for Vickers' design, which became the Valiant. Although not fully meeting the requirements of the specification, the Valiant design posed little risk of failure and could therefore reach service earlier. The HP.80's crescent wing was tested on a ⅓-scale glider, the HP.87, and a modified Supermarine Attacker, the Handley Page HP.88. The HP.88 crashed on 26 August 1951 after completing only about thirty flights and little useful data was gained during its brief two months of existence. By the time the HP.87 was ready, the HP.80 wing had changed such that the former was no longer representative. At any rate, the design of the HP.80 had sufficiently advanced that the loss of the HP.88 had little effect on the programme.

The nose of a Victor, around 1960

Two HP.80 prototypes, *WB771* and *WB775*, were built. The Victor was a futuristic-looking, streamlined machine, with four turbojet engines buried in the thick wing roots. Distinguishing features of the Victor were its highly swept T-tail with considerable dihedral on the horizontal stabilisers, and a prominent chin bulge that contained the targeting radar, cockpit, nose landing gear unit and an auxiliary bomb aimer's position. Unlike the Vulcan and Valiant, the Victor's pilots sat at the same level as the rest of the crew, thanks to a larger pressurised compartment that extended all the way to the nose. As with the other V-bombers, only the pilots were provided with ejection seats; the three systems operators relying on "explosive cushions" inflated by a CO2 bottle that would help them from their seats and towards a traditional bail out in the event of high g-loading, but despite this, escape for the three backseaters was extremely difficult. It was originally required by the specification that the whole nose section could be detached at high altitudes to act as an escape pod, but the Air Ministry abandoned this demand in 1950.

The Victor's bomb bay was much larger than that of the Valiant and Vulcan, which allowed heavier weapon loads to be carried, but over shorter ranges. As an alternative to the single "10,000 lb" nuclear bomb as required by the specification, the bomb bay was designed to carry a single 22,000 lb (10,000 kg) Grand Slam or two 12,000 lb (5,500 kg) Tallboy earthquake bombs, up to forty-eight 1,000 lb (450 kg) bombs or thirty-nine 2,000 lb (900 kg) sea mines. Underwing panniers that could carry a further 28 1,000 lb bombs were planned although never built.

HP.80 prototype *WB771* was broken down at the Handley Page factory at Radlett and transported by road to RAF Boscombe Down for its first flight. Bulldozers were used on the route to create new paths around obstacles. The sections of the aircraft were hidden under wooden framing and tarpaulins printed with "GELEYPANDHY / SOUTHAMPTON" to make it appear to be a boat hull in transit. GELEYPANDHY was an anagram of "Handley Pyge" marred by a signwriter's error. It made its maiden flight on 24 December 1952.

The HP.80 prototypes performed well, but there were a number of design miscalculations that lead to the loss of *WB771* on 14 July 1954, when the tailplane detached whilst making a low-level pass over the runway at Cranfield, causing the aircraft to crash with the loss of the crew. Attached to the fin using three bolts, the tailplane was subject to considerably more stress than had been anticipated and the three bolts failed due to metal fatigue. Additionally, the aircraft were considerably tail heavy. This was remedied by large ballast weights in the HP.80 prototypes. Production Victors had a lengthened nose that also served to move the crew escape door further from the engine intakes. The fin was shortened to eliminate the potential for flutter while the tailplane attachment was changed to a stronger four-bolt fixing.

Victor B.1

Victor B.1 (*XA922*) on a landing approach

Production *B.1* Victors were powered by the Armstrong Siddeley Sapphire ASSa.7 turbojets rated at 11,000 lbf (49 kN), and was initially equipped with the Blue Danube nuclear weapon, re-equipping with the more powerful Yellow Sun weapon when it became available, although Victors also carried U.S.-owned Mark 5 nuclear bombs (made available under the Project E programme) and the British Red Beard tactical nuclear weapon. A total of 24 were upgraded to *B.1A* standard by the addition of Red Steer tail warning radar in an enlarged tailcone and a suite of radar warning receivers and electronic countermeasures (ECM) from 1958 to 1960.

On 1 June 1956, a production Victor *XA917* flown by test pilot Johnny Allam inadvertently exceeded the speed of sound after Allam let the nose drop slightly at a higher power setting. Allam noticed a cockpit indication of Mach 1.1 and ground observers from Watford to Banbury reported hearing a sonic boom. The Victor was the largest aircraft to have broken the "sound barrier" at that time.

Victor B.2

The RAF required a higher ceiling for its bombers, and a number of proposals were considered for improved Victors to meet this demand. At first, Handley Page proposed use of the 14,000 lbf (62.4 kN) Sapphire 9 engines to produce a "Phase 2" bomber, to be followed by "Phase 3" Victors with much greater wingspan (137 ft (42 m)) and powered by Bristol Siddeley Olympus turbojets or Rolls-Royce Conway turbofans. The Sapphire 9 was cancelled, however, and the heavily modified Phase 3 aircraft would have delayed production, so an interim "Phase 2A" Victor was proposed and accepted, to be powered by the Conway and having minimal modifications.

The "Phase 2A" proposal was accepted by the Air Staff as the *Victor B.2*, with Conway RCo.11 engines providing 17,250 lbf (76.7 kN). This required enlarged and redesigned intakes to provide greater airflow. The wingtips were extended, increasing the wingspan to 120 ft (36.6 m). Unlike the B.1, the B.2 featured distinctive retractable "elephant ear" intakes on the rear fuselage forward of the fin. These scoops fed ram air to turbine-driven alternators, thus their name "Ram Air Turbine" (RAT) scoops. In the event of a high-altitude flameout, the loss of electrical or hydraulic power would trigger the RATs to open and provide sufficient electrical power to work the flight controls until the main engines could be re-lit. The right wing root also incorporated a Blackburn *Artouste* airborne auxiliary power plant (AAPP) or airborne auxiliary power unit (AAPU). This small "5th" engine provided high-pressure air for engine starting, and provided electrical power on the ground, or in the air as an emergency back-up in the event of main engine failures or flameout. The APU was also a useful feature to support operations away from specialist Victor support equipment. The aircraft also featured an extension at the base of the fin containing ECM cooling equipment.

The first prototype Victor B.2, serial number *XH668* made its maiden flight on 20 February 1959. It had flown 100 hours by 20 August 1959, when, while high-altitude engine tests were being carried out by the Aeroplane and Armament Experimental Establishment (A&AEE), it disappeared from radar screens, crashing into the sea off the coast of Pembrokeshire. An extensive search operation was initiated to locate and the wreckage of *XH668* to determine the cause of the crash. It took until November 1960 to recover most of the aircraft, with the accident investigation report concluding that the starboard pitot head had failed during the flight, causing the aircraft's flight control system to force the aircraft into an unrecoverable dive. Only minor changes were needed to resolve this problem, allowing the Victor B.2 to enter service in February 1962.

A total of 21 B.2 aircraft were upgraded to the B.2R standard with Conway RCo.17 engines (20,600 lbf/92 kN thrust) and facilities to carry a Blue Steel stand-off nuclear missile. The aircrafts' wings were modified to incorporate two "speed pods" or "Küchemann carrots". These were anti-shock bodies; bulged fairings that reduced wave drag at transonic speeds (see area rule), which were also used as a convenient place to house chaff dispensers. Handley Page proposed to build a further refined "Phase 6" Victor, with more fuel and capable of carrying up to four Skybolt (AGM-48) ballistic missiles on standing airborne patrols, but this proposal was rejected although it was agreed that some of the Victor B.2s on order would be fitted to carry two Skybolts. This plan was abandoned when the U.S. cancelled the whole Skybolt programme in 1963. With the move to low-level penetration missions, the Victors were fitted with air-to-air refuelling probes above the cockpit, large underwing fuel tanks, and received a two-tone camouflage finish in place of the Anti-flash white. Trials were also conducted with terrain-following radar and a side scan mode for the bombing and navigation radar but neither became operational.

Victor B.2 Strategic Reconnaissance

Nine B.2 aircraft were converted for strategic reconnaissance purposes to replace Valiants withdrawn due to wing fatigue, with delivery beginning in July 1965. They received cameras, a bomb bay-mounted radar mapping system and wing top sniffers to detect particles released from nuclear testing.

Victor tankers

An RAF Victor tanker (*XM717*) being refuelled at the Civil Air Terminal, a Second World War RAF Air Station, at NAS Bermuda *ca.* 1985.

The withdrawal of the Valiant fleet due to metal fatigue in December 1964 meant that the RAF had no front line tanker aircraft, so the B.1/1A aircraft, now judged to be surplus in the strategic bomber role, were refitted for this duty. To get some tankers into service as quickly as possible, six B.1A aircraft were converted to *B(K).1A* standard (later redesignated *B.1A (K2P)*), receiving a two-point system with a hose and drogue carried under each wing, while the bomb bay remained available for weapons. Handley Page worked day and night to convert these six aircraft, with the first being delivered on 28 April 1965, and 55 Squadron becoming operational in the tanker role in August 1965.

While these six aircraft provided a limited tanker capability suitable for refuelling fighters, the Mk 20A wing hosereels could only deliver fuel at a limited rate, and were not suitable for refuelling bombers. Work therefore continued to produce a definitive three-point tanker conversion of the Victor Mk.1. Fourteen further B.1A and 11 B.1 were fitted with two permanently fitted fuel tanks in the bomb bay, and a high-capacity Mk 17 centreline hose dispenser unit with three times the fuel flow rate as the wing reels, and were designated *K.1A* and *K.1* respectively.

The remaining B.2 aircraft were not as suited to the low-level strike mission as the Vulcan with its strong delta wing. This, combined with the switch of the nuclear deterrent from the RAF to the Royal Navy (with the Polaris missile) meant that the Victor was now surplus to requirements. Hence, 24 B.2 were modified to *K.2* standard. Similar to the K.1/1A conversions, the wing was trimmed to reduce stress and had the nose glazing plated over. The glazing was reintroduced, on some aircraft, for reconnaissance missions during the Falklands War. The K.2 could carry 91,000 lb (41,000 kg) of fuel. It served in the tanker role until withdrawn in October 1993.

Operational history

The Victor was the last of the V bombers to enter service, with deliveries of B.1s to No. 232 Operational Conversion Unit RAF based at RAF Gaydon, Warwickshire before the end of 1957. The first operational bomber squadron, 10 Squadron, formed at RAF Cottesmore in April 1958, with a second squadron, 15 Squadron forming before the end of the year. Four Victors, fitted with Yellow Astor reconnaissance radar, together with a number of passive sensors, were used to equip a secretive unit, the Radar Reconnaissance Flight at RAF Wyton. The Victor bomber force continued to build up, with 57 Squadron forming in March 1959 and 55 Squadron in October 1960. The Victor proved popular in service, having good handling and excellent performance. One unusual characteristic of the early Victor was its self landing capability, where once lined up with the runway, the aircraft would naturally flare as the wing was in ground effect while the tail continued to sink, giving a cushioned landing without any intervention by the pilot.

The improved Victor B.2 started to be delivered in 1961, with the first B.2 Squadron, 139 Squadron forming in February 1962, and a second, 100 Squadron in May 1962. These were the only two bomber squadrons to form on the B.2, as the last 28 Victors on order were cancelled. The prospect of Skybolt ballistic missiles, with which each V-bomber could strike at two separate targets, meant that less bombers would be needed, while the government were unhappy with Sir Frederick Handley Page's resistance to their pressure to merge his company with competitors. In 1964–1965, a series of detachments of Victor B.1As was deployed to RAF Tengah, Singapore as a deterrent against Indonesia during the Borneo conflict, the detachments fulfilling a strategic deterrent role as part of Far East Air Force, while also giving valuable training in low-level flight and visual bombing. In September 1964, with the confrontation with Indonesia reaching a peak, the detachment of four Victors was prepared for rapid dispersal, with two aircraft loaded with live conventional bombs and held on one-hour readiness, ready to fly operational sorties, but they were not required to fly combat missions, with the high readiness alert finishing at the end of the month.

Following the discovery of fatigue cracks, developing due to their low-altitude usage, the B.2R strategic bombers were retired by the end of 1968 with the intention that these would be converted to tankers. Handley Page prepared a modification scheme that would see the Victors fitted with tip tanks, the structure modified to limit further fatigue cracking in the wings, and ejection seats provided for all six crewmembers. The Ministry of Defence delayed signing the order for conversion of the B2s until after Handley Page went into liquidation. The contract for conversion was instead awarded to Hawker Siddeley, who produced a much simpler conversion than that planned by Handley Page, with the wingspan shortened to reduce wing bending stress and hence extend airframe life. The reconnaissance aircraft remained in use until 1974 (one of their last missions was to monitor French nuclear tests in the South Pacific) when they followed the bombers into the tanker conversion line. However, the Victor would be the last V-bomber to retire in 1993, nine years after the last Vulcan (although the Vulcan survived longer in its original role as a bomber). It saw service in the Falklands War and 1991 Gulf War as an in-flight refuelling tanker.

Variants

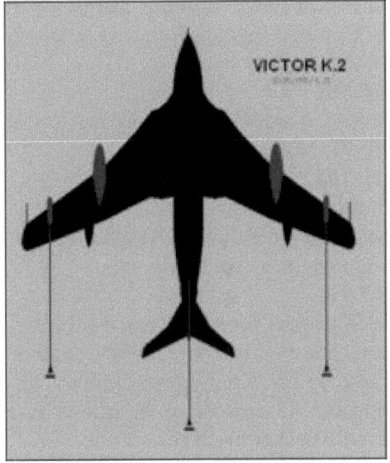

Ventral plan of a Victor K Mk.2

HP.80
Prototype, two aircraft built.
Victor B.1
Strategic bomber aircraft, 50 built.
Victor B.1A
Strategic bomber aircraft, B.1 updated with Red Steer tail warning radar and ECM suite, 24 converted.
Victor B.1A (K.2P)
2 point in-flight refuelling tanker retaining bomber capability, six converted.
Victor BK.1
3 point in-flight refuelling tanker (renamed *K.1* after bombing capability removed), 11 converted.
Victor BK.1A
3 point in-flight refuelling tanker (renamed *K.1A* as for K.1), 14 converted.
Victor B.2
Strategic bomber aircraft, 34 built.
Victor B.2RS
Blue Steel-capable aircraft with RCo.17 Conway 201 engines, 21 converted.
Victor B(SR).2
Strategic reconnaissance aircraft, nine converted.

Victor K.2
In-flight refuelling tanker. 24 converted from B.2 and B(SR).2.

HP.96
Proposed military transport of 1950 with new fuselage carrying 85 troops. Unbuilt.

HP.97
1950 civil airliner project. Not built.

HP.98
Proposed pathfinder version with remotely operated tail guns and powered by Conway engines. Rejected in favour of Valiant B.2.

HP.101
Proposed military transport version of HP.97. Not built.

HP.104
Proposed "Phase 3" bomber of 1955 powered by Bristol Olympus or Sapphire engines. Not built.

HP.111
1958 project for military or civil transport, powered by four Conway engines. Capacity for 200 troops in military version or 145 passengers in airliner in a double-decker fuselage.

HP.114
Proposed "Phase 6" bomber designed for standing patrols carrying two or four GAM-87 Skybolt ballistic missiles.

HP.123
Proposed military tactical transport based on HP.111 and fitted with blown flaps. Rejected in favour of Armstrong Whitworth AW.681.

Operators

Victor B.1A (K.2P) *XH648* preserved at the Imperial War Museum Duxford

- Royal Air Force
  - No. 10 Squadron RAF operated B.1 from April 1958 to March 1964 at RAF Cottesmore.
  - No. 15 Squadron RAF operated B.1 from September 1958 to October 1964 at RAF Cottesmore.
  - No. 55 Squadron RAF operated B.1 and B.1As from RAF Honington from October 1960, moving to RAF Marham and receiving B.1(K)A tankers in May 1965. These were replaced by K.2 in July 1975, with the squadron continuing to operate Victors in the tanker role until disbanding in October 1993.
  - No. 57 Squadron RAF operated B.1As, K.1 & K.2s from March 1959 to 1992.
  - No. 100 Squadron RAF operated B.2s at RAF Wittering from May 1962 to September 1968.
  - No. 139 (Jamaica) Squadron RAF operated B.2s from February 1962 to December 1968.
  - No. 214 Squadron RAF operated K.1 tankers from July 1966 to January 1977.
  - No. 543 Squadron RAF operated B(SR).2s from December 195 to May 1974.
  - No. 232 Operational Conversion Unit RAF.
  - Radar Reconnaissance Flight RAF Wyton.

Accidents and incidents

- 20 August 1959: *XH668* a B2 of the A&AEE lost a pitot head and dived into the sea off Milford Haven, Pembrokeshire.
- 19 June 1960: *XH617* a B1A of 57 Squadron caught fire in the air and was abandoned near Diss, Norfolk.
- 23 March 1962: *XL159* a B2 of the A&AEE stalled and dived into a house at Stubton, Lincolnshire.
- 14 June 1962: *XH613* a B1A of 15 Squadron lost power on all engines and was abandoned on approach to RAF Cottesmore.
- 16 June 1962: *XA929* a B1 of 10 Squadron overshot the runway and broke up at RAF Akrotiri following an aborted takeoff.
- 2 October 1962: *XA934* a B1 of 'A'Squadron, 232 OCU had an engine fail on takeoff from RAF Gaydon after which two engines failed on approach. The aircraft crashed into a copse several miles from RAF Gaydon. Of the four crew on board only the co-pilot survived.
- 20 March 1963: *XM714* a B2 of 100 Squadron stalled after takeoff from RAF Wittering.
- 29 June 1966: *XM716* a SR2 of 543 Squadron was giving a demonstration flight for the press and television at RAF Wyton. The aircraft had made one high-speed circuit and was flying low in a wide arc to return back over the airfield when the starboard wing was seen to break away and both it and the rest of the aircraft burst into flames. All four crew were killed. The aircraft was the first SR2 to enter service with the squadron, and released evidence suggests that it was overstressed.
- 19 August 1968: Victor K1 *XH646* of 214 Squadron collided in midair near Holt, Norfolk in bad weather with a 213 Squadron English Electric Canberra *WT325*; all four crew members of the Victor died
- 10 May 1973: *XL230* a SR2 of 543 Squadron bounced during landing at RAF Wyton and exploded.
- 24 March 1975: Victor K1A *XH618* of 57 Squadron was involved in a midair collision with Hawker Siddeley Buccaneer *XV156* during a simulated refuelling. The Buccaneer hit the Victor's tailplane causing the aircraft to crash into the sea 95 mi (153 km) east of Sunderland, County Durham.
- 19 June 1986 *XL191* a K2 of 57 Squadron undershot approach in bad weather at Hamilton, Ontario.
- 3 May 2009: During a "fast taxi" run at Bruntingthorpe Aerodrome, *XM715* made an unplanned brief flight, reaching a height of about 30 ft (9 m) at maximum. The aircraft did not have a permit to fly; however, the Civil Aviation Authority (CAA) stated that they would not be conducting an investigation. The

co-pilot had failed to reply to the command "throttles back", the pilot then had to control the throttles himself, the confusion temporarily disrupting firm control of the aircraft.

Survivors

XH648, 2001

Victor K.2 *XM715* preserved at the British Aviation Heritage Centre, Bruntingthorpe

Five Victors have survived (as of 2010) plus a few cockpit sections.

Victor B.1A
- *XH648*: a B.1A (K.2P) at the Imperial War Museum Duxford, Cambridgeshire. The only Mark 1 to survive and the only one with bombing capability preserved (bomb doors and bomb aimer's positions are visible signs of this).

Victor K.2
- *XH672*: *Maid Marian*, at the Royal Air Force Museum, Cosford, Shropshire, in the new Cold War building.
- *XH673*: Gate guardian at RAF Marham, Norfolk, the Victor's last home.
- *XL231*: *Lusty Lindy*, at the Yorkshire Air Museum, York. The prototype for the B.2 to K.2 conversion.
- *XM715*: *Teasin' Tina*/*Meldrew*, at the British Aviation Heritage Centre, Bruntingthorpe, Leicestershire.

The names, and accompanying nose art, were applied during the 1991 Gulf War. Of these, *Lindy* and *Tina* are the only "live" aircraft. They are run up regularly, performing high speed taxi runs with parachute braking at annual events.

Specifications (Handley Page Victor B.1)

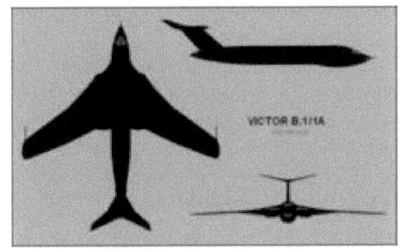

3-view of Victor B.1

3-view of Victor B.2

Data from Handley Page Aircraft since 1907

General characteristics
- **Crew:** 5
- **Length:** 114 ft 11 in (35.05 m)
- **Wingspan:** 110 ft 0 in (33.53 m)
- **Height:** 28 ft 1½ in (8.57 m)
- **Wing area:** 2,406 sq ft (223.5 m²)
- **Empty weight:** 89,030 lb (40,468 kg)
- **Max takeoff weight:** 205,000 lb (93,182 kg)
- **Powerplant:** 4 × Armstrong Siddeley Sapphire A.S.Sa.7 turbojets, 11,050 lb (49.27 kN) each

Performance
- **Maximum speed:** 627 mph (545 knots, 1,009 km/h) at 36,000 ft (11,000 m)
- **Range:** 6,000 mi (5,217 nmi, 9,660 km)
- **Service ceiling:** 56,000 ft (17,000 m)

Armament
- Up to 35 × 1,000 lb (450 kg) bombs *or*
- 1× Yellow Sun free-fall nuclear bomb

Notable appearances in media

A Handley Page Victor features prominently in the 1962 British movie comedy *The Iron Maiden*. A number of sequences show the aircraft in closeup, taxiing, taking off, climbing, flying past and landing with parachute deployed. Although a bomber, in the film it purports to be a prototype supersonic jetliner designed by the protagonist.

Source (edited): "http://en.wikipedia.org/wiki/Handley_Page_Victor"

Hawker Siddeley Harrier

The **Hawker Siddeley Harrier**, colloquially the "Harrier Jump Jet", was the first generation of the Harrier series, the first operational close-support and reconnaissance fighter aircraft with Vertical/Short Takeoff and Landing (V/STOL) capabilities. Developed in the 1960s, the Harrier was the only truly successful V/STOL design of the many that arose in the era. The Harrier was produced directly from the Hawker Siddeley Kestrel prototypes following the cancellation of a more advanced supersonic aircraft, the Hawker Siddeley P.1154. The Royal Air Force ordered the Harrier GR.1 and GR.3 variants in the late 1960s. It was exported to the United States for use by the US Marine Corps (USMC), as the AV-8A Harrier, in the 1970s.

The Royal Air Force (RAF) positioned the bulk of their Harriers in West Germany to defend against a potential invasion of Western Europe by the Soviet Union; the unique abilities of the Harrier allowed the RAF to disperse their forces away from vulnerable and well-known airbases. The USMC deployed their Harriers as a close air support platform, and as naval aircraft on board amphibious assault ships. Harrier squadrons saw several deployments overseas to deter regional aggression. The Harrier's ability to operate with minimal ground facilities and very short runways allowed it to be used at locations unavailable to other fixed-wing aircraft.

In the 1970s, the British Aerospace Sea Harrier was spawned from the Harrier for use by the Royal Navy on Invincible class aircraft carriers. The Sea Harrier and the Harrier were crucial to the 1982 Falklands War, in which the aircraft proved to be flexible and versatile. Sea Harriers provided fixed-wing air defense while the RAF Harriers focused on ground-attack missions in support of the advancing British land force. The Harrier was also extensively redesigned as the AV-8B Harrier II and British Aerospace Harrier II by the team of McDonnell Douglas and British Aerospace. The innovative Harrier family and its Rolls-Royce Pegasus vectorable-thrust engine have generated long-term interest in V/STOL aircraft. Similar V/STOL operational aircraft include the contemporary Soviet Yakovlev Yak-38 and one variant of the developing Lockheed Martin F-35 Lightning II.

Development

Origins

The Harrier's lineage began with the Hawker P.1127. Prior to working on the P.1127, Hawker Aviation had been working on a replacement for the Hawker Hunter—the Hawker P.1121. However, the P.1127 was cancelled after the release of the 1957 Defence White Paper, which advocated a policy shift away from manned aircraft and towards missiles. This policy resulted in the termination of the majority of aircraft development projects then underway. Hawker sought to quickly move on to a new project, and became interested in the field of Vertical Take Off/ Landing (VTOL) aircraft, which did not need runways. According to Air Chief Marshal Sir Patrick Hine, this interest may have been stimulated by the presence of Air Staff Requirement 345, which sought a V/STOL ground attack fighter for the Royal Air Force.

Design work on the P.1127 was formally started in 1957 by Sir Sydney Camm, Ralph Hooper of Hawker Aviation and Stanley Hooker (later Sir Stanley) of the Bristol Engine Company. The close cooperation between the airframe company, Hawker, and the engine company, Bristol, was viewed by Gordon Lewis, the project engineer, as one of the key factors that allowed the development of the Harrier to continue in spite of technical obstacles and political setbacks. Rather than using rotors or a direct jet thrust, the P.1127 had an innovative vectored thrust turbofan engine, the Pegasus. The Pegasus I, rated at 9,000 pounds (4.1 kN) of thrust, first ran on September 1959. A contract for two development prototypes was signed in June 1960, and the first flight followed in October 1960. Of the six prototypes built, three crashed—including one one during an air display at the 1963 Paris Air Show.

Tripartite Evaluation

Hawker Siddeley XV-6A Kestrel in later USAF markings

The immediate development of the P.1127 was the Kestrel FGA.1, which appeared after Hawker Siddeley Aviation was formed. In 1961, the United Kingdom, United States, and West Germany jointly agreed to purchase nine P.1127 aircraft, to be named Kestrels, for the evaluation of the performance and potential of V/STOL aircraft. The Kestrel was strictly an evaluation aircraft; to save money the Pegasus 5 engine was not fully developed as intended, and only had 15,000 pounds (6.8 kN) of thrust instead of the projected 18,200 pounds (8.3 kN). The Tripartite Evaluation Squadron numbered ten pilots, four each from the UK and US, and two from West Germany. The Kestrel's first flight took place on 7 March 1964.

A total of 960 sorties were made during the trials, including 1,366 take-offs and landings, by the end of evaluations in November 1965. One Kestrel was destroyed in an accident. One aircraft was destroyed in an accident and six of the remainder were redesignated as XV-6A Kestrels and transferred to the United States for evaluation. The two remaining British-based Kestrels were assigned for further trials and experimentation at RAE Bedford; one was modified to use the uprated Pegasus 6 engine.

P.1154

At the time of the development of the P.1127, Hawker and Bristol had also undertaken a considerable amount of development work on a supersonic version, the Hawker Siddeley P.1154, to meet a North Atlantic Treaty Organisation (NATO) requirement issued for such an aircraft. The design used a single Bristol Siddeley BS100 engine with four swivelling nozzles in a fashion similar to the P.1127, and required the use of plenum chamber burning (PCB) to achieve supersonic speeds. The P.1154 won the competition to meet the requirement despite several rival bids from other aircraft manufacturers such as Dassault Aviation. The project was cancelled in 1965 after the French government withdrew following the selection of the P.1154 over the Dassault Mirage IIIV.

The Royal Air Force and the Royal Navy planned to develop and introduce the supersonic P.1154 independently of the cancelled NATO requirement. This ambition was complicated, however, by the conflicting requirements between the two services—while the RAF wanted a low level supersonic strike aircraft, the Navy sought a twin-engined air defence fighter. Following the election of the Labour Government of 1964, the P.1154 was cancelled as the Royal Navy had already begun procurement of the McDonnell Douglas Phantom II and the RAF placed a greater importance on the BAC TSR-2's ongoing development. Elements of the project, such as a supersonic PCB-equipped Pegasus engine, continued to be worked on with the intention of developing a future Harrier variant for decades following cancellation.

Production

Following the collapse of the P.1154's development, the RAF began examining the adoption of a simple upgrade of the existing subsonic Kestrel for service and issued Requirement ASR 384 for a V/STOL ground attack jet. Hawker Siddeley received an order for six pre-production aircraft, designated *P.1127 (RAF)*, in 1965, of which the first made its maiden flight on 31 August 1966. An order for 60 production aircraft, designated as Harrier GR.1, was received in early 1967.

AV-8C Harrier undergoing flight deck evaluation tests

The Harrier GR.1 made its first flight on 28 December 1967. It officially entered service with the RAF on 18 April 1969 when the Harrier Conversion Unit at RAF Wittering received its first aircraft. The aircraft were built in two factories—one in Kingston upon Thames, southwest London, and the other at Dunsfold, Surrey—and underwent initial testing at Dunsfold. The ski-jump technique for launching Harriers from Royal Navy aircraft carriers was extensively trialled at RNAS Yeovilton from 1977. Following the conclusion of these tests, from 1979 onwards ski-jumps were added to the flight decks of all Royal Navy aircraft carriers.

In the late 1960s, the British and American governments entered into talks about commencing production of Harriers in the United States. Hawker Siddeley and McDonnell Douglas formed a partnership in 1969 in preparation for American production. However, Congressman Mendel Rivers and the House Appropriations Committee held the view that it would be cheaper to produce the AV-8A on the pre-existing production lines in the United Kingdom—hence all AV-8A Harriers were purchased from Hawker Siddeley. Improved Harrier versions with better sensors and more powerful engine versions were subsequently developed in later years. A total of 102 AV-8A and 8 TAV-8A Harriers were ordered and received by the USMC between 1971 and 1976.

Design

Overview

The Harrier's role was typically a ground attack aircraft, though its manoeuvrability also allowed for effective close range air-to-air combat. The Harrier is powered by a single Pegasus turbofan engine mounted in the fuselage. The engine is fitted with two intakes and four vectorable nozzles for directing the thrust generated; two for the bypass flow and two for the jet exhaust. Several smaller reaction nozzles are also fitted in the nose, tail, and wingtips for the purpose of balancing during vertical flight. It has two landing gear on the fuselage and two outrigger landing gear on the wings. The Harrier is equipped with four wing and three fuselage pylons for carrying a variety of weapons and external fuel tanks.

An RAF Harrier GR.1, on loan to the USMC, displaying its underside, several weapons are outfitted to the aircraft

The Kestrel and the Harrier were similar in appearance, though approximately 90% of the Kestrel's airframe was redesigned for the Harrier. The Harrier was powered by the more powerful Pegasus 6 engine; new air intakes with auxiliary blow-in doors were added to produce the required airflow at low speed. Its wing was modified to increase area, and the undercarriage was strengthened. Additional hardpoints for weapons were added (with two under each wing, one plumbed for carrying fuel tanks and a centreline hardpoint), two 30 mm (1.2 in) ADEN cannon could be carried in pods under the fuselage. The Harrier was outfitted with modern avionics to replace the basic systems used in the Kestrel; a navigational-attack system incorporating an Inertial navigation system originally for the P.1154 was installed; information was presented to the pilot by a head-up display and a moving map display.

The Harrier's VTOL abilities allowed it to be deployed from very small prepared clearings or helipads as well as normal airfields. It was believed that in a high intensity conflict, air bases would be vulnerable and likely to be quickly knocked out. The capability to scatter Harrier squadrons to dozens of small "alert pads" on the front lines was seen as highly prized to military strategists; the USMC procured the aircraft on this basis. Hawker Siddeley noted that STOL operations were advantageous in saving fuel and carrying greater levels of ordnance over operating exclusively as a VTOL aircraft.

Engine

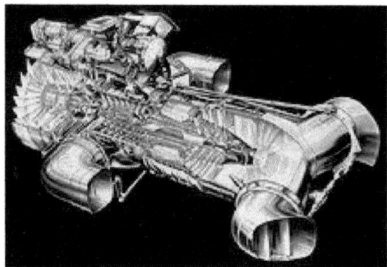

Drawing of the Rolls-Royce Pegasus with cutaway view

The Rolls-Royce Pegasus turbofan jet engine, developed in tandem with the Harrier, was designed specifically for VSTOL manoeuvering. Originally developed by Bristol Siddeley, it was a development of the earlier conventional Orpheus turbofan engine, the main difference being the thrust generated is directed through four rotatable nozzles. The engine is equipped for water injection to increase thrust and takeoff performance in hot and high conditions, in normal STOVL operations the system would be used in landing vertically with a heavy weapons load. The water injection function had originally been added following the input of USAF Colonel Bill Chapman, who worked for the *Mutual Weapons Development Team*.

The primary focus through development was upon the issue of achieving high performance for as little weight as possible; tempered by the amount of funding that was available. Following the Harrier's entry to service, the focus switched to improving reliability and extending engine life; a formal joint US/UK Pegasus Support Program operated for many years, spending a £3 million annual budget to investigate and develop engine improvements. The version used in the initial production Harriers was the Pegasus 6, the majority of Harriers were powered by the later Pegasus 11. Several variants improving on the original engine have been released, the Pegasus 11-61/Mk.107 is the latest and most powerful version of the engine, providing 23,800 lbf (106 kN).

Controls and handling

Piloting a Harrier requires a high level of skill and understanding; pilots described it as being "unforgiving". The aircraft is capable of both forward flight (where it behaves in the manner of a typical fixed-wing aircraft above its stall speed), and VTOL and STOL manoeuvres (where the traditional lift and control surfaces are useless). This requires skills and understanding more usually associated with helicopters. Most services demand great aptitude and extensive training for Harrier pilots, as well as experience of piloting both types of aircraft. Trainee pilots are often drawn from highly experienced and skilled helicopter pilots.

In addition to normal flight controls, the Harrier has a lever for controlling the direction of the four vectorable nozzles. It had been viewed as a significant design success that the cockpit only required the addition of a single lever over that of a conventional aircraft. The nozzles point rearward with the lever in the forward position for horizontal flight; when the lever was rearwards the nozzles point directly downward for vertical takeoff or landing.

Thrust vectoring nozzle on a Sea Harrier

The Harrier has two control elements that a fixed-wing aircraft does not usually have. These are the thrust vector and reaction control system. The thrust vector refers to the slant of the four engine nozzles and can be set between 0° (horizontal, pointing directly back) and 98° (pointing down and slightly forwards). The 90° vector is normally deployed for VTOL manoeuvring. The reaction control is achieved by manipulating the control stick and is similar in action to the cyclic control of a helicopter. While irrelevant during forward flight mode, these controls are essential during VTOL and STOL manoeuvres. Wind direction in reference to the aircraft is crucial during VTOL manoeuvres.

The procedure for vertical takeoff involves facing the aircraft into the wind. The thrust vector is set to 90° and the throttle is brought up to maximum; at which point the aircraft leaves the ground rapidly. The throttle is trimmed until a hover state is achieved at the desired altitude. The short takeoff procedure involves proceeding with normal takeoff and then applying a thrust vector (less than 90°) at a runway speed below normal takeoff speed, usually the point of application would be around 65 knots. For lower take off speeds the thrust vector would be greater.

The technique of vectoring in forward flight, or "VIFFing", involves rotating the vectored thrust nozzles into a forward-facing position during normal flight. It was a dog-fighting tactic, allowing for both higher turns rates than would normally be possible for an aircraft with such a short wing-span, and for sudden braking. The latter could cause a chasing aircraft to overshoot and present itself as a target for the Harrier it was chasing—a combat technique formally developed by the USMC in the Harrier in the early 1970s.

Differences between versions

The two largest users of the Harrier were the United States Marine Corps (USMC) and the Royal Air Force. In the USMC, the exported model of the Harrier operated was designated the *AV-8A Harrier*. These were broadly similar to the RAF's Harrier GR.1; changes included the removal of all magnesium components, the integration of American radios and Identification Friend or Foe (IFF) systems, and the outer pylons (unlike the RAF aircraft) were designed from delivery to be equipped with self-defence AIM-9 Sidewinder heat-seeking air to air missiles. Most of the AV-8As had been delivered with the more powerful Pegasus engine used in the GR.3 instead of the one used in the earlier GR.1.

The RAF GR.1 and the initial AV-8As were fitted with the Ferranti FE541 inertial navigation/attack suite, but these were replaced in the USMC Harriers by a simpler Interface/Weapon Aiming Computer in order to aid quick turn around between missions; the Martin-Baker ejection seats were also replaced by the Stencel SEU-3A in the American aircraft. The RAF had their GR.1 aircraft upgraded to an improved standard, the *Harrier GR.3*, featuring improved sensors, a nose-mounted laser tracker, the integration of electronic countermeasure (ECM) systems, and a further upgraded Pegasus Mk 103. The USMC also upgraded their AV-8As to the *AV-8C* configuration; this programme involved the installation of ECM equipment and adding a new inertial navigation system to the aircraft's avionics. Substantial changes were the Lift Improvement Devices, to increase VTOL performance, at the same time several airframe components were restored or replaced to extend the life of the aircraft. Spain's Harriers, designated AV-8S or VA.1 Matador for the single-seater, and TAV-8S or VAE.1 for the two-seater, were almost identical to USMC Harriers, differing only in the radios fitted.

The Royal Navy's Fleet Air Arm (FAA) operated a substantially modified variant of the Harrier, the British Aerospace Sea Harrier. This version was not intended for ground-attack duties and, unlike the standard Harrier, equipped with a radar and Sidewinder missiles for air combat duties and fleet air defence. The Sea Harrier was also fitted with navigational aids for maritime landing upon carriers, corrosion resistance, and a raised bubble-canopy for greater visibility. Later on, the Sea Harrier was equipped to use AIM-120 AMRAAM Beyond Visual Range anti-aircraft missiles and the more advanced *Blue Vixen* radar for longer range air-to-air combat; Sea Eagle missiles were also added for conducting anti-ship missions.

The McDonnell Douglas AV-8B Harrier II is the latest Harrier variant, a second-generation series to replace the first generation of Harrier jets already in service; all the above variants of the Harrier have mainly been retired with the Harrier II taking their place in the RAF, USMC, and FAA. In the 1970s, the United Kingdom considered two options for replacing their existing Harriers: joining McDonnell Douglas (MDD) in developing the *BAE Harrier II*, or the development of an independent *Big Wing Harrier*. The "Big Wing" Harrier would have increased the wing area from 200 to 250 square ft, allowing for significant increases in weapons load and internal fuel reserves. The option of cooperation with MDD was chosen over the more risky isolated approach in 1982.

Operational history

Royal Air Force

A RAF Harrier GR.3 of *No. 233 OCU* hovering over RAF Mildenhall, Suffolk in 1984

The first RAF squadron to be equipped with the Harrier GR.1, No. 1 Squadron, started to convert to the aircraft at RAF Wittering in April 1969. An early demonstration of the Harrier's capabilities was shown by the participation of two aircraft in the *Daily Mail* Transatlantic Air Race in May 1969, flying between St Pancras railway station, London and downtown Manhattan with the use of aerial refuelling, the time taken was 6 hours 11 minutes. Two further squadrons were established at RAF Wildenrath as part of RAF Germany in 1970, with a fourth squadron forming at Wildenrath in 1972. In 1977, the German based Harrier force was moved forwards to RAF Gütersloh, closer to the prospective front line in the event of an outbreak of a European war, with one of the squadrons being disbanded with its aircraft being distributed between the other two.

In RAF service, the Harrier was used in close air support (CAS), reconnaissance, and other ground attack roles. The flexibility of the Harrier led to a long-term heavy deployment in West Germany as a conventional deterrent and potential strike weapon against Soviet aggression; from camouflaged rough bases the Harrier was expected to launch attacks on advancing armour columns coming from East Germany. Harriers were also deployed abroad, to bases in Norway and Belize. No. 1 Squadron was specifically earmarked for Norwegian operations in the event of war, operating as part of Allied Forces Northern Europe, possibly in support of 3 Commando Brigade. The Harrier's capabilities were necessary in the Belize deployment, it was the only RAF combat aircraft capable of safely operating from the airport's short runway; British forces had been stationed in Belize for several years due to tensions over Guatemalan claim to Belizean territory, finally being withdrawn in 1993.

A RAF Harrier GR.3 in Belize, 1990

A defining combat experience for the Harrier was during the Falklands War, in which ten Harrier GR.3s of No. 1 Squadron RAF operated from the aircraft carrier HMS *Hermes*. As the RAF Harrier GR.3 had not been designed for the naval environment, prior to the task force being dispatched they were rapidly modified; special sealants against corrosion were applied and a new deck-based inertial guidance aid was devised to allow RAF Harriers to land as easily as their RN Sea Harrier equivalents. Transponders to guide aircraft back to the carriers during night time operations and flares/chaff dispensers were also installed.

As there was little space on board the carriers, two requisitioned merchant container ships, the *Atlantic Conveyor* and *Atlantic Causeway*, were modified with temporary flight decks, and used to carry Harriers and helicopters to the combat area. The Harrier GR.3s focused on providing close air support to the ground forces on the Falklands and attacking Argentine positions; suppressing enemy artillery was often a high priority. Sea Harriers were also heavily used in the war, primarily conducting fleet air defence and combat air patrols against the threat of attacking Argentine fighters; however, both the Sea Harriers and Harrier GR3s were used in ground attack missions upon the runway at Stanley.

A former RAF Harrier GR.3 on display near Bletchley Park, 2005

If most of the Sea Harriers had been lost, the GR.3s would have replaced them in air patrol duties, even though the Harrier GR.3 was not designed for air defence operations; as such the GR.3s quickly had their outboard weapons pylons modified to take air-to-air Sidewinder missiles. From 10 to 24 May, before the British landed in the Falklands, a detachment of three GR.3s provided air defence for Ascension Island until three F-4 Phantom IIs arrived to take on this responsibility. During the fighting over and near the Falklands four Harriers GR.3s and six Sea Harriers were lost to ground fire, accidents, or mechanical failure; more than 2,000 Harrier sorties were conducted during the conflict, or six sorties per day per aircraft. The greatest threat to the Harriers over the Falklands were surface-to-air missiles (SAMs) and small arms fire from the ground.

Following the Falklands War, the first generation of RAF Harriers did not see further combat, although they continued to serve in the RAF for several more years—as a deterrent against further Argentine invasion attempts No. 1453 Flight RAF was deployed to the Falklands Islands from August 1983 to June 1985. However the second generation Harrier IIs saw action in Bosnia, Iraq, and Afghanistan. The first generation Hawker Siddeley airframes were replaced by the improved Harrier II, which had been developed jointly between McDonnell Douglas and British Aerospace.

United States Marine Corps
Major General Joe Anderson.
The United States Marine Corps began showing a significant interest in the Harrier around the same time the first RAF Harrier squadron was established in 1969, and this motivated Hawker Siddeley to further develop the aircraft in hope of encouraging a purchase. Although there were concerns in Congress about multiple coinciding projects in the Close Air Support role, the Marine Corps were enthusiastic about the Harrier and managed to overcome efforts to obstruct its procurement.

The AV-8A entered service with the Marine Corps in 1971 and attack squadrons converted to the Harrier. The service became interested in performing ship-borne operations with the Harrier. Admiral Elmo Zumwalt promoted the concept of a Sea Control Ship, a 15,000-ton light carrier equipped with Harriers and helicopters, to supplement the larger aircraft carriers of the US Navy. An amphibious assault ship, the USS *Guam* was converted into the *Interim Sea Control Ship* and operated as such between 1971 and 1973; with the purpose of studying the limits and possible obstacles for operating such a vessel. Since then, the Sea Control Ship concept has been subject to periodic re-examinations and studies, often in the light of budget cuts and questions over the usage of supercarriers.

A USMC AV-8A from *VMA-231* in camouflage paint; two napalm bombs are equipped under its wing.

Other exercises were performed to demonstrate the AV-8A's suitability for operating from various amphibious assault ships and aircraft carriers; the tests showed, amongst other things, that the Harrier was capable of performing in weather where conventional carrier aircraft could not. The USMC also developed a stand-by system, known as *Arapaho*, which would rapidly convert civilian cargo ships into sea-going platforms for operating and maintaining a handful of Harriers.

The Marines' concept for deploying the Harriers in a land-based expeditionary role focuses on aggressive speed; Harrier forward bases and light maintenance facilities were to be set up in under 24 hours on any perspective battle area. The forward bases, containing one to four Harriers, were to be located 20 miles from the forward edge of battle (FEBA), while a more established permanent airbase would be located around 50 miles from the FEBA. Supplies lines, including armaments, would be regularly ferried by Sikorsky CH-53E Super Stallion from the main base to the dispersed forward bases. The close proximity of forward bases, as opposed to conventional aircraft operating from airfields, allowed for a far greater sortie rate and reduced fuel consumption.

A pair of USMC AV-8A Harriers refuelling from a Lockheed Martin KC-130 tanker.

Other operators

An AV-8S Matador flies over the Spanish aircraft carrier *Dédalo*(R01).

Stern view of HMTS *Chakri Naruebet*, a single Harrier is on deck.

The AV-8A's abilities in combat with other aircraft were tested by the Marine Corps by conducting mock dog-fights with McDonnell Douglas F-4 Phantom IIs, these exercises trained pilots to use the *VIFF* capability to out-manoeuver their opponents, and showed that the Harriers could act as effective air-to-air fighters at close range. The operational experience with the Harrier and its flexibility convinced officers within the Corps of the need for further investment in this field, and that the military advantages outweighed any political issues in this pursuit.

Starting in 1979 the USMC began upgrading their AV-8As to the *AV-8C* configuration, mainly the work focused on extending their useful service lives and improving VTOL performance. The AV-8C and the remaining AV-8A Harriers were retired when the Harrier II, designated as *AV-8B*, was introduced from the mid-1980s onwards. The performance of the Harrier in USMC service led to calls for the United States Air Force to procure Harrier IIs in addition to the USMC's own plans, but these never resulted in Air Force orders.

Due to the Harrier's unique characteristics it attracted a large amount of interest from other nations, often as attempts to make their own V/STOL jets were unsuccessful, such in the cases of the American XV-4 Hummingbird or the German VFW VAK 191B. Operations by the RAF and RN in the Falklands Conflict, and by the USMC aboard the USS *Nassau* in 1981, proved that the aircraft were highly effective in combat. These operations also demonstrated that 'Harrier Carriers' provided a powerful presence at sea without the expense of big deck carriers.

Due to the display of usefulness of the Harrier on small carriers, the navies of Spain and later Thailand also bought the Harrier for use as their main carrier-based fixed-wing aircraft. Spain's purchase of Harriers was complicated by long standing political friction between the British and Spanish governments of the era; even though the Harriers were manufactured in Britain they were sold to Spain by the US acting as an intermediary. The Spanish Navy operated the AV-8S Matador from their aircraft carrier Dédalo (formerly the USS Cabot), the Harriers providing both air defense and strike capabilities for the Spanish fleet starting in 1976. Spain later bought five Harriers directly from the British government to replace losses.

Hawker Siddeley aggressively marketed the Harrier for export, at one point the company was holding talks with Australia, Brazil, Switzerland, India and Japan, however, out of these only India would emerge as a later customer, for the Sea Harrier. At one point China came very close to becoming an operator of the first generation Harrier. Following an approach by the UK in the early 1970s, while relations with the West were warming, China was interested in the aircraft and sought to modernise the Chinese military. The deal did not come to pass despite progress, the trade was cancelled by the UK as part of a diplomatic backlash over the Sino-Vietnamese War in 1979, a military invasion of Vietnam by China.

The Spanish Navy, Royal Air Force and United States Marine Corps, have since retired their Harrier Is. Spain sold seven single-seat and two two-seat Harriers to Thailand in 1998. The Royal Thai Navy still operates a small number of the AV-8S Matador on the light aircraft carrier HTMS *Chakri Naruebet*. The Thai Navy has had significant logistical problems keeping the Harriers operational, due to a shortage of funds for spare parts and equipment, leaving only a few Harriers serviceable at a time. Thailand considered acquiring ex-Royal Navy Sea Harriers around 2003, more suitable for maritime operations and better equipped for air defense, to replace their AV-8S Harriers, however, this investigation did not proceed to a purchase.

Variants

A Royal Air Force Harrier GR.3 aircraft parked on the flight line during Air Fete '84 at RAF Mildenhall.

A USMC TAV-8A Harrier from *VMAT-203* on the flight line.

Harrier GR.1, GR.1A, GR.3
Single-seat versions for RAF. The RAF ordered 118 of the GR.1/GR.3 series, with the last production aircraft delivery in December 1986.

AV-8A, AV-8C Harrier
Single-seat versions for the U.S. Marine Corps. The USMC ordered 102 AV-8As. The AV-8C was an upgrade to the AV-8A.

AV-8S Matador
Export version of the AV-8A Harrier for the Spanish Navy, which designated them as *VA-1 Matador*.

Harrier T.2, T.2A, T.4, T.4A
Two-seat training versions for the RAF, with a stretched body and taller tail fin.

Harrier T.4N, T.8, T.60
Two-seat training versions for the Royal Navy and Indian Navy, avionics fitting based on Sea Harrier.

TAV-8A Harrier
Two-seat training version for the USMC, powered by a Pegasus Mk 103.

TAV-8S Matador
Two-seat training version for the Spanish Navy, and later Royal Thai Navy.

Operators

Current operator

 **Thailand**
- Royal Thai Navy
  - Squadron 1 Wing3 (HTMS Chakri Naruebet Flying Unit) - AV-8S and TAV-8S.

Former operators

 **India**
- Indian Navy
  - Operated the Harrier T.4 for Sea Harrier training.

A Spanish Navy AV-8S Matador aircraft.

United States Marine Corps AV-8A of VMA-231 in 1980

Spain
- Spanish Navy
  - No. 008 Escuadrilla - AV-8S and TAV-8S Matador.

United Kingdom
- Royal Air Force
  - No. 1 Squadron RAF re-equipped with Harrier GR.1s between July and October 1969 at RAF Wittering. It started to replace its first generation Harriers with Harrier GR.5s in 1988, discarding its last GR.3 on 31 March 1989.
  - No. 3 Squadron RAF formed at RAF Wildenrath with the Harrier GR.1A on 1 January 1971, moving to RAF Gütersloh in 1977. It re-equipped with Harrier GR.5s in 1989.
  - No. 4 Squadron RAF converted to Harriers at RAF at RAF Wittering in early 1970, moving to Wildenrath in Germany in June that year. It moved to RAF Gütersloh in January 1977 and replaced its GR.3s with Harrier GR.7s in 1990.
  - No. 20 Squadron RAF reformed at RAF Wittering in October 1970, moving to Wildenrath later that year. It disbanded in February 1977, with its aircraft being shared between the other two Germany based squadrons.
  - No. 233 Operational Conversion Unit RAF formed at Wittering from the Harrier Conversion Unit in October 1970. No 233 OCU was assigned the numberplate 20(R) Squadron in 1992, with the unit flying GR.3 until 1994 and the T.4 until 1996.
  - No. 1417 Flight RAF - Deployed to the Central American nation of Belize from 1980 to 1993.
  - No. 1453 Flight RAF - Deployed to Stanley, in the Falklands Islands from August 1983 to June 1985.
- Royal Navy
  - 899 Naval Air Squadron operated the Harrier T.4A and T.4N for training purposes for the Sea Harrier.

United States
- United States Marine Corps
  - VMA-231 - AV-8A/C Harrier. 1973–1985.
  - VMA-513 - AV-8A/C Harrier. 1971–1986.
  - VMA-542 - AV-8A/C Harrier. 1972–1986.
  - VMAT-203 - Training squadron, equipped with AV-8A and TAV-8A Harrier. 1975–1987.

Aircraft on display

Former Harrier GR.1 that crashed in 1971 and used as a static engine test bed by Rolls-Royce, on display at the Bristol Aero Collection, Kemble, England

- GR.1 XV277 is on display at the National Museum of Flight, East Fortune, Scotland.
- GR.1 XV278 is on display at the Luftwaffenmuseum der Bundeswehr, Gatow, Germany.
- GR.3 XV748 is on display at the Yorkshire Air Museum, Elvington, England.
- GR.3 XV751 is on display at the Gatwick Aviation Museum, Surrey, England.
- GR.3 XV752 is on display at Bletchley Park, Buckinghamshire, England.
- GR.3 XV779 is on display at the gate to RAF Wittering, England.
- GR.1 XV798 is on display at the Bristol Aero Collection, Kemble, Gloucestershire, England.
- GR.3 XW919 is on display at the Polish Aviation Museum, Kraków, Poland.
- T.4 XW934 is on display at the Farnborough Air Sciences Trust, Farnborough, Hampshire, United Kingdom.
- GR.3 XZ129 is on display at the Ashburton Aviation Museum, Ashburton, New Zealand.
- GR.3 XZ133 is on display at the Imperial War Museum Duxford, England.
- GR.3 XZ968 is on display outside the Muckleburgh Collection, Norfolk.
- GR.3 XZ997 is on display at the Royal Air Force Museum, Hendon, England.
- GR.3 XZ998 is on display at the Flugausstellung Leo Junior at Hermeskeil, Germany.
- Mk 52 G-VTOL is on display at the Brooklands Museum, Surrey, England.
- AV-8A 158966 is on display at the Canada Aviation and Space Museum, Ottawa, Ontario, Canada.
- AV-8A 159233 is on display at the Imperial War Museum North, Manchester, England.

Specifications (Harrier GR.3)

Data from Jane's All The World's Aircraft 1988–89

General characteristics

- **Crew:** One
- **Length:** 46 ft 10 in (14.27 m)
- **Wingspan:** 25 ft 3 in (7.70 m)
- **Height:** 11 ft 11 in (3.63 m)
- **Wing area:** 201.1 ft² (18.68 m²)
- **Empty weight:** 13,535 lb (6,140 kg)
- **Max takeoff weight:** 25,200 lb (11,430 kg)
- **Powerplant:** 1 × Rolls-Royce Pegasus 103 turbofan with four swivelling nozzles, 21,500 lbf (95.6 kN) Four vertical flight puffer jets use engine bleed air, mounted in the nose, wingtips, and tail.

Performance

- **Maximum speed:** 730 mph (635 knots, 1,176 km/h) at sea level
- **Combat radius:** 230 mi (200 nmi, 370 km) lo-lo-lo with 4,400 lb (2,000 kg) payload
- **Ferry range:** 2,129 mi (1,850 nmi, 3,425 km)
- **Endurance:** 1 hr 30 min (combat air patrol - 115 mi (185 km) from base)
- **Service ceiling:** 51,200 ft (15,600 m)
- **Climb to 40,000 ft (12,200 m):** 2 min 23 s

Armament

- **Guns:** 2× 30 mm (1.18 in) ADEN cannon pods under the fuselage
- **Hardpoints:** 4× under-wing & 1× under-fuselage pylon stations with a capacity of 5,000 lb (2,268 kg) and provisions to carry combinations of:
  - **Rockets:** 4× Matra rocket pods with 18× SNEB 68 mm rockets each
  - **Missiles:** 2× AIM-9 Sidewinders Air-to-air missiles
  - **Bombs:** A variety of unguided iron bombs, BL755 cluster bombs or laser guided bombs
  - **Others:**
    - 1× Reconnaissance pod
    - 2× drop tanks for extended range/loitering time

Source (edited): "http://en.wikipedia.org/wiki/Hawker_Siddeley_Harrier"

Hawker Siddeley Nimrod

The **Hawker Siddeley Nimrod** is a military aircraft developed and built in the United Kingdom. It is an extensive modification of the de Havilland Comet, the world's first jet airliner. It was originally designed by de Havilland's successor, Hawker Siddeley, now part of BAE Systems.

It was designed as a Royal Air Force maritime patrol aircraft, the **Nimrod MR1/MR2**, with the major role being anti-submarine warfare (ASW), although it also had secondary roles in maritime surveillance and anti-surface warfare. It served in this role from the early 1970s until March 2010. The current Nimrod series was due to be replaced by the now cancelled Nimrod MRA4.

The RAF also uses the **Nimrod R1** variant in an electronic intelligence gathering (ELINT) role.

Development

Five separate marks of the Nimrod have been developed during the period of the type's service with the RAF. Of these, three have been successfully in service;

- MR1 - the initial maritime reconnaissance variant
- MR2 - an upgraded version of the MR1
- R1 - a Mark 1 Nimrod optimised for the signals intelligence role

The other two were unsuccessful and were eventually cancelled before they could enter front-line service;
- AEW3 - an airborne early warning version cancelled in 1986 in favour of the E-3 Sentry
- MRA4 - an upgraded version of the MR2 cancelled in 2010 in a defence review

The development of the Nimrod patrol aircraft began in 1964 as a project to replace the Avro Shackleton. The Nimrod design was based on that of the Comet 4 civil airliner which had reached the end of its market life (the first two RAF aircraft were unfinished Comets). The Comet's turbojet engines were then replaced with Rolls-Royce Spey turbofans for better fuel efficiency, particularly at the low altitudes required for maritime patrol. Major fuselage changes were made, including an internal weapons bay, an extended nose for radar, a new tail with electronic warfare (ESM) sensors mounted in a bulky fairing, and a MAD (Magnetic anomaly detector) boom. After the first flight in May 1967, the RAF ordered 46 Nimrod MR1s. The first example (XV230) entered service in October 1969. Five squadrons were eventually equipped with the MR1.

R1

Three Nimrod aircraft were adapted for the signals intelligence role, replacing the Comet C2s and Canberras of No. 51 Squadron in May 1974. The R1 is distinguished from the MR2 by the lack of a MAD boom. Only since the end of the Cold War has the role of the aircraft been officially acknowledged; they were once described as "radar calibration aircraft". The R1s have not suffered the same rate of fatigue and corrosion of the MR2s. One R1 was lost in a flying accident since the type's introduction; this occurred in May 1995 during a flight test after major servicing, at RAF Kinloss. To replace this aircraft an MR2 was selected for extensive conversion, undertaken by BAE Systems at the Woodford factory, to R1 standard, and entered service in December 1996.

The Nimrod R1 is based at RAF Waddington in Lincolnshire, England and flown by 51 Sqn. The two remaining Nimrod R1s were originally planned to be retired at the end of March 2011, but operational requirements forced the RAF to deploy one to RAF Akrotiri, Cyprus on 16 March in support of Operation Ellamy. They will now be kept in service for at least another 3 months until June 2011. The R1 will be replaced by ex-USAF Boeing RC-135W *Rivet Joint* aircraft starting in 2014, known as Air Seeker.

MR2

Nimrod MR2 XV231 at NAS Norfolk (USA) in 1984

Starting in 1975, 32 aircraft were upgraded to MR2 standard, including modernisation of the electronic suite and (as the **MR2P**) provision for in-flight refuelling and additional ESM pods on the wingtips. The in-flight refuelling capability was introduced during the Falklands War, as well as hardpoints to allow the Nimrod to carry the AIM-9 Sidewinder missile for use against Argentine Air Force Boeing 707 which were configured for maritime patrol/surveillance duties shadowing the British naval task force. Eventually all MR2s gained refuelling probes and the "P" designation was dropped.

The Nimrod MR2 carried out three main roles - Anti-Submarine Warfare (ASW), Anti-Surface Unit Warfare (ASUW) and Search and Rescue (SAR). Its extended range enabled the crew to monitor maritime areas far to the north of Iceland and up to 4,000 km out into the Western Atlantic. With Air-to-Air Refuelling (AAR), range and endurance was greatly extended. The MR2 was a submarine killer carrying up to date sensors and data processing equipment linked to the weapon systems. In addition to weapons and sonobuoys, a searchlight was mounted in the starboard wing pod for Search and Rescue (SAR) operations.

Nose of a Nimrod MR2 at RIAT 2009

The crew consisted of two pilots and one flight engineer, two navigators (one tactical navigator and a routine navigator), one Air Electronics Officer (AEO), the sonobuoy sensor team of two Weapon System Operators (WSOp ACO) and four Weapon System Operators (WSOp EW) to manage passive and active electronic warfare systems. Two of the WSOps were used as observers positioned at the port and starboard beam lookout windows when flying in dense air traffic. The MR2 had the longest bomb bay of any NATO aircraft.

The Nimrod MR2 was based at RAF Kinloss in Scotland and flown by 201, 120 and 42(R) Squadrons. First maintenance of the MR2 was carried out by the Nimrod Line Sqn. Software support for the MR2 was carried out by the Nimrod Software Team also based at RAF Kinloss. The Nimrod MR2 aircraft was withdrawn on 31 March 2010, a year earlier than planned, for financial reasons. The last official flight of the MR2 Nimrod took place on 26 May 2010, with XV229 flying from RAF Kinloss to Kent International Airport, Manston in Kent, where it will be used by the nearby MOD Defence Fire Training and Development Centre as an evacuation training airframe.

AEW3

Nimrod AEW3

In the mid-1970s a modified Nimrod was proposed for the Airborne Early Warning (AEW) mission — again as a replacement for the Lancaster-derived, piston-engined Shackleton AEW.2. Eleven existing Nimrod airframes were to be converted by British Aerospace at the former Avro plant at Woodford to house the GEC Marconi radars in a bulbous nose and tail. The **Nimrod AEW3** project was plagued by cost over-runs and problems with the GEC 4080M computer used. Eventually, the MoD recognised that the cost of developing the radar system to achieve the required level of performance was prohibitive and the probability of success very uncertain, and in December 1986 the project was cancelled. The RAF eventually received seven Boeing E-3 Sentry aircraft instead.

MRA4

BAE Systems Nimrod MRA4

The Nimrod MRA4 was intended to replace the capability provided by the MR2. It was essentially a new aircraft, with current-generation Rolls-Royce BR710 turbofan engines, a new larger wing, and fully refurbished fuselage. However the project was subject to delays, cost over-runs, and contract re-negotiations. It was cancelled in 2010 as a result of the Strategic Defence and Security Review at which point it was £789 million over-budget and nine years late. The prototype aircraft, produced at a cost of over £1bn each, have been scrapped.

Design

The Nimrod is the first jet-powered Maritime Patrol Aircraft (MPA). Earlier MPA designs used piston engines or turboprop engines to improve fuel economy and to allow for lengthy patrols at low altitudes, as with the Lockheed P-3 Orion. Jet engines are most economical at high altitudes and less economical at low altitudes; the aircraft can travel to the operational area at high altitude which is economical on fuel and fast compared to earlier piston aircraft. On reaching the patrol area the Nimrod descends to its working altitude.

On patrol at high weight all four engines are used, but as fuel is consumed and weight is reduced first one and then a second engine is shut down, allowing the remaining engines to be run at an efficient RPM rather than running all engines at less efficient RPM. A "rapid start" system is fitted should the closed-down engines need to be restarted quickly; instead of relying only on ram air for restarting an engine, compressor air from a live engine is used in a starter turbine which rapidly accelerates the engine being started. All engines are used for travel back to base at high altitude.

Operational history

At first the crews, who were transferred to the Nimrod from the piston-engine Avro Shackletons, were not enthusiastic with the craft, mainly because its sensor suite was only marginally superior to the Shackleton's. In fact most sensors were the same, although the aircraft had a new digital data fusion computer. The Nimrod gave sterling service during the "Cod Wars" between Iceland and the UK over fishing rights. During the Falklands war (Operation Corporate), several Nimrods combed the sea for enemy submarines. The Nimrods took part in Operation Granby (the Gulf War 1990/1991), the NATO operations against Serbia in 1999, Operation Telic (the Iraq war in 2003 and beyond), the campaign in Afghanistan, and over Libya in 2011. They also were a routine component of British search and rescue (SAR) operations in the North Sea.

Search and rescue

While the Nimrod MR1/MR2 was in service, one aircraft from each of the squadrons on rotation was available for search and rescue operations at one-hour standby. The standby aircraft carried two sets of Lindholme Gear in the weapons bay. Usually one other Nimrod airborne on a training mission would also carry a set of Lindholme Gear. As well as using the aircraft sensors to find aircraft or ships in trouble, it was used to find survivors in the water, with a capability to search areas of up to 20,000 square miles (52,000 km). The main role would normally be to act as on-scene rescue coordinator to control ships, fixed-wing aircraft, and helicopters in the search area.

Because of the search and rescue role, Nimrod aircraft often appeared in the media in connection with major rescue incidents. In August 1979 a number of Nimrods were involved in finding competitors in distress in the disaster-stricken 1979 Fastnet race, and directing helicopters to the scene. The *Alexander L. Kielland* was a Norwegian semi-submersible drilling rig that capsized whilst working in the Ekofisk oil field in March 1980 killing 123 people. Six different Nimrods searched for survivors and took it in turn to provide a rescue co-ordination role, involving the control of 80 surface ships and 20 British and Norwegian helicopters; control became particularly important as the visibility deteriorated. In an example of the search capabilities, in September 1977 when an attempted crossing of the North Atlantic in a Zodiac inflatable dinghy went wrong, a Nimrod found the collapsed dinghy and directed a ship to it.

Offshore Tapestry

Tapestry is a codeword for the activities by ships and aircraft that protect the United Kingdom's Sovereign Sea Areas, including the protection of fishing rights and oil and gas extraction. Following the establishment of a 200 nautical miles (370 km) Exclusive Economic Zone (EEZ) at the beginning of 1977 the Nimrod fleet was tasked with patrolling the 270,000 square miles (700,000 km) area. The aircraft would locate, identify, and photograph vessels operating in the EEZ. The whole area was normally covered every week, with each vessel being photographed. The aircraft would also check and communicate with all oil and gas platforms. In 1978 a Nimrod arrested an illegal fishing vessel from the air in the Western Approaches and made the vessel proceed to Milford Haven for further investigation. During the Icelandic Cod Wars of 1972 and 1975-1976 the Nimrod aircraft operated with Royal Navy surface vessels protecting British fishing fleets.

Operators

United Kingdom
- Royal Air Force

Aircraft on display

MR2 variants
- XV226 - Bruntingthorpe Aerodrome
- XV231 - Manchester Airport viewing park
- XV232 - Coventry airport
- XV240 - Gate guardian at RAF Kinloss
- XV241 - National Museum of Flight, East Fortune, Scotland
- XV250 - Yorkshire Air Museum
- XV254 - Highland Aviation Museum, Inverness Airport (Forward 54 feet (16 m) of fuselage preserved)
- XV255 - City of Norwich Aviation Museum

AEW3
- Cockpit at Solway air Museum, Carlisle

Accidents and incidents

Five Nimrods have been lost in accidents :
- On 17 November 1980, a Nimrod MR2 XV256 crashed near RAF Kinloss after three engines failed following multiple birdstrikes. Both pilots were killed but the remaining crew survived.
- On 3 June 1984, a Nimrod MR2 XV257 stationed at RAF St Mawgan suffered extensive damage when a reconnaissance flare ignited in the bomb bay during flight. The aircraft successfully returned to base but was subsequently written-off due to fire damage. There were no casualties.
- On 16 May 1995, XW666, a Nimrod R1 from RAF Waddington, ditched in the Moray Firth 4.5 miles (7.2 km) from Lossiemouth after an engine caught fire during a post-servicing test flight from RAF Kinloss. The Ministry of Defence (MoD) inquiry identified a number of technical issues as the cause. There were no casualties.
- On 2 September 1995, a Nimrod MR2 XV239 crashed into Lake Ontario while participating in the Canadian International Air Show, killing the seven crew members.
- On 2 September 2006, a Nimrod MR2 XV230 crashed near Kandahar in Afghanistan, killing 12 airmen, one marine and one soldier — the largest single day loss of UK personnel since the Falklands War. This was the first Nimrod to enter operational service, originally as a MR1 but upgraded to MR2 standard in the 1980s. On 23 February 2007, the Ministry of Defence grounded all MR2 aircraft while fuel pumps were inspected. The MoD stressed that this was not necessarily related to the crash in Afghanistan.
- On 5 November 2007, XV235 was involved in a midair incident over Afghanistan when the crew noticed a fuel leak during air-to-air refuelling. After transmitting a mayday call, the crew landed the aircraft successfully. The incident came only a month before the issue of the report of a Board of Enquiry into the 2 September 2006 fatal accident to XV230 in (likely) similar circumstances. The RAF subsequently suspended air-to-air refuelling operations for this type.

RAF Nimrod MR2 taxis for takeoff

MR2

General characteristics
- **Crew:** 12
- **Capacity:** 24
- **Length:** 38.65 m (126 ft 9 in)
- **Wingspan:** 35.00 m (114 ft 10 in)
- **Height:** 9.14 m (31 ft)
- **Wing area:** 197.05 m² (2,121 sq ft)
- **Empty weight:** 39,009 kg (86,000 lb)
- **Max takeoff weight:** 87,090 kg (192,000 lb)
- **Powerplant:** 4 × Rolls-Royce Spey turbofans, 54.09 kN (12,160 lbf) each

Performance
- **Maximum speed:** 923 km/h (575 mph)
- **Cruise speed:** 787 km/h (490 mph)
- **Range:** 8,340-9,265 km (5,180-5,755 mi)
- **Service ceiling:** 13,411 m (44,000 ft)

Armament
- **Guns:** None
- **Hardpoints:** 2× under-wing pylon stations and an internal bomb bay with a capacity of 20,000 lb (9,100 kg) and provisions to carry combinations of:
  - **Rockets:** None
  - **Missiles:**
    - Air-to-air missile: 2× AIM-9 Sidewinder (non-standard in RAF service, only mounted on the MR2 during the Falklands War)
    - Air-to-surface missile: Nord AS.12, Martel missile, AGM-65 Maverick, AGM-84 Harpoon
  - **Bombs:**

- Depth charges, US-owned B57 nuclear depth bombs (2) (until 1992)
- **Other:**
- Air-dropped Mk.46 torpedoes, Sting Ray torpedoes
- Naval mines
- Sonobuoys

Source (edited): "http://en.wikipedia.org/wiki/Hawker_Siddeley_Nimrod"

IAI Nesher

The **Israel Aircraft Industries Nesher** (Hebrew: נשר, "Vulture" - often mistranslated as "Eagle") is the Israeli version of the Dassault Mirage 5 multi-role fighter aircraft. Most were later sold to the Argentine Air Force as **Daggers**, and later upgraded as **Fingers**.

Design and development

Dassault Aviation had developed the Mirage 5 at the request of the Israelis, who were the main foreign customers of the Mirage III. The Israeli Air Force (IAF) wanted the next version to have less all-weather capability in exchange for improved ordnance carrying capacity and range as the weather in the Middle East is mostly clear.

The French government arms embargo on Israel (on the eve of the Six Day War and afterwards) prevented the first 30 Mirage 5 aircraft (which were already paid for by Israel) plus optional 20 from being delivered and cut off support for the existing Mirage IIICJ fleet. Officially, Israel built the aircraft after obtaining complete blueprints. However, some sources claim Israel received 50 Mirage 5s in crates from French Air Force (AdA), while the AdA took over the 50 aircraft originally intended for Israel.

The Nesher was identical to the Mirage 5, except for the use of some Israeli avionics, a Martin-Baker zero-zero ejection seat, and provisions for a wider range of AAMs (Air-to-Air Missiles), including the Israeli Shafrir heat-seeking missile. Fifty-one Nesher fighters (Nesher S) and ten Nesher two-seat trainers (Nesher T) were built in all.

The Nesher had simpler avionics than the Mirage IIIC, and was found by Israeli pilots to be slightly less maneuvrable. However, it had longer range and bigger payload. The reduced maneuvrability did not prevent the Nesher from giving a good account of itself in air combat during the Yom Kippur war.

Nesher production was phased out from 1978 to make way for an improved Mirage derivative that had been in planned in parallel, in which the Atar engine was replaced by an Israeli-built General Electric J79 engine, the engine used on the American F-104 Starfighter and F-4 Phantom II fighters. The result was the IAI Kfir.

Operational history

Israel

The first Nesher prototype flew in September 1969, with production deliveries to the IAF beginning in May 1971, ending in February 1974. These aircraft performed well during the 1973 Yom Kippur War, claiming over a hundred kills. An estimated 15 Neshers were lost in combat or otherwise.

Argentina

Argentine Air Force Dagger, Jujuy Airport, 1981

Survivors of Israeli aircraft were refurbished and exported to the Argentine Air Force in two batches, 26 in 1978 and 13 in 1980, under the name **Dagger**, comprising 35 *Dagger A* single-seat fighters and 4 *Dagger B* two-seat trainers.

They form a new unit, 6th Air Group, and they were immediately listed with the help of the 8th Air Group (Mirage IIIEA) and the Peruvian Air Force, already a user of the Mirage 5, due the escalating crisis with Chile of that year.

During the 1982 Falklands War (Spanish: *Guerra de las Malvinas*), they were deployed to the southern naval airbase of Río Grande, Tierra del Fuego, and an airfield in Puerto San Julián and despite the distance to their targets and lack of aerial refueling capability, managed to make 153 sorties against both ground and naval targets on the 45 days of operations. In the last role they damaged HMS Antrim (D18), HMS Brilliant (F90), HMS Broadsword (F88), HMS Ardent (F184), HMS Arrow (F173) and HMS Plymouth (F126). Eleven Daggers were lost in combat (nine by AIM-9L Sidewinders fired from Sea Harriers and two by Surface to Air Missiles).

IAI Finger, Tandil, 1999

In the 1979 contract with IAI, the Argentine Air Force stipulated that the *Daggers* would be equipped with new avionics and HUD systems to take them to the Kfir C.2 (and beyond in some subsystems) standard. The program, named **Finger**, was underway in 1982 when the Falklands War broke out. With the war over, as some of these systems were made by the British Marconi Electronic Systems, they needed to be replaced after an arms embargo was imposed by the UK. The replacement of such systems took the planes to the final *Finger IIIB* standard mainly by replacing the British equipment with French-built Thomson-CSF.

Variants

- **Nesher S**: Single-seat ground-attack fighter version for the Israeli

Air Force.
- **Nesher T**: Two-seat training version for the Israeli Air Force.
- **Dagger A**: Refurbished single-seat fighter version for the Argentine Air Force.
- **Dagger B**: Refurbished two-seat training version for the Argentine Air Force.
- **Finger I**:
- **Finger II**:
- **Finger III**:

Operators

 Argentina
- Argentine Air Force

Former operator

 Israel
- Israeli Air Force

Specifications
General characteristics
- **Crew:** 1
- **Capacity:** 4200kg
- **Length:** 15.65 ()
- **Wingspan:** 8.22 ()
- **Height:** 4.25m ()
- **Wing area:** 34.8 ()
- **Empty weight:** 6,600kg ()
- **Max takeoff weight:** 13,500kg ()

Performance
- **Maximum speed:** mach 2.1 (39,370ft)
- **Range:** 1,300km () 1186 with 4700 litre's of auxiliary fuel in drop tanks plus 2 Air to Air missiles and 2600lb of bombs
- **Service ceiling:** 17,680 (55,775ft)
- **Rate of climb:** 16,400ft/min ()

Armament
up to 4200kg of disposable stores

Source (edited): "http://en.wikipedia.org/wiki/IAI_Nesher"

Learjet 35

The **Learjet Model 35** and **Model 36** are a series of American multi-role business jets and military transport aircraft. When used by the United States Air Force they carry the designation **C-21A**.

The aircraft are powered by two Garrett TFE731-2 turbofan engines. Its cabin can be arranged for 6-8 passengers. The Model 36 has a shortened passenger area in the fuselage, in order to provide more space in the aft fuselage for fuel tanks. It is designed for longer-range mission capability.

The engines are mounted in nacelles on the sides of the aft fuselage. The wings are equipped with single-slotted flaps. The wingtip fuel tanks distinguish the design from other aircraft having similar functions.

Development

The concept which became the LJ35 began as the Learjet 25BGF (with GF referring to "Garrett Fan"), a Learjet 25 with a then-new TFE731 turbofan engine mounted on the left side in place of the 25's General Electric CJ610 turbojet engine. This testbed aircraft first flew in May, 1971. As a result of the increased power and reduced noise of the new engine, Learjet further improved the design, and instead of being simply a variant of the 25, it became its own model, the 35.

Operational history

In 1976 American professional golfer Arnold Palmer used a Learjet 36 to establish a new round-the-world class record of 22,894 miles (36990 km) completed in 57 hours 25 minutes 42 seconds.

Learjet 35s made the bulk of Escuadrón Fénix during the 1982 Falklands War mainly on diversion flights.

Production on the 35/36 series ceased in 1994.

As of January, 2007, the U.S. National Transportation Safety Board database lists 19 fatal accidents for the 35/35A, and two for the 36/36A.

Variants

The Learjet 35A.

The Learjet 35AS.

Learjet 35

The original **Model 35** was powered by two TFE731-2-2A engines and was 13 inches longer than its predecessor, the Model 25. First flight of the prototype Model 35 was on 22 August 1973, and the aircraft was FAA certified in July, 1974. It could carry up to eight passengers. There were 64 base-model 35s built.

Learjet 35A

The **Model 35A** is an upgraded Model 35 with TFE731-2-2B engines and a range of 2,789 miles, with a fuel capacity of 931 US gallons (3,524 L) with refueling accomplished at ground level through each wingtip tank. It was introduced in 1976, replacing the 35. Over 600 35As were built, with a production line that ended with serial number 677, in 1993.

On February 12, 1996, a Learjet 35A piloted by Mark E. Calkins, Charles Conrad, Jr., Paul Thayer, and Daniel Miller completed an around-the-world flight in record time. The record remains standing as of 2011. This aircraft is now on display in Terminal C of Denver International Airport.

Variants

A C-21A Learjet attached to the North Dakota Air National Guard's (NDANG) 119th Fighter Wing.

C-21A

The **C-21A** is an "off the shelf" military variant of the Learjet 35A, with room for eight passengers and 42 ft³ (1.26 m³) of cargo. In addition to its normal role, the aircraft is capable of transporting litters during medical evacuations. Delivery of the C-21A fleet began in April 1984 and was completed in October 1985. Dyncorp International provides full contractor logistics support at seven worldwide locations.

There are 38 Air Force active duty aircraft, and 18 Air National Guard aircraft in the C-21A fleet. On 1 April 1997, all continental U.S.-based C-21As were realigned under Air Mobility Command, with the 375th Airlift Wing at Scott Air Force Base, Illinois, as the lead command. C-21As stationed outside the continental United States are assigned to the theater commanders.

EC-21A

Not a U.S. military designation. Electronic warfare training version of the Learjet 35A.

PC-21A

Not a U.S. military designation. Maritime patrol, anti-submarine warfare version of the Learjet 35A, equipped with a search radar, FLIR, infra-red linescanner, ESM and MAD systems, high-resolution TV, plus a hardpont under each wing, able to carry up to 454-kg (1,000-lb) in weight.

RC-21A

Not a U.S. military designation. Reconnaissance version of the Learjet 35A, equipped with a long-range oblique photography cameras, side-looking synthetic aperture radar, podded surveillance camera systems.

U-36

A Combat support variant of the Learjet 35A for the Japan Air self Defense Force (JASDF)

Learjet 36

The **Model 36** is essentially identical to the 35, except that it has a larger fuselage fuel tank, giving it 500 miles longer range, but reducing the passenger area's length by 18 inches (0.46 m). It was certified, along with the 35, in July, 1974.

Learjet 36A

Like the 35A, the **Model 36A** has upgraded engines and a higher maximum gross weight. It was introduced in 1976, replacing the 36.

R-21A

Not a U.S. military designation. Reconnaissance version of the Learjet 36A, equipped with a long-range oblique photography cameras, SLAR and a surveillance camera system.

U-21A

Not a U.S. military designation. Utility transport, training version of the Learjet 36A. Four were built for the Japan Maritime Self-Defense Force.

After-Market Modifications

Raisbeck Engineering offers two after-market modifications to the Learjet 35 and 36 series of aircraft. The Aft Fuselage Locker offered by this company is an external storage container mounted below the rear fuselage that can hold 300 lb of baggage. The addition of the locker imposes no performance penalties on the aircraft. This company also offers the ZR LITE performance improvement package. This modification reduces the cruise drag of the aircraft resulting in 25% less time-to-climb, 3000 to 4000 feet higher initial cruise altitude, .02+ increase in cruise Mach at equal power settings, 1% decrease in N1 and 15° ITT reduction at equal Mach and a 5-10% increase in range.

Avcon Industries also offers two after-market modifications to the Learjet 35 and 36 series of aircraft. The Avcon Fins are delta fins mounted n the aft fuselage, similar to those used on the Learjet 31 which improve directional stability when installed on Lear 35 & 36 models, and eliminate the FAA requirement for operable yaw dampers. The Avcon R/X modifications adds 750 pounds of usable fuel in the tip tanks, which provides up to 40 minutes of additional flight time at normal cruise speeds and altitudes.

Notable accidents and incidents

- On 7 June 1982, Argentine Air Force Learjet 35A serial T-24 was shot down by Sea Dart surface to air missile fired by HMS *Exeter* during the Falklands War killing all 5 on board.
- On 13 February 1983 a LearJet 35A carrying Sri Lankan business tycoon Upali Wijewardene disappeared (exploded) over Straits of Malacca (Malaysia). The wreckage has never been found, as well as any trace of Wijewardene and his top executives and crew.
- On 17 April 1995, a C-21 crashed into a wooded area near Alexander City, Alabama killing the two pilots and six passengers, including Clark G. Fiester, assistant secretary of the Air Force for acquisition, and Major General Glenn A Profitt II.
- The 1996 New Hampshire Learjet crash on Christmas Eve, 24 December 1996, in which a Learjet 35A crashed in New Hampshire, leading to the longest missing aircraft search in that state's history, lasting almost three years, and eventually resulted in Congressional legislation mandating improved emergency locator transmitters (ELTs) be installed in U.S.-registered business jets.
- On 29 August 1999, a U.S. registered Learjet 35A owned by Corporate Jets, Inc., was shot down near Adwa, Ethiopia, while flying

from Luxor, Egypt, to Nairobi, Kenya, with the loss of three persons.
- On 25 October 1999, professional golfer Payne Stewart was killed in the crash of a Learjet 35. The plane apparently suffered a loss of cabin pressure at some point early in the flight. All on board are thought to have died of hypoxia, lack of oxygen. The plane, apparently still on autopilot, continued flying until one engine flamed out, most likely due to fuel starvation crashed near Aberdeen, South Dakota after an uncontrolled descent. The exact cause of the pressurization failure and the reason behind the crew's failure or inability to respond to it has not been definitively determined.
- On 2 May 2000, F1 racing driver David Coulthard survived a Learjet 35 crash. His chartered aircraft was traveling from Farnborough Airfield to Côte d'Azur International Airport when it developed engine trouble, and crashed while making an emergency landing at Saint-Exupéry International Airport near Lyon, France. While Coulthard received only minor injuries, the front of the aircraft disintegrated upon impact, killing both pilots.
- On 9 March 2006 Argentine Air Force Learjet 35A serial T-21 struck terrain and broke up shortly after takeoff from El Alto International Airport in La Paz, Bolivia killing all 6 on board. The Learjet was sent to Bolivia to deliver humanitarian aid.
- On 4 November 2007, a Learjet 35A crashed in São Paulo, Brazil, after a failed takeoff attempt. It destroyed a house in a residential area near the Campo de Marte Airport, killing the pilot, co-pilot and 6 people of the same family who were in the house.
- On 5 January 2010 a Learjet 35A, registered to Royal Air Freight Inc. of Waterford, Michigan, crashed into the Des Plaines River on final approach to Chicago Executive Airport near Wheeling, IL, killing both pilot and co-pilot.

Operators

Civilian operators

German Air Rescue (DRF Stiftung Luftrettung gAg), AirMedical Ltd, Oxford, England

Raytheon Australia EWTS

Pelair (Australia) Defence and government related aviation support, Medivac, Executive Charter, Freight, Special Mission activities for international aid organisations

Air Affairs (Australia) Corporate Charter, Medivac, Target Towing

Líder Aviação (Brazil) Corporate Charter and Medivac -Líder Aviação

Rent Jets (Republic of Moldavia) Executive Charter -Rent Jets

Military operators

Argentina
- Argentine Air Force

Bolivia
- Bolivian Air Force

Brazil
- Brazilian Air Force

Chile
- Chilean Air Force

Finland
- Finnish Air Force

Japan
- Japan Maritime Self Defense Force

Mexico
- Mexican Air Force

Namibia
- Namibian Air Force

Switzerland
- Swiss Air Force

United States
- United States Air Force

Thailand
- Royal Thai Air Force

Specifications (C-21A)

Data from {GlobalSecurity}

General characteristics

- **Crew:** two (pilot and co-pilot)
- **Capacity:** 8 passengers and 3,153 lb (1,433 kg) of cargo
- **Length:** 48 ft 7 in (14.71 m)
- **Wingspan:** 39 ft 6 in (11.97m)
- **Height:** 12 ft 3 in (3.71 m)
- **Wing area:** 253.3ft² (23.53m²)
- **Empty weight:** 10,119 lb (4,590kg)
- **Loaded weight:** lb (kg)
- **Useful load:** lb (kg)
- **Max takeoff weight:** 18,300 lb (8,235 kg)
- **Powerplant:** 2 × Garrett TFE731-2-2B turbofan, 3,500 lb (16kN) each
- ***Unit cost**: $3.1 million (fiscal 1996 constant dollars)

Performance

- **Never exceed speed:** 350 knots indicated (KIAS) (403 mph, 648 km/h or 0.81M (These numbers differ based on altitude))
- **Maximum speed:** 461 knots at 41,000 ft (12,500 m) (530 mph, 853 km/h, Mach 0.81)
- **Stall speed:** 100 knots (mph, km/h)
- **Range:** 2,004 nm (2,306 mi, 3,690 km)
- **Service ceiling:** 45,000 ft (13,700 m)
- **Rate of climb:** 8000 ft/min (m/s)
- **Wing loading:** lb/ft² (kg/m²)

Source (edited): "http://en.wikipedia.org/wiki/Learjet_35"

Lockheed C-130 Hercules

The **Lockheed C-130 Hercules** is a four-engine turboprop military transport aircraft designed and built originally by Lockheed, now Lockheed Martin. Capable of using unprepared runways for takeoffs and landings, the C-130 was originally designed as a troop, medical evacuation, and cargo transport aircraft. The versatile airframe has found uses in a variety of other roles, including as a gunship (AC-130), for airborne assault, search and rescue, scientific research support, weather reconnaissance, aerial refueling, maritime patrol and aerial firefighting. It is the main tactical airlifter for many military forces worldwide. Over 40 models and variants of the Hercules serve with more than 60 nations.

During its years of service, the Hercules family has participated in countless military, civilian and humanitarian aid operations. The family has the longest continuous production run of any military aircraft in history. In 2007, the C-130 became the fifth aircraft—after the English Electric Canberra, B-52 Stratofortress, Tupolev Tu-95, and KC-135 Stratotanker—to mark 50 years of continuous use with its original primary customer, in this case, the United States Air Force. The C-130 is also the only military aircraft to remain in continuous production for 50 years with its original customer, as the updated C-130J Super Hercules.

Design and development

Background and requirements

The Korean War, which began in June 1950, showed that World War II-era piston-engine transports—C-119 Flying Boxcars, C-47 Skytrains and C-46 Commandos—were inadequate for modern warfare. Thus on 2 February 1951, the United States Air Force issued a General Operating Requirement (GOR) for a new transport to Boeing, Douglas, Fairchild, Lockheed, Martin, Chase Aircraft, North American, Northrop, and Airlifts Inc. The new transport would have a capacity for 92 passengers, 72 combat troops or 64 paratroopers in a cargo compartment that is approximately 41 feet (12 m) long, 9 feet (2.7 m) high, and 10 feet (3.0 m) wide. Unlike transports derived from passenger airliners, it was to be designed from the ground-up as a combat transport with loading from a ramp at the rear of the fuselage. This innovation for military cargo aircraft was first pioneered on the WW II German Junkers Ju 252 and Ju 253 "Hercules" transport prototypes in WWII. The Boeing C-97 also had a retracting ramp through clamshell doors, but could not be used for airdrops of cargo.

The Hercules also resembled a larger four-engine brother to the C-123 Provider with a similar wing and cargo ramp layout. That plane evolved from the Chase XCG-20 Avitruc, which was first designed and flown as a cargo glider in 1947. The rear ramp not only makes it possible to drive vehicles onto the plane (also possible with forward ramp on a C-124), but to airdrop or use low-altitude extraction for Sheridan tanks or even dropping improvised "daisy cutter" bombs.

A key feature was the introduction of the T56 turboprop, which was first developed specifically for the C-130. At the time, the turboprop was a new application of turbine engines that used exhaust gases to turn a shafted propeller, which offered greater range at propeller-driven speeds compared to pure turbojets, which were faster but thirstier. As was the case on helicopters of that era such as the UH-1 Huey, turboshafts produced much more power for their weight than piston engines. Lockheed would subsequently use the same engines and technology in the Lockheed L-188 Electra. That plane failed to perform efficiently in its civilian configuration but quite successfully adapted as the P-3 Orion patrol plane where speed and endurance of turboprops excelled.

The new Lockheed cargo plane design possessed a range of 1,100 nmi (1,300 mi; 2,000 km), takeoff capability from short and unprepared strips, and the ability to fly with one engine shut down. Fairchild, North American, Martin and Northrop declined to participate. The remaining five companies tendered a total of 10 designs: Lockheed two, Boeing one, Chase three, Douglas three, and Airlifts Inc. one. The contest was a close affair between the lighter of the two Lockheed (preliminary project designation L-206) proposals and a four-turboprop Douglas design.

The two YC-130 prototypes; the blunt nose was replaced with radar on later production models.

The Lockheed design team was led by Willis Hawkins, starting with a 130 page proposal for the *Lockheed L-206*. Hall Hibbard, Lockheed vice president and chief engineer, saw the proposal and directed it to Kelly Johnson, who did not care for the low-speed, unarmed aircraft, and remarked, "If you sign that letter, you will destroy the Lockheed Company." Both Hibbard and Johnson signed the proposal and the company won the contract for the now-designated Model 82 on 2 July 1951.

The first flight of the *YC-130* prototype was made on 23 August 1954 from the Lockheed plant in Burbank, California. The aircraft, serial number *53-3397*, was the second prototype but the first of the two to fly. The YC-130 was piloted by Stanley Beltz and Roy Wimmer on its 61-minute flight to Edwards Air Force Base; Jack Real and Dick Stanton served as flight engineers. Kelly Johnson flew chase in a P2V Neptune.

Production

C-130H Hercules flight deck

After the two prototypes were completed, production began in Marietta, Georgia, where over 2,300 C-130s have been built through 2009.

The initial production model, the *C-130A*, was powered by Allison T56-A-9 turboprops with three-blade propellers. Deliveries began in December 1956, continuing until the introduction of the *C-130B* model in 1959. Some A models were re-designated *C-130D* after being equipped with skis. The newer C-130B had ailerons with increased boost—3,000 psi (21 MPa) versus 2,050 psi (14 MPa)—as well as uprated engines and four-bladed propellers that were standard until the J-model's introduction.

C-130A model

Mexican Air Force C-130A

The first production C-130s were designated as A-models, with deliveries in 1956 to the 463d Troop Carrier Wing at Ardmore AFB, Oklahoma and the 314th Troop Carrier Wing at Sewart AFB, Tennessee. Six additional squadrons were assigned to the 322d Air Division in Europe and the 315th Air Division in the Far East. Additional airplanes were modified for electronics intelligence work and assigned to Rhein-Main Air Base, Germany while modified RC-130As were assigned to the Military Air Transport Service (MATS) photo-mapping division. Airplanes equipped with giant skis were designated as C-130Ds, but were essentially A-models except for the conversion. Australia became the first non American force to operate the C130A Hercules with 12 examples being delivered during late 1958-early 1959. These aircraft were fitted with three-blade AeroProducts propeller of 15' diameter. As the C-130A became operational with Tactical Air Command (TAC), the C-130's lack of range became apparent and additional fuel capacity was added in the form of external pylon-mounted tanks at the end of the wings. The A-model continued in service through the Vietnam War, where the airplanes assigned to the four squadrons at Naha AB, Okinawa and one at Tachikawa Air Base, Japan performed yeoman's service, including operating highly classified special operations missions such as the BLIND BAT FAC/Flare mission and FACT SHEET leaflet mission over Laos and North Vietnam. The A-model was also provided to the South Vietnamese Air Force as part of the Vietnamization program at the end of the war, and equipped three squadrons based at Tan Son Nhut AFB. The last operator in the world is the Honduran Air Force, which is still flying one of five A model Hercules (FAH *558*, c/n 3042) as of October 2009.

C-130B model

The C-130B model was developed to complement the A models that had previously been delivered, and incorporated new features, particularly increased fuel capacity in the form of auxiliary tanks built into the center wing section and an AC electrical system. Four-bladed Hamilton Standard propellers replaced the Aero Product three-bladed propellers that distinguished the earlier A-models. B-models replaced A-models in the 314th and 463rd Troop Carrier Wings. During the Vietnam War four squadrons assigned to the 463rd Troop Carrier/Tactical Airlift Wing based at Clark Air Force Base and Mactan Air Force Base in the Philippines were used primarily for tactical airlift operations in South Vietnam. In the spring of 1969, 463rd crews commenced COMMANDO VAULT bombing missions dropping "daisy cutter" M-121 10,000 lb (4,534 kg) bombs to clear "instant LZs" for helicopters. These would later be used by South Vietnam forces in a last-ditch air support effort to turn back communist troops. As the Vietnam War wound down, the 463rd B-models and A-models of the 374th Tactical Airlift Wing were transferred back to the United States where most were assigned to Air Force Reserve and Air National Guard units. Another prominent role for the B model was with the United States Marine Corps, where Hercules initially designated as GV-1s replaced C-119s. After Air Force C-130Ds proved the type's usefulness in Antarctica, the US Navy purchased a number of B-models equipped with skis that were designated as LC-130s. The Royal Canadian Air Force became another early user of the C130 with the delivery of its first B model in 1960.

An electronic reconnaissance variant of the C-130B was designated C-130B-II. A total of 13 aircraft were converted and operated under the SUN VALLEY program name. They were operated primarily from Yokota Air Base, Japan. All reverted to standard C-130B cargo aircraft after their replacement in the reconnaissance role by other aircraft. The C-130B-II was distinguished by its false external wing fuel tanks, which were disguised signals intelligence (SIGINT) receiver antennas. These pods were slightly larger than the standard wing tanks found on other C-130Bs. Most aircraft featured a swept blade antenna on the upper fuselage, as well as extra wire antennas between the vertical fin and upper fuselage not found on other C-130s. Radio call numbers on the tail of these aircraft were regularly changed so as to confuse observers and disguise their true mission.

C-130E model

Brazilian Air Force C-130E

The extended range *C-130E* model entered service in 1962 after it was developed as an interim long-range transport for the Military Air Transport Service. Essentially a B-model, the new designation was the result of the installation of 1,360 US gal (5,150 L) *Sargent Fletch-*

er external fuel tanks under each wing's mid-section and more powerful Allison T56-A-7A turboprops. The hydraulic boost pressure to the ailerons was reduced back to 2050 psi as a consequence of the external tanks weight in the middle of the wingspan. The E model also featured structural improvements, avionics upgrades and a higher gross weight. Australia took delivery of 12 C130E Hercules during 1966-67 to supplement the 12 C-130A models already in service with the RAAF. Sweden and Spain fly the TP-84T version of the C-130E fitted for aerial refueling capability.

C-130F / KC-130F / C-130G models

The *KC-130* tankers, originally *C-130F*s procured for the US Marine Corps (USMC) in 1958 (under the designation *GV-1*) are equipped with a removable 3,600 US gal (13,626 l) stainless steel fuel tank carried inside the cargo compartment. The two wing-mounted hose and drogue aerial refueling pods each transfer up to 300 US gal per minute (19 l per second) to two aircraft simultaneously, allowing for rapid cycle times of multiple-receiver aircraft formations, (a typical tanker formation of four aircraft in less than 30 minutes). The US Navy's *C-130G* has increased structural strength allowing higher gross weight operation.

C-130H model

Japan Air Self-Defense Force C-130H

The *C-130H* model has updated Allison T56-A-15 turboprops, a redesigned outer wing, updated avionics and other minor improvements. Later *H* models had a new, fatigue-life-improved, center wing that was retro-fitted to many earlier H-models. The H model remains in widespread use with the US Air Force (USAF) and many foreign air forces. Initial deliveries began in 1964 (to the RNZAF), remaining in production until 1996. An improved C-130H was introduced in 1974, with Australia purchasing 12 of type in 1978 to replace the original 12 C-130A models which had first entered RAAF Service in 1958.

The United States Coast Guard employs the HC-130H for long range search and rescue, drug interdiction, illegal migrant patrols, homeland security, and logistics.

C-130H models produced from 1992 to 1996 were designated as C-130H3 by the USAF. The 3 denoting the third variation in design for the H series. Improvements included ring laser gyros for the INUs, GPS receivers, a partial glass cockpit (ADI and HSI instruments), a more capable APN-241 color radar, night vision device compatible instrument lighting, and an integrated radar and missile warning system. The electrical system upgrade included Generator Control Units (GCU) and Bus Switching units (BSU)to provide stable power to the more sensitive upgraded components.

C-130K model

Royal Air Force C-130K (C.3)

The equivalent model for export to the UK is the *C-130K*, known by the Royal Air Force (RAF) as the *Hercules C.1*. The *C-130H-30* (*Hercules C.3* in RAF service) is a stretched version of the original Hercules, achieved by inserting a 100 in (2.54 m) plug aft of the cockpit and an 80 in (2.03 m) plug at the rear of the fuselage. A single C-130K was purchased by the Met Office for use by its Meteorological Research Flight, where it was classified as the *Hercules W.2*. This aircraft was heavily modified (with its most prominent feature being the long red and white striped atmospheric probe on the nose and the move of the weather radar into a pod above the forward fuselage). This aircraft, named *Snoopy*, was withdrawn in 2001 and was then modified by Marshall of Cambridge Aerospace as flight-test bed for the A400M turbine engine, the TP400. The C-130K is used by the RAF Falcons for parachute drops. Three C-130K (Hercules C Mk.1P) were upgraded and sold to the Austrian Air Force in 2002.

Later C-130 models & variants

The *MC-130E Combat Talon* was developed for the USAF during the Vietnam War to support special operations missions throughout Southeast Asia, and spawned a family of special missions aircraft. 37 of the earliest models currently operating with the United States Special Operations Command are scheduled to be replaced by new-production MC-130J versions. The EC-130 and EC-130H Compass Call versions are also Special variants but are assigned to Air Combat Command (ACC).

USAF HC-130P refuels a HH-60G Pavehawk helicopter

The *HC-130* is a family of long-range search and rescue variants used by the USAF and the US Coast Guard. Equipped for deep deployment of Pararescuemen (PJs), survival equipment, and aerial refueling of combat rescue helicopters, HC-130s are usually the on-scene command aircraft for combat SAR missions. Early versions were equipped with the Fulton surface-to-air recovery system, designed to pull a person off the ground using a wire strung from a helium balloon. The John Wayne movie *The Green Berets* features its use. The Fulton system was later removed when aerial refueling of helicopters proved safer and more versatile. The movie *The Perfect Storm* depicts a real life SAR mission involving aerial refueling of a New York Air National Guard HH-60G by a New York Air National Guard HC-130P.

The *C-130R* and *C-130T* are US Navy and USMC models, both equipped with underwing external fuel tanks. The USN C-130T is similar, but has additional avionics improvements. In both models, aircraft are equipped with Allison T56-A-16 engines. The USMC versions are designated *KC-130R* or *KC-130T* when equipped with underwing refueling pods and pylons and are fully night vision system compatible.

The RC-130 is a reconnaissance version. A single example is used by the Islamic Republic of Iran Air Force, the aircraft having originally been sold to the former Imperial Iranian Air Force.

The *Lockheed L-100 (L-382)* is a civilian variant, equivalent to a C-130E model without military equipment. The L-100 also has two stretched versions.

Next generation

In the 1970s, Lockheed proposed a C-130 variant with turbofan engines rather than turboprops, but the US Air Force preferred the takeoff performance of the existing aircraft. In the 1980s, the C-130 was intended to be replaced by the Advanced Medium STOL Transport project. The project was canceled and the C-130 has remained in production.

In the 1990s, the improved C-130J Super Hercules was developed by Lockheed (later Lockheed Martin). This model is the newest version and the only model in production. Externally similar to the classic Hercules in general appearance, the J model has new turboprop engines, six-bladed propellers, digital avionics, and other new systems.

Improvements and upgrades

In 2000, Boeing was awarded a US$1.4 billion contract to develop an Avionics Modernization Programme kit for the C-130. The program was beset with delays and cost overruns until project restructuring in 2007. On 2 September 2009, Bloomberg news reported that the planned Avionics Modernization Program (AMP) upgrade to the older C-130s would be dropped to provide more funds for the F-35, CV-22 and airborne tanker replacement programs. However, in June 2010, the Pentagon approved funding for the initial production of the AMP upgrade kits. Under the terms of this agreement, the USAF has cleared Boeing to begin low-rate initial production (LRIP) for the C-130 AMP. A total of 198 aircraft are expected to feature the AMP upgrade. The current cost per aircraft is US$14 million although Boeing expects that this price will drop to US$7 million for the 69th aircraft.

A Hercules deploying flares, sometimes referred to as *Angel Flares* due to the characteristic shape

USMC KC-130F Hercules performing takeoffs and landings aboard the aircraft carrier USS *Forrestal* (CVA-59) in 1963. The aircraft is now displayed at the National Museum of Naval Aviation.

The Hercules holds the record for the largest and heaviest aircraft to land on an aircraft carrier. In October and November 1963, a USMC KC-130F (BuNo *149798*), loaned to the US Naval Air Test Center, made 29 touch-and-go landings, 21 unarrested full-stop landings and 21 unassisted take-offs on the USS *Forrestal* at a number of different weights. The pilot, LT (later RADM) James H. Flatley III, USN, was awarded the Distinguished Flying Cross for his role in this test series. The tests were highly successful, but the idea was considered too risky for routine "Carrier Onboard Delivery" (COD) operations. Instead, the C-2 Greyhound was developed as a dedicated COD aircraft. The Hercules used in the test, most recently in service with Marine Aerial Refueler Squadron 352 (VMGR-352) until 2005, is now part of the collection of the National Museum of Naval Aviation at NAS Pensacola, Florida.

The C-130 Hercules were used in the Battle of Kham Duc, when the North Vietnamese army forced U.S.-led forces to abandon the Kham Duc Special Forces Camp.

In 1958, a US reconnaissance C-130A-II was shot down over Armenia by MiG-17s.

While the C-130 is involved in cargo and resupply operations daily, it has been a part of some notable offensive operations.

In 1964 C-130 crews from the 6315th Operations Group at Naha AB, Okinawa commenced FAC/Flare missions over the Ho Chi Minh Trail in Laos supporting USAF strike aircraft. In April 1965 the mission was expanded to North Vietnam where C-130 crews led formations of B-57 bombers on night reconnaissance/strike missions against communist supply routes leading to South Vietnam. In early 1966 Project BLIND BAT/LAMPLIGHTER was established at Ubon RTAFB, Thailand. After the move to Ubon the mission became a four-engine forward air controller (FAC) mission with the C-130 crew searching for targets then calling in strike aircraft. Another little-known C-130 mission flown by Naha-based crews was COMMANDO SCARF, which involved the delivery of chemicals onto sections of the Ho Chi Minh Trail in Laos that were designed to produce mud and landslides in hopes of making the truck routes impassable.

In November 1964, on the other side of the globe, C-130Es from the 464th Troop Carrier Wing but loaned to 322d Air Division in France, flew one of the most dramatic missions in history in the former Belgian Congo. After a Congolese rebel group named "Simba" took white residents of the city of Stanleyville hostage, the US and Belgian developed a joint rescue mission that used the C-130s to airlift and then drop and air-land a force of Belgian paratroopers to rescue the hostages. Two missions were flown, one over Stanleyville and another over Paulis during Thanksgiving weeks. The headline-making mission resulted in the first award of the prestigious MacKay Trophy to C-130 crews.

In October 1968 a C-130B from the 463rd Tactical Airlift Wing dropped a pair of M121 10,000 pound bombs that had been developed for the massive B-36 bomber but had never been used. The US Army and US Air Force resurrected the huge weapons as a means of clearing landing zones for helicopters and in early 1969 the 463rd commenced Commando Vault missions. Although the stated purpose of COMMANDO VAULT was to clear LZs, they were also used on enemy base camps and other targets.

The MC-130 Combat Talon variant carries and deploys the among the largest conventional bombs in the world, the BLU-82 "Daisy Cutter" and GBU-43/B Massive Ordnance Air Blast bomb, also known as the MOAB. Daisy Cutters were used during the Vietnam War to clear landing zones and to eliminate mine fields. The weight and size of the weapons make it impossible or impractical to load them on conventional bombers. The GBU-43/B MOAB is a successor to the BLU-82 and can perform the same function, as well as perform strike functions against hardened targets in a low air threat environment.

The AC-130 also holds the record for the longest sustained flight by a C-130. From 22 October to 24 October 1997, two AC-130U gunships flew 36.0 hours nonstop from Hurlburt Field Florida to Taegu (Daegu), South Korea while being refueled 7 times by KC-135 tanker aircraft. This record flight shattered the previous record longest flight by over 10 hours while the 2 gunships took on 410,000 lb (190,000 kg) of fuel. The gunship has been used in every major U.S. combat operation since Vietnam, except for Operation El Dorado Canyon, the 1986 attack on Libya.

In the Indo-Pakistani War of 1965, the Pakistan Air Force modified/improvised several aircraft for use as heavy bombers, and attacks were made on Indian bridges and troop concentrations with some successes. No aircraft were lost in the operations, though one was slightly damaged.

It was also used in the 1976 Entebbe raid in which Israeli commando forces carried a surprise assault to rescue 103 passengers of an airliner hijacked by Palestinian and German terrorists at Entebbe Airport, Uganda. The rescue force—200 soldiers, jeeps, and a black Mercedes-Benz (intended to resemble Ugandan Dictator Idi Amin's vehicle of state)—was flown 2,200 nmi (2,532 mi; 4,074 km) from Israel to Entebbe by four Israeli Air Force (IAF) Hercules aircraft without mid-air refueling (on the way back, the planes refueled in Nairobi, Kenya).

During the Falklands War (Spanish: *Guerra de las Malvinas*) of 1982, Argentine Air Force C-130s undertook highly dangerous, daily re-supply night flights as blockade runners to the Argentine garrison on the Falkland Islands. They also performed daylight maritime survey flights. One was lost during the war. Argentina also operated two KC-130 tankers during the war, and these refueled both the Skyhawk and Navy Super Etendards which sank 6 British ships. The British also used their C-130s to support their logistical operations.

During the Gulf War of 1991 (Operation Desert Storm), the C-130 Hercules was used operationally by the US Air Force, US Navy and US Marine Corps, along with the air forces of Australia, New Zealand, Saudi Arabia, South Korea and the UK.

Recent history

During the invasion of Afghanistan in 2001 and the ongoing support of the International Security Assistance Force (Operation Enduring Freedom), the C-130 Hercules has been used operationally by Australia, Belgium, Canada, Denmark, France, Italy, the Netherlands, New Zealand, Norway, Portugal, South Korea, Spain, the UK and the United States.

During the 2003 invasion of Iraq (Operation Iraqi Freedom), the C-130 Hercules has been used operationally by Australia, the UK and the United States. After the initial invasion, C-130 operators as part of the Multinational force in Iraq used their C-130s to support their forces in Iraq.

One RAF C-130 was shot down on 30 January 2005, when an Iraqi insurgent brought it down firing with a ZU-23 anti-aircraft artillery gun while the plane was flying at 164 ft (50 m) after it had dropped SAS special forces paratroopers.

USMC C-130T *Fat Albert* performing a JATO

A prominent C-130T aircraft named *Fat Albert* serves as the support aircraft for the US Navy Blue Angels flight demonstration team. Although Fat Albert supports a Navy squadron, it is operated by the US Marine Corps (USMC) and its crew consists solely of USMC personnel. At some air shows featuring the team, Fat Albert takes part, performing flyovers and sometimes demonstrating its jet-assisted takeoff (JATO) capabilities, but the JATO demonstration ended in 2009 due to dwindling supplies of rockets.

Civilian use

A C-130E fitted with a MAFFS dropping fire retardant

The U.S. Forest Service developed the Modular Airborne FireFighting System for the C-130 in the 1970s, which allows regular aircraft to be temporarily converted to an airtanker for fighting wildfires. In the late 1980s, 22 retired USAF C-130As were removed from storage at Davis-Monthan Air Force Base and transferred to the U.S. Forest Service who then sold them to six private companies to be converted into air tankers (see U.S. Forest Service airtanker scandal). After one of these aircraft crashed due to wing separation in flight as a result of fatigue stress cracking, the entire fleet of C-130A air tankers was permanently grounded in 2004 (see 2002 airtanker crashes). C-130s have been used to spread chemical dispersants onto the massive oil slick in the Gulf Coast in 2010.

Variants

(foreground to background) C-130s from the: US, Canada, Australia and Israel.

Significant military variants of the C-130 include:

C-130A/B/E/F/G/H/K/T
Tactical airlifter basic models
C-130J Super Hercules
Tactical airlifter, with new engines, avionics, and updated systems
C-130K
Designation for RAF Hercules C1/W2/C3 aircraft (C-130Js in RAF service are the Hercules C.4 and Hercules C.5)
AC-130A/E/H/U Spectre/Spooky
Gunship variants
C-130D/D-6
Ski-equipped version for snow and ice operations United States Air Force / Air National Guard
CC-130E/H/J Hercules
Designation for Canadian Forces Hercules aircraft
DC-130A/E
Drone control
EC-130
EC-130E/J Commando Solo - USAF / Air National Guard psychological operations version
EC-130E - Airborne Battlefield Command and Control Center (ABCCC)
EC-130E Rivet Rider - Airborne psy-

chological warfare aircraft
EC-130H Compass Call - Electronic warfare and electronic attack.
EC-130V - Airborne early warning and control (AEW&C) variant used by USCG for counter-narcotics missions
GC-130
Permanently Grounded "Static Display"
HC-130
HC-130B/E/H - Early model combat search and rescue
HC-130P/N Combat King - USAF aerial refueling tanker and combat search and rescue
HC-130J Combat King II - Next generation combat search and rescue tanker
HC-130H/J - USCG long-range surveillance and search and rescue
JC-130
Temporary conversion for flight test operations
KC-130F/R/T/J
United States Marine Corps aerial refueling tanker and tactical airlifter
LC-130F/H/R
USAF / Air National Guard - Ski-equipped version for Arctic and Antarctic support operations.
MC-130
MC-130E/H Combat Talon I/II - Special operations infiltration/extraction variant
MC-130W Combat Spear/Dragon Spear - Special operations tanker/gunship
MC-130P Combat Shadow - Special operations tanker
MC-130J Combat Shadow II - Special operations tanker Air Force Special Operations Command
YMC-130H - Three modified under Operation Credible Sport for second Iran hostage crisis rescue attempt
NC-130
Permanent conversion for flight test operations
PC-130
Maritime patrol
RC-130
Surveillance aircraft for reconnaissance
SC-130
Search and rescue
TC-130
Aircrew training
VC-130
VIP transport
WC-130A/B/E/H/J
Weather reconnaissance ("Hurricane Hunter") version for USAF / Air Force Reserve Command in support of the NOAA/National Weather Service's National Hurricane Center

Operators

Countries operating the C-130 in December 2006

Philippine Air Force and Army servicemen unload a C-130 of supplies for transfer to waiting U.S. helicopters for delivery to Panay Island.

Accidents and losses

The C-130 Hercules has had a low accident rate in general. The Royal Air Force recorded an accident rate of about one aircraft loss per 250,000 flying hours over the last forty years, placing it behind Vickers VC10s and Lockheed TriStars with no flying losses. USAF C-130A/B/E-models had an overall attrition rate of 5 percent as of 1989 as compared to 1 to 2 percent for commercial airliners in the U.S., according to the NTSB, 10 percent for B-52 bombers, and 20 percent for fighters (F-4, F-111), trainers (T-37, T-38), and helicopters (H-3).

A total of 70 aircraft were lost by the United States Air Force and the United States Marine Corps during combat operations in the Vietnam War in Southeast Asia. By the nature of the Hercules' worldwide service, the pattern of losses provides an interesting barometer of the global hot spots over the past fifty years.

Aircraft on display

Australia
- C-130A RAAF A97-214 used by 36 Squadron from early 1959, withdrawn from use late 1978; now at RAAF Museum, RAAF Base Williams, Point Cook.
- C-130E RAAF A97-160 used by 37 Squadron from August 1966, withdrawn from use November 2000; to RAAF Museum, 14 November 2000, cocooned as of September 2005.

Canada
- CC-130E RCAF 10314 (later 130314) is on display at the National Air Force Museum of Canada, CFB Trenton

Norway
- C-130H Royal Norwegian Air Force 953 retired 10 June 2007 and moved to the Air Force museum at Oslo Gardermoen in May 2008.

Saudi Arabia
- C-130H RSAF 460 was operated by 4 Squadron Royal Saudi Air Force, December 1974 until January 1987. It was damaged in a fire at Jeddah in December 1989. Restored for ground training by August 1993. At Riyadh Air Base Museum, November 2002, restored for ground display by using a tail from another C-130H.

United States
- AC-130A USAF 53-3129, one of the first seven AC-130A aircraft deployed to Vietnam, named *First Lady* in November 1970. This aircraft was a conversion of the first production C-130. On 25 March 1971, it took an anti-aircraft artillery hit in the belly just aft of the nose gear wheel well over the Ho Chi Minh trail in Laos. The 37 mm shell destroyed everything below the crew deck and barely missed striking two crew members. In 1975, after the conclusion of US involvement in the

Vietnam war, it was transferred to the Air Force Reserve, where it served with the 711th Special Operations Squadron of the 919th Special Operations Wing. In 1980 the aircraft was upgraded from the original three-bladed propellers to the quieter four-bladed propellers and was eventually retired in late 1995. The retirement also marked an end to the Air Force Reserve Command flying the AC-130A. The aircraft now sits on display in the final Air Force Reserve Command configuration with grey paint, black markings, the four-bladed Hamilton Sunstrand 54H60-91 props at the Air Force Armament Museum at Eglin Air Force Base, Florida, USA.

- C-130A USAF 55-0037 was used by the 773 TCS, 483 TCW, 315 AD, 374 TCW, 815 TAS, 35 TAS, 109 TAS, belly-landed at Duluth, MN., April 1973, repaired; 167 TAS, 180 TAS, to Chanute Technical Training Center as GC-130A, May 1984; now displayed at Octave Chanute Aerospace Museum, Rantoul Aviation Complex, Rantoul, Illinois. as of November 1995.
- C-130A USAF 56-0518 was by the 314 TCW, 315 AD, 41 ATS, 328 TAS; to South Vietnamese Air Force 435 Transport Squadron, November 1972; holds the C-130 record for taking off with the most personnel on board, during evacuation of SVN, 29 April 1975, with 452. Returned to USAF, 185 TAS, 105 TAS; gate guard at Little Rock AFB Visitor Center by March 1993.
- C-130A USAF 57-0453 operated from 1958 to 1991, last duty with 155th TAS, 164th TAG, Tennessee Air National Guard, Memphis International Airport, Tennessee, 1976–1991, named "Nite Train to Memphis"; to AMARC in December, 1991, then sent to Texas for modification into replica of C-130A-II 56-0528, shot down by Russian fighters over Soviet Yerevan, Armenia on 2 September 1958, while on ELINT mission with loss of all crew, displayed in National Vigilance Park, National Security Agency grounds, Fort George Meade, Maryland.
- C-130D USAF 57-0490 was used by the 61st TCS, 17th TCS, 139th TAS with skis, July 1975-April 1983; to MASDC, 1984–1985, GC-130D ground trainer, Chanute AFB, Illinois, 1986–1990; When Chanute closed in September 1993 it moved to the Octave Chanute Aerospace Museum, Rantoul, Illinois. In July 1994 it moved to the Empire State Air Museum, Schenectady County Airport, New York, until placed on the gate at Stratton ANGB in October 1994.
- NC-130B USAF 57-0526 was the second B model manufactured, initially delivered as JC-130B; assigned to 6515th Organizational Maintenance Squadron for flight testing at Edwards AFB, California on 29 November 1960; turned over to 6593rd Test Squadron's Operating Location No. 1 at Edwards AFB and spent next seven years supporting Corona Program; "J" status and prefix removed from aircraft Oct 1967; transferred to 6593rd Test Squadron at Hickam AFB, Hawaii and modified for mid-air retrieval of satellites; acquired by 6514th Test Squadron at Hill AFB in Jan 1987 and used as electronic testbed and cargo transport; aircraft retired Jan 1994 with 11,000+ flight hours and moved to Hill Aerospace Museum by January 1994.
- KC-130F USMC BuNo 149798 was used in tests in October–November 1963 by the U.S. Navy for unarrested landings and unassisted take-offs from the carrier USS *Forrestal*, it remains the record holder for largest aircraft to operate from a carrier flight deck, and carried the name "Look Ma, No Hook" during the tests. Retired to the National Museum of Naval Aviation, NAS Pensacola, Florida in May, 2003.
- C-130G USMC BuNo 151891 was modified to EC-130G, 1966, then testbed for EC-130Q in 1981. To TC-130G in May 1990 and assigned as Blue Angels support craft, serving as "Fat Albert Airlines" from 1991 to 2002. Retired to the National Museum of Naval Aviation at NAS Pensacola, Florida, November 2002.
- C-130E USAF 64-0525 is on display at the 82nd Airborne Division War Memorial Museum at Fort Bragg, North Carolina. Aircraft was the last assigned to the 43rd AW at Pope AFB, NC prior to retirement from the USAF.
- C-130E USAF 69-6579 was operated by the 61st TAS, 314th TAW, 50th AS, 61st AS; at Dyess AFB as maintenance trainer as GC-130E, March 1998;to Dyess AFB museum, January 2004.
- MC-130E Combat Talon AFSOC 64-0567 was unofficially known as "Wild Thing". It transported captured Panamanian dictator Manuel Noreiga in 1989 during Operation Just Cause, and participated in Operation Eagle Claw, the unsuccessful attempt to rescue US hostages from Iran in 1980. Wild Thing was also the first fixed-wing aircraft to employ night-vision goggles. On display at Hurlburt Field, in Florida.
- C-130E USAF 69-6580 was operated by the 61st TAS, 314th TAW, 317th TAW, 314th TAW, 317th TAW, 40th AS, 41st AS, 43rd AW, retired after center wing cracks were detected in April 2002; to the Air Mobility Command Museum, Dover AFB on 2 February 2004.
- C-130E USAF 70-1269 was used by the 43rd AW and now on display at the Pope Air Park, Pope AFB, 2006.
- C-130H USAF 74-1686 was used by the 463rd TAW; one of three C-130H airframes modified to YMC-130H for aborted rescue attempt of Iranian hostages, Operation Credible Sport, with rocket packages blistered onto fuselage in 1980, but these were removed after mission was canceled. Subsequent duty with the 4950th Test Wing, then donated to the Robins AFB museum, Georgia, in March 1988.

Specifications (C-130H)

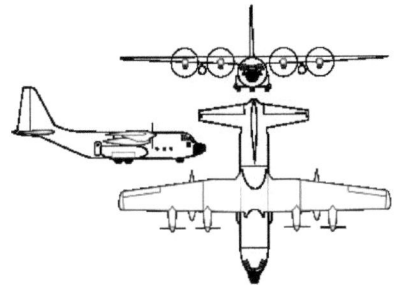

Data from USAF C-130 Hercules fact sheet, International Directory of Military Aircraft, Complete Encyclopedia of World Aircraft, Encyclopedia of Modern Military Aircraft

General characteristics
- **Crew:** 5 (two pilots, navigator, flight engineer and loadmaster)
- **Capacity:**
  - 92 passengers *or*
  - 64 airborne troops *or*
  - 74 litter patients with 2 medical personnel *or*
  - 6 pallets *or*
  - 2–3 HMMWVs *or*
  - 2 M113 armored personnel carrier
- **Payload:** 45,000 lb (20,000 kg)
- **Length:** 97 ft 9 in (29.8 m)
- **Wingspan:** 132 ft 7 in (40.4 m)
- **Height:** 38 ft 3 in (11.6 m)
- **Wing area:** 1,745 ft² (162.1 m²)
- **Empty weight:** 75,800 lb (34,400 kg)
- **Useful load:** 72,000 lb (33,000 kg)
- **Max takeoff weight:** 155,000 lb (70,300 kg)
- **Powerplant:** 4× Allison T56-A-15 turboprops, 4,590 shp (3,430 kW) each

Performance
- **Maximum speed:** 320 knots (366 mph, 592 km/h) at 20,000 ft (6,060 m)
- **Cruise speed:** 292 kn (336 mph, 540 km/h)
- **Range:** 2,050 nmi (2,360 mi, 3,800 km)
- **Service ceiling:** 33,000 ft (10,060 m) empty; 23,000 ft (7,077 m) with 42,000 pounds (19,090 kilograms) payload ()
- **Rate of climb:** 1,830 ft/min (9.3 m/s)
- **Takeoff distance:** 3,586 ft (1,093 m) at 155,000 lb (70,300 kg) max gross weight; 1,400 ft (427 m) at 80,000 lb (36,300 kg) gross weight

Avionics
- Westinghouse Electronic Systems (now Northrop Grumman) AN/APN-241 weather and navigational radar

Source (edited): "http://en.wikipedia.org/wiki/Lockheed_C-130_Hercules"

Lockheed L-188 Electra

The **Lockheed Model 188 Electra** is an American turboprop airliner built by Lockheed. First flying in 1957, it was the first large turboprop airliner produced in the United States. Initial sales were good, but after two fatal crashes which prompted an expensive modification program to fix a design defect, no further orders were placed. The type was soon replaced by turbojet airliners but many were modified as freighters and the type continues to operate in various roles into the 21st Century. The airframe was also used as the basis for the Lockheed P-3 Orion maritime patrol aircraft.

Development

Lockheed had established a strong position in airliner production with its piston-engined Constellation series and was approached by Capital Airlines to develop a turboprop airliner, but with no interest from other American carriers the company did not produce a design; Capital Airlines went on to order 60 British Vickers Viscount four-engined turboprop airliners. In 1954 the company offered a twin-engined design, the CL-303, to meet an American Airlines requirement; it was a high-wing design for 60 to 70 passengers but again the design failed to interest other carriers.

American Airlines then revised its requirement and specified a four-engine design for 75 passengers and a range of 2000 miles (3220 km). To meet this Lockheed proposed a new design, the CL-310 with a low wing and either four Rolls-Royce Darts or Napier Elands. The CL-310 design met the American Airlines requirement but Eastern Airlines wanted an aircraft with more range and 85 to 90 seats. Lockheed modified and enlarged the CL-310 design to use the Allison 501-D13, a civilian version of the T56 originally developed for the prototype Lockheed C-130 Hercules military transport.

This design was launched as the Model 188 with an order for 35 aircraft by American Airlines on June 8, 1955, this was followed by an Eastern Airlines order for 40 on September 27, 1955. The first aircraft took 26 months to complete and by that time Lockheed had orders for 129 aircraft. The prototype, a Model 188A, first flew on December 6, 1957. and a was awarded a type certificate by the Federal Aviation Administration (FAA) on 22 August 1958. The first delivery was to Eastern Airlines on October 8, 1958 although it did not enter service until January 1959.

In 1957 the United States Navy issued a requirement for an advanced maritime patrol aircraft. Lockheed proposed a development of the Electra which was later placed into production as the P-3 Orion, which saw much greater success. The Orion approaches nearly 50 years of front-line service.

Design

The Model 188 Electra is a low-wing cantilever monoplane powered by four wing-mounted Allison 501-D13 turboprops. It has a retractable nose-wheel landing gear and a conventional tailplane. It has a cockpit crew of three and can carry 66 to 80 passengers in a mixed-class arrangement, although 98 could be carried in a high-density configuration. The first variant was the Model 188A which was followed by the longer-range Model 188C with increased fuel load and a higher take-off weight.

Operational history

Civil operations

L188C Electra of KLM Royal Dutch Airlines operating a passenger service at Manchester Airport in 1963

American Airlines was the launch customer, followed by Eastern Airlines and Braniff Airways. The Electra suffered a troubled start in service. Passengers of early aircraft complained of high noise levels in the cabin forward of the wings, caused by propeller resonance. To solve this problem, Lockheed redesigned the engine nacelles to tilt the engines upwards by three degrees. The changes were incorporated on the production line by mid-1959 or as modification kits for the aircraft already built, and resulted in much-improved performance as well as increased passenger comfort. Much worse, three were lost in fatal accidents in 14 months between February 1959 and March 1960. Following the third crash the FAA restricted the maximum speed at which Electras could be flown until the cause could be determined.

After an extensive investigation, two of the crashes (in September 1959 and March 1960) were found to be caused by an engine mount problem. They were not strong enough to dampen a whirling mode that affected the outboard engine nacelles. When the oscillation was transmitted to the wings they were attached to, a severe up-and-down vibration escalated until the wings would tear themselves off the aircraft.The company implemented an expensive modification program labelled the Lockheed Electra Achievement Program or LEAP, in which the engine mounts and the wing structures supporting the mounts were strengthened, and some of the wing skins replaced with thicker material. Each of the survivors of the 145 Electras built to that time was modified at Lockheed's expense at the factory, the modifications taking 20 days for each aircraft; and the changes were incorporated in subsequent aircraft as they were built. However the damage had been done, the public lost confidence in the type; this and the smaller jets that were being introduced eventually relegated Electras to only the smallest airlines. Production ended in 1961 after only 170 aircraft had been built. Losses to Lockheed have been estimated as high as $57 million, not counting an additional $55 million in lawsuits. Although their use continued throughout the 1970s and 1980s for passenger operations, most of the aircraft currently in service are operated as freighters.

Many airlines in the US flew Electras, but the only European airline to order the type was KLM. In the South Pacific, Tasman Empire Airways Limited (TEAL) and its successor Air New Zealand flew the Electra. In Australia Trans Australia Airlines (TAA) and Ansett each operated three Electras on the trunk routes between the Australian mainland state capital cities, and later to Port Moresby, from 1959 until 1971. Ansett had its three Electras converted to freighters in 1970-71 and continued to fly them until 1984. Qantas also operated four Electras on its routes to Hong Kong and Japan; to New Caledonia; and to New Guinea (until the New Guinea route was handed to Ansett and TAA); then later across the Indian Ocean to South Africa, and across the Tasman in competition with TEAL after that airline became 100% New Zealand-owned. The divestiture of TEAL's 50%- Australian shareholding was itself prompted by the Electra order, as TEAL wanted jet aircraft, but was forced by the Australian government to order Electras instead to standardise with Qantas. Three of Qantas' Electras were retired in the mid-1960s and the fourth in 1971.

Lockheed L-188 Electra of Bolivian airline Lloyd Aéreo Boliviano operated until 1975.

Some Electras were sold to South-American airlines such as Bolivian airline Lloyd Aéreo Boliviano which allowed to fly non-stop international destinatios until it took delivery on its first jet airliner, displacing the Electra, and Varig, operating the Rio de Janeiro-São Paulo shuttle service (the so-called *Ponte Aérea* - air bridge, in Portuguese) before being sold to Zaire in 1992. Others were retired from passenger service into air cargo use, 40 airframes being modified by a subsidiary of Lockheed from 1968 with either one or two large doors in the left side of the fuselage and a reinforced cabin floor.

Of the total of 170 Electras built, as of March 2011 58 have been written off because of crashes and other accidents.

Military use

In 1973, the Argentine Navy bought three Electras equipped with cargo doors. These were used during the "Dirty War" to toss political prisoners into the Rio de La Plata, in the infamous death flights. The Electras were also used in transport duties during the Falklands War in 1982.

In 1983, after the retirement of its last SP-2H Neptunes the Argentine Navy bought further civilian Electra airframes, modified several for maritime patrol, and widely used them until their replacement by P-3s in 1994. One of the Argentine Navy's Electras, known locally as **L-188W Electron** (for electronic warfare), is preserved at the Argentine Naval Aviation Museum (MUAN) at Bahía Blanca.

Variants

An L-188CF of Atlantic Airlines

L-188A
Initial production version
L-188AF (All Freight version)
Unofficial designation for freighter conversions of L-188A carried out under a supplementary type certificate.
L-188PF (Passenger-Freight version)
Unofficial designation for freighter conversions of L-188A carried out under a supplementary type certificate.
L-188C
Long-range version with increased fuel capacity (6,940 gallon fuel capacity from 5,450 gallons on L-188A) and a higher operating gross weight (Maximum takeoff weight is 116,000 lb compared to 113,000 lb of the "A" version)
L-188CF
Unofficial designation for freighter conversion of L-188C carried out under a supplementary type certificate.
YP-3A Orion
One Orion aerodynamic test bed, fuselage shortened by seven feet.

Operators

Current operators

As of August 2010 a total of 11 Lockheed L-188 Electra aircraft (all variants) were reported in airline service, with Atlantic Airlines (7) and Buffalo Airways (3) operating cargo variants and Trans Service Airlift operating a passenger 188A. As of March 2011, Atlantic Airlines' fleet numbers five, while another 13 Electras are registered to Canadian company Air Spray, converted into firefighting airtankers with a 3000 US gallon capacity tank; and two to Conair Group, also configured as an airtanker.

Military operators

Argentina
- Argentine Naval Aviation

Bolivia
- Bolivian Air Force

Ecuador
- TAME

Honduras
- Honduran Air Force - one 188A from 1979

Mexico
- Mexican Air Force - one 188A from 1978 to 1987.

Panama
- Panamanian Air Force - One 188C from 1973 to 1984.

Orders
Model 188A
- Eastern Airlines ordered 40 188As which were delivered between November 1958 and August 1959, the last five as 188Cs.
- American Airlines ordered 35 188As which were delivered between November 1958 and March 1960.
- National Airlines ordered 14 188As which were delivered between April 1959 and January 1961.
- Ansett-ANA ordered three 188As which were delivered to Australia in February 1959, April 1959 and February 1960.
- Braniff ordered nine 188As which were delivered between April 1959 and January 1960.
- Western Airlines ordered 12 188As which were delivered between May 1959 and February 1961.
- Trans Australia Airlines ordered three 188As which were delivered to Australia between June 1959 and August 1960.
- General Motors ordered one 188A which was delivered in July 1958.

Model 188C
- Northwest Orient Airlines ordered 18 188Cs which were delivered between July 1959 and June 1961.
- Pacific Southwest Airlines ordered three 188Cs which were delivered in November and December 1959.
- Capital Airlines ordered five 188Cs but later cancelled the order, the five aircraft were sold to other operators.
- Qantas ordered four 188Cs which were delivered to Australia between October and December 1959.
- KLM ordered 12 188Cs which were delivered to the Netherlands between September 1959 and December 1960.
- Tasman Empire Airways ordered three 188Cs which were delivered to New Zealand in October and December 1959.
- Garuda ordered three 188Cs which were delivered to Indonesia in January 1961.

Accidents and incidents
- On February 3, 1959, American Airlines Flight 320 en route from Chicago to New York City crashed on approach, killing 65 of 73 on board.
- On September 29, 1959, a Braniff Electra (Braniff Flight 542) crashed in Buffalo, Texas en route to Dallas, Texas from Houston, Texas. All Twenty-nine passengers and five crew members died in the crash. The Civil Aeronautics Board blamed the crash on the "whirl-mode" prop theory and in-flight separation of a wing from the aircraft.
- Just under six months later, on March 17, 1960, an Electra operated as Northwest Orient Flight 710, en route from Chicago to Miami, Florida, broke apart in flight over Perry County, Indiana, in the second "whirl-mode" crash. All 63 people on board were killed (57 passengers and six crew members).
- On October 4, 1960, Eastern Air Lines Flight 375 crashed on takeoff from Boston, Massachusetts's Logan International Airport, killing 62 of 72 on board. The crash was eventually determined to be the result of bird ingestion in three engines rather than structural failure.
- On June 12, 1961, KLM Flight 823 crashed short of the runway at Cairo killing 20 out of the 36 on board.
- On September 17, 1961, Northwest Orient Airlines Flight 706 crashed on takeoff from Chicago-O'Hare In-

ternational Airport, killing all 37 on board. The crash was eventually determined to be the result of mechanical failure in the aileron primary control system due to an improper replacement of the aileron boost assembly.
- On April 22, 1966, an American Flyers Airline L-188 crashed into a hill on approach to Ardmore Municipal Airport, killing all 5 crew and 78 of the 93 passengers on board.
- On February 16, 1967, Garuda Indonesia Airways Flight 708 crashed while attempting to land at Manado-Sam Ratulangi Airport. 22 of 92 passengers and crew on board were killed. The crash was eventually determined to be the result of an awkward landing technique resulting in an excessive rate of sink on touchdown. Marginal weather at the time of landing was a contributing factor.
- On May 3, 1968, Braniff Flight 352, which was en route from Houston to Dallas, disintegrated over Dawson, Texas. All 80 passengers and five crew members were killed. This was the worst air disaster in Texas at the time. The Probable Cause found by the National Transportation Safety Board was excessive loads put upon the aircraft structure while attempting to recover from an unusual attitude resulting from loss of control in thunderstorm turbulence; the operation in the turbulence resulted from a decision to penetrate an area of known severe weather.
- On August 9, 1970, LANSA Flight 502 crashed shortly after takeoff, killing 99 of the 100 people on board, plus two people on the ground.
- On December 24, 1971, LANSA Flight 508, which was en route from Lima to Pucallpa, Peru, entered an area of strong turbulence and lightning and disintegrated in mid air due to structural failure following a lightning strike and fire. Of the 92 people on board, 91 were killed. One passenger, Juliane Köpcke, survived the crash.
- On June 4, 1976, an Air Manila 188A (RP-C1061) crashed just after takeoff from the Guam Naval Air Station.
- On January 21, 1985 chartered Galaxy Airlines Flight 203 crashed after takeoff from Reno-Cannon International Airport en-route to Minneapolis, Minnesota with 71 people on board.
- On December 18, 1995 an overloaded 188C of Trans Service Airlift crashed near Cahungula, Angola with the loss of 141 of the 144 occupants.

Specifications (Model 188A)

Data from Lockheed Aircraft since 1913

General characteristics
- **Crew:** Five (3 flight deck)
- **Capacity:** 98 passengers
- **Length:** 104 ft 6 in (31.85 m)
- **Wingspan:** 99 ft 0 in (30.18 m)
- **Height:** 32 ft 10 in (10.00 m)
- **Wing area:** 1,300 sq ft (120.8 m²)
- **Empty weight:** 57,400 lb (26,036 kg)
- **Max takeoff weight:** 113,000 lb (51,256 kg)
- **Powerplant:** 4× Allison 501-D13 turboprop engines, 3,750 eshp (2,800 kW) each

Performance
- **Maximum speed:** 390 knots (448 mph, 721 km/h) at 12,000 ft (3,660 m)
- **Cruise speed:** 324 knots (373 mph, 600 km/h)
- **Range:** 1,913 nmi (2,200 mi, 3,540 km) with maximum payload, 2,409 nmi, 2,770 mi, 4,455 km with 17,500 lb (7,938 kg) payload
- **Service ceiling:** 28,400 ft (8,665 m)
- **Rate of climb:** 1,970 ft/min (10 m/s)

Source (edited): "http://en.wikipedia.org/wiki/Lockheed_L-188_Electra"

Lockheed P-2 Neptune

The **Lockheed P-2 Neptune** (originally designated **P2V** until September 1962) was a Maritime patrol and ASW aircraft. It was developed for the United States Navy by Lockheed to replace the Lockheed PV-1 Ventura and PV-2 Harpoon, and being replaced in turn with the Lockheed P-3 Orion. Designed as a land-based aircraft, the Neptune never made a carrier landing, although a small number of aircraft were converted for carrier use and successfully launched. The type was successful in export and saw service with several armed forces.

Design and development

XP2V-1 prototype in 1945

A P2V takes off from the *USS Franklin D. Roosevelt* (CVA 42) in 1951

P2V-2 of VP-18 over NAS Jacksonville, 1953

Development began early in World War II, but compared to other aircraft in development at the time, it was considered a low priority. It was not until 1944 that the program went into full swing. A major factor in the design was ease of manufacture and maintenance, and this may have been a major factor in the type's long life and worldwide success. The first aircraft flew in 1945. Production began in 1946, and the aircraft was accepted into service in 1947.

It was one of the first aircraft to be fitted in operational service with both piston and jet engines. The Convair B-36, several Boeing C-97 Stratofreighter, Fairchild C-123 Provider, and Avro Shackleton aircraft were also so equipped. The jet engines were fitted with intake doors that could be closed for economical piston-engine only searching operations. The jet engines could be employed for sprint or short field take-off, but were seldom used in typical operations.

Normal crew access was via a ladder on the aft bulkhead of the nose wheel well to a hatch on the left side of the wheel well, then forward to the observer nose or up through another hatch to the main deck. There was also a hatch in the floor of the after fuselage, near the sonobuoy chutes.

Operational history

Early Cold War

Prior to the introduction of the P-3 Orion in the mid-1960s the Neptune was the primary US land-based anti-submarine patrol craft, intended to be operated as the hunter of a "'Hunter-Killer"

group, with Destroyers employed as killers. Several features aided this task:
- Sonobuoys could be launched from a station in the aft portion of the fuselage and monitored by radio
- Some models were equipped with "pointable" twin .50 caliber machine guns in the nose, most had a forward observation bubble with an observer seat, a feature seen in several of the images.
- A Magnetic Anomaly Detector was fitted in an extended tail, producing a paper chart. Unmarked charts were not classified, but those with annotations were classified as secret.
- A belly-mounted surface search radar enabled detection of surfaced and snorkeling submarines at considerable distances.

As the P-2 was replaced in the U.S. Navy by the P-3A Orion in active Fleet squadrons in the early and mid-1960s, the P-2 continued to remain operational in the Naval Air Reserve through the mid 1970s, primarily in its SP-2H version. As active Fleet squadrons transitioned to the P-3B and P-3C in the mid- and late-1960s and early 1970s, the Naval Reserve P-2s were eventually replaced by P-3As and P-3Bs and the P-2 exited active US naval service. VP-23 was the last active duty patrol squadron to operate the SP-2H, retiring its last Neptune on 20 February 1970.

Covert operations P2V-7U/RB-69A variants

In 1954 under Project Cherry, the US Central Intelligence Agency (CIA) obtained five newly built P2V-7 (7047/135612/54-4037, 7097/140438/54-4038, 7099/140440/54-4039, 7101/140442/54-4040, 7105/141233/54-4041) and converted these into P2V-7U/RB-69A variants by Lockheed's Skunk Works at Hangar B5 in Burbank, California, for the CIA's own private fleet of covert ELINT/ferret aircraft. Later to make up P2V-7U/RB-69A operational losses, the CIA obtained and converted two existing US Navy P2V-7s (7286/150283 in September 1962, 7021/135564 in December 1964) to P2V-7U/RB-69A Phase VI standard, and also acquired an older

P2V-5(128355) from US Navy as training aircraft in 1963. Test flights done by lead aircraft (7047) at Edwards AFB from 1955 to 1956, all the aircraft painted with dark sea blue color but with USAF markings. In 1957 P2V-7U (7047) was sent to Eglin AFB for testing aircraft performance at low level and under adverse conditions. The initial two aircraft (7097, 7099) were sent to Europe, based at Wiesbaden, West Germany, but were later withdrawn in 1959 when the CIA reduced its covert aircraft assets in Europe. The CIA sent the other two P2V-7U/RB-69As to Hsinchu Air Base, Taiwan, where by December 1957, they were given to a "Black Op" unit, the 34th Squadron, better known as the Black Bat Squadron, of the Republic of China Air Force (|ROCAF/Taiwan); these were painted in ROCAF/Taiwan markings. The ROCAF/Taiwan P2V-7U/RB-69A's mission was to conduct low level penetration flights into mainland China to conduct ELINT/ferret missions including mapping out China's air defense networks, inserting agents via airdrop, and dropping leaflets and supplies. The agreement for plausible deniability between US and ROC government meant the RB-69A would be manned by ROCAF/Taiwan crew while conducting operational missions, but would be manned by CIA crew when ferrying RB-69A out of Taiwan or other operational area to US.

The P2V-7U/RB-69A flew with ROCAF/Taiwan Black Bat Squadron over China from 1957 to November 1966. All five original aircraft (two crashed in South Korea, three shot down over China) lost with all hands on board. In January 1967, two remaining RB-69As flew back to NAS Alameda, California, and were converted back to regular US Navy P2H/P2V-7 ASW aircraft configurations.Most of the 34th Squadron's Black Op missions still remain classified by the CIA, although a CIA internal draft history, *Low-Level Technical Reconnaissance over Mainland China (1955-66)*, reference CSHP-2.348, written in 1972 that covers CIA/ROCAF/Taiwan 34th

Squadron's Black Op missions is known to be in existence but would not be declassified by the CIA until after 2022.

Vietnam War

During the Vietnam War, the Neptune was used by the US Navy as a gunship, an overland reconnaissance and sensor deployment aircraft, and in its traditional role as a maritime patrol aircraft. The Neptune was also utilized by the U.S. Army's 1st Radio Research Company (Aviation), call sign "Crazy Cat," located at Cam Ranh Bay, as an electronic "ferret" aircraft. Observation Squadron 67 (VO-67), call sign "Lindy", was the only P-2 Neptune aircraft squadron to ever receive the Presidential Unit Citation. VO-67 lost three aircraft and 20 aircrew to ground fire during its secret missions into Laos and Vietnam in 1967–68. The ROCAF/Taiwan's secret 34th Squadron's RB-69A/P2V-7U ELINT/SIGINT aircraft flew a low level electronic reconnaissance from Da Nang, flying over Thanh Hoa province on 20 August 1963 to investigate a air resupply drop zone that turned out to be a set trap for a Republic of China Air Force (ROCAF) C-123B airdrop mission 10 days earlier due to the air-inserted agents having been captured and turned. Next year, an air defense radar mapping mission was also flown by 34th Squadron's RB-69A/P2V-7U aircraft into North Vietnam and Laos on the night of 16 March 1964. The RB-69A took off from Da Nang, flew up the Gulf of Tonkin before coasting in near Haiphong, then flew down North Vietnam and the Laos border. The mission was requested by SOG for helping plan the insert or resupply of agents. Seven AAA sites, 14 early warning radar sites and two CGI radar signals were detected.

Falklands War

The Argentine Naval Aviation had received at least 16 Neptunes in different variants since 1958 including eight ex-RAF for use in the Escuadrilla Aeronaval de Exploración (English: *Naval exploration squadron*). They were intensively used in 1978 during the Operation Soberania against Chile including over the Pacific Ocean.

During the Falklands War (Spanish: *Guerra de las Malvinas*) in 1982, the last two airframes in service (2-P-111 and 2-P-112) played a key role of reconnaissance and aiding Dassault Super Étendards, particularly on the 4 May attack against HMS *Sheffield*. The lack of spare parts, caused by the US having enacted an arms embargo in 1977 due to the *Dirty War*, led to the type being retired before the end of the war; Argentine Air Force C-130 Hercules took over the task of searching for targets for strike aircraft.

In 1983, the unit was reformed with Lockheed L-188 Electras modified for maritime surveillance; in 1994 these were replaced with P-3B Orions.

Other military operators

The Canadian version, the Lockheed CP-127 (P2V-7) Neptune served in the RCAF Maritime Air Command from 1955, as an anti-submarine, anti-shipping and maritime reconnaissance aircraft, being fitted with piston engines initially. In 1957, the CP-127s had two underwing Westinghouse jet engine pods installed. This conversion provided additional thrust for an improved takeoff, increased endurance by allowing higher weights of fuel and generally improved the overall performance of the aircraft. Armament included two torpedoes, mines, depth charges, bombs carried internally plus unguided rockets mounted externally underwing. A total of 25 Neptunes served with nos. 404, 405 and 407 squadrons until the type was replaced by the Canadair CP-107 Argus in 1968.

The Royal Air Force Coastal Command operated 52 P2V-5s, designated Neptune MR.1s as a stop-gap modern maritime patrol aircraft until the Avro Shackletons could enter service. They were used from between 1952 and March 1957, being used for Airborne Early Warning experiments as well as for maritime patrol.

In Australia, the Netherlands, and the US Navy, its tasks were taken over by the larger and more capable P-3 Orion, and by the 1970s, it was only in use by patrol squadrons in the US Naval Reserve. The US Naval Reserve abandoned its last Neptunes in 1978, those aircraft also having been replaced by the P-3 Orion. By the 1980s, the Neptune had fallen out of military use in most purchasing nations, replaced by newer aircraft.

Neptune Aviation Services' P-2V Neptune drops Phos-Chek on the 2007 WSA Complex fire in Oregon.

In Japan, the Neptune was license-built from 1966 by Kawasaki as the P-2J, with the piston engines replaced by IHI turboprops. Kawasaki continued their manufacture much later than Lockheed did; the P-2J remained in service until 1984.

Civilian firefighting

P-2/P2Vs are currently employed in aerial firefighting roles by operators such as Aero Union and Neptune Aviation Services and can carry 2,400 gal (9,084 l) of retardant with a service life of 15,000 hours. Neptune proposes to replace them with Bombardier Q200 and Q300 aircraft which are estimated to have a service life of 80,000 hours.

"Truculent Turtle"

The third production **P2V-1** was chosen for a record-setting mission, ostensibly to test crew endurance and long-range navigation but also for publicity purposes: to display the capabilities of the Navy's latest patrol bomber. Its nickname was "The Turtle," which was painted on the aircraft's nose (along with a cartoon of a turtle smoking a pipe pedaling a device attached to a propeller). However, in press releases immediately before the flight, the Navy referred to it as The Truculent Turtle.

Lockheed P-2 Neptune - page 149

P2V-1 *Turtle* in 1946

P2V-5 with nose turret in 1952

US Navy AP-2H of VAH-21

Loaded with fuel in extra tanks fitted in practically every spare space in the aircraft, the *Turtle* set out from Perth, Australia to the United States. With a crew of four (and a nine-month-old gray kangaroo, a gift from Australia for the Washington, D.C. zoo) the aircraft set off on 9 September 1946, with a RATO (rocket-assisted takeoff). Two and a half days (55h, 18m) later, the "Turtle" touched down in Columbus, Ohio, 11,236.6 mi (18,083.6 km) from its starting point. It was the longest unrefueled flight made to that point - 4,000 mi (6,400 km) longer than the USAF's B-29 Superfortress record. This would stand as the absolute unrefueled distance record until 1962 (beaten by a USAF B-52 Stratofortress), and would remain as a piston-engined record until 1986 when Dick Rutan's Voyager would break it in the process of circumnavigating the globe. The "Truculent Turtle" is preserved at the National Museum of Naval Aviation at NAS Pensacola.

Variants

P2V-3 of VP-5 in 1953

An OP-2E of VO-67 in 1967/68 over Laos

P-2H of VP-56 in 1963

Restored French P-2H in Australia, 2004

Minden Air's Tanker 55, formerly an SP-2H, at Fox Field

RB-69A of the CIA in USAF markings

Lockheed produced seven main variants of the P2V. In addition, Kawasaki built the turboprop-powered P-2J in Japan. Model names after the 1962 redesignation are given in parentheses.
XP2V-1
Prototype, one produced.
P2V-1
First production model; 15 built.
P2V-2
Second production model; 81 built.
P2V-2N "Polar Bear"
Modified Neptune with ski landing gear and early MAD gear; one1 built.
P2V-3
Upgraded powerplant; 83 built.
P2V-3C
Carrier-based Neptune; 11 built.
P2V-3B
Conversions from other P2V-3 models, including P2V-3C and -3W, fitted with

the ASB-1 Low Level Radar Bombing System; 16 converted.

P2V-3W
Airborne Early Warning variant, APS-20 search radar; 30 built.

P2V-3Z
VIP combat transport; two built.

P2V-4 (P-2D)
Upgraded powerplant and fuel capacity; 52 built.

P2V-5
Replaced solid nose with turret, APS-20 and APS-8 search radars standard, jettisonable wingtip fuel tanks. Late models featured observation nose and MAD gear in place of nose and tail turrets; 424 built.

P2V-5F (P-2E)
Modification with J34 jet engines, deleted wing rocket stubs, increased bombload.

AP-2E
Designation applied to P2V-5F with special SIGINT/ELINT equipment used by the US Army's 1st Radio Research Company at Cam Ranh Bay.

P2V-5FD (DP-2E)
P2V-5F with target towing or drone launch capability, various defensive equipment and all weaponry deleted.

P2V-5FE (EP-2E)
P2V-5F with Julie/Julie ASW gear but without other changes of P2V-5FS (SP-2E). Assigned almost exclusively to USNR.

P2V-5FS (SP-2E)
P2V-5F with Julie/Jezebel ASW gear.

OP-2E
Modified for use as part of Operation Igloo White with Observation Squadron 67 (VO-67); only 12 converted.

P2V-6 (P-2F)
Aerial mine delivery capability, APS-70 search radar, upgraded powerplant; 83 built.

P2V-6B
AUM-N-2 Petrel missile launch capability.

P2V-6M (MP-2F)
Formerly P2V-6B, 16 produced; note that originally the M mission modifier prefix stood for missile carrier, but was eventually dropped, becoming the role-modifier for multi-mission aircraft.

P2V-6F (P-2G)
P2V-6/P-2F refitted with J34 jet engines.

P2V-6T (TP-2F)
Trainer version with armament deleted, wingtip tanks often deleted.

P2V-7 (P-2H)
Last Neptune variant produced by Lockheed, upgraded powerplant, jet pods standard, improved wingtip tanks, APS-20 search radar, bulged cockpit canopy, early fitted with nose and tail turrets, but replaced with observation nose and MAD tail, dorsal turret also fitted early and replaced with observation bubble; 311 built.

P2V-7LP (LP-2H)
Ski landing gear, JATO provisions; four built.

P2V-7S (SP-2H)
Additional ASW/ECM equipment including Julie/Jezebel gear.

P2V-7U
Naval designation of the RB-69A variant.

AP-2H
Specialized ground attack variant for Heavy Attack Squadron 21 (VAH-21); only four converted.

RB-69A
Least known of the P2V Neptune family. Five built, two converted for CIA covert operations, obtained with USAF help and operated by ROCAF/Taiwan's 34th Squadron. Aerial reconnaissance/ ELINT platform, modular sensor packages fitted depended on the mission needs. Originally fitted with Westinghouse APQ-56 Side Looking Airborne Radar (SLAR), the APQ-24 search radar, the Fairchild Mark IIIA cameras, the APR-9/13 radar intercept receiver, the QRC-15 DF system, the APA-69A DF display, the APA-74 pulse analyser, the Ampex tape recorder, the System 3 receiver to intercept enemy communications, the APS-54 RWR, a noise jammer, the RADAN system doppler radar navigation, and others. In May 1959, a upgrade program known as Phase VI was approved, and added the ATIR air-to-air radar jammer, replacing APR-9/13 with ALQ-28 ferret system, the QRC-15, 3 14-channel recorders and 1 7-channel high speed recorder to record ELINT systems, the K-band receiver, the ASN-7 navigation computer replacing RADAN, and Fulton Skyhook system.

C-139
The C-139 designation was applied to a planned transport version of the Neptune, which was cancelled before any aircraft were built.

Neptune MR.1
British designation of P2V-5; 52 delivered.

CP-122 Neptune
RCAF designation of P2V-7.(jet pod not initially fitted to 25 P2V-7 aircraft delivered to RCAF, but subsequently retrofitted)

Kawasaki P-2J (P2V-Kai)
Japanese variant produced by Kawasaki with T64 turboprop engines, various other improvements; 82 built.

Operators

A RAAF SP-2H with a USN P-5 and a RNZAF *Sunderland* in 1963

A Neptune MR.1 of 217 Sqn Coastal Command RAF in 1953

Lockheed P-2 Neptune - page 151

Aero Union P-2 Tanker 16 at Fox Field in 2003, without jet engines

Neptune Aviation Services' Tanker 44 takes off from Fox Field to fight the California wildfires of October 2007

Military operators

Argentina
- Argentine Navy - Argentine Naval Aviation (eight units)
  - Escuadrilla Aeronaval de Exploracion

Australia
- Royal Australian Air Force
  - No. 10 Squadron RAAF
  - No. 11 Squadron RAAF

Brazil
- Brazilian Air Force (14 Units)
  - 1°/7° Grupo de Aviação

Canada
- Royal Canadian Air Force
  - No. 404 Squadron RCAF
  - No. 405 Squadron RCAF
  - No. 407 Squadron RCAF

Chile

France
- French Navy

Japan
- Japan Maritime Self Defense Force

Netherlands
- Dutch Naval Aviation Service

Portugal

Republic of China
- Republic of China Air Force
  - 34th Black Bat Squadron

United Kingdom
- Royal Air Force
  - No. 36 Squadron RAF
  - No. 203 Squadron RAF
  - No. 210 Squadron RAF
  - No. 217 Squadron RAF
  - No. 236 Operational Conversion Unit RAF

United States
- United States Army
- United States Navy
- Central Intelligence Agency operated 7 RB-69A in USAF colors.

Civilian operators
- Aero Union
- Minden Air
- Neptune Aviation Services

Survivors

There are a few Neptunes that have been restored and are on display in museums and parks.

SP-2E
- Historic Aircraft Restoration Projects, Brooklyn, New York, USA; Bureau Number (BuNo)131542* SP-2E is at Floyd Bennett Field Brooklyn, Hangar "B"
- United States Army Aviation Museum, Fort Rucker, Alabama, USA; Army serial number 131485 / Navy BuNo 131485

SP-2H
- Museo Aeronaval (MUAN) of Argentine Naval Aviation: SP-2H serial 2-P-112 is the one which tracked HMS Sheffield
- National Museum of Naval Aviation, NAS Pensacola, Florida, USA; BuNo 141234 and BuNo 141561
- NAS Jacksonville Memorial Park, NAS Jacksonville, Florida, USA; BuNo 131410
- Gate guard, former NAS Brunswick, Maine, USA; BuNo 128392
- Gate guard, Moffett Federal Airfield (former NAS Moffett Field), California, USA; BuNo 128393
- Gate guard, Marine Corps Base Hawaii (former MCAS Kaneohe Bay), Hawaii, USA; BuNo 150279 (relocated from former NAS Barbers Point, Hawaii)
- Gate guard, MVK De Kooy, The Netherlands. (Reg. 216/V)
- In storage, awaiting restoration. Militaire Luchtvaart Museum Soesterberg, The Netherlands. (Reg. 201/V)
- One tailsection. Hato, Curaçao.
- SP-2H, former Dutch Navy, number 204, on display on grounds of RAF Cosford Museum, Shropshire, England.

P-2H
- Mid-Atlantic Air Museum. Reading, Pennsylvania; BuNo 144683
- Museum of Aviation Robins AFB, Georgia, USA ; BuNo 147954. The P-2 Neptune is painted to represent a USAF/CIA/Taiwan RB-69A.
- Pima Air and Space Museum, Tucson, Arizona, USA; aircraft configured as an AP-2H, BuNo 135620

P2V
- P2V-1 "Truculent Turtle" aircraft, National Museum of Naval Aviation, NAS Pensacola, Florida, USA; BuNo 89082
- Pima Air and Space Museum, Tucson, Arizona, USA; BuNo 147957
- Veterans of Foreign Wars Post 3761, Baltimore, Ohio, USA; on display on grounds; BuNo unknown
- P2V-7 Tillamook Air Museum, Tillamook, Oregon, USA; BuNo unknown, Airworthy
- P2V-7, Historical Aircraft Restoration Society, Illawarra Regional Airport, New South Wales, Australia. Ex-Royal Australian Air Force A89-273, now civil registered VH-IOY. BuNo 149073, Airworthy.

Specifications

P2V-3

Data from Combat Aircraft since 1945

General characteristics
- **Crew:** 9-11
- **Length:** 77 ft 10 in (23.72 m)
- **Wingspan:** 100 ft 0 in (30.48 m)
- **Height:** 28 ft 4 in (8.56 m)
- **Wing area:** 1,000 ft² (92.9 m²)
- **Empty weight:** 34,875 lb (15,819

- **Max takeoff weight:** 64,100 lb (29,076 kg)
- **Powerplant:** 2× Wright R-3350-26W Cyclone-18 radial engine, 3,200 hp (2,386 kW) wet each
- **Propellers:** 3 bladed propeller, 1 per engine

Performance
- **Maximum speed:** 278 kn (313 mp/h) (515 km/h)
- **Cruise speed:** 155 kn (174 mp/h) (286 km/h) (max)
- **Range:** 3,458 nmi (3,903 mi) (6,406 km)

Armament
- **Rockets:** 2.75 in (70 mm) FFAR in removable wing-mounted pods
- **Bombs:** 8,000 lb (3,629 kg) including free-fall bombs, depth charges, and torpedoes

P-2H (P2V-7)

Data from Combat Aircraft since 1945

General characteristics
- **Crew:** 7-9
- **Length:** 91 ft 8 in (27.94 m)
- **Wingspan:** 103 ft 10 in (31.65 m)
- **Height:** 29 ft 4 in (8.94 m)
- **Wing area:** 1,000 ft² (92.9 m²)
- **Empty weight:** 49,935 lb (22,650 kg)
- **Max takeoff weight:** 79,895 lb (35,240 kg)
- **Powerplant:** 2× Westinghouse J34 Wright R-3350-32W Cyclone Turbo-compound radial engine, 3,700 hp (2,759 kW) wet each
- **Propellers:** 4 bladed propeller, 1 per engine

Performance
- **Maximum speed:** 316 kn (363 mp/h) (586 km/h) (all engines)
- **Cruise speed:** 180 kn (207 mp/h) (333 km/h) (max)
- **Range:** 1,912 nmi (2,157 mi) (3,540 km)
- **Service ceiling:** 22,400 ft ()

Armament
- **Rockets:** 2.75 in (70 mm) FFAR in removable wing-mounted pods
- **Bombs:** 8,000 lb (3,629 kg) including free-fall bombs, depth charges, and torpedoes

Accidents and incidents
- On 6 November 1951, a P2V of VP-6 carrying out a 'weather reconnaissance mission over international waters off Vladivostok' was attacked and shot down by a number of MiG-15s. All 10 crew were killed.
- On 18 January 1953, a P2V of VP-22 was shot down off Swatow in the Formosa Straits by Chinese anti-aircraft fire. Eleven of thirteen crewmen were rescued by a US Coast Guard PBM-5 under fire from shore batteries on Nan Ao Tao island. Attempting to takeoff in 8 to 12 foot swells, the PBM crashed. Ten survivors out of 19 total (including five from the P2V) were rescued by USS *Halsey Powell* (DD-686). During the search effort, a PBM-5 from VP-40 received fire from a small-caliber machine gun, and *Gregory* (DD 802) received fire from shore batteries.
- On 4 September 1954, a P2V-5 of VP-19 operating from NAS Atsugi ditched in the Sea of Japan, 40 miles off the coast of Siberia after an attack by two Soviet Air Forces MiG-15 *Fagots*. One crewmen was lost, and the other nine were rescued by a USAF SA-16 amphibian.
- On 22 June 1955, a P2V-5 of VP-9 (BuNo 131515), flying a patrol mission from Kodiak, Alaska, was attacked over the Bering Straits by two Soviet Air Forces MiG-15s. The P2V crash-landed on St. Lawrence Island after an engine was set afire. Of the eleven crew members, including pilot Richard F. Fischer, co-pilot David M. Lockhard, Donald E. Sonnek, Thaddeus Maziarz, Martin E. Berg, Eddie Benko, David Assard and Charles Shields, four sustained injuries due to gunfire and six were injured during the landing. The US demanded $724,947 in compensation; the USSR finally paid half this amount.
- On 25 March 1960, an RB-69A/P2V-7U(7101/140442/54-4040) crashed into a hill near Kunsan Air Base, South Korea, during a low level ferry flight from Hsinchu, Taiwan to stage area in Kunsan, South Korea. All 14 aircrew on board were killed.
- On 6 November 1961, an RB-69A/P2V-7U(7099/140440/54-4039) conducting a low level penetration flight over mainland China was shot down by ground fire over Liaodong peninsula. All 14 aircrew on board were killed in action.
- On 8 January 1962, a RB-69A/P2V-7U(7097/140438/54-4038) crashed into the Korea Bay while conducting ELINT and leaflet dropping missions. All 14 aircrew on board were killed in action.
- On 19 June 1963, a RB-69A/P2V-7U(7105/141233/54-4041) was conducting ELINT mission over mainland China, and was shot down by PLAAF MiG-17PF over Linchuan, Jiangxi, after intercepted repeatedly by multiple MiG-17PFs and Tu-4Ps. All 14 aircrew on board were killed in action.
- On 11 June 1964, a RB-69A/P2V-7U (7047/135612/54-4037) was conducting ELINT mission over mainland China, and was shot down by PLAN-AF MiG-15 over Shandong peninsula, after intercepted by MiG-15s and Il-28s. All 13 aircrew on board were killed in action.
- On 5 September 2008, a Neptune Aviation Services Lockheed Neptune N4235T crashed soon after takeoff from Reno/Stead Airport, Reno, Nevada. The left engine and then left wing were seen to catch fire before the aircraft crashed. All three crew members on board were killed.

Source (edited): "http://en.wikipedia.org/wiki/Lockheed_P-2_Neptune"

Short SC.7 Skyvan

The **Skyvan** is a 19-seater twin turboprop aircraft manufactured by Short Brothers of Belfast, Northern Ireland. It is used mainly for short-haul freight and skydiving.

The Skyvan is a high wing twin-engined all-metal monoplane with a high semi-cantilever tailplane with twin rudders. The first flight of the Skyvan, the Skyvan 1, was on 17 January 1963.

The Shorts 330 and Shorts 360 are stretched model of the original SC-7 which were designed as regional airliners.

Design and development

In 1958, Shorts were approached by F.G. Miles Ltd (successor company to Miles Aircraft) who were seeking backing to produce a development of the H.D.M.106 Caravan design with a Hurel Dubois high aspect ratio wing. Shorts acquired the design and data gathered from trials of the Miles Aerovan based H.D.M.105 prototype. After evaluating the Miles proposal, Shorts rejected the Caravan. They developed their own design for a utility all-metal aircraft which was called the **Short SC.7 Skyvan**. It was popular with freight operators compared to other small aircraft because of its large rear door for loading and unloading freight. Its fuselage resembles the shape of a railroad boxcar for simplicity and efficiency.

Construction started at Sydenham, Belfast in 1960 and the first flight of the prototype occurred on 17 January 1963, powered by two Continental piston engines. The prototype was re-engined with the intended Turbomeca Astazou turboprop engines later in 1963. The Skyvan is an all-metal, high-wing monoplane, with a braced, high aspect ratio wing (similar to that used on Hurel-Dubois aircraft), and an unpressurised, square section fuselage. Production switched in 1968 to the Skyvan Series 3 aircraft, which replaced the Astazous with Garrett AiResearch TPE331 turboprops. A total of 153 Skyvans (plus the prototype) were produced by the time production ended in 1986.

Operational history

Skyvans served widely in both military and civilian operations, with the type remaining in service with a number of civilian operators, and in military service in Guyana and Oman.

Invicta Aviation Skyvan on parachuting duties at the Cotswold Air Show. (2010).

In 1982, two Skyvans of the Argentine Naval Prefecture participated in the Falklands War. Both aircraft were ferried to Port Stanley in April 1982. One aircraft was damaged by British naval gunfire on Stanley racecourse and did not fly again; it was finally destroyed by shellfire during British bombardments on the 12/13 June. The second aircraft was used at Pebble Island where it became bogged down in the soft ground and destroyed by British fire on 15 May 1982 (see Raid on Pebble Island).

Skyvans are sometimes used for air to air photography and for skydiving operations.

Production

All built by Short in Belfast.
- **Skyvan 1** : prototype, one built. 2 x Continental GTSIO-520 engines.
- **Skyvan 1A** : re-engined prototype. 2 x 388 kW (520 hp) Turboméca Astazou engines.
- **Skyvan 2** : Astazou powered production. 8 series 2 produced.
- **Skyvan 3** : Garrett TPE331 powered production. 145 produced (all series 3 models)
- **Skyvan 3A** : higher gross weight version of Skyvan Series 3.
- **Skyvan 3M** : military transport version. It can be used for supply dropping, assault transport, dropping paratroops, troop transport, cargo transport, casualty evacuation, plus search and rescue missions.
- **Skyvan 3M-200** : high gross weight version of Skyvan 3M (M-TOW 6,804 kg, 15,000 lb).
- **Skyliner** : deluxe all-passenger version.

Civilian operators

As of July 2009 a total of 39 Skyvan aircraft remain in airline service, with Sonair (1), Swala Airlines (2), Transway Air Services (1), Deraya Air Taxi (3), Layang Layang Aerospace (1), Macair Airlines (1), Malaysia Air Charter (1), Olympic Airways (1), Pan-Malaysian Air Transport (1), Wirakris Udara (1), CAE Aviation (1), Deltacraft (1), Invicta Aviation (2), Pink Aviation Services (4), Advanced Air (1), Allwest Freight (2), Arctic Circle Air Service (3), GB Airlink (1), North Star Air Cargo (5), Skylift Taxi Aereo (1), Skydive Arizona (4), Sydney Skydivers (2) and Summit Air (2)., Sustut Air (1), Ryan Air (Alaska)

Military operators

Company military demonstrator in 1982

Argentina
- Argentine Coast Guard, Bought five in 1971 Two lost in 1982 in Falklands War. Rest retired in 1995 and replaced with 5 CASA C-212 Aviocar. Picture

Austria
- Austrian Air Force

▬ **Botswana**
- Botswana Defence Force Air Wing

▬ **Ecuador**
- Ecuadorian Army - Former operator

▬ **Gambia**
[*Military of Gambia

▬ **Ghana**
- Ghana Air Force

▬ **Guyana**
- Guyana Defence Force

▬ **Indonesia**
- Indonesian Air Force

▬ **Japan**
- Japan Coast Guard

▬ **Lesotho**
- Lesotho Defence Force

▬ **Malawi**

▬ **Mauritania**
- Military of Mauritania

▬ **Mexico**
- Mexican Air Force

▬ **Nepal**
- Nepalese Army
  - Nepalese Army Air Service

▬ **Oman**
- Royal Air Force of Oman

▬ **Singapore**
- Republic of Singapore Air Force
  - 121 Squadron, Republic of Singapore Air Force operated Skyvan 3M for Utility transport and Search-and-locate duties from 1973 to 1993.

▬ **Thailand**
- Thai Border Patrol Police

▬ **United Arab Emirates**
- United Arab Emirates Air Force

▬ **United Kingdom**
- British Army
  - Lend lease for Parachute Regiment and Airborne Forces to fill gap of the C-130 Hercules.

▬ **Yemen**
- Yemen Air Force

Specification (Short Skyvan 3)
Data from Jane's Civil and Military Upgrades 1994-95

General characteristics
- **Crew:** 1-2
- **Capacity:** 19 passengers
- **Length:** 12.21 m (40 ft 1 in)
- **Wingspan:** 19.79 m (64 ft 11 in)
- **Height:** 4.6 m (15 ft 1 in)
- **Wing area:** 35.12 m² (378 ft²)
- **Empty weight:** 3,331 kg (7,344 lb)
- **Max takeoff weight:** 5,670 kg (12,500 lb)
- **Powerplant:** 2× Garrett AiResearch TPE-331-201 Turboprops, 533 kW (715 hp) each

Performance
- **Never exceed speed:** 402 km/h (250 mph)
- **Maximum speed:** 324 km/h (202 mph)
- **Cruise speed:** 315 km/h (170 knots, 197 mph)
- **Stall speed:** 111 km/h (69 mph)
- **Range:** 1,200 km (694 miles)
- **Service ceiling** 6858m (22,500 ft)
- **Rate of climb:** 500 m/min (1,640 ft/min)
- **Wing loading:** 136.6 kg/m² (33.5 lb/ft²)

Source (edited): "http://en.wikipedia.org/wiki/Short_SC.7_Skyvan"

Sikorsky SH-3 Sea King

The **Sikorsky SH-3 Sea King** (company designation **S-61**) is a twin-engined anti-submarine warfare (ASW) helicopter. It served with the United States Navy and other forces, and continues to serve in many countries around the world. The Sea King has been built under license in Italy and Japan, and in the United Kingdom as the Westland Sea King. The major civil versions are the **S-61L** and **S-61N**.

Design and development

SH-3As of HS-6 above USS *Kearsarge* in the early 1960s

In 1957, Sikorsky was awarded a contract to develop an all-weather amphibious helicopter. It would combine submarine hunter and killer roles. It was designed for shipboard operations, as the five main rotor blades as well as tail section with its five blades can be folded for easy stowage. Because of its amphibious hull, the Sea King has the ability to land on water. The sponsons were fitted with deployable airbags to enhance flotation.

The prototype flew on 11 March 1959. Armament and equipment of Sea Kings vary widely with their role. Typical armaments can be four torpedoes, four depth charges or two anti-ship missiles (Sea Eagle or Exocet). It can also readily be configured to deploy the B57 tactical nuclear weapon. A large Chaff Pod is sometimes carried for anti-ship missile defense of the Carrier Battle Group. ASW equipment includes AQS-13B/E dipping sonar with a 500 foot cable, 5000 watts of power and a Sonar Data Computer for processing sonar and sonobuoy data, 21 sonobuoys (various models), ARR-75 Sonobuoy Receivers, ASQ-81 Magnetic Anomaly Detector (MAD Bird) and AKT-22 Data link to transmit sonar and sonobuoy data to the rest of the Fleet. In the search and rescue role the cabin can accommodate 22 survivors or nine stretchers and two medical officers. In the troop transport role 28 soldiers can be accommodated.

Sikorsky SH-3 Sea King - page 155

Operational history

Sea King as Marine One

The Sea King first flew on 11 March 1959; it became operational with the United States Navy in June 1961 as the HSS-2. The designation for the aircraft was changed with the introduction of the unified aircraft designation system in 1962 to the SH-3A. It was used primarily for anti-submarine warfare, but also served in anti-ship, search and rescue, transport, communications, executive transport and Airborne Early Warning roles. Aircraft carriers always deployed the Sea King as the first aircraft in the air and the last to land serving in air operations as plane guard and SAR for the fixed winged aircraft. An SH-3A, operating from the USS *New Orleans* amphibious assault ship, was used in the February 1971 Apollo 14 recovery mission.

In the US Navy, it was replaced in the ASW and SAR roles by the SH-60 Sea Hawk during the 1990s, but continues in service for other roles, for ASW in the reserves, and around the world. All H-3 aircraft in US Navy service are used in the logistics support, range support, Search and Rescue, test, and VIP transport roles. The H-3 was finally retired on 27 January 2006 in a Final Flight ceremony in NAS Norfolk, Virginia, by Helicopter Combat Support Squadron 2 (HC-2), the Fleet Angels. HH-3 variants based on the SH-3 airframe were built for the US Air Force.

Sea Kings are used as one of the official helicopters of the President of the United States and are operated by the United States Marine Corps. Sea Kings use the call sign Marine One when the president is aboard.

Variants

A SH-3D Sea King during Apollo 17 recovering operations, with the USS *Ticonderoga* in the background

HH-3A on the *USS Bon Homme Richard*

The President's VH-3A "Sea King" helicopter on permanent display at Nixon Library, Presidential fleet from 1961 to 1976

SH-3G in 1981

SH-3H of HS-8 dipping sonar

Several UH-3H Sea Kings taking off

US military
XHSS-2
The only prototype of the H-3 Sea King.
YHSS-2
Prototype and trials aircraft. Seven helicopters were built for the US Navy.
SH-3A
Anti-submarine warfare helicopter for the US Navy (245 built); originally designated HSS-2.
HH-3A
Search and rescue helicopter for the US Navy (12 converted from SH-3A).
CH-3A
Military transport version for the US Air Force (three converted from SH-3A later became CH-3B).

NH-3A (S-61F)
Experimental high speed compound helicopter, with extensive streamlining, no floats, short wings carrying two turbojet engines for extra speed.(1 Converted from SH-3A). Later modified with a tail rotor able to rotate 90° to serve as a pusher propeller.

RH-3A
Minesweeper helicopter for the US Navy (9 converted from SH-3A).

VH-3A
VIP transport helicopter for the US Army and Marine Corps (eight built, plus 2 SH-3A (STAKE) conversions which were rebuilt from damaged helicopters (one YHSS-2 and one SH-3A); originally designated VHSS-2. One (Army operated) was given to Egypt in 1972 and one (also Army operated) crashed at Walker Key, Bahamas in 1973; the rest were returned to the US Navy (HC-6) in 1975/6) and replaced by the VH-3D. At least 2 have subsequently been placed in museums.

CH-3B
Military transport helicopter for the US Air Force.

SH-3D (S-61B) (HSS-2A)
Anti-submarine warfare helicopter for the US Navy (73 built and two conversions from SH-3As).

SH-3D (S-61B)
Anti-submarine warfare helicopter for the Spanish Navy (six built).

SH-3D-TS
Anti-submarine warfare version.

VH-3D
VIP transport helicopter for the US Army (until 30 June 1976) and the US Marine Corps.

SH-3G
Cargo, utility transport helicopter for the US Navy (105 Conversions from SH-3A and SH-3D).

SH-3H (HSS-2B)
Anti-submarine warfare helicopter for the US Navy (Conversions from older versions).

SH-3H AEW
Airborne early warning version for the Spanish navy.

UH-3H
cargo, utility transport version for the US Navy.

Sikorsky designations
S-61
Company designation for the H-3 Sea King.

S-61A
Export version for the Royal Danish Air Force. Wider pontoons w/o flotation bags, a 530 liter centre tank instead of a dipping sonar and no automatic powered folding system.

S-61A-4 Nuri
Military transport, search and rescue helicopter for the Royal Malaysian Air Force. It can seat up to 31 combat troops (38 built).

S-61A/AH
Utility helicopter for survey work and search and rescue in the Antarctic.

S-61B
Export version of the SH-3 anti-submarine warfare helicopter for the Japanese Maritime Self Defense Force.

S-61D-3
Export version for the Brazilian Navy.

S-61D-4
Export version for the Argentine Navy.

S-61NR
Search and rescue version for the Argentine Air Force.

S-61L/N
Civil versions of the Sea King.

S-61R
The S-61R served in the United States Air Force as the CH-3C/E Sea King and the HH-3E Jolly Green Giant, and with the United States Coast Guard and the Italian Air Force as the HH-3F Sea King (more commonly referred to by the nickname "Pelican").

S-61V
Company designation for the VH-3A, (1 built for Indonesia).
S-61V-1 : Export version of the VH-3A, one built for Indonesia.

United Aircraft of Canada

Canadian Sikorsky CH-124A Sea King.

CH-124
Anti-submarine warfare helicopter for the Royal Canadian Navy (41 assembled by United Aircraft of Canada).

CH-124A
The Sea King Improvement Program (SKIP) added modernized avionics as well as improved safety features.

CH-124B
Alternate version of the CH-124A without a dipping sonar but formerly with a MAD sensor and additional storage for deployable stores. In 2006, the 5 aircraft of this variant were converted to support the Standing Contingency Task Force (SCTF), and were modified with additional troop seats, and frequency agile radios. Plans to add fast-rope capability, EAPSNIPS (Engine Air Particle Separator / Snow & Ice Particle Separator) did not come to fruition.

CH-124B2
6 CH-124B's were upgraded to the CH-124B2 standard in 1991-1992. The revised CH-124B2 retained the sonobuoy processing gear to passively detect submarines but, the aircraft was now also fitted with a towed-array sonar to supplement the ship's sonar. Since anti-submarine warfare is no longer a major priority within the Canadian Forces, the CH-124B2 were refitted again to become improvised troop carriers for the newly formed Standing Contingency Task Force.

CH-124C
One CH-124 operated by the Helicopter Operational Test and Evaluation Facility located at CFB Shearwater. Used for testing new gear, and when not testing new gear, it is deployable to any Canadian Forces ship requiring a helicopter.

CH-124U
Unofficial designation for 4 CH-124's that were modified for passenger/freight transport. One crashed in 1973, and the survivors were later refitted to become CH-124A's.

Westland

Westland Sea King AEW.2A of the Royal Navy in 1998

The **Westland Sea King** variant was manufactured under license by Westland Helicopters Ltd in the United Kingdom, who developed a specially modified version for the Royal Navy. It is powered by a pair of Rolls-Royce Gnome turbines (license-built T58s), and has British avionics and ASW equipment. This variant first flew in 1969, and entered service the next year. It is also used by the Royal Air Force and has been sold around the world.

Agusta
AS-61
Company designation for the H-3 Sea King built under licence in Italy by Agusta.
AS-61A-1
Italian export model for the Royal Malaysian Air Force.
AS-61A-4
Military transport helicopter, search and rescue helicopter.
AS-61N-1 Silver
License built model of the S-61N, with a shortened cabin.
AS-61VIP
VIP transport helicopter.
ASH-3A (SH-3G)
Utility transport helicopter
ASH-3D
Anti-submarine warfare helicopter. Flown by the Italian, Brazilian, Iranian, Peruvian and Argentinian navies.
ASH-3TS
VIP, executive transport mission helicopter. Also known as the ASH-3D/TS.
ASH-3H
Anti-submarine warfare helicopter

Mitsubishi
S-61A
Licence built-version of the S-61A as Search-and-Rescue and Utility helicopters for the Japan Maritime Self Defense Force (18 Built)
HSS-2
Licence built version of the S-61B as an Anti-submarine warfare helicopter for the Japan Maritime Self Defense Force (55 Built).
HSS-2A
Licence built version of the S-61B(SH-3D) as an Anti-submarine warfare helicopter for the Japan Maritime Self Defense Force (28 Built).
HSS-2B
Licence built version of the S-61B(SH-3H) as an Anti-submarine warfare helicopter for the Japan Maritime Self Defense Force (23 Built).

Operators

Royal Danish Air Force S-61A

Brazilian Navy SH-3 Sea King in company with a USN Sea King of HS-9

LASD's **Rescue 5**, a Sikorsky SH-3H Sea King helicopter, flies offshore near Point Vincente Park in Rancho Palos Verdes.

Royal Air Force Westland Sea King helicopter, a licensed derivative of the Sea King with a number of new systems

Argentina
- Argentine Naval Aviation - 5 S61D4, 9 H-3, 2 AS61D, 2 AS61H

Brazil
- Brazilian Navy - 6 S61D3, 8 H-3, 4 AS61D

Canada
- Canadian Forces Maritime Command
- Canadian Forces Air Command
- Canadian Forces Land Command

Denmark
- Royal Danish Air Force

Egypt
- Egyptian Air Force

India
- Indian Navy - US-built SH-3 Sea Kings.

Iran
- Imperial Iranian Air Force
- Islamic Republic of Iran Air Force
- Imperial Iranian Navy
- Islamic Republic of Iran Navy

Iraq
- Iraqi Air Force

158 - Westland Lynx

🇮🇪 **Ireland**
- Coast Guard

🇮🇹 **Italy**
- Italian Air Force
- Italian Navy

🇯🇵 **Japan**
- Japan Maritime Self Defense Force - Mitsubishi built Sea kings.

🇲🇾 **Malaysia**
- Royal Malaysian Air Force

🇵🇪 **Peru**
- Peruvian Navy

🇸🇦 **Saudi Arabia**
- Royal Saudi Air Force

🇪🇸 **Spain**
- Spanish Navy

🇻🇪 **Venezuela**
- Army of Venezuela

🇺🇸 **United States**
- Los Angeles County, California Sheriff's Department (former United States Navy examples)
- United States Air Force
- United States Coast Guard
- United States Marine Corps
- United States Navy

Aircraft on Display

- SH-3G, BuNo 149932, display aboard USS *Yorktown* (CV-10), Patriot's Point Naval and Maritime Museum, Charleston, South Carolina
- SH-3H, BuNo 149695, permanent static display, NAS Jacksonville, Florida
- SH-3H, BuNo 148042, permanent static display, NS Norfolk/Chambers Field (formerly NAS Norfolk), Virginia adjacent to Gate #4
- SH-3H, BuNo 149738, Quonset Air Museum, Quonset State Airport (former NAS Quonset Point), North Kingston, Rhode Island
- UH-3H, BuNo 149711, display aboard USS *Midway* (CV-41) Museum, San Diego, California
- VH-3A, BuNo 150613, National Museum of Naval Aviation, NAS Pensacola, Florida
- VH-3A, BuNo 150611, Ronald Reagan Presidential Library, Simi Valley, California
- VH-3A, BuNo 150617, Richard Nixon Presidential Library and Museum, Yorba Linda, California

Specifications (SH-3)

General characteristics

- **Crew:** 4 (2 pilots, 2 ASW systems operators)
- **Capacity:** 3 passengers
- **Length:** 54 ft 9 in (16.7 m)
- **Rotor diameter:** 62 ft (19 m)
- **Height:** 16 ft 10 in (5.13 m)
- **Disc area:** ft² (m²)
- **Empty weight:** 11,865 lb (5,382 kg)
- **Loaded weight:** 18,626 lb (8,449 kg)
- **Max takeoff weight:** 22,050 lb (10,000 kg)
- **Powerplant:** 2× General Electric T58-GE-10 turboshafts, 1,400 shp (kW) each

Performance

- **Maximum speed:** 166 mph (267 km/h)
- **Range:** 621 mi (1,000 km)
- **Service ceiling:** 14,700 ft (4,481 m)
- **Rate of climb:** 1,310-2,220 ft/min (400-670 m/min)

Armament

- 2× Mk 46/44 anti-submarine torpedoes (SH-3H)
- Various sonobuoys and pyrotechnic devices
- B-57 Nuclear depth charge
- Door guns and gun turrets on some variants (see *Main article: U.S. Helicopter Armament Subsystems*)

Source (edited): "http://en.wikipedia.org/wiki/Sikorsky_SH-3_Sea_King"

Westland Lynx

The **Westland Lynx** is a British multi-purpose military helicopter designed and built by Westland Helicopters at its factory in Yeovil. Originally intended as a utility craft for both civil and naval usage, military interest led to the development of both battlefield and naval variants. The Lynx went into operational usage in 1977 and was later adopted by the armed forces of over a dozen nations, primarily serving in the battlefield utility, anti-armour, search and rescue and anti-submarine warfare roles. In 1986 a specially modified Lynx set the current Fédération Aéronautique Internationale's official airspeed record for helicopters. The helicopter is now produced and marketed by AgustaWestland.

Development

The initial design (then known as the Westland WG.13) was started in the mid-1960s as a replacement for the Westland Scout and Wasp, and a more advanced alternative to the UH-1 Iroquois. As part of the Anglo-French helicopter agreement signed in February 1967, the French company Aérospatiale were given a work share in the manufacturing programme. Aérospatiale received 30% of production with Westland performing the remainder. It was intended that France would buy Lynxes for its Navy and as an armed reconnaissance helicopter for the French Army, with the United Kingdom in return buying Aérospatiale Gazelles and Pumas for its armed forces. The French Army cancelled its requirement for Lynxes in October 1969.

The original Lynx design was powered by two Rolls-Royce Gem 2 turboshaft engines, and used many components derived from the Scout and Wasp. However, the rotor was new, being of a semi-rigid design with honeycomb sandwich blades. The first Lynx prototype took its maiden flight on 21 March 1971.

XX153 which broke the Helicopter speed record in 1972

In 1972, a Lynx broke the world speed record over 15 and 25 km by flying at 321.74 km/h (199.92 mph). It also set a new 100 km closed circuit record shortly afterwards, flying at 318.504 km/h (197.91 mph).

The British Army ordered over 100 Lynxes, designated the **Lynx AH.1** (*Army H*elicopter Mark 1), for different roles, such as transport, armed escort, anti-tank warfare (with eight TOW missiles), reconnaissance and evacuation. The Army has fitted a Marconi Elliot AFCS system onto the Lynx for automatic stabilisation on three axes. Deliveries of production Lynxes began in 1977.

An improved Lynx AH.1 with Gem 41-1 or Gem 42 engines and an uprated transmission was referred to as the **Lynx AH.5**; only five were built for evaluation purposes. The AH.5 led to the **Lynx AH.7**, which added a new tail rotor derived from that of the Westland 30, a reinforced airframe, improved avionics and defensive aids. These received further upgrades in service, including British Experimental Rotor Programme (BERP) rotor blades.

The initial naval variant of the Lynx, known as the **Lynx HAS.2** in British service, or **Lynx Mk.2(FN)** in French service, differed from the Lynx AH.1 in being equipped with a tricycle undercarriage and a deck restraint systems, folding main rotor blades, an emergency flotation system and a nose-mounted radar. An improved Lynx for the Royal Navy, the **Lynx HAS.3**, had Gem 42-1 Mark 204 engines, an uprated transmission, a new flotation system and an Orange Crop ESM system. The Lynx HAS.3 also received various other updates in service. A similar upgrade to the French Lynx was known as the **Lynx Mk.4(FN)**. Many different export variants based on the Lynx HAS.2 and HAS.3 were sold to other air arms.

In 1986, the former company demonstrator Lynx, registered *G-LYNX*, was specially modified with Gem 60 engines and BERP rotor blades. On 11 August 1986 the helicopter was piloted by Trevor Egginton when it set an absolute speed record for helicopters over a 15 and 25 km course by reaching 400.87 km/h (249.09 mph); an official record it currently holds.

Lynx-3

Announced in 1984, the **Lynx-3** was an enhanced Lynx development, with a stretched fuselage, a redesigned tailboom and tail surfaces, Gem 60-3/1 engines and a new wheeled tricycle undercarriage. The Lynx-3 also included BERP rotor blades, and increased fuel capacity. Both Army and Naval variants were proposed. The project was ended in 1987 due to insufficient orders. Only one Army Lynx-3 prototype was built.

Super Lynx and Battlefield Lynx

ZD252 a Royal Navy Lynx HMA.8 about to land

A development of the Lynx AH.7 with the wheeled undercarriage of the Lynx-3 was marketed by Westland as the **Battlefield Lynx** in the late 1980s. The prototype first flew in November 1989 and deliveries began in 1991. This variant entered British Army service as the **Lynx AH.9**.

In the early 1990s, Westland incorporated some of the technology from the Naval Lynx-3 design into a less-radical **Super Lynx**. This featured BERP rotor blades, the Westland 30-derived tail rotor, Gem 42 engines, a new undernose 360-degree radar installation and an optional nose-mounted electro-optical sensor turret. Royal Navy Lynx HAS.3s upgraded to Super Lynx standard were known in service as the **Lynx HMA.8**, and several export customers ordered new-build or upgraded Super Lynxes. Later, Westland offered the **Super Lynx 200** with LHTEC CTS800 engines and the **Super Lynx 300**, which also had a new cockpit and avionics derived from the AgustaWestland EH101. Both of these models have achieved several export sales.

Future Lynx/Lynx Wildcat

The British Army and Royal Navy Lynx fleets are due to be upgraded to a new common advanced Lynx variant based on the Super Lynx 300, with a new tailboom, undercarriage, cockpit, avionics and sensors. Initially referred to as the Future Lynx, this type has since been renamed by AgustaWestland as the AW159 Lynx Wildcat.

Design

The Lynx is a multi-purpose helicopter design with a side by side cockpit for pilot and observer. It features a large sliding crew door on each side giving access to the cabin which can be used to accommodate up to nine equipped troops dependent on seating configuration, or alternatively radio equipment when used in the command post role or surplus fuel for long journeys. Its twin Rolls Royce Gem turboshaft engines power a four-blade semi-rigid main rotor system. The Lynx is an agile helicopter, capable of performing loops and rolls.

Operational history

A Lynx HAS.3 of HMS *Cardiff* in March 1982 prior to the Falklands War practising search and rescue.

Lynx HAS.3 of the Black Cats (Royal Navy) display team

The Lynx Mk.2(FN) entered service with the French Navy's Aviation navale in 1979. In British service, the Lynx is used by the Army Air Corps (AAC) and the Fleet Air Arm (FAA). The Lynx AH.1 entered service with the AAC in 1979, followed by the Lynx HAS.2 with the FAA in 1981. The FAA Lynx fleet was upgraded to Lynx HAS.3 standard during the 1980s, and again to Lynx HMA.8 standard in the 1990s. Most Army Lynx were later upgraded to Lynx AH.7 standard.

As of 2009, the AAC operate the Lynx AH.7 and AH.9 as utility helicopters. Army owned Lynx AH.7 and AH.9 are also in service with the FAA where they operate as attack/utility helicopters in support of the Royal Marines. Lynx HAS.3 and HMA.8 operate as anti-submarine warfare and maritime attack helicopters equipped with the Stingray torpedo, Sea Skua anti-ship missile and depth charge for Royal Navy warships. HAS.3 and HMA.8 are also capable of anti-trafficking and anti-piracy roles when carrying boarding parties and when fitted with the FN Herstal M3M pintle mounted heavy machine gun.

The Lynx's most prominent combat role was operating the Sea Skua to devastating effect against the Iraqi Navy during the 1991 Gulf War. The Lynx also saw service with British Army forces during that conflict. The HAS.2 naval ASW variant had already taken part in combat operations in British service during the Falklands War in 1982. Although none were shot down, three were lost aboard vessels hit in Argentine air attacks, two from iron bombs on HMS *Coventry* and HMS *Ardent*, and one to Exocets on MV *Atlantic Conveyor*.

The Lynx was used during Operation Barras to rescue 11 British soldiers in Sierra Leone on 10 September 2000.

The most recent wartime mission for the Lynx was during the invasion of Iraq in 2003. It has also seen extensive service during peacekeeping operations and exercises, and it is standard equipment for most Royal Navy surface combatants when they deploy.

A British Lynx from 847 Naval Air Squadron was shot down over Basra, Iraq on 6 May 2006. The helicopter was downed by a surface-to-air missile (using a Man Portable Air Defence System). The Lynx crashed into a house and burst into flames, killing all five on board, including the Commanding Officer of 847 NAS. A riot followed with locals celebrating the downing of the helicopter and surrounding the crash site as British troops rushed to the scene. This was the first British helicopter and only the second British aircraft downed (the first was an RAF Hercules) due to enemy fire in the war. A flight of either AAC or RM Lynx AH.7s are based at Basra Air Station under command of the Joint Helicopter Force (Iraq) on a rotational basis, but are restricted operationally during the summer months due to the very high daytime temperatures which affect lifting capacity and endurance dramatically.

The Super Lynx has been used extensively by the Portuguese Navy in Operation Ocean Shield. It operates from NRP Alvares Cabral and has been fitted with a FN M3M 12.7 mm machine gun.

On 28 February 2011, one Royal Netherlands Navy Naval Aviation Service Lynx was captured in Libya during an evacuation mission. Three navy personnel were taken prisoner by Libyan troops and two civilians were evacuated by other means.

Variants

Land-based variants

A British Army Lynx AH.7 in Bosnia during Operation Joint Endeavor - Peace Implementation Force (IFOR), 7 May 1996

Army Air Corps Lynx AH.7 at RIAT 2010

Westland WG.13
Prototype, first flight 21 March 1971. Thirteen prototypes built.
Lynx AH.1
Initial production version for the British Army Air Corps, powered by 671 kW (900 hp) Gem 2 engines, with first production example flying 11 February 1977, and deliveries continuing until February 1984, with 113 built. Used for a variety of tasks, including tactical transport, armed escort, anti-tank warfare (60 were equipped with eight TOW missiles as **Lynx AH.1 (TOW)** from 1981), reconnaissance and casualty evacuation.

Lynx AH.1GT
Interim conversion of the AH.1 to partial AH.7 standard for the Army Air Corps with uprated engines and revised tail rotor.

Lynx HT.1
Planned training version for Royal Air Force. Cancelled.

Lynx AH.5
Upgraded version for the Army Air Corps, with 835 kW (1,120 shp) Gem 41-1 engines and uprated gearbox. Three built as **AH.5 (Interim)** as Trials aircraft for MoD. Eight ordered as AH.5s for Army Air Corps, of which only two built as AH.5s, with remaining six completed as AH.7s. Four were later upgraded to AH.7 standard and one was retained for trials work as an **AH.5X**.

Lynx AH.6
Proposed version for the Royal Marines with undercarriage, folding tail and deck harpoon of Naval Lynx. Not built.

Lynx AH.7
Further upgraded version for the Army Air Corps, with Gem 41-1 engines and uprated gearbox of AH.5 and new, larger, composite tail rotor. Later refitted with BERP type rotor blades. Twelve new build, with 107 Lynx AH.1s converted. A small number also used by the Fleet Air Arm in support of the Royal Marines. Now replaced by the WAH-64 Apache as the main attack helicopter.

Lynx AH.7(DAS)
AH.7 with Defensive Aids Subsystem.

Lynx AH.9 (*"Battlefield Lynx"*)
Utility version for Army Air Corps, based on AH.7, but with wheeled undercarriage and further upgraded gearbox. Sixteen new-built plus eight converted from AH.7s.

Lynx AH.9A
AH.9 with uprated LHTEC CTS800-4N 1,015 kW (1,362 shp) engines. 22 are to be upgraded.

Naval variants

Royal Navy Lynx HAS.3(ICE(S)) supporting an Antarctic research base

Lynx HAS.2 / Mk.2(FN)
Initial production version for the Royal Navy (HAS.2) and the French Navy (Mk.2(FN)), powered by Gem 2 engines and with wheeled undercarriage, folding rotors and tail and deck harpoon. HAS.2 equipped with British Sea Spray radar, with Mk.2(FN) having French radar and dipping sonar. When it is used in the anti-submarine role, it can carry two torpedoes or depth charges. For anti-surface warfare, it is equipped with either four Sea Skua missiles (Royal Navy) or four AS.12 missiles (French Navy). 60 built for Royal Navy, and 26 for France.

Lynx HAS.3
Improved version of HAS.2 powered by Gem 42-1 engines and with upgraded gearbox. Thirty built from new, with deliveries starting in March 1982 and all remaining HAS.2s (53 aircraft) converted to HAS.3 standards.

Lynx HAS.3S
Improved version of the HAS.3 for the Royal Navy fitted with secure radio systems.

Lynx HAS.3GM
Modified helicopters for the Royal Navy, for service in the Persian Gulf, with improved electronic warfare equipment, revised IFF and provision for Forward looking infrared (FLIR) under fuselage. Originally deployed for 1990-91 Gulf War. Designated HAS.3S/GM when fitted with secure radios. (GM denotes **G**ulf **M**odification).

Lynx HAS.3ICE
HAS.3 modified for Antarctic service aboard ice patrol ship HMS *Endurance*. Designated HAS.3SICE when fitted with secure radios.

Lynx HAS.3CTS
HAS.3 upgraded with avionics system proposed for HMA.8. Seven converted as test beds.

Lynx Mk.4(FN)
Upgraded version for the Aéronavale, with Gem 42-1 engines. Fourteen built.

Lynx HMA.8
Upgraded maritime attack version based on Super Lynx 100. Gem 42-200 engines, BERP type main rotors and larger tail rotor of AH.7. Fitted with FLIR in turret above nose, with radar moved to radome below nose.

Lynx HMA.8(DSP)
Digital **S**ignal **P**rocessor.

Lynx HMA.8(DAS)
Defensive **A**ids **S**ubsystem. (DSP aircraft modified).

Lynx HMA.8(SRU)
SATURN (**S**econd-generation **A**nti-jam **T**actical **U**HF **R**adio for **N**ATO) **R**adio **U**pgrade. (DAS aircraft modified. Incorporates SIFF (**S**uccessor to **IFF**)).

Lynx HMA.8(CMP) see note below
Combined **M**ods **P**rogramme. (SRU aircraft modified with improved comms and defensive systems).

Note: At the time of writing, all HMA.8 aircraft have been upgraded to CMP standard and as such HMA.8(CMP) aircraft have since been re-designated back to HMA.8(SRU). The Lynx HAS.8 fleet are currently undergoing further modifications, by the Lynx Operational Support Team, to improve self-defense, mission execution and survivability. These modifications will not effect the SRU designation.

Export variants

A boarding team rappel onto their ship from a Brazilian Navy Super Lynx Mk.21A

Lynx Mk.90B landing on Royal Danish Navy THETIS-class

Lynx of the German Navy

Cockpit of a Lynx of the German Navy

Super Lynx of the Brazilian Navy

Lynx Mk.21
Export version of the HAS.2 for the Brazilian Navy. Brazilian navy designation **SAH-11**. Nine delivered.

Super Lynx Mk.21A
Version of the Super Lynx (based on HAS.Mk.8) for the Brazilian navy, with Gem 42 engines and 360° traverse Seaspray 3000 radar under nose. Nine new build helicopters plus upgrades of remaining five original Mk.21s.

Lynx Mk.22
Unbuilt export version for the Egyptian Navy.

Lynx Mk.23
Export version of the HAS.2 for the Argentine Navy. Two built. Grounded due to British embargo on spares following Falklands War. Single surviving helicopter later sold to Denmark.

Lynx Mk.24
Unbuilt export utility version for the Iraqi army.

Lynx Mk.25
Export version of the HAS.2 for the Royal Netherlands Navy. Designated **UH-14A** in Dutch service. Used for utility and SAR roles.

Lynx Mk.26
Unbuilt export armed version for the Iraqi army.

Lynx Mk.27
Export version for the Royal Netherlands Navy with 836 kW (1,120 kW) Gem 4 engines. Equipped for ASW missions with dipping sonar. Designated **SH-14B** in Dutch service. 10 built.

Lynx Mk.28
Export version of the AH.1 for the Qatar Police. Three built.

Lynx Mk.64
Export version of the Super Lynx for the South African Air Force.

Lynx Mk.80
Export version for the Royal Danish Navy based on the HAS.3 but with non-folding tail. Eight built.

Lynx Mk.81
Upgraded ASW version for the Royal Netherlands Navy, powered by Gem 41 engines with no sonar but fitted with towed Magnetic anomaly detector. Designated **SH-14C** in Dutch service, and mainly used for training and utility purposes. Eight built.

SH-14D
UH-14A/SH-14B/SH-14C Lynx upgraded to a common standard by the Royal Netherlands Navy under the STAMOL programme with Gem 42 engines, provision for dipping sonar and FLIR. 22 upgraded.

Lynx Mk.82
Unbuilt export version for the Egyptian army.

Lynx Mk.83
Unbuilt export version for the Saudi Arabian army.

Lynx Mk 84
Unbuilt export version for the Qatar army.

Lynx Mk 85
Unbuilt export version for the United Arab Emirates army.

Lynx Mk.86
Export SAR version of the HAS.2 for the Royal Norwegian Air Force.

Lynx Mk.87
Embargoed export version for the Argentine navy. Two completed and sold to Denmark as Mk.90 other six not built

Lynx Mk.88
Export version for the German Navy with Gem 42 engines, and dipping sonar. Nineteen built. **Super Lynx Mk.88A** is an upgraded version with

Gem 42 engines, under-nose radome with 360°traverse radar and FLIR above nose. Seven new build helicopters plus conversion of Mk.88s.

Lynx Mk.89
Export version of HAS.3 for the Nigerian navy. Three built.

Lynx Mk.90
Export version for the Royal Danish Navy, modified from embargoed Argentine Mk.87s. Lynx Mk.90A is the upgraded version. The Lynx Mk.90 and Mk.90A were upgraded to Super Lynx standard and designated Mk.90B.

Lynx Mk.95
Version of Super Lynx for the Portuguese Navy, with Bendix radar in undernose radome, dipping sonar but no FLIR. Three new build plus two converted ex-Royal Navy HAS.3s.

Super Lynx Mk.99
Version of Super Lynx for the South Korean Navy, with Seaspray 3 radar in undernose radome, dipping sonar, and FLIR, for anti-submarine and anti-ship operations. Twelve were built. Super Lynx Mk.99A is the upgraded version with improved rotor, with a further 13 built. Hulls were produced in the United Kingdom while South Korea supplied domestic ISTAR, electro-optical, electronic warfare, and fire-control systems, as well as flight control actuators and undercarriage.

Super Lynx Mk.100
Super Lynx for the Royal Malaysian Navy, with 990 kW (1,327 hp) CTS-800-4N engines. Six built.

Super Lynx Mk.110
Super Lynx 300 for Thai Navy. Four ordered.

Super Lynx Mk.120
Export version for the Royal Air Force of Oman. 16 built.

Super Lynx Mk.130
Export version for the Algerian Navy. Four ordered.

Super Lynx 300
Advanced Super Lynx with CTS-800-4N engines.

Projects
Lynx HT.3
Proposed training version for the Royal Air Force, not built.

Lynx-3
Enhanced Lynx variant with Westland 30 tail boom and rotor, Gem 60 engines, new wheeled tricycle undercarriage and MIL-STD-1553 databus. Only one prototype built (serial/registration *ZE477* / G-17-24) in 1984.

Battlefield Lynx
Proposed export version of Lynx AH.9.

Battlefield Lynx 800
Proposed export version of Lynx AH.9 with LHTEC T800 engines, the project was suspended in 1992. One demonstrator helicopter was built and flight tested.

Lynx ACH
Proposed **A**dvanced **C**ompound **H**elicopter technology demonstrator, partly funded by the Ministry of Defence. Announced in May 1998, the ACH was planned to be powered by RTM322 engines with variable area exhaust nozzles and a gearbox from the Westland 30-200, have wings attached at cabin roof level and BERP rotor blades. It was predicted to fly approximately 50% faster than a standard Lynx.

Derivatives
Westland 30
medium helicopter based on the Lynx, using some dynamic systems with a new, enlarged fuselage for up to 22 passengers.

AgustaWestland AW159 Lynx Wildcat
a development of the Super Lynx with two LHTEC CTS800 engines; previously known as the **Future Lynx**.

NOTES: AH = Army Helicopter, HAS = Helicopter, Anti-Submarine, HMA = Helicopter, Maritime Attack, IFF = Identification Friend or Foe, (GM) = Gulf Modification, (S) = Secure speech radio, and SIFF = Successor to IFF.

Operators

Lynx of the Royal Danish Navy

Lynx of the Portuguese Navy

Westland Super Lynx Mk.21A of the Brazilian Navy

Military operators

Algeria
- Algerian Air Force: Super Lynx 4 Mk.300 (to be delivered in 2010)

Argentina
- Argentine Navy: The Argentine Naval Aviation ordered ten Mk.23s but only two were delivered before the outbreak of the Falklands War and the ensuing arms embargo imposed by the British. To make up for the undelivered aircraft, the Argentines ordered the Eurocopter Fennec. The two delivered helicopters in addition to the undelivered helicopters were later sold to the Danish Navy and Brazilian Navy.

Brazil
- Brazilian Navy: 12 Lynx Mk.21A

Denmark
- Royal Danish Air Force: 8 Super Lynx Mk.90Bs used for various missions. These were originally operated by the Royal Danish Navy

until January 2011.

France
- French Navy - French Naval Aviation: 31 Lynx HAS.4

Germany
- German Navy: 22 Sea Lynx Mk.88A

Malaysia
- Royal Malaysian Navy: 6 Super Lynx Mk.100

Netherlands
- Royal Netherlands Navy: 20 Super Lynx SH-14D. Originally received 6 search and rescue (UH-14A/Mk.25) and 18 anti-submarine warfare models (SH-14B/Mk.27 and SH-14C/Mk.81), which have all been upgraded to SH-14D standard for both SAR and ASW duties.

Nigeria
- Nigerian Navy: 3 Lynx Mk.89 (One caught fire and was destroyed) - used for anti-submarine warfare. Retired from service.

Norway
- Royal Norwegian Air Force: 6 Lynx Mk.86 - operated on on behalf of the Norwegian Coast Guard. 337 Skvadron operates from the Nordkapp Class cutters.

Oman
- Royal Air Force of Oman: 15 Super Lynx Mk.120

Pakistan
- Pakistan Navy - Pakistan Naval Air Arm: 3 Lynx Mk.3 - used for anti-ship / anti-submarine / transport duties. These aircraft have been retired from service since 2003.

Portugal
- Portuguese Navy 5 Lynx Mk.95 - operated from the *"Vasco da Gama class frigates"*.

South Africa
- South African Air Force: 4 Super Lynx Mk.64. Operates from the South African Navy Valour class frigates.

British Army Air Corps AH.7 at RIAT 2010.

South Korea
- Republic of Korea Navy: 12 Super Lynx Mk.99 and 13 Super Lynx Mk.99A. Used for anti-submarine and surface warfare.

Thailand
- Royal Thai Navy had 2 Super Lynx 300s in use in January 2010. Operated by 203 Squadron at U-Tapao RTNS, Chonburi Province, Thailand.

United Kingdom
- British Army - Army Air Corps: 120 Lynx AH.1 / AH.5 / AH.7 / AH.9.
- Royal Navy - Fleet Air Arm: 80 Lynx HAS.2 / HAS.3 / HMA.8.

Law Enforcement operators

Qatar
- Qatar State Police

Specifications (Super Lynx Series 100)

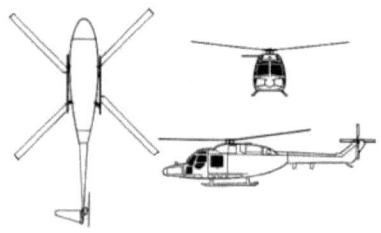

Data from Flight International World Aircraft and Systems Directory (3rd ed.)

General characteristics
- **Crew:** 2 or 3
- **Capacity:** 10 troops
- **Payload:** 737 kg ()
- **Length:** 15.241 m (50 ft)
- **Rotor diameter:** 12.80 m (42 ft)
- **Height:** 3.734 m for mk7; 3.785 m for mk9 (12.25 ft for mk7; 12.41 ft for mk9)
- **Disc area:** 128.71 m² (1,385 ft²)
- **Empty weight:** 3,291 kg (7,255 lb)
- **Max takeoff weight:** 5,330 kg (11,750 lb)
- **Powerplant:** 2× Rolls-Royce Gem turboshaft, 835 kW (1,120 shp) each

Performance
- **Maximum speed:** 324 km/h (201 mph)
- **Range:** 528 km (328 miles) with standard tanks

Armament
- Naval: 2 x torpedoes *or* 4x Sea Skua missiles *or* 2 x depth charges.
- Attack: 2 x 20mm cannons, 2 x 70mm rocket pods CRV7, 8 x TOW ATGM
- General: 7.62mm General Purpose Machine Guns (AH.7 and AH.9), Browning AN/M3M .50 calibre heavy machine gun (HAS.3 and HMA.8)

Source (edited): "http://en.wikipedia.org/wiki/Westland_Lynx"

Westland Scout

The **Westland Scout** was a general purpose military light helicopter developed by Westland Helicopters. It was closely related to the Westland Wasp naval helicopter.

Design and development

Both the Scout and the Wasp were developed from the Saunders-Roe P.531, itself a development of the Saunders-Roe Skeeter. With the acquisition of Saunders Roe, Westland took over the

P.531 project, which became the prototype for the Scout (originally called Sprite) and the Wasp.

The P.531 was developed with the 635 shp (474 kW) Bristol Siddeley Nimbus and the 685 shp (511 kW) de Havilland Gnome H.1000 engine, which flew from 3 May 1960. The production Scout AH.1 used a 1,050 shp (780 kW) Rolls-Royce (RR having acquired Bristol Siddeley by then) Nimbus 101 engine, torque limited to 685 shp (511 kW), and achieved its first flight on 29 August 1960. The Nimbus power ratings were 1,050 shp (780 kW) for five minutes, 685 shp (511 kW) for one hour and 650 shp (480 kW) could be maintained up to 7,000 ft (2,100 m) at 30 degrees Celsius.

The Scout has a rigid tubular skid undercarriage with two oleos connecting the rear cross-tube to the fuel tank rear bulkhead. Despite appearances the oleos act in tension, not compression, damping the reflex action to prevent the aircraft bouncing when landing. Energy absorption on landing is mainly through the two cross-tubes. Additional rigidity is given to the undercarriage through diagonal struts connecting the rear cross tube to the main fuselage longitudinal webs. These struts also help stiffen the airframe vertically and laterally, and are fitted with quick release pins to allow access to the fuselage access panels. The rear cross-tube is anchored centrally and the front cross-tube is fixed to the two main fuselage longitudinal webs. The port skid also acted as a storage tube for the long HF aerial, the skid was accessed via a screw-fixed cap at the rear. The vertical spigot at the front of each skid is used to mount ballast weights to alter the aircraft's centre of gravity.

Behind the two front seats was a three-seat bench, although this could be replaced with a four-seat bench when fitted with modified rear doors (see main photograph). It was used for general light work including observation, liaison, training, and search and rescue. When fitted as a light attack helicopter it carried either two, skid-mounted, forward-firing machine gun (L8A1 GPMG) packs or a single pintle mounted machine gun in the rear cabin. The pintle mount was available in both port and staboard mountings. The gunpacks, which were both aimed at a preset convergence angle, carried 200 rounds of ammunition and were mounted on a tubular spar that was fixed between the front and rear undercarriage legs. In the anti-tank role it could carry four guided missiles (the Nord SS.11). The sighting unit was the AF.120, the result of a joint venture between Avimo and Ferranti and had x2.5 and x10 magnification. The APX Bezu sight unit was also evaluated but rejected, although it was adopted for use on the Westland Wasp. Additional testing and trials were carried out with the Hawkswing(initially known as Airstrike Swingfire) missile. Initial firings were carried out in early 1972, to test the system for the Westland Lynx, the associated AF.530 sight was subsequntly trialled in 1974. The Hawkswing system was cancelled in 1975 due to its manual control system (MCLOS) compared to the semi-automatic (SACLOS) system utilised by its rivals HOT and TOW. In the casualty evacuation role (CASEVAC), the Scout could carry two stretchers internally or two on externally mounted pods, the co-pilots seat could also be reversed to allow an attendant to face the casualties.

Although the general design of the aircraft was robust, with an airframe fatigue life of 7200 hours, the cockpit ergonomics were less than perfect. An example of this was the cabin heater switch being mounted next to the fuel cock. Unfortunately this led to the loss of at least four aircraft when the pilot misadvertantly closed the fuel cock instead of switching off the cabin heater, causing the engine to shut down. The autorotational qualities of the Scout have also been described by some pilots as 'startling'. In service trials and testing were carried out by the AAC's Development Wing at Middle Wallop, Hampshire. A wide variety of weapons and equipment were evaluated, although many were never adopted. Amongst these were the 7.62mm General Electric Minigun and the two inch rocket pod. The rocket pods were mounted either side of the central fuselage section on the multi-spar weapon booms and both smooth tube and fin-stabilised rockets were tested, although the accuracy was described as 'indifferent'. Studies were also carried out for a pintle mounted M2 Browning machine gun in place of the standard 7.62 GPMG, and the French AME.621 20mm cannon. Another was the installation of a Bendix R.100 lightweight weather and ground-mapping radar, which had a range of eight and forty miles. This was mounted behind the fibreglass nose access panel along with a small viewing screen in the cockpit. The radar antenna was moved further forward later in the development and a small, pronounced nose cone was fitted onto the panel.

During the development of the WG.13 Westland Lynx, two Scouts were used as testbeds and fitted with full-scale, semi-rigid Lynx main rotor heads, despite the fact that the WG.13 rotor diameter was greater by around three metres . The first test flight was achieved 31 August 1970. A prototype MBB BO 105 also used a Scout main rotor head and blades during the development phase, unfortunately this aircraft was destroyed due to ground resonance during its initial trials.

About 150 Scouts were built through 1968, primarily at the Fairey Aviation Division factory at Hayes.

Scout AH.1 at Farnborough 1962

Operational history

The Scout formed the backbone of the Army Air Corps throughout the 1960s and well into the 1970s; the first Scout flew on 29 August 1960 and an initial order for 66 aircraft followed a month after its first flight. Engine problems delayed the introduction of the Scout until 1963, and as an interim measure the Army Air Corps received a small number of Allouette II helicopters. Although the aircraft's entry into service was delayed, the Scout still had a number of teething troubles when it was introduced. One of the earliest losses was XR596, which crashed into the jungle near Kluang airfield in Southern Malaya, 16 July 1964, following a fuel pump failure. The two crew died in the incident. Engine failures were responsible for the loss of at least eleven military and civilian registered aircraft. The engine life of the Nimbus during the early part of its service was notoriously low, with four to six flying hours being the norm. A competition was allegedly held, with a prize to the first unit that could achieve an engine life of twenty-five flying hours. Operational experience and development work steadily improved the reliability of the Nimbus and by 1964 engine life had improved to two/three engine changes per 1,000 flying hours.

The Scout AH Mk 1 was operated by the Army Air Corps on general light work, including observation and liaison. Like the Wasp, the Scout could be fitted out with different role equipment including flotation gear and a Lucas, air-driven hoist which had a lift capacity of 600 lb (270 kg). In the light attack role it was capable of carrying one pintle machine gun in the rear cabin (it is possible to carry two pintle mounted GPMGs in the cabin, although this would, unsurprisingly, be somewhat cramped) or two forward-firing 7.62mm L7 General Purpose Machine Guns (GPMGs) fixed to the undercarriage skid. These GPMG combinations were sometimes used in unison to great effect.

The forward firing GPMGs were electrically operated, being fired by the pilot and aimed using a rudimentary system of drawing a small cross on the windscreen with a chinagraph pencil. In sandy conditions these weapons could jam, which necessitated one of the free crew to lean out of the cockpit door and 'boot' the offending weapon in hope of clearing it. This procedure was not strictly in accordance with the flight reference cards. The L7A1 pintle mounted weapon was operated by a door gunner.

8 Flight Scout AH.1 at Habilayn, Radfan 1967

In the anti-tank role four SS.11 ATGWs were carried, these could be carried in conjunction with the pintle mounted GPMG. During the Falklands campaign the SS.11 achieved some success, being used to attack Argentine positions 14 June 1982. For night time reconnaissance the Scout could carry four 4.5-inch (110 mm) parachute flares mounted on special carriers. In addition, two smaller parachute flares could be carried to allow emergency landings at night. These were fitted on the starboard rear fuselage on a special attachment point. About 150 Scout helicopters were acquired for the Army Air Corps and were operated by them up until 1994.

The way British Military Aviation has been established has meant that the Royal Marines have never actually "owned" their own aircraft. The larger Whirlwind, Wessex and Sea King helicopters have been "Royal Navy" Helicopters and, like today's Lynx AH Mk 7, the Scout AH Mk 1s operated by 3 Commando Brigade Air Squadron (3 CBAS) were British Army helicopters on loan. 3 CBAS flew the Scout from 1979 through to 1982, when the Scout was replaced by the Westland Lynx, and the squadron was eventually renumbered as 847 Naval Air Squadron.

The Scout saw operational service in Borneo, Aden, Oman, Rhodesia, Northern Ireland and then in the South Atlantic.

The territorial army (aac) formed 666sqn with a number of scouts in the late 1980s.

Borneo

Mystery still surrounds a Scout that went missing 20 September 1965. XR599 set off for a 40-nautical-mile (74 km) night flight from Lundu to Kuching, the mission being to transport a local communist suspect to the Sarawak capital for interrogation. At 23:00 hrs the aircraft was posted as missing and a search and rescue mission was mounted. Although the aircraft and the remains of the pilot, the escort rifleman and the suspect were never found, a fisherman later dredged up small parts of the aircraft wreckage. On 23 September a local newspaper, The Strait Times, printed a story speculating that the Scout had been hi-jacked by the prisoner who had somehow managed to capture his escort's weapon and then ordered the pilot to either fly out to sea or over the jungle towards the Indonesian border until they ran out of fuel. Tragedy struck a second time on 25 September when an RAF Westland Whirlwind HAR.10 of 225 Sqn, searching over jungle for XR599, crashed killing the five crew.

Aden and Radfan

In Aden and Radfan a number of Scouts were shot down, although these usually resulted in a forced landing and the aircraft were recovered, repaired and returned to service. A example of this occurred 26 May 1964 when the CO of 3 Para, Lt Col Anthony Farrar-Hockley, used a Scout to reconnoitre the Wadi Dhubsan area, Radfan. The aircraft was hit by enemy fire, the pilot made an emergency landing and the aircraft was subsequently recovered. Three Scouts were written off during the campaign, the first, XR634, was through pilot error whilst landing, 16 May 1966. Although initially repairable this aircraft was subsequently damaged beyond economic repair when it was dropped by the RAF Westland Wessex sent to recover it. The second aircraft, XT635, flew into a hillside during a night patrol at Jebal, 5 May 1967, killing the two crew and the two passengers. The third aircraft,

XT641, was destroyed on the ground in an incident where the pilot, and his F.O. intelligence officer passenger were captured and shot dead by the NLF after landing in a wadi bed whilst on a flight from Ataq to Mayfa'ah on 3 September 1967. The NLF then set fire to and destroyed the aircraft. Dropping recovered aircraft from helicopters is not the preserve of the Royal Air Force. On 1 August 1968, Westland Sioux *XT123* crashed at Sharjah, Oman, and was subsequently written off when it was dropped by the Westland Scout that was attempting the recovery.

Lt David John Ralls, RCT, was awarded the DFC for counter-attacking a large group of enemy which had previously attacked an army road repair party on the road to Habilayn. Lt Ralls attack, on 30 May 1967, utilised both the forward-firing and pintle mounted weapons, forcing the enemy to retreat. Despite his aircraft being hit a number of times, he then directed three Hawker Hunter airstrikes onto the target.

Falklands War

At the start of "Operation Corporate" six Scouts from 3 Commando Brigade Air Squadron were operating alongside three machines from No. 656 Squadron AAC, and when 5 Infantry Brigade landed they were joined by another three Scouts from 656 Squadron. During the Falklands conflict the Scout was engaged in CASEVAC, re-supply and Special Forces insertion roles. One aircraft, *XT629*, was one of two Scouts of B Flight 3 Commando Brigade Air Squadron, that was attacked by two FMA IA 58 Pucarás (the only Argentine air-to-air victory in the war) of Grupo 3 near Camilla Creek House, North of Goose Green. *XT629* was hit by cannon fire and crashed, killing the pilot and severing the leg of the crewman, who was thrown clear of the wreckage on impact. The second Scout evaded the Pucarás and later returned to the site to CASEVAC the survivor. Another Scout, *XR628*, of 656 Sqn AAC, suffered a main rotor gearbox failure whilst in a low hover over MacPhee Pond, 8 June 1982. *XR628* had taken cover as two pairs of A-4 Skyhawks from Grupo 5 approached, these aircraft later attacked the RFA LSLs *Sir Galahad* and *Sir Tristram* at Bluff Cove. Once the threat had passed and the pilot began to climb away, the main gearbox failed at the main input drive and the aircraft made a forced landing at the lakeside in around four feet of water. The two crew were picked up another 656 Sqn Scout piloted by Capt J G Greenhalgh later that day. The aircraft was eventually recovered and airlifted to Fitzroy by Seaking on 11 June, but was subsequently written off on its return to the UK. Following research at the National Archive, Kew, it has been determined that *XR628* was the same aircraft that was shot down, 26 May 1964, carrying 3 Para CO Lt Col Farrar-Hockley.

Scouts armed with SS.11 anti-tank missiles were used to great effect during the Falklands campaign. On 14 Jun 1982, an Argentine 105 mm Pack Howitzer battery dug in to the West of Stanley Racecourse was firing at the Scots Guards as they approached Mount Tumbledown. As the guns were out of range of the Milan ATGWs of nearby 2 Para, their 2IC, Major Chris Keeble, contacted Capt J G Greenhalgh of 656 Sqn AAC on the radio and requested a HELARM using SS.11 missiles to attack on them. As he was engaged in ammunition re-supply, his Scout was not fitted with missile booms. This was in order to reduce weight and increase the aircraft lift capability. Capt Greenhalgh then returned to Estancia House, where his aircraft was refuelled, fitted out, and armed with four missiles in 20 minutes with the rotors still turning. An 'O' group was then held with the crews of two Scouts of 3 CBAS and Capt Greenhalgh took off on a reconnaissance mission, while the other aircraft were fitted out and readied. Within 20 minutes he had located the target and carried out a detailed recce of the area. He fired two missiles at the enemy positions and then returned to a pre-arranged RV to meet up and guide in the other two Scouts. The three aircraft, positioned 100 metres apart, then fired a total of ten missiles (nine missiles hit, one failed) from the ridge overlooking the Argentine positions 3000m away and succeeded in hitting the howitzers, nearby bunkers, an ammunition dump and the command post. The Argentine troops returned mortar fire, a round landing directly in front of Capt Greenhalgh's Scout.

Northern Ireland

In Northern Ireland the Scout pioneered the use of the Heli-Tele aerial surveillance system, having a gyro-stabilised Marconi unit shoe-horned into the rear cabin. The Heli-Tele unit weighed some 700 lb (320 kg), although later developments reduced this significantly. The aircraft was also used for mounting Eagle patrols. In this role the rear cabin doors and seats were removed and four troops sat in the rear cabin with their feet resting on the skids. Operating with two aircraft in unison, this allowed an eight man patrol to be quickly inserted into an area and mount snap Vehicle Check Points (VCPs) if necessary. Up until 1973, the standard tail rotor colour scheme for the Scout were bands of red and white. On 14 September 1973 a soldier died during training at Gosford Castle, Armagh, after coming into contact with the tail rotor blades whilst the aircraft was on the ground. Following this accident the tail rotor blade colour scheme was changed to the distinctive black and white bands.

Because of the specialist nature of operations in Northern Ireland, a particularly important piece of role equipment was introduced in the form of the 'Nightsun' 3.5 million candle power searchlight. Operations at night were greatly enhanced with the introduction of Night Vision Goggles (NVGs), although these missions could still be hazardous. This was evident on the night of 2 December 1978, when the pilot of XW614, 659 Sqn, became disorientated during a sortie and crashed into Lough Ross, killing the two crew. XW614 was the last of five Scouts written off during operations in the Province.

Exports

Unlike its naval counterpart, the Scout did not achieve the same export success as the Wasp, with the Royal Jordanian Air Force acquiring three helicopters, two were operated in Uganda, and Bahrain had two helicopters which were operated by the Bahrain Public Security Force in police service roles. The Scout never received civilian air worthiness certification which prevented it from being sold to civilian operators, the design being utilised purely for army use from the outset. All current operators require an 'Experimental' certificate to fly them.

Two Scout helicopters were acquired by the Royal Australian Navy (RAN) in April 1963 and were operated by the 723 Naval Air Squadron, with the aircraft being rotated aboard the hydrographic survey ship HMAS *Moresby*. The RAN Scouts proved the practicalities of operating helicopters from small ships for the RAN, and the RAN operated these helicopters up until 1973, when they were replaced by Bell 206B-1 Kiowas. The RAN experience with the Scouts aboard HMAS *Moresby* illustrated the need for a higher-level maintenance regime as a result of operating the helicopters in areas with high concentrations of abrasive coral sand encountered around the Australian coastline and the detrimental effect that it had on the rotor blades, airframe and engine components. Despite the additional effort to maintain the helicopters, the Scouts were considered to be superior to the seaplanes and flying boats that had previously been used in this role. One of the Scouts ditched in Wewak Harbour whilst taking off from HMAS *Moresby*, April 1967, although it was subsequently recovered the aircraft was written off.

Survivors

Although the operational flying days are behind them, there are still Scouts in the air; mainly in the UK; at the present time there are six Scouts remaining on the UK Civil Register along with the Army Air Corps Historic Flights aircraft. Outside the UK, the last of six Scouts that were taken down to New Zealand has been withdrawn from use, leaving ZS-HAS flying in South Africa.

Military

- XP851 10 May 1963: While serving with 651 Sqn, aircraft suffered an engine failure during winching trials at Yeovil, Somerset. It force landed into a field adjacent to the airfield and rolled upside down. The pilot was uninjured but the aircraft was later deemed to be damaged beyond repair.
- XP892 17 November 1964: While serving with 3 Flt, Cyprus, the aircraft crash landed at Ktima landing pad, following a tail rotor failure at 40 feet (12 m). The main rotor subsequently struck the cockpit injuring both crew.
- XP889 23 February 1965: While serving with AAC Centre, the aircraft crashed and rolled onto its side following an engine failure during take off, at Sidbury Hill near Everleigh, Wiltshire. The pilot had made a precautionary landing to re-select radio channels. The engine failure was caused by a blocked fuel pipe.
- XP854 23 March 1965: While serving with 18 Flt, Oberhausen, West Germany, the engine failed due to blocked oil filters. During the subsequent autorotation the pilot pulled up the collective lever early to avoid houses, causing the loss of main rotor speed, resulting in a heavy landing. Of the three crew the pilot was slightly injured. The aircraft was initially sent to Westlands for repair but was declared a write off. Airframe allocated to ground instruction at Middle Wallop (TAD043).
- XR638 3 January 1966: While serving with 21 Flt, UK, the aircraft encountered engine problems caused by the inadvertent closure of the fuel cock in mistake for the heater control, during a delivery flight from Wroughton to Middle Wallop. The aircraft subsequently lost height and crashed tail first at Marlborough, Wiltshire. It then caught fire and burnt out killing the two crew.
- XT621 14 January 1966: While serving with 665 Sqn, West Malaysia, the pilot became disorientated during a landing in 'brown out' conditions at night. The aircraft rolled to starboard, crashed onto its side and overturned, injuring one of the three crew on board.
- XT619 10 March 1966: While serving with 21 Flt, UK, the aircraft was carrying a soldier in a stretcher pod as part of a casevac scenario, during Exercise 'Baker's Dozen, Stanford PTA, Norfolk . The pilot inadvertently shut off the fuel cock instead of the cabin heater. The pilot reopened the fuel cock, but during the subsequent attempted emergency landing, the main rotors struck a tree and the aircraft crashed in a ploughed field near Thetford. The two crew and the soldier were injured.
- XR633 7 September 1966: While serving with 4 Wing, the aircraft suffered an engine failure and ditched in the Straits of Malacca, Malaysia. The airframe was subsequently sold to a private owner in Suffolk.
- XP895 11 November 1966: While serving with 21 Flt, the aircraft crash-landed into a ploughed field at Overton, Hampshire following engine failure at 700 feet (210 m). Although the aircraft was written off, the two crew were uninjured.
- XR598 20 March 1967: While serving with 11 Flt, Bakalalan, Borneo, the pilot was unable to control a yaw to the right while on approach. The aircraft struck a tree breaking off the tail rotor and damaging the main rotor. The aircraft crashed injuring two of the four occupants.
- XV120 6 June 1967: While serving with 10 Flt, the aircraft crashed into the ground at the corner of Long Cross housing estate at Felton near Bristol Airport, just before 9 am, killing the pilot, Capt Norman Wallace, 28, and the two other occupants, Brigadier George Butler, 49, and L/Cpl John Carr, 19.
- XT625 30 January 1968: While serving with 11 Flt, Borneo, the aircraft suffered an engine failure and force landed into the jungle near

Gerik, ten miles (16 km) from Butterworth, Malaysia, killing Cpl Christopher Galloway REME, and injuring the other two occupants.

- XT615 2 February 1968: While serving with 13 Flt, Oman, the aircraft suffered an engine failure at 900 feet (270 m), near Sharjah. During the subsequent autorotation and landing, the port skid touched down first on sloping soft ground, causing the aircraft to bounce and land on its starboard side. Two of the four occupants were injured.
- XT622 23 April 1968: While serving with 7 Flt, Malaysia, suffered an engine failure on approach to Kangar Kahang, Johore State, injuring two of the four occupants in the subsequent heavy landing.
- XR640 14 May 1969: While serving with 6 Flt, the aircraft was involved in a mid-air collision during take-off at Chattendon Barracks, Rochester, Kent. The pilot of the Scout, and the two occupants of the Sioux, XT802 of 3 RTR Air Sqn, were killed. L/Cpl Sindall and Spr Pedley Royal Engineers were awarded the BEM for gallantry in attempting to rescue the occupants.
- XV125 16 December 1969: While serving with 651 Sqn, Germany, the aircraft suffered a tail rotor blade failure during a test flight and subsequently suffered a heavy landing near Verden. The three occupants were unhurt.
- XP896 20 November 1973: While serving with 663 Sqn, Northern Ireland, the aircraft suffered an engine failure during take off from Armagh. During the subsequent forced landing it struck a recovery vehicle in a vehicle park, injuring the five crew.
- XR636 12 April 1974: While serving with 664 Sqn, Northern Ireland, the aircraft flew into rising ground at Rich Hill near Portadown, County Armagh, killing the pilot, WO2 David Christopher Rowat.
- XR631 19 June 1974: While serving with 652 Sqn, Germany, the aircraft crashed and caught fire following a wire strike at Vogelsang, during a photographic sortie. The four crew subsequently escaped without injury.
- XV133 9 January 1976: While serving with 662 Sqn, Northern Ireland, the aircraft crashed near Crossmaglen, Armagh, after the pilot became disorientated flying into low cloud at night. Both the pilot, WO2 Brian Anthony Jackson, and the passenger, Cpl Arthur Kenneth Ford Royal Signals, were killed.
- XV132 10 April 1978: While serving with 655 Sqn, Northern Ireland, the aircraft crashed into Lough Neagh after flying into a snow storm. Both the pilot, Capt Michael James Kett Royal Artillery, and the passenger, a 17 year old cadet, were killed.
- XP904 12 May 1978: While serving with 654 Sqn, Germany, the aircraft crashed into trees and caught fire at Lemgo, near Lippstadt. The aircraft was in a near vertical descent with virtually no rotor speed, killing the two crewmen. The possible cause was the inadvertent closure of the fuel cock in mistake for the heater control.
- XR604 8 February 1979: While serving with 7 Regt, prior to take off from Hereford, Herefordshire, the pilot inadvertently operated the fuel shut off cock instead of the cabin heater. The engine failed at 800 feet (240 m) and the aircraft overturned during the subsequent forced landing in a school playing field. The pilot was slightly injured.
- XR601 26 August 1979: While serving in BATUS, Suffield, Canada, following an engine failure during a hover at 50 feet (15 m), the main rotor severed the tailboom in the subsequent heavy landing. One of the two crew was badly injured. The airframe was allocated to ground instruction at SEAE, Arborfield, England and then to Whittington Barracks for display.
- XP890 6 October 1981: While serving with ARWF, Middle Wallop, Hants, the aircraft was badly damaged when it was landed on by a Bristow Helicopters Ltd Westland Bell 47G-4, registration G-AXKT, which was written off. The Scout was stripped for spares in 1987.
- XT647 28 September 1982: While serving with A&AEE, Boscombe Down, Wiltshire, control was lost during take off due to misalignment of the pilot valve in the starboard cyclic control system. The aircraft was subsequently destroyed on impact. The two crew escaped injury.
- XP901 18 January 1983: While serving with 660 Sqn, Hong Kong, the aircraft was badly damaged and written off in a heavy engine off landing at Sek Kong. The two crewmen were slightly injured.
- XP906 12 March 1985: While serving with 660 Sqn, Hong Kong, the aircraft rolled over on take off from Crest Hill, Sheung Shui, after loss of main rotor rpm, killing Maj Richard Balkwill, Royal Artillery, and injuring three others. The airframe was subsequently disposed of on the Sek Kong fire dump.
- XP909 19 February 1991: While serving with 658 Sqn, at the Yakama range, Washington, USA, the aircraft ran out of fuel. During the subsequent heavy landing at the bottom of a canyon, it bounced and came to rest 70 feet (21 m) up the side of the canyon. Both crew were severely injured.

Civilian
- G-BXRL 16 October 1999: Pilot inadvertently reduced power and mis-interpreted an engine failure. The aircraft (ex-AAC XT630) descended and landed in a water-filled quarry. The three occupants received minor injuries.
- G-BZBD 23 August 2000: Pilot felt an increase in cyclic control forces and mis-interpreted a hydraulic failure. After switching off the hydraulic system the aircraft (ex-AAC XT632) manoeuvred violently and impacted the ground.

- G-BYNZ 24 September 2000: Pilot carried out an emergency landing due to deteriorating weather conditions. As he descended in a right-hand, descending spiral, the aircraft (ex-AAC XW281) struck the ground tail first and rolled onto its port side. The aircraft was written off.
- G-BXSL 19 November 2001: Following an in-flight engine failure, the aircraft (ex-AAC XW799) impacted the ground and rolled over. The subsequent report found the most likely cause of the engine failure to be fuel contamination. None of the two occupants were hurt.

Popular culture

- The Scout featured in the 1982 film, Who Dares Wins, starring Lewis Collins. Some of the flying scenes caused consternation for co-star Maurice Roëves, due to his chronic fear of heights. The aircraft were provided and flown by No. 656 Squadron AAC.
- A 'wrecked' Scout featured on a beach scene in a 2008 Royal Marine recruitment film. The 45 second advert was filmed in Brunei and featured Malay actors posing as terrorists. The film, which cost £1million, was later withdrawn due to the inference that Malaysians could be involved with terrorism.
- The hulk of a Scout is featured on the Channel 4 series, 'Scrapheap Challenge'.

Variants

Saunders-Roe P.531
Prototype.
Saunders-Roe P.531-2 Mk.1
Pre-production aircraft.
Scout AH.1
Five/six-seat light utility helicopter for the British Army

Operators

Military operators

Scout at the SAAF museum, Port Elizabeth, South Africa

Australia
- Royal Australian Navy
  - Fleet Air Arm (RAN) operated 2 helicopters in 723 Squadron RAN.

Jordan
- Royal Jordanian Air Force operated 3 helicopters.

South Africa
- South African Air Force

United Kingdom
- British Army Air Corps
- Royal Marines

Law enforcement operators

Bahrain
- Bahrain State Police operated 2 helicopters.

Uganda
- Uganda Police Force Air Wing - operated 2 helicopters.

Specifications (Scout)

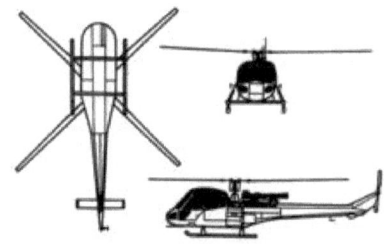
Westland Scout 3-view drawing

Westland Scout and Wasp Silhouettes

Data from Jane's All The World's Aircraft 1965–66

General characteristics

- **Crew:** 1/2
- **Capacity:** 4/5 passengers
- **Payload:** 1,500 lb (680 kg) (slung load)
- **Length:** 30 ft 4 in (9.25 m)
- **Rotor diameter:** 32 ft 3 in (9.83 m)
- **Height:** 8 ft 11 in (2.72 m)
- **Disc area:** 816.9 ft² (85.90 m²)
- **Empty weight:** 3,232 lb (1,465 kg)
- **Max takeoff weight:** 5,300 lb (2,405 kg)
- **Powerplant:** 1× Rolls-Royce Nimbus 101 turboshaft, 1,050 shp (783 kW) (derated to 685 shp (511 kW))

Performance

- **Never exceed speed:** 132 mph (115 knots, 213 km/h)
- **Maximum speed:** 131 mph (114 knots, 211 km/h) at sea level
- **Cruise speed:** 122 mph (106 knots, 196 km/h)
- **Range:** 315 mi (274 nmi, 507 km)
- **Service ceiling:** 17,700 ft (5,400 m)
- **Hover ceiling:** 12,500 ft (3,800 m) (in ground effect)
- **Rate of climb:** 1,670 ft/min at sea level (8.50 m/s)
- **Disc loading:** 6.48 lb/ft² (31.6 kg/m²)
- **Power/mass:** 0.13 hp/lb (0.21 kW/kg)

Armament

- **Guns:** 1 or 2 x L7 GPMG machine guns
- **Missiles:** 4 x SS.11 anti-tank guided missiles

Source (edited): "http://en.wikipedia.org/wiki/Westland_Scout"

Westland Sea King

The **Westland WS-61 Sea King** is a British licence-built version of the American Sikorsky S-61 helicopter of the same name, built by Westland Helicopters. The aircraft differs considerably from the American version, with Rolls-Royce Gnome engines (licence-built General Electric T58s), British made anti-submarine warfare systems and a fully computerised control system. The Westland Sea King was also produced as the **Commando** troop transport version for export.

Design and development

Westland Helicopters, which had a long standing licence agreement with Sikorsky to allow it to build Sikorsky's helicopters, extended the agreement to cover Sikorsky Sea King soon after the Sea King's first flight in 1959. In 1966 the British Royal Navy selected the Sea King to meet a requirement for an anti-submarine warfare helicopter to replace the Westland Wessex, placing an order with Westland for 60 Sea Kings on 27 June 1966. The prototype and pre-production aircraft were constructed with Sikorsky-built components. The first Westland-built aircraft, the first production aircraft for the Royal Navy, designated the **Sea King HAS1**, first flew on the 7 May 1969 and was delivered to the navy in the same year.

Over 300 Westland Sea Kings were produced, the last to be built at Westland were Mk 43B SAR versions for the Royal Norwegian Air Force. The last of the Royal Navy's Sea King ASW helicopters was retired in 2003, being replaced by the AgustaWestland Merlin HM1. The Airborne Surveillance and Control (ASaC) (formerly Airborne Early Warning) variant is expected to be replaced in time for the two *Queen Elizabeth*-class aircraft carriers, some time in the 2010s. The types in contention are a Merlin derivative, a V-22 Osprey variant or a derivative of the E-2C Hawkeye. The UK is also expected to replace the HC4 and Search and Rescue variants in the 2010s.

Anti-submarine warfare

The basic ASW Sea King has been upgraded numerous times, becoming the **HAS2**, **HAS5** and **HAS6**, the latter of which has been replaced by the AgustaWestland Merlin ASW helicopter. Surviving aircraft are having the mission equipment removed and the aircraft are being used in the utility role.

Troop transport

A troop carrying version marketed as the **Commando** was developed for the Egyptian Air Force. A Commando variant, but retaining the folding blades and tail of the ASW variants, was designated the **Sea King HC4** by the Royal Navy and is still in service as an important asset for amphibious assaults under the command of Commando Helicopter Force. It is capable of transporting 27 fully equipped troops with a range of 400 miles (640 km). Current Royal Naval Air Squadrons that operate the Commando variant are 845 Naval Air Squadron, 846 Naval Air Squadron and 848 Naval Air Squadron. The Sea King HC4 has been involved in operations in the Falklands, the Balkans, Gulf War I, Sierra Leone, Lebanon, Gulf War II and Afghanistan.

Some of the HAS6 fleet were re-purposed, by removing the ASW equipment, as Royal Marine troop transports. These aircraft were retired in 2010.

Search and rescue

German SAR Sea King

A dedicated Search and Rescue version (**Sea King HAR3**) was developed for the RAF Search and Rescue Force, and the first of 15 entered service from September 1977 to replace the Westland Whirlwind HAR.10. A sixteenth aircraft was ordered shortly after, and following the Falklands War of 1982, three more aircraft were purchased to enable operation of a SAR flight in the islands, initially from Navy Point on the north side of Stanley harbour, and later from RAF Mount Pleasant. In 1992 six further aircraft were ordered to replace the last remaining Westland Wessex helicopters in the Search and Rescue role. The six (**Sea King HAR3A**) had updated systems including, uniquely amongst all the marks of Sea King in UK service, a digital autopilot with coupled navigation system. Search and rescue versions of the Sea King were also produced for the Royal Norwegian Air Force, the German Navy and the Belgian Air Force.

Some Royal Navy HAS5 ASW variants were adapted for the Search and Rescue role and are currently in service with 771 Naval Air Squadron, Culdrose and HMS Gannet SAR Flight at Prestwick Airport in Scotland. They are expected to remain in service until 2018.

Airborne early warning

The Royal Navy airborne early warning (AEW) capability had been lost when the Fairey Gannet aeroplane was withdrawn after the last of the RN's fleet carriers, HMS *Ark Royal*, was decommissioned in 1978. During the Falklands War, a number of warships were lost, with casualties, due to the lack of an indigenous AEW presence. The proposed fleet cover by the RAF Shackleton AEW.2 was too unresponsive and at too great a distance to be practical. Consequently, two Sea King HAS2s were modified in 1982 with the addition of the Thorn-EMI ARI 5930/3 Searchwater radar, attached to the side of the fuselage on a swivel arm and protected by an inflatable dome. This allowed the helicopter to lower the radar below the fuselage in flight and to raise it for landing. These prototypes, designated Sea King HAS2(AEW), were both flying within 11 weeks and deployed with 824

"D" Flight on HMS *Illustrious*, serving in the Falklands after the cessation of hostilities. A further seven HAS2s were modified to a production standard, known as the **Sea King AEW2**. These entered operational service in 1985, being deployed by 849 Naval Air Squadron. Four Sea King HAS5s were also later converted to to AEW role as **AEW5**s, giving a total of thirteen AEW Sea Kings.

An upgrade programme, Project Cerberus, resulted in the Sea King AEW fleet being upgraded with a new mission system based around the improved Searchwater 2000AEW radar from 2002 onwards. This variant was initially referred to as the **Sea King AEW7**, but soon renamed **ASaC7** (Airborne Surveillance and Control Mk.7). The main role of the Sea King ASaC7 is detection of low flying attack aircraft. It also provides interception/attack control and over-the-horizon targeting for surface launched weapon systems. In comparison to older versions, the new radar enables the ASaC7 to simultaneously track 400 targets instead of the earlier 250 targets.

The ASaC7s will remain in service until they are replaced under the Future Organic Airborne Early Warning (FOAEW) programme, which will operate from the UK's future Queen Elizabeth class aircraft carrier.

Operational history

Falklands War

The Sea King was deployed during the Falklands War, performing mainly anti-submarine search and attack, and also replenishment, troop transport, and Special Forces insertions into the occupied islands. On 23 April 1982, a Sea King HC4 was ditched while performing a risky transfer of supplies to a ship at night, operating from the flagship HMS *Hermes*.

Another Sea King was lost, again from ditching into the sea, due to a systems malfunction. All of the Sea King's crew were rescued. Five days later, a Sea King, again from *Hermes*, crashed into the sea due to an altimeter problem; all crew were rescued.

On 17 May 1982 a Sea King HC4 landed at Punta Arenas, Chile, and was subsequently destroyed by its crew. The three crew later gave themselves up to Chilean authorities. They were returned to the UK and were given gallantry awards for the numerous dangerous missions that they had undertaken. The official story was that the crew had become lost, although it was widely speculated that the helicopter had actually been inserting Special Air Service (SAS) soldiers onto the Argentine mainland.

On 19 May 1982, a Sea King had been transporting SAS troops to HMS *Intrepid* from *Hermes* and was attempting to land on *Intrepid*. A thump was heard, and the Sea King dipped and crashed into the sea, killing 22 men. However, nine survived this accident, but only after jumping out of the Sea King just before the helicopter crashed. Bird feathers were found in the debris of the crash, which suggested that this accident was the result of a bird strike, though this theory is debated. The SAS lost 18 men in the crash, their highest number of casualties on one day since the Second World War. The Royal Signals lost one man and the RAF one man. The latter was the only RAF fatality of the campaign.

Gulf War I

During the 1991 Gulf War Sea Kings roles included air-sea rescue, inter-ship transporting duties and transporting Royal Marines onto suspect ships that refused to turn around during the enforced embargo on Iraq. In addition two Sea King Mk5s from 826 Naval Air Squadron had their ASW sonar equipment removed and were equipped with a system for hunting sea mines called "Demon Camera". Six Sea King Mk4 helicopters from 845 Naval Air Squadron and six from 848 Squadron (which had been reformed and recommissioned that December) were deployed independently of the fleet. They provided support for the 1st Armoured Division. Initially based near King Khalid Military City, they followed the ground advance through Iraq into Kuwait.

Balkans

The Sea King participated in the UN's intervention in Bosnia, with Sea Kings operated by 820 Naval Air Squadron and 845 Naval Air Squadron. The Sea Kings from 820 NAS were deployed from Royal Fleet Auxiliary ships *Fort Grange* (since renamed *Fort Rosalie*) and *Olwen*. They provided logistical support, rather than the ASW role that the Squadron was geared towards, ferrying troops as well as supplies across the Adriatic Sea. They performed over 1,400 deck landings, flying in excess of 1,900 hours. The Sea Kings from 845 NAS performed vital casualty evacuation and other tasks. Their aircraft were hit numerous times, though no casualties were incurred.

During NATO's intervention in Kosovo, a British led operation, Sea Kings from 814 Naval Air Squadron, operated aboard HMS *Ocean* and RFA *Argus* and also on destroyers and frigates. They provided search and rescue (SAR), as well as transporting troops and supplies.

Gulf War II

A Sea King in service with the Royal Norwegian Air Force

During the 2003 invasion of Iraq, Sea King ASaC7 from 849 NAS operated off the flagship of the Royal Navy Task Force HMS *Ark Royal*. Sea King HC.4s also deployed from HMS *Ocean* (operated by 845 Naval Air Squadron) landing the lead invasion forces on the Al-Faw Peninsula, as well as Sea King HAS.6 from RFA *Argus* (operated by 820 Naval Air Squadron).

On 22 March 2003, two AEW Sea Kings from 849 NAS operating from

Ark Royal collided over the Persian Gulf, killing six British and one American military personnel.

During the Gulf Wars the Sea Kings provided logistical support, transporting Royal Marines from their off-shore bases on *Ark Royal*, *Ocean* and other ships on to land in Kuwait.

Lebanon

In July 2006, Sea King HC.4 helicopters from RNAS Yeovilton were deployed to Cyprus to assist with the evacuation of British citizens from Lebanon. The UK mission was codenamed Operation Highbrow.

Australia

Several RAN Sea Kings embarked aboard HMAS *Melbourne* prepare to launch

The Sea King replaced the Westland Wessex HAS31 as the Royal Australian Navy's Anti-Submarine Warfare helicopter from 1974. The aircraft were typically fitted with Racal ARI 5955/2 lightweight radar, Racal Navigation System RNS252, Racal Doppler 91, ADF Bendix/King KDF 806A and Tacan AN/ARN 118. All surviving Mk50 airframes were upgraded to Mk50A standard, through a mid-life extension. In 1995, the AQS-13B sonar was removed and since then, the Sea King's main role changed to maritime utility support. During the first five years of operation, a number of aircraft were lost due primarily to a loss of main gearbox oil.

The Fleet Air Arm's Sea King fleet will be replaced earlier than was originally planned in response to the loss of a Sea King providing humanitarian aid in Indonesia in April 2005 due to mechanical failure. The crash resulted in the deaths of nine Australian military personnel. Australian Sea Kings played an integral part in the relief effort for the December 2004 Indian Ocean Tsunami, particularly in Indonesia's Aceh province where they delivered medical teams and aid supplies from Royal Australian Navy ships. The Australian Sea Kings will be replaced by the MRH 90.

Variants

Indian Navy Sea King Mk.42B on INS *Mumbai* at Portsmouth, UK

Royal Navy Sea King AEW.2A in 1998

Sea King HAS.6 on *HMS Invincible* in 2004

RAN Sea King Mk50, Shark 09, launches from HMAS *Melbourne*, 1980

RAF Rescue Sea King HAR.3 at RIAT 2010

Sea King HAS.1
The first anti-submarine version for the Royal Navy. The Westland Sea King first flew in 1969.

Sea King HAS.2
Upgraded anti-submarine version for the Royal Navy. Some were later converted for AEW (Airborne Early Warning) duties.

Sea King AEW.2
Nine Sea King HAS.2s were converted into AEW aircraft, after lack of AEW cover was revealed during the Falklands War.

Sea King HAR.3
Search and rescue version for the Royal Air Force.

Sea King HAR.3A
Upgraded search and rescue version of the Sea King HAR.3 for the Royal Air Force.

Sea King HC.4 / Westland Commando
Commando assault and utility transport version for the Royal Navy. Capable of transporting 28 fully equipped troops.

Sea King Mk.4X
Two helicopters for trials at the Royal Aircraft Establishment at Farnborough.

Sea King HAS.5
Upgraded anti-submarine warfare version for the Royal Navy, some later converted into the HAR.5 for Search and Rescue.

Sea King HAR.5
Search and rescue version for the Royal Navy.

Sea King AEW.5
Four Sea King HAS.5s were converted into AEW helicopters for the Royal Navy.

Sea King HU.5
Surplus HAS.5 ASW helicopters converted into utility role for the Royal Navy.

Sea King HAS.6
Upgraded Anti-submarine warfare version for the Royal Navy.

Sea King HAS.6(CR)
Five surplus HAS.6 ASW helicopters converted into the utility role for the Royal Navy. The last of the Royal Navy's HAS.6(CR) helicopters was retired from service with 846 NAS on 31 March 2010.

Sea King ASaC7
Upgraded AEW2/5 for the Royal Navy with Searchwater 2000AEW replacing original Searchwater radar.

Sea King Mk.41
Search and rescue version of the Sea King HAS.1 for the German Navy, with longer cabin; 23 built, delivered between 1973 and 1975. A total of 20 were upgraded from 1986 onwards with additional Ferranti Seaspray radar in nose and capability to carry four Sea Skua Anti-ship missiles.

Sea King Mk.42
Anti-submarine warfare version of the Sea King HAS.1 for the Indian Navy; 12 built.

Sea King Mk.42A
Anti-submarine warfare version of the Sea King HAS.2 for the Indian Navy, fitted with haul-down system for operating from small ships; three built.

Sea King Mk.42B
Multi-purpose version for the Indian Navy, equipped for anti-submarine warfare, with dipping sonar and advanced avionics, and anti-shipping operations, with two Sea Eagle missiles; 21 built (one crashing before delivery).

Sea King Mk.42C
Search and rescue/utility transport version for the Indian Navy with nose mounted Bendix search radar; six built.

Sea King Mk.43
Search and rescue version of the Sea King HAS.1 for the Royal Norwegian Air Force, with lengthened cabin; 10 built.

Sea King Mk.43A
Uprated version of the Sea King Mk.43 for the Royal Norwegian Air Force, with airframe of Mk.2 but engines of Mk.1. Single example built.

Sea King Mk.43B
Upgraded version of the Sea King Mk.43 for the Royal Norwegian Air Force. Upgraded avionics, including MEL Sea Searcher radar in large dorsal radome, weather radar in nose and FLIR turret under nose. Three new-build plus upgrade of remaining Mk.43 and Mk.43A helicopters.

Sea King Mk.45
Anti-submarine and anti-ship warfare version of the Sea King HAS.1 for the Pakistan Navy. Provision for carrying Exocet anti-ship missile; six built.

Sea King Mk.45A
One ex-Royal Navy Sea King HAS.5 helicopter was sold to Pakistan as part of a follow-on order.

Sea King Mk.47
Anti-submarine version of the Sea King HAS.2 for the Egyptian Navy; six built.

Sea King Mk.48
Search and rescue version for the Belgian Air Force. Airframe similar to HAS.2 but with extended cabin; five built, delivered 1976.

Sea King Mk.50
Multi-role version for the Royal Australian Navy, equivalent to (but preceding) HAS.2; 10 built.

Sea King Mk.50A
Two improved Sea Kings were sold to the Royal Australian Navy as part of a follow-on order in 1981.

Sea King Mk.50B
Upgraded multi-role version for the Royal Australian Navy.

Commando Mk.1
Minimum change assault and utility transport version for the Egyptian Air Force, with lengthened cabin but retaining sponsons with floation gear. Five built.

Egyptian Westland Commando Mark 2

Commando Mk.2
Improved assault and utility transport version for the Egyptian Air Force, fitted with more powerful engines, non-folding rotors and omitting undercarriage sponsons and floatation gear; 17 built.

Commando Mk.2A
Assault and utility transport version for the Qatar Emiri Air Force, almost identical to Egyptian Mk.2; three built.

Commando Mk.2B
VIP transport version of Commando Mk.2 for the Egyptian Air Force; two built.

Commando Mk.2C
VIP transport version of Commando Mk.2A for the Qatar Emiri Air Force; one built.

Commando Mk.2E
Electronic warfare version for the Egyptian Air Force, fitted with integrated ESM and jamming system, with radomes on side of fuselage; four built.

Commando Mk.3
Anti-ship warfare version for the Qatar Emiri Air Force, fitted with dorsal radome and capable of carrying two Exocet missiles.

Operators

Belgian Air Component Sea King Mk.48

German Navy Mk.41 at RIAT 2010.

Sea King of the German Navy

Australia
- Royal Australian Navy - Fleet Air Arm (RAN)
  - 817 Squadron RAN

Belgium
- Belgian Air Component

Egypt
- Egyptian Air Force
- Egyptian Navy

Germany
- German Navy

India
- Indian Navy - Indian Naval Air Arm

Malaysia
- Royal Malaysian Air Force

Norway
- Royal Norwegian Air Force
  - 330 Squadron (SAR), scheduled for replacement with AW101 Merlin, EC225 Super Puma, NH-90, S-92 Superhawk or V-22 Osprey in 2020.

Pakistan
- Pakistan Navy - Pakistan Naval Air Arm

Qatar
- Qatar Emiri Air Force

Sierra Leone
- Military of Sierra Leone

United Kingdom
- Royal Air Force
  - No. 22 Squadron RAF
  - No. 202 Squadron RAF
  - No. 203(R) Squadron RAF
  - No. 1564 Flight RAF

Royal Navy SAR Sea King

- Royal Navy - Fleet Air Arm
  - 771 Naval Air Squadron
  - 845 Naval Air Squadron
  - 846 Naval Air Squadron
  - 848 Naval Air Squadron
  - 849 Naval Air Squadron
  - 854 Naval Air Squadron
  - 857 Naval Air Squadron
  - HMS Gannet SAR Flight
- Royal Aircraft Establishment

Specifications (Sea King HAS.5)
Data from Omnifarious Sea King

General characteristics
- **Crew:** Two to four, depending on the mission
- **Length:** 55 ft 10 in (17.02 m)
- **Rotor diameter:** 62 ft 0 in (18.90 m)
- **Height:** 16 ft 10 in (5.13 m)
- **Disc area:** 3,020 ft² (280 m²)
- **Empty weight:** 14,051 lb (6,387 kg)
- **Loaded weight:** 21,000 lb (9,525 kg)
- **Max takeoff weight:** 21,400 lb (9,707 kg) (overload weight)
- **Powerplant:** 2× Rolls-Royce Gnome H1400-2 turboshafts, 1,660 shp (1,238 kW) each
- **Propellers:** Five bladed rotor

Performance
- **Maximum speed:** 129 mph (112 knots, 208 km/h) (max cruise at sea level)
- **Range:** 764 mi (664 nmi, 1,230 km)
- **Service ceiling:** 10,000 ft (3,050 m)
- **Rate of climb:** 2,020 ft/min (10.3 m/s)

Armament
- 4× Mark 44, Mark 46 or Sting Ray torpedos, or 4× Depth charges

Source (edited): "http://en.wikipedia.org/wiki/Westland_Sea_King"

Westland Wasp

The **Westland Wasp** was a British small first-generation, gas-turbine powered, shipboard anti-submarine helicopter. Produced by Westland Helicopters, it came from the same P.531 programme as the British Army Westland Scout, and was based on the earlier piston-engined Saunders-Roe Skeeter. It fulfilled the requirement of the Royal Navy for a helicopter small enough to land on the deck of a frigate and carry a useful load of two homing torpedoes.

Design and development

The increasing speed and attack range of the submarine threat, and the increased range at which this threat could be detected led to a Royal Navy requirement for a "MAnned Torpedo-Carrying

Helicopter" (MATCH). Contemporary shipboard weapons did not have the necessary range, therefore MATCH was in essence a stand-off weapon with the helicopter carrying the torpedo or other weapon to the target and being instructed when and where to drop it. Unlike the larger Wessex, the Wasp carried no sonar of it own, and was limited strictly to working in partnership with its parent ship, other ships or other ASW units.

The first Wasp at the SBAC show 1962, a month before the first flight

The first prototype Saro P.531 flew on 20 July 1958, with the prototypes being subject to detailed testing by the Royal Navy, including the evaluation of several different undercarriage layouts, before settling on the definitive arrangement. An order for a pre-production batch of two "Sea Scouts" was placed in September 1961. The first flight of the two pre-production Wasp took place on 28 October 1962. Full production soon commenced, 98 in total being procured for the RN. The Wasp successfully exported to Brazil, the Netherlands, Indonesia, Malaysia, New Zealand and South Africa. 133 aircraft were built in total.

Front undercarriage of Wasp at IWM Duxford

Rear undercarriage of Wasp at IWM Duxford

Wasp was essentially a navalised Scout, indeed it was originally to be called the *Sea Scout*, and differed mainly in design details. It had a unique 4-wheeled castering undercarriage that allowed the aircraft to be manoeuvred on small, pitching flightdecks. The Wasp had the ability of "negative pitch" from the rotorblades which enabled the aircraft to "adhere" to the deck until the lashings were attached. Additional fuel tankage was installed in the cabin floor and both the tail boom and main rotor blades were foldable to allow stowage in the small hangars fitted to the first generation helicopter-carrying escorts. It was fitted with a winch above the starboard rear door, and also had the capacity to carry under-slung loads from the semi automatic cargo release unit mounted under the fuselage. With a crew of 2 (Pilot and Missile Aimer/Aircrewman) and the capacity to seat 3 passengers Wasp was useful for short-range transport missions, and for casualty evacuation with room for one stretcher fitted across the rear cabin area.

Later modifications included the ability to carry the Nord SS.11 wire-guided missile, with the fitting of the Aimers sight in the left cockpit roof and the installation of large inflatable emergency floats in sponsons on either side of the cabin to prevent capsizing of the top-heavy aircraft in the event of ditching. The SS.11 had limited range to target small surface targets such as patrol boats or shore positions and this was later replaced by the AS.12, which effectively had double the range.

Operational history

Royal Navy

Privately-owned Westland Wasp HAS.1 (*XT781*) at the Classic-Jet Air Show, Kemble, England, in 2003. On the UK Civil Register, in Royal Navy markings, as *G-KAWW*.

The **Wasp HAS.1** (HAS Mk 1) was introduced to service in the *small ships* role in 1964, after an intensive period of trials by 700(W) IFTU between June 1963 and March 1964. It served in this primary role with 829 Naval Air Squadron, but also in training units to supply crews for the front line with 706 NAS between 1965 and 1967 and in 703 NAS between 1972 and 1981. Single airframes also served for light liaison duties in the Commando Assault squadrons, 845 NAS and 848 NAS until 1973. Although effective as a submarine killer, it was best deployed paired with a Wessex HAS.3 submarine hunter. In the late 1970s, the Westland Lynx started to replace the Wasp.

On 25 April 1982 the Argentinian submarine ARA *Santa Fe* was spotted by a Wessex helicopter from HMS *Antrim*. The Wessex and a Westland Lynx HAS.2 from HMS *Brilliant* then attacked it with depth charges, a Mk 46 torpedo, and also strafed it with GPMG. A Wasp launched from HMS *Plymouth* and two Wasps launched from HMS *Endurance* fired AS.12 antiship missiles at the submarine, scoring hits. Santa Fe was damaged badly enough to prevent her from submerging. The crew abandoned the submarine at the jetty on South Georgia and surrendered to the British forces, thus becoming the first casualty of the sea war, as well as the first direct engagement by the Royal Navy Task Force.

The last Wasp was finally withdrawn from service in 1988 when the last of the Type 12 Rothesay class frigates was decommissioned.

Royal Malaysian Navy

The Wasp came into service with the Royal Malaysian Navy quite late, compared to the others nations who procured the aircraft. She joined the RMN on 8 April 1988. The Wasp had a relatively short career with that Navy, being phased out just ten years later when they were replaced by the Eurocopter Fennec.

Royal New Zealand Navy

The first four of an eventual nineteen Kiwi Wasps were purchased in 1966 being immediately assigned to the new Leander class frigate of the Royal New Zealand Navy (RNZN), HMNZS *Waikato*. They provided numerous tasks, as well as taking part in the Armilla Patrol in the Persian Gulf during the 1980s. The Wasps were flown by RNZN pilots but maintained by ground crews of No. 3 Squadron RNZAF.

In 1997, four Wasps performed a flypast, marking the arrival of the new ANZAC class frigate, HMNZS *Te Kaha*.

The Wasp served 32 years with the RNZN, retiring in 1998, the same year HMNZS *Waikato*, which first operationally deployed the Wasp in New Zealand, was herself decommissioned. They were replaced by the SH-2 Seasprite as a stop gap until the Arrival of their SH-2G(NZ).

Royal Netherlands Navy

With the Royal Netherlands Navy beginning in the late 1960s, after the fire onboard HNLMS *Karel Doorman*, NATO anti-submarine commitments were taken over by a squadron of Westland Wasp helicopters, operated from six Van Speijk class anti-submarine frigates. The Royal Netherlands Navy 860 Naval Air Squadron received 12 Wasp helicopters between November 1966 and June 1967, operated from Van Speijk class frigates as AH-12A's and flown in the ASW role. The last of the Dutch Wasps were eventually withdrawn from service in 1981 when they were replaced by the Westland Lynx.

Other operators

The Wasp was also in service with the Brazilian, Indonesian, and South African navies. The Indonesian aircraft are all former Dutch aircraft and were the last of the type in active service.

The last of the ten Surplus Dutch Navy Helicopters refurbished by Westland's for the Indonesian Navy was grounded in 1998. Flown by 400 Squadron (RON 400) from NAS Juanda, and when at sea were embarked upon the Indonesian Navy's ex UK Royal Navy Tribal class and ex-Dutch Navy Van Spiejk class frigates.

The Brazilian Navy operated the Wasp as the UH-2 & UH-2A taking delivery of three new build helicopters in April 1966 and a further seven ex-Royal Navy helicopters in 1977. 1º Esquadrão de Helicópteros de Emprego Geral (HU-1) flew the helicopters from Navy's Gearing and Allen M. Sumner class destroyers and the Niterói class frigates.

The South African Navy received their first batch of ten new build airframes in 1963, which was followed by the delivery of a second batch of further 8 from 1973. Although only six were delivered due to the International arms embargo placed on South Africa during the apartheid regime. The Wasps were flown by 22 Flight, from Ysterplaat, the unit subsequently became 22 Squadron, Maritime Command in 1976. The helicopters were operated from the navy's President class frigates. The South African Navy also acquired one ex Bahrain Public Security Force airframe as an instructional airframe to support its Wasp programme. The South African Navy withdrew their last Wasp in 1990.

Variants

Westland Wasp HAS.1

Sea Scout HAS.1
The Sea Scout HAS.1 was the original Royal Navy designation for the Wasp.

Wasp HAS.1
Shipboard anti-submarine warfare helicopter for the Royal Navy.

Operators

Brazil
- Brazilian Navy

Indonesia
- Indonesian Navy

Malaysia
- Royal Malaysian Navy

Netherlands
- Royal Netherlands Navy - Dutch Naval Aviation Service

New Zealand
- Royal New Zealand Navy
  - No. 3 Squadron RNZAF.

South Africa
- South African Navy

United Kingdom
- Royal Navy - Fleet Air Arm
  - 700W Intensive Flying Trials Unit
  - 703 Naval Air Squadron
  - 706 Naval Air Squadron
  - 829 Naval Air Squadron
  - 845 Naval Air Squadron
  - 848 Naval Air Squadron

Survivors

Brazil
On display
- Wasp HAS.1 *N-7039*, which was *XT433* in the Royal Navy from 1965 to 1978, is on display at Campo Dos Afonsos.

Malaysia
On display
- Wasp HAS.1 *M499-07*, which was *XT426* in the Royal Navy from 1965 to 1992, is on display at the Maritime Museum, Melacca.

New Zealand
On display
- Wasp HAS.1 *NZ3906* is on display at the Royal New Zealand Air Force Museum in Christchurch.

United Kingdom
Airworthy
- G-BYCX a former South African WASP Mk 1B is based at Bembridge, Isle of Wight.
- G-BZPP a Wasp HAS.1 (was RN serial number *XT793*) is privately owned in Surrey and flies in Royal Navy markings as *XT793*.
- G-CBUI a Wasp HAS.1 (was RN serial number *XT420*) is privately owned in Surrey and flies in Royal Navy markings as *XT420*.
- G-KAXT a former Royal Navy (*XT787*) and Royal New Zealand Navy (*NZ3905*) Wasp HAS.1 is flown from North Weald Airfield and flown in Royal Navy markings as *XT787*.

On display
- Wasp HAS.1 *XS463* is on display at Gatwick Aviation Museum, Gatwick.
- Wasp HAS.1 *XS527* is on display at Fleet Air Arm Museum, Yeovilton.
- Former Endurance Flight Wasp HAS.1 *XS567* is on display at the Imperial War Museum Duxford.
- Wasp HAS.1 *XT443* is on display at The Helicopter Museum, Weston-super-Mare.
- Wasp HAS.1 *XT788* is based in Devon, England but is displayed at various locations around the United Kingdom as a focal point for charity collection.

Stored or under restoration
- G-KANZ a former RN (*XT782*) and RNZN (*NZ3909*) Wasp HAS.1 is under restoration at North Weald in RNZN markings as *NZ3909*.
- G-RIMM a Wasp HAS.1 (was RNZN *NZ3907* and RN *XT435*) flew marked as *XT435* but does not have a current Permit to Fly.
- Wasp HAS.1s *XT427* and *XT778* are held in storage by the Fleet Air Arm Museum, Yeovilton.
- Former 829 NAS Wasp HAS.1 *XT434* is privately owned.
- Former 829 NAS Wasp HAS.1 *XT439* is privately owned in Hertfordshire.
- Wasp HAS.1 *XT437* is held by the Boscombe Down Aviation Collection at Boscombe Down.

A small number of helicopters are still used by the military and technical colleges for maintenance and engineering training.

Specifications (Wasp HAS.1)

Westland Scout and Wasp silhouettes

Data from Westland Aircraft since 1915

General characteristics
- **Crew:** One pilot, one Aircrewman
- **Capacity:** up to four passengers
- **Length:** inc rotor 40 ft 4 in (12.30 m)
- **Rotor diameter:** 32 ft 3 in (9.83 m)
- **Height:** 8 ft 11 in (2.72 m)
- **Disc area:** 816.9 ft² (75.9 m²)
- **Empty weight:** 3,452 lb (1,569 kg)
- **Max takeoff weight:** 5,500 lb (2,500 kg)
- **Powerplant:** 1× Rolls-Royce Nimbus 103 turboshaft, 1,050 shp (783 kW)

Performance
- **Maximum speed:** 120 mph (104 knots, 193 km/h)
- **Cruise speed:** 110 mph (96 knots, 177 km/h)
- **Range:** 303 miles (263 NM, 488 km)
- **Service ceiling:** 12,200 ft (3,720 m)
- **Rate of climb:** 1,440 ft/min (7.3 m/s)
- **Disc loading:** 6.75 lb/ft² (33 kg/m²)
- **Power/mass:** 0.19 hp/lb (0.31 kW/kg)

Armament
- Naval: 2 x Mk 44 *or* 1 x Mk 46 torpedo *or* 2 x Mk 44 depth charges *or* WE.177 600lb Nuclear Depth Bomb.
- Attack: 4 x SS-11 *replaced by* 2 x AS.12 missiles.
- General: GPMG, 4.5 Flares, Smoke/flame floats.

Source (edited): "http://en.wikipedia.org/wiki/Westland_Wasp"

Westland Wessex

The **Westland Wessex** is a British turbine-powered version of the Sikorsky S-58 "Choctaw", developed under license by Westland Aircraft (later Westland Helicopters), initially for the Royal Navy, and later for the Royal Air Force. The Wessex was built at Westland's factory at Yeovil in Somerset.

Design and development
An American-built Sikorsky HSS-1 was shipped to Westland in 1956 to act as a pattern aircraft. It was re-engined with a Napier Gazelle turboshaft engine, and first flew in that configuration on 17 May 1957. The first Westland-built Wessex *XL727*, a **Wessex HAS.1** first flew on 20 June 1958, and they entered anti-submarine duties in 1961 with the Royal Navy Fleet Air Arm. The Royal Navy's anti-submarine examples (HAS Mk.1, HAS Mk.3) also used the Gazelle engine.

The design was adapted in the early 1960s for the RAF, and later Royal Marines, to become a general-purpose helicopter capable of troop-carrying, air ambulance and ground support roles. In contrast with the HAS.1, it used twin Rolls-Royce Gnome engines. These marks (HC.2, HCC.4, HU.5) had a single large exhaust on each side of the nose, the Gazelle-powered examples having a pair of smaller exhausts on either side.

Operational history
The Wessex was first used by the RN, the RAF first used the helicopter in

1962, and did not finally retire until January 2003, being the main transport helicopter until the introduction of the Aérospatiale Puma. The bright yellow RAF machines used for air-sea or mountain rescue duties became especially famous and saved many lives.

The Navy pressed the development of the HAS.1 into the improved **HAS.3**, coming into service in 1967. It saw embarked service on the County Class destroyers. The HAS Mk.3 could be identified by a dorsal radome and strake extending behind the "hump".

Wessex helicopters were also used by the Queen's Flight of the RAF to transport VIPs including members of the British Royal Family, from 1969 to 1998. Those Royal helicopters were designated **HCC.4** and were essentially similar to the **HC.2** but with an upgraded interior, additional navigation equipment and enhanced maintenance programmes. A later version used by the Royal Marine Commandos was the **HU.5**.

Counter-insurgency operations

A crisis arose in 1962 as Brunei was not included in the newly formed Federation of Malaya and Indonesia threatened confrontation, including a continuation of the effort started by the North Kalimantan Liberation Army. By February 1964, RAF and Royal Navy Helicopters including some Westland Wessex operating from bases in Sarawak and Sabah to assist Army and Marine detachments fighting guerilla forces infiltrated by Indonesia over its one thousand mile frontier with Malaysia. In Borneo, the helicopter played a major role in fortifying the frontier and maintaining the frontier strong points by airlifting supplies in.

Wessex were also used in Oman to support British operations in Dhofar. Three of them transported SAS reinforcements in the Battle of Mirbat.

Falklands War

Around fifty-five Westland Wessex HU.5s went to the Falklands War in the South Atlantic in 1982, though a few of these, sent as replacements, did not arrive until after the end of hostilities. Their prime role was the landing, and moving forward, of Rapier missile systems, fuel, artillery and ammunition.

On 21 May 1982, 845 Squadron's Wessex HU.5s supported British landings on East Falkland. Some days later short-term SAS observation posts were inserted, with help from Wessex HU.5s, on the mountains behind Stanley. All six of 848 Squadron's Wessex HU.5s were lost when the container ship *Atlantic Conveyor* was sunk.

A Wessex of the Uruguayan Navy

Uruguay

16 former RAF Wessex HC.2 were supplied to Uruguay. The Uruguayan Navy received 5 helicopters in 1998, with the Uruguayan Air Force taking delivery of 11 helicopters in three batches from 2000 until 2003. Today, the Uruguayan Naval Aviation has a single Westland Wessex HC2 still in service. It is the last of the type flying with any air arm in the world.

Variants

A *Wessex HAS1* at the Imperial War Museum at Duxford (UK)

A *Wessex* at the Australian National Mairitme Museum

Wessex HAS1
RN utility, anti-submarine warfare, later air-sea rescue only, 140 built, some later converted to HAS3.
Wessex HC2
RAF Troop carrier for up to 16 troops, One prototype converted from HAS1 and 73 built.
Wessex HAR2
RAF search and rescue conversions.
Wessex HAS3
RN anti-submarine version with improved avionics with a radome on the rear fuselage, 3 new-build development aircraft and 43 converted from HAS.1
Wessex HCC4
VVIP transport for the Queens Flight, two built
Wessex HU5
RN service troop transporter, carried 16 Royal Marines, 101 built
Wessex HAS31
Royal Australian Navy anti-submarine warfare model, 27 built.
Wessex HAS31B
Updated anti-submarine warfare model for the Royal Australian Navy.
Wessex 52
military transport version of the HC2 for the Iraqi Air Force, 12 built.
Wessex 53
Military transport version of the HC2 for the Ghana Air Force, two built.
Wessex 54
Military transport version of the HC2 for the Brunei Air Wing, two built
Wessex 60
Civilian version of the Wessex HC2, 20 built.

Notable accidents

- G-ASWI - Bristow Helicopters.

Crashed (North Sea) August 1981; no survivors

Operators

Military Operators

Australia
- Royal Australian Navy Fleet Air Arm
  - No. 723 Squadron RAN
  - No. 725 Squadron RAN
  - No. 816 Squadron RAN
  - No. 817 Squadron RAN

Brunei
- Brunei Air Wing

Egypt
- Egyptian Air Force

Ghana
- Ghana Air Force

Iraq
- Iraqi Air Force

Oman
- Royal Air Force of Oman - Four ex-RAF HC.2s

United Kingdom
- Royal Air Force
  - No. 18 Squadron RAF
  - No. 22 Squadron RAF
  - No. 28 Squadron RAF
  - No. 32 Squadron RAF
  - No. 60 Squadron RAF
  - No. 72 Squadron RAF
  - No. 78 Squadron RAF
  - No. 84 Squadron RAF
  - No. 103 Squadron RAF
  - No. 2 Flying Training School RAF
  - Queen's Flight
  - SAR Training Squadron RAF
  - Wessex Operational Conversion Flight RAF
- Royal Navy Fleet Air Arm
  - 700 Naval Air Squadron
  - 706 Naval Air Squadron
  - 707 Naval Air Squadron
  - 737 Naval Air Squadron
  - 771 Naval Air Squadron
  - 772 Naval Air Squadron
  - 781 Naval Air Squadron
  - 814 Naval Air Squadron
  - 815 Naval Air Squadron
  - 819 Naval Air Squadron
  - 820 Naval Air Squadron
  - 824 Naval Air Squadron
  - 826 Naval Air Squadron
  - 829 Naval Air Squadron
  - 845 Naval Air Squadron
  - 846 Naval Air Squadron
  - 847 Naval Air Squadron
  - 848 Naval Air Squadron
  - RFA Regent Flight
  - RFA Resource Flight

Uruguay
- Uruguayan Air Force
- Uruguayan Navy

Civil Operators

United Kingdom
- Bristow Helicopters

Specifications (Wessex HC.2)

General characteristics

- **Crew:** Two pilots (civilian type 60 Wessex cleared for single pilot operation in UK)
- **Capacity:** 16 troops or 8 stretchers
- **Length:** 65 ft 8 in (20.03 m)
- **Rotor diameter:** 56 ft 0 in (17.07 m)
- **Height:** 16 ft 2 in (4.93 m)
- **Disc area:** 2,463 ft² (229 m²)
- **Empty weight:** 8,304 lb (3,767 kg)
- **Loaded weight:** lb (kg)
- **Max takeoff weight:** 13,500 lb (6,123 kg)
- **Powerplant:** 2× Rolls-Royce Gnome turboshaft, 1,535 shp (1,150 kW) each

Performance

- **Maximum speed:** 133 mph (212 km/h)
- **Range:** 480 miles (772 km)
- **Service ceiling:** 10,000 ft (3,050 m)
- **Rate of climb:** ft/min (m/s)
- **Disc loading:** 5.5 lb/ft² (26.7 kg/m²)
- **Power/mass:** 0.11 hp/lb (0.19 kW/kg)

Source (edited): "http://en.wikipedia.org/wiki/Westland_Wessex"